Introduction to

RECREATION AND LEISURE SERVICES

Eighth Edition

Introduction to
RECREATION AND LEISURE SERVICES

Eighth Edition

Karla A. Henderson

M. Deborah Bialeschki

John L. Hemingway

Jan S. Hodges

Beth D. Kivel

H. Douglas Sessoms

Venture Publishing, Inc.
State College, Pennsylvania

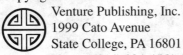
Production Manager: Richard Yocum
Manuscript Editing: Valerie Paukovits, Michele L. Barbin
Cover Design and Illustration: Echelon Design

Printing and Binding: Jostens Printing and Publishing, Inc.

Library of Congress Catalogue Card Number 2001091774
ISBN 1-892132-23-0

Dedicated to the individuals who provided the
foundation for recreation and leisure studies
at the University of North Carolina—Chapel Hill

Harold D. Meyer
H. Douglas Sessoms
Thomas Stein
Lee E. Meyer

TABLE OF CONTENTS

Unit Four: Trends and Issues in Recreation and Leisure Services 285

List of Tables and Figures

Preface

This textbook, *Introduction to Recreation and Leisure Services*, focuses on the growing and changing meanings of recreation and leisure services in communities. This book addresses all sectors of this field, including public, not-for-profit, and private commercial entities. Underlying any recreation service is the mandate to address the meanings of leisure and to examine inclusion and social justice as vital components of the quality of life. Many perspectives could be taken to provide an introduction to recreation and leisure, but we offer one appropriate to our vision regarding the benefits of recreation and leisure for individuals and within communities.

We believe in the value of recreation as a means to optimize human development and create communities that provide a high quality of life for all residents and visitors. We believe that inclusion and social justice must be considered regardless of the sector in which services are offered.

Inclusion refers to ensuring that all individuals—regardless of attributes such as race, class, religion, economic (dis)advantage, physical or mental abilities, sexual orientation, gender, or any other defining characteristics—have the right to leisure. *Social justice* refers to the means for providing equitable and fair opportunities.

This book is divided into four units. The first unit focuses on leisure and its value. We explore the meanings of leisure and how our understandings have evolved. In the second unit we concentrate on historical and comparative roots of recreation and leisure. Without an understanding of how leisure involvement and recreation services have evolved, we cannot explore what the future might hold. In the third unit, we examine the broad range of community recreation services, including government roles, the value of not-for-profit groups, and the impact that market-driven commercial recreation has on society. The final unit addresses trends and issues. The opportunities for involvement in recreation and leisure, whether as a participant or in a career, create challenges. The ability to confront issues with facts and information and to think critically will be important if recreation and leisure services are to further human development, social change, and environmental justice.

Whether you are considering a career in this field or want to be a more informed citizen, we hope the value of recreation and leisure services becomes apparent. The structured approach to facilitating leisure through recreation services now has a century of history in the United States and around the world. As we begin the twenty-first century, the opportunities for leisure as a vehicle for social transformation are limitless. A critical exploration of the meanings of recreation and leisure for individuals within communities is a logical step toward the advancement of this field of study.

In 1948, Harold D. Meyer and Charles K. Brightbill wrote the first edition of this book, *Community Recreation: A Guide to Its Organization and Administration*. That text was revised several times until 1969 when H. Douglas Sessoms joined Meyer as an author for the fourth edition. They changed the title to *Introduction to Leisure Services*. Sessoms was the sole author of the text until 1994 when Karla A. Henderson became second author for the seventh edition. This eighth edition of the book marks a transition again with major changes in format and content, added authors, and a new title, *Introduction to Recreation and Leisure Services*. The new authors also honor the enormous contributions of Sessoms to the development of the field of recreation and leisure services in North Carolina and across the United States. The foundation that Sessoms laid through several earlier editions of this book will be the cornerstone of the recreation and leisure services field for years to come, even as approaches and topics in this field change.

We are deeply indebted to many colleagues in the preparation of this work. They have been sources of information, helpful critics, and understanding friends. Our support staff at the University of North Carolina—Chapel Hill, Summer Montgomery and Meg Dawson, have provided encouragement and technical assistance. We also acknowledge the contributions from Richard Gitelson, Mark Havitz, and Leandra Bedini who gave us a foundation for this new edition based on their work on the seventh edition. Several graduate students have been helpful to us, including Mike Thonnereiux, Sonja Hodges, Mary Stevens, Owen Daniels, Amber Correll, and Jessica Irven. We also want to acknowledge the support of our partners and friends, Anne Sessoms, Delaine Deal, Jennie Hemingway, Rhonda Mickelson, and Liz Young. Most of all we are indebted to those professionals such as Meyer and Brightbill who paved the way for us, and to our colleagues who continue to move recreation and leisure services forward with their insight, commitment, and compassion.

UNIT ONE: LEISURE AND SOCIETY

Leisure is an important issue for most people whether they realize it or not. Many people feel they have too little leisure, while some folks have too much. Having time and money to do what one really wants to do is significant to most people. For most people, leisure is necessary for having a good quality of life.

Recreation and leisure are major forces in the economic and social life of the United States. Expenditures for vacation trips, ocean cruises, tennis and golf matches, weekend outings, and other forms of recreation behavior are several billion dollars greater than expenditures for national defense. Statistics suggest that by 2020 over 40% of the jobs in the United States will be in the area of leisure and tourism. This figure is expected to grow to 50% by 2050 (Begun, 2000).

Work and leisure are often discussed as interrelated activities. The exact nature of this relationship has been the subject of speculation among economists, sociologists, and other social and behavioral scientists. Past research indicated that people would work no longer than it took to maintain their desired lifestyle, that most workers would be content with subsistence, and most would stop working when their incomes rose beyond that level (US Department of Labor, 1980). That theory has not held true because many workers seem to enjoy the acquisition of goods made possible by higher wages (Schor, 1991). At the same time, Americans today generally perceive they have less leisure than desired.

In this perceived scarcity of leisure, however, is hope. Recreation and leisure have become valued as a desirable alternative for expression and satisfaction. Most Americans want a quality of life that includes adequate free time and meaningful activities. The margin of preference for more income over free time is evolving, as we will explore throughout this unit. We will also examine the ways that people find recreation and leisure opportunities in their communities.

1.1   Changes in Society

Recreation and leisure services are a product of industrialization and the leisure-work trade-off. With increased industrialism people actively sought leisure. A system of services and activities in the public, not-for-profit, and private commercial sectors evolved to meet their needs, expectations, and desires. This system in the United States began as a social movement during the early 1900s and reached full maturity by the latter half of the 20th century.

Nearly every city and town in the United States has an organized recreation and parks service available to its citizens. Billions of tax dollars are spent each year for the acquisition, construction, and operation of recreation programs, areas, and facilities (National Recreation and Park Association, 2001). Not-for-profit organizations and private commercial offerings also are common in most communities and comprise numerous opportunities within the leisure service industry. Few industries have expanded more rapidly in the late 20th century than those businesses that cater to recreation. The demand for recreation equipment, vacation areas, and recreation settings exceeds the supply. Theme parks, jogging trails, and lighted tennis courts dot the landscape. Denim, the cloth traditionally associated with workers' clothing, has become the fabric of recreation participants. Ball caps, sweatshirts, fleece vests, and running shoes are standard wearing apparel for millions of recreating youth and adults.

Whether the desire for more free-time activities will replace work as North Americans' dominant activity is a matter of speculation. Many factors influence recreation behavior. We examine briefly some of the changing societal issues and trends that currently affect the evolving nature of recreation and leisure services. These economic, social, and environmental changes influence how people in the United States think about and value leisure. These values translate into contemporary recreation and leisure service delivery in the public, not-for-profit, and private commercial sectors.

The Changing Society

All of us are aware of the changing face of the United States and the global society. We know about the baby boomer generation through Generation Y, the changing nature of the family, the ever-widening gap between the haves and the have nots, the questioning of traditional values, changing gender roles, the recognition of race and ethnicity, and the visibility of violence. Familiarity with the continuously changing environment is imperative to understand the value of recreation and leisure. Most of the following data used to describe the changing society came from the US Department of Health and Human Services website (1998) where the statistics are continually being updated.

Family Structure and Income

Society seems to be less stable than before in many ways, and family structure reflects this instability. For example, between 1970 and 1997, the proportion of children in two-parent families decreased from 85% to 68%. While negative connotations often exist for children in single-parent families, the great majority of these children do well (Zill, Morrison & Coiro, 1993). The decline in two-parent families was found for African-American, European-American, Latino/Latina, Asian-American, and American-Indian families, although the decline was somewhat steeper for African-American families. Another indicator of this decreasing stability is how frequently a child has moved. Frequent moves are associated with negative outcomes such as dropping out of school, delinquency, depression, and teen births. Some researchers suggest that a lack of rootedness in a local community may be an underlying cause of these problems (Wood, Halfon, Scarlata, Newacheck & Nessim, 1993). Of the children who had moved, the largest percentage was Latino/Latina (23%).

At the end of the 20th century, over 37% of all families in the United States lived below the poverty level, while over half of the female-headed single-parent families lived below the poverty level. The more educated the parents, the more likely they were to maintain two-parent families and have higher incomes. A concern has existed for children born to single women because some data suggest that these children are more likely to grow up poor and become single parents themselves (Ventura, 1995). A considerable increase has been seen in the percentage of births to single women from 1960 (5%) to 1994 (33%) before stabilizing in 1996 (32%).

Median incomes are a good way to assess the economic well-being of society. These statistics enable us to measure the ability of a family at the midpoint of the income distribution to purchase goods and services required to raise children and have a desired quality of life. Between 1975 and 1996, the median income has narrowly fluctuated around the $40,000 mark (in 1996 dollars). A detailed look at the data, however, shows some interesting discrepancies. For example, the median income of female-headed families in 1996 was $16,400 compared to $26,500 for male-headed families, and $51,800 for married couple families. When analyzed by race and ethnicity, the medians are substantially higher for White families. For example, in 1996 the median income for White families was $44,500 as compared to $22,900 for Black families and $24,600 for Latino/Latina families (US

Department of Health and Human Services, 1998). Although some of this difference can be attributed to the fact that more African-American and Latino/Latina families tend to be headed by single women, the discrepancy is problematic.

The number of people working has also continued to grow over the past two decades as more women have entered the labor force and as the number of single-parent families has increased. For example, in 1996 over 71% of all children between 6–17 years living in two-parent homes had both parents in the labor force. When analyzed by race and ethnicity, Black children have the highest rate of parental involvement in the labor force, followed closely by Whites, and then Latino/Latina families.

Baby boomers will also continue to impact North American society in the coming decades. This generation waited longer to have children, and when they did start families they were often smaller than in the past. Projections show that the growth in numbers of school-age children will slow during the first two decades of the 21st century, and the median age of the population will continue to increase. By 2011 the boomers will move into their senior years and become a population bulge for the next twenty years. These seniors will likely be more active, have more money, and live longer than older adults previously have in our society.

Health Conditions

Several health issues have been identified for American society, including the prevalence of overweight children and adults. This concern has received attention as more medical data link being overweight with hypertension, coronary heart disease, diabetes, and some cancers. In 1999 almost two-thirds of males and almost one-half of females were overweight and one out of five people were obese. At the current rate, by 2025 three-fourths of all males and females in the United States will be overweight with over one-third classified as obese (Begun, 2000). The 1996 Report from the Surgeon General indicated that over 60% of Americans do not exercise regularly despite the known benefits of physical activity (US Department of Health and Human Services, 1996). A pattern of decreasing activity with age was consistent in all areas of physical activity. The data also indicated that males across all age groups consistently had 16–26% higher rates of involvement in exercise or sport than women.

Child abuse and suicide are also growing health concerns in our society. Almost one million cases of child neglect or abuse were documented in 1995, with estimates as high as 2.5 million when undocumented cases were considered (US Department of Health and Human Services, 1998). The rate rose by 18% from 1990 to 1996. As one possible response to abuse or other stress, 24% of all children in grades 9–12 had seriously considered suicide during the past 12 months, while 1 in 11 of them had actually attempted suicide during that time. White and Latino/Latina youth were more likely to consider suicide, and females were more likely to have serious thoughts of suicide. However, the actual rates of suicide, particularly among 15–19 year olds, are four times higher for males than females (US Department of Health and Human Services, 1998).

Social Development

Health problems are often mitigated through a focus on social development. A snapshot of the social and personal life of today's high school students indicates a sense of priorities for the future. Having a good marriage and family life and being successful in work have been cited as extremely important by about 80% and 66% of the high school seniors, respectively. Having lots of money and making a contribution to society were the next likely goals (20% and 30%), followed by goals to work to correct social and economic inequalities (12%) and becoming a leader in the community (15%). Black high school students attached more importance than did White students to being successful at work, having lots of money, and correcting social and economic inequalities. Few differences were found by gender except that females place more importance on having a good marriage and family life and felt having a lot of money was less important than other goals (US Department of Health and Human Services, 1998).

Individual problem behaviors of adolescents are also telling statistics about the social development of a society (Moore & Glei, 1994). These risky behaviors include problems in school, sexual intercourse, use of illegal drugs, use of alcohol, and cigarette smoking. As one might imagine, the number of children never engaging in any risky behaviors declines significantly as they move through adolescence. Across the adolescent years, more girls report being free of any risk behaviors, as do children from two-parent families and children from mid- to high-income families.

A concern about violence is also escalating in US society. Carrying a weapon is associated with the most serious forms of violence and increases the risk of death or serious injury if a violent argument occurs (Public Health Reports, 1993). The insidiousness of violence lies not only in the physical harm that occurs but also in how the fear or perception of violence also changes people's behavior. When fear of assault or violence curtails activities, it diminishes quality of life. Whyte and Shaw (1994) describe how many young women were fearful in all aspects of their lives and how it affected where they went, when they went, and with whom they participated during leisure. Although fear may not stop people from work or leisure, it can diminish the freedom people perceive they have. Further, violence in US society is feared not only from strangers but also from family and friends as evidenced by the rise of domestic violence in the home and the workplace.

Another social trend is the increased diversity of US society. Statistics support a growing population of African Americans, Latino/Latinas, and Asian/Pacific Islanders. For the past three decades the United States has been influenced by growing numbers of immigrants who come from primarily Asia, Latin America, and the Caribbean. These different cultural values, languages, attitudes, and behaviors bring challenges as well as positive attributes to an increasingly diverse society. They will affect how people live and how providers facilitate leisure services.

Environmental Concerns

Along with these social trends is an increased ambivalence about the environment. An alarmist concern in the 1970s with environmental degradation has led to some complacency about environmental issues today. Because some problems (e.g., highway littering) have been addressed, people believe the imminent dangers are over. Evidence of urban sprawl in many cities in the United States, however, is a growing concern. People live as if land will always be plentiful. Although many of the species that faced extinction in the latter half of the twentieth century have now experienced some repopulation, a concern about habitat preservation is still omnipresent.

The tension between economic development and sustainability is an issue in local municipalities as well as tourism environments. Many tourism opportunities depend on the environment, yet many tourism operators have not made environmental preservation a priority. A focus on sustainable tourism gains impetus for structural change by moving away from a strictly economic focus in the present to planning for the future. This planning involves consuming natural resources only at a rate that they can be replaced, maintaining biological diversity, recognizing and valuing aesthetic appeal, and respecting the people who live where tourism takes place.

Values as a Basis for Change

Statistics paint a picture of a changing society with many potential implications for recreation and leisure. Future positive change, especially applied to inclusive and socially just recreation and leisure services, requires an examination of people's value systems.

Sociologists refer to social and personal values as those beliefs and behaviors that an individual or a society deems important to its welfare. A person's value system gives direction for choosing between alternative forms of behavior and determining the relative importance of any experience.

Every society develops a social value system and socializes young people to honor those things considered essential. As societies change, different interest groups develop and the value system is altered. Because each person has a different perception of what life ought to be, different behaviors emerge. It is not surprising, therefore, to find social drinking acceptable in some groups but not in others, or that some groups place a premium on family activity while others stress individual pursuits and interests. In a heterogeneous society, a multitude of value structures exist, yet most reflect the dominant values of a society.

Although the pastoral existence of the small town and farm community way of life is often romanticized, the United States is an urban society with an urban value system. The values of conspicuous consumption (e.g., buying products to show how wealthy one is whether you need them or not) and conspicuous display (e.g., wearing only expensive name brand clothing) as well as most people's desire for immediate action and convenience packaging have had their effects on personal and social behaviors and the concomitant attitudes about recreation and leisure. For example, most people expect campsites to have electricity, indoor plumbing, sewage disposal, and concrete slabs for the RVs. For the less hearty, "roughing it" now takes place in a plush motel or in a comfortable cottage at a seaside or mountain resort.

Time and its use have had great impact on values and the changing American lifestyle. Traditionally, time has been measured and valued in its economic sense. Labor is paid for by the hour, wages by the week, and pensions according to the number of years worked. For many, the pleasures derived from a recreation outing are directly related to the amount of time required for that experience. Americans have been and continue to be time conscious.

Supporters of organized recreation systems have always held that recreation, leisure, and play experiences are of value. They advocate recreation programs because they build character, improve quality of life, instill feelings of democracy and self-reliance, and help individuals become disciplined and productive persons. Furthermore, recreation activities have been seen as a form of education and as a means to refresh the industrial worker. Consequently, most of the early recreation programs were highly active, designed for children, and generally promoted to prevent delinquency. Though little scientific evidence supports these claims, conventional wisdom suggests that if a person knows how to play fairly, he or she will be a good worker and citizen.

Even with a greater appreciation of leisure as a right to be enjoyed, the work ethic remains at the heart of the Western value system. Most Americans believe that one should earn leisure, be self-supporting, and take pride in achievements. Although the hobo and drifter are often portrayed by novelists as living a leisurely life, society continues to disdain people who are homeless or on welfare because they are not a part of the employment system. Success is valued and people believe that those who use their skills wisely and for the advancement of business and industry should be highly rewarded. Not surprisingly our industrial and economic leaders are the highest paid occupational group.

Values shape changes in recreation and leisure interests. Values also dictate the procedures to be used in providing recreation and leisure services opportunities. To a large extent our society has approached the provision of recreation services in much the same way that it has handled its educational and welfare programs. It has blended not-for-profit and private commercial resources with those of government, and for the most part this combination has worked. To meet the changing interests and needs of society, recreation and leisure service providers must use the information available about human characteristics, values, and behaviors to meet the challenge of recreation as a means for personal and societal growth.

Challenges to Leisure

Although having a good time is an American tradition, recreation and leisure are not always highly valued. Few nations have exhibited more respect for the work ethic than has the United States. Work has been treated as sacred, and most other activities have been secondary to economic productivity and consumption. Because of this attitude, some philosophers and social scientists have viewed leisure as a threat, as something for which we are not prepared. Juliet Schor (1991) noted:

> The danger of increasing leisure time voluntarily is that it could replace one inequity with another—as inequality of income creates inequality of time. The poorest third would work just as many hours as ever—or more, as more work became available—while the top two-thirds would gradually become a leisured class. The people who would gain free time would be those who already had the financial resources that make it possible—education, homes, and a bank account. They would be mainly White and mainly upper and middle class.

A "leisure socicty" has been predicted for many years but has been slow to materialize. The 40-hour workweek has been accepted as the standard, although some people question whether the workweek is really 40 hours, since people now spend more time traveling to and from the job than they did in former years. Further, with the increase in technology, people are doing more work at home at all times of the day. Technology has also raised the expectation that if one can work faster, he or she should also get more work done. With more than 70% of US females in the work force, more hours are spent in the "second shift" doing housework after spending the day at work (Hoschild & Machung, 1990). Some scholars (e.g., Schor, 1991) even describe us as "the overworked American(s)." In addition, the number of temporary or part-time workers who may hold two or more jobs has risen.

Other scholars (e.g., Robinson & Godbey, 1999) have argued that people have more leisure today than in the past. Their time budget analyses show this conclusion to be true. A problem arises, however, when people may have more time, but feel like they do not. These people feel stressed and under pressure most of the time. Scheduling of one's leisure has become increasingly difficult for the American family with two adults working, children in year-round schools, and multigenerational family responsibilities. When people have free time, they are frequently too exhausted to seek out opportunities other than watching television. Oddly enough, this television watching is generally not perceived as leisure by a majority of people.

Although Congress enacted legislation in 1968 designating that certain holidays (e.g., Memorial Day, President's Day, Martin Luther King, Jr.'s Birthday) were to be celebrated on Mondays, thereby giving federal employees several long weekends each year, America still ranks below almost all industrial nations in the average number of vacation days granted workers. The US average of 20 days of holiday *and* vacation per year is half the number taken by workers in most European countries.

The challenges to meet the needs and interests of a wide spectrum of youth and adults in communities are often daunting. Changing trends and values influence the recreation and leisure services provided. Recreation and leisure, as inherent dimensions of people's lives and guaranteed as rights in our society, can help address some of the social and environmental problems.

Recreation and Leisure Services and Change

The third unit of this book provides an in-depth look at the spectrum of recreation and leisure services, including public, not-for-profit, and private commercial organizations. The services, programs, and facilities offered by recreation and leisure providers include a vast number of opportunities that continually evolve. For example, in the United States more than 70 federal agencies develop programs and policies that affect recreation and leisure behaviors or supervise and maintain recreation resources. These services extend from regulatory agencies such as the Fish and Wildlife

Service (which regulates the use and conservation of wildlife resources) to the direct service agencies such as the National Park Service and the Department of Defense (with their multiprogram emphases).

Recreation resource management and the offering of technical assistance to local communities are major responsibilities of state recreation agencies. All 50 states have designated recreation and park services involved in the overall planning and development of outdoor recreation facilities. Many state governments have recreation divisions offering consulting services to local communities and private groups. All states have one or more departments promoting their tourism potential and attractions.

The demand for all types of activities has been felt also at the local level. No longer are local public park and recreation departments content merely to offer the traditional athletic leagues and playground programs. They have responded by developing services and partnerships for older adults, childcare and after-school programs for youth, and self-supporting aquatic and fitness centers. In addition to their traditional role of operating playgrounds, parks, and community buildings, some public recreation departments have assumed responsibility for the management of sports arenas, cultural centers, and nature museums.

Amusement, diversion, and technology have contributed to the growth of mass leisure. Advances in the production and the distribution of goods and an increased level of affluence have resulted in new forms of entertainment and amusement. The development of electronic technologies has given us a variety of new ways to play and socialize, including virtual reality, HDTV, palm pilots, and cellular telephones that serve as computers. Tourism has become a year-round activity. In many areas resort motels no longer offer an off-season price since "off-season" simply no longer exists. Theme parks such as Walt Disney World and Busch Gardens have had a huge impact upon local economies. They have expanded the range of recreation opportunities available to those seeking the commercial recreation experience. Central to this growth of the recreation in all sectors is the desire for diversion, the need to escape, and a growing interest in having many choices in one's personal life.

Accompanying the growth of the amusement industry has been the acceleration of opportunities for more personalized participant expression. Americans have the equipment and ability to "just do it" with whatever "turns them on." The only limiting factors are knowledge of the resources available and attitudes toward their free-time expressions. Boats, SUVs, digital cameras, geographic positioning systems, computers, synthetic fabrics, and freeze-dried foods are readily available. The problem among affluent Americans is not that they lack something to do, but rather so much is available that they do not know where to begin. For individuals with disabilities or who are restricted by various forms of discrimination or economic difficulty, however, the situation may be different. Accessibility and opportunity exist for many people in American society but not for all.

Americans are not the only ones benefiting from new recreation and leisure opportunities. In Japan, multitiered golf driving ranges have been constructed. Each weekend millions of people crowd into trains to leave the city for the tranquility of the countryside. In Europe, growing recreation concerns have given rise to a variety of leisure movements. Factories close for weeks so their employees may take holidays. The countryside and sports arena programs are well-supported in England and Germany. Even the so-called developing countries such as the People's Republic of China, with their rapidly changing technology, are aware of the importance of recreation and leisure. They are taking steps to make sure their citizens and visitors have ample opportunities for enjoyment and their wildlife and resources are protected.

This chapter has introduced how societal trends as well as people's values shape the ways that recreation and leisure are embodied in the United States. Recreation and leisure should be the right of all individuals and inclusive opportunities should exist in communities through the provision of services by the public, not-for-profit, and private commercial sectors. These services will have little meaning, however, unless leisure is understood and valued.

Reflection Questions

1. What are the significant demographic changes influencing how leisure is valued and how recreation is embodied in US society?

2. What is meant by a leisure society? In what ways would you consider the United States to be a leisure society? In what ways is it not a leisure society?

3. How have values shaped views of leisure?

4. How have you developed your values about work and leisure?

1.2   Descriptions and Definitions of Recreation and Leisure

As in most fields of study, some basic terms and concepts need interpretation. These descriptions and definitions are useful for several reasons: (1) to help professionals who study recreation and leisure understand and measure the leisure phenomenon; (2) to predict the consequences and actions of the services provided more accurately; (3) to understand the roles and responsibilities in providing leisure services; and (4) to research specific leisure benefits and allocate resources more effectively.

Leisure

The concept of leisure is difficult to limit to a single definition. As an experience interpreted by individuals within varied contexts, the study of leisure has evolved into three basic approaches: time, activity, and state of mind. Some individuals view leisure as a period of time they call free time. Other people see leisure as a set of activities that generally occur outside of work activities. In this context, leisure is earned; it is time freed by and from work and therefore cannot occur when one is at work. Other people conceive of leisure as an attitude toward existence or a state of mind. Leisure as a state of mind is philosophical in nature, while leisure as time or activity is easily measured (e.g., number of activities or time spent) and based in scientific theory and practice.

None of these approaches, however, provide a perfect definition. For example, free or nonobligated time and activity participation can be measured, but determining when one is at leisure is difficult. You may have unobligated time between classes. If you read a book for your English class, is that leisure? If we define leisure as certain types of nonwork activity, we still have a similar problem. For example, many people would categorically define jogging as a leisure activity. However, if you were asked to run with a friend on a 20-mile marathon-training run, would that be leisure for you? To a passerby who defines leisure as a specific type of activity, they would likely say that running was leisure for you.

Perhaps the closest we can come to a universal definition is when one accepts leisure as a psychological or state of mind experience. In this view, time and type of activity have little to do with the experience achieved. According to Neulinger (1981), the possibility exists for one to be at leisure even when at work (i.e., engaged in some activity for which one is obligated or paid money). Leisure may come from any experience where one's motives, rather than the activity or the time in which the activity is pursued, are of prime importance. In this context a person is at leisure when in harmony with his or her own rhythms, when the experience is chosen in relative freedom, and when the person is intrinsically motivated. In this text we consider *leisure* to be a state of mind where activity is chosen in relative freedom for its quality of intrinsic satisfaction. We accept leisure time as nonwork time and agree that while a leisure experience is more likely to occur during one's free time, it is not limited to a specific time or activity.

Recreation and Play

Leisure and recreation are frequently used interchangeably, especially when defined as free-time experiences or something done for pleasure in one's free time. Ask people what they do in their leisure, and they will often give you the same response as when you ask what they do for recreation. Yet leisure and recreation are not necessarily synonymous. Both are seen as experiences undertaken because of the end results; however, recreation is also viewed as a means to an end, especially among therapeutic recreation professionals who use the recreation experience as a treatment modality. Generally, however, we define *recreation* as a voluntary, organized, socially redeeming, and fun activity that occurs during free time.

Some people also use play interchangeably with either recreation or leisure. We can, however, make some distinctions in this concept from recreation or leisure. Most people associate characteristics like spontaneity, purposelessness, and the creation of an imaginary world with play. Play is almost always pleasurable, self-expressive, and can range from fairly aimless, disorganized activity to very complex involvements. Almost everyone links play to children. However, we know that adults also like to be spontaneous and find "childlike play" a refreshing break from the structure and reality of our everyday world. The definition of *play* within the context of this book refers to spontaneous and expressive activity that is done for its own sake.

For most people, the distinction between leisure and recreation is seldom an issue. As we discuss the provision of recreation and leisure services throughout this book, however, we need to understand how the general public as well as professionals in this field view these concepts. Therefore, we will discuss leisure as a broad umbrella term that includes the pleasurable activity dimensions of recreation. The critical components of leisure are choice and intrinsic motivation. Recreation falls under the umbrella of leisure because it includes those organized activities engaged in during free time for personal and social benefits. Play is the expression of recreation and leisure.

Recreation and Leisure Services Sectors

The recreation and leisure service delivery system consists of three basic sectors or providers: public services, not-for-profit agencies, and private commercial businesses. Each type of provider has its own features and mission that appeal to individuals in varied situations. Together they provide society's system for meeting the leisure interests of the entire community. A comparison of different aspects of each element is presented in Table 1.2 (page 18).

The role of the leisure services profession is often viewed in two ways. One perspective, often associated with the parks approach, suggests that recreation and leisure professionals should be primarily concerned with the management of selected natural resources or facilities for individuals' recreation pursuits. For example, the agency provides an opportunity (e.g., a park), and the participant plans and directs his or her recreation activities (e.g., goes for a run). The second view, the recreation approach, acknowledges the responsibility of recreation and parks services for the development and administration of recreation opportunities. For example, the agency directs or schedules the activities of participants (e.g., organizes a softball tournament). The parks approach is more often associated with the private commercial sector and the natural resource segment of public recreation services. The recreation approach is more commonly associated with the not-for-profit sector and public recreation programs.

Great strides have been made during the past half century to establish recreation and leisure services as a distinct field with unique characteristics and social roles. Leisure service professionals are not physical educators, social workers, or physical therapists. As professionals, they are knowledgeable about human needs, economic and community development, program planning, and administration and management. Their professional expectations often depend on three things: (1) the public's perception of recreation and leisure; (2) the past experience of the managing agency that employs recreation specialists; and (3) the educational biases of the professors who teach in leisure service curricula.

The merger in the 1960s of the parks approach movement and the recreation approach movement was accomplished at the professional level primarily by the formation of the National Recreation and Park Association (NRPA). Differences in background, training, and perceptions of professionals, however, have made the standardization of basic concepts and mandates difficult.

Park and recreation services can be found in all leisure services sectors, but they are most closely allied with the public (governmental) sector. The public has generally supported the view that all governmental entities should provide basic opportunities for recreation activities to every member of the community. This public mandate includes the development and maintenance

Table 1.2:   Comparison between Elements of Recreation and Leisure Services

	Public	Not-for-Profit	Commercial
Service Philosophy	Enrich the lives of the community by providing opportunities for the meaningful use of leisure	Enrich the lives of participating members by providing opportunities for the meaningful use of leisure, frequently with emphasis on the group and individual	Satisfy public demand for recreation experiences and services in an effort to produce a profit
Service Objectives	Provide leisure opportunities that contribute to the social, physical, educational, cultural, and general well-being of the community	Provide leisure opportunities that appeal to participating members and allow for close group association, emphasizing citizenship, behavior, and social values	Provide leisure opportunities that appeal to customers, encourage competition, and net a profit while serving the public
Agencies	Federal, state, county, and local government units, such as parks and recreation departments, recreation and park districts, and state park departments	Boy Scouts, Girl Scouts, Camp Fire, Y organizations, tennis clubs, swim clubs, neighborhood recreation associations	Corporations, franchises, partnerships, resorts, theme parks, professional sports
Finance	Taxes (primarily), gifts, grants, trust funds, fees	Gifts, grants, endowments, donations, fundraisers, membership fees	Investment of the owner or promoters, admission fees paid by users
Facilities	Community buildings, national, state, and local parks, athletic fields, playgrounds, stadiums, camps, beaches, museums, zoos, golf courses	Community centers, youth centers, athletic facilities, play areas, clubs, camps, aquatic areas	Theaters, clubs, taverns, night clubs, lounges, racetracks, bowling lanes, amusement parks, stadiums
Leadership	Professionally prepared individuals (professionals and volunteers) provide and manage comprehensive recreation programs	Professionally prepared individuals (professionals and volunteers) provide programs frequently on a social group-work basis	Professionally prepared business and sales-oriented individuals design and manage services to produce a profit
Membership	Unlimited and open to all	Limited by organizational mission, such as age, gender, religion	Limited by economics to those participants who pay for the service or product

of natural resources, the provision of programs and services, and the promotion and care of cultural activities and historic sites. Citizens generally expect the not-for-profit and private commercial recreation sectors to meet any other remaining recreation needs that exist in communities.

When you ask people what they do for recreation, they typically answer with some activity. People have accepted certain activities as recreation, especially those activities normally organized for fun during one's free time. More often than not, the basic skills for these activities are learned during childhood and are enjoyed on the weekend, after work or school, or on a holiday. Classes to learn recreational skills, sports, and social occasions are typically described as recreation. People in communities have come to expect and define recreation in terms of these activities. Consequently, communities have organized their recreation and park agencies to offer these types of programs to accommodate the free-time interests of the public.

The Provider and the Participant

As the leisure services profession develops, specific terms emerge to distinguish people who provide the recreation service from people who participate. Individuals who provide recreation, parks, and leisure services are generally referred to as recreation professionals or leisure services professionals or specialists. Some of these professionals choose to become certified. People acquire this professional designation by meeting academic eligibility requirements, passing a national test, and maintaining professional status through continuing professional education. Recreation professionals who become certified by the National Recreation and Park Association were formerly called Certified Leisure Professionals (CLP); in 2000 the title was changed to Certified Park and Recreation Professionals (CPRP). Therapeutic recreation professionals can become Certified Therapeutic Recreation Specialists (CTRS).

A recreation or leisure services professional is professionally prepared to further the goals of recreation and leisure services. Those individuals participating in the recreation experience generically are called participants regardless of whether the public, not-for-profit, or private commercial sectors are addressed. In some areas of the recreation and leisure service fields, participants may be referred to as clients, consumers, recipients, or recreationists.

Recreation and leisure are understood in a number of ways. The provision of recreation services occurs in public, not-for-profit, and private commercial organizations that have somewhat different mandates with a variety of organizational structures. At this point, it is useful to have a broad understanding of the descriptions and definitions used in helping to understand why recreation and leisure services are valued in US society.

Reflection Questions

1. How would you distinguish the terms *recreation*, *leisure*, and *play*?

2. Describe the two views of the role of the leisure services professional.

3. What are the three primary categories of leisure services? Describe the purpose of each.

4. Why is it important to develop definitions of concepts such as recreation and leisure? For whom are these conceptual distinctions important?

5. Why is professionalization important to the field of recreation and leisure?

1.3   Leisure and Work

Leisure and work are cultural adaptations to material and social needs (Chick, 1998). Material needs like food, shelter, or clothing are universal, but the ways that people satisfy them differ from culture to culture. Social needs include individual and group identity, status, and desirable forms of leisure and work. As cultures become more complex, people tend to understand their activities more in terms of their social environments than their material environments.

Cultural and Historical Dimensions of Leisure and Work

When patterns of activity are stable for a long time, they seem natural to people. Life is arranged around these patterns. People might even have difficulty conceiving how life might be arranged any differently even if they had unlimited alternatives.

In contemporary Western society, for example, work and leisure generally form distinct spheres in people's lives. Activities and experiences deemed appropriate to each sphere occur for the most part in different places at different times with different people. This way of thinking affects the organization of daily life—most people distinguish between free time and work time. It also influences our assumptions about the stages in the life span. The transition from the spontaneity of childhood through adolescence to adulthood, for example, consists of increasingly structured preparation for an adult life of productive work (interrupted by intervals of leisure) and a transition to retirement ideally devoted to the cultivation of leisure. This pattern seems to most people as natural as the sun rising in the east and setting in the west, but it is actually a relatively recent development in Western history. We get a sense of the changes that shape people in their leisure and work by looking at the interconnected issues of time sense and the organization of work.

Time Sense

Time sense refers to how people comprehend time. Every culture organizes the passage of time in some fashion, distinguishing between how time is reckoned and how it is experienced. Time reckoning often uses natural phenomena like the solar year or the lunar month to denote units of time. People experience time culturally, reflecting the relation between human activity and natural phenomena. What matters is not the interval between one full moon and the next, but during which moon the fruit ripens. Human activities are cued by the cultural meanings of these phenomena, not the phenomena themselves. Time sense is not "telling time" but understanding the meaning of time within a specific cultural context.

Two broad types of time sense exist: cyclical and linear. In *cyclical time* sense, people organize the experience of time around cycles or recurring events from the natural world or daily life. The annual cycle of the year's seasons is a natural cycle that has cultural meanings. Such recurring events in daily life as tending livestock, going to draw water at the village well, beginning work, or starting the fire for the evening meal are often socially or ritually complex activities with meanings absorbed into time sense. We get a sense of duration, or time reckoning, from knowing how long it takes to do something like roast an ear of corn. All societies have cycles in daily life. For example, we do not need a calendar or clock to know whether it is Sunday or Monday morning in a large city. Distinctive rhythms of traffic patterns, the ways people move along the sidewalk, or go in and out of buildings are characteristic of specific days in the weekly cycle. They are meaningful to us because we understand their cultural context.

Linear time is organized around definite beginning and ending points. Linear time reckoning measures time as a succession of discrete, standardized increments. Each increment occurs once and none is ever repeated. Tomorrow may be another day, but the day we are experiencing right now will never return. Lacking reference to natural cycles or events in daily life, linear time is given meaning by its uses. Therefore, in linear time sense we experience time as something that can be used well or poorly. Benjamin Franklin's remonstrance against idleness in *Poor Richard's Almanac* captures this aspect of linear time sense: "Dost thou love life? Then do not squander time, for that's the stuff life is made of" (Franklin, 2000). To see how linear time sense structures daily life in Western society, glance around you in class. How many of your classmates are wearing watches? How many carry appointment books, planners, or electronic schedulers? It is not by accident that one of the most popular brands of appointment calendars and planners is named "The Franklin Planner."

The Organization of Work

Cyclical time sense is usually most characteristic of preindustrial and agricultural societies, while linear time sense occurs in industrial societies. Elements of cyclical time sense remain, however, even in highly industrialized settings. After AD 1300, a change in time sense became steadily more evident in Europe. Change in time sense related to the changing organization of work, even though other factors such as technological innovation and urbanization were involved.

Work can be classified as task-oriented or time-disciplined. An association exists between cyclical time sense and task orientation, and between linear time sense and time discipline. Task-oriented work is organized around features inherent in the tasks to be performed. Some tasks can be set aside today and taken up tomorrow without any ill effects. A button can be sewed on a new coat tomorrow as well as today without harming the coat. Other tasks, once started, must be carried to completion. For example, a person cannot leave cloth for our new coat in the dyeing vat overnight without ruining it. An internal necessity rising from the nature of the task itself governs task-oriented work. An element of task orientation is also governed by natural cycles. Tides dictate when fishing boats must leave and return to port and weather cycles determine when crops must be planted and harvested. The urgency lies within the tasks themselves and are not imposed by a calendar or clock.

Task-oriented work, even if it involves intense labor, allows the integration of work into the rest of life. Thompson (1967) commented that in task-oriented work,

> Social intercourse and labour are intermingled—the working day lengthens or contracts according to the task—and there is no great sense of conflict between labour and 'passing the time of day.' (p. 60)

Once the task is completed, the sense of urgency associated with work is reduced. Societies where task orientation is prevalent are thus characterized by alternating periods of hard work and slack time. This rhythm is experienced as natural because it is based on necessities seemingly imposed by the structure of work itself.

Time-disciplined work began with the spread of industrialization. Large-scale enterprises require synchronizing the activities of many workers engaged in different tasks. Supervisors want to predict the work to be done so they can schedule and control it. The unpredictable work rhythms found in smaller workshops are not acceptable because they jeopardize the higher profits that can be realized from enterprises of greater size. To synchronize the activities of many workers, new meanings of time were necessary. Workers who enjoyed irregular hours, even skipping work altogether on Mondays and Tuesdays, had to be organized to work not by the internal necessities of the task, but by external clock time. They had to arrive at a set time, work a set number of hours, put down their work only when permitted, and go home at a set time. Submitting to the discipline of clock time was a new experience for most of workers as industrialization began. It created a distinction between work time and nonwork time that was alien to them.

Contemporary Conceptualizations of Leisure

Definitions of leisure have implications for programming and planning, recreation and leisure services, and leisure research. Since time discipline has been central to the evolution of modern work, it is not surprising that leisure is commonly defined as free time. Leisure is also frequently defined as activity people do for enjoyment or fun. Enjoyment, fun, and motivation suggest a further definition of leisure as a psychological experience or state of mind. An additional emerging approach conceptualizes leisure as a cultural construct integrating values and expectations about time and activity.

Leisure as Time

Time-based definitions of leisure appeared because of the transition to the modern organization of work. The motivation to work was assumed to be the desire for wages received in exchange for surrendering control over one's activities for a specified time at a specified place. Leisure came to be defined as time when one was not paid, away from the work place, and in control of one's own undertakings. This definition reflects two important elements of modern work: the distinction between work time and nonwork time and the separation of paid work from other life activities. To define leisure as free time, then, is to define it in terms of what it is not rather than as what it is.

Early economists who regarded leisure as a threat to economic stability were among the first to define leisure as unpaid time and the opposite of paid time at work. One problem with this definition is the unspoken assumption that only paid work away from the home has value. The definition overlooks socially vital activities like childrearing, household management, personal care, and community volunteering. Since women performed most of these activities, this definition excluded their contributions and the structures of their time. Today most economists recognize that many factors affect time use.

Sociologists have also distinguished between paid time and unpaid time but generally have been more sensitive to the different activities occurring during nonwork time. Leisure was distinguished not only from paid work but also from nonwork activities made necessary by work, such as commuting and even eating and sleeping. The French sociologist Dumazedier (1967) noted the discretionary nature of both time and activity. Parker (1971) concluded that defining leisure as nonwork activity was satisfactory as long as possible limits on free choice and the preeminent social value of work were acknowledged.

Anthropologists have studied time use in a wide range of societies. Not all cultures distinguish between work time and nonwork time, but all have some organization of time and activity that permits analysis of the relation between leisure and work (Gross, 1984; Munn, 1992). Anthropologists have also studied the effects of industrialization on work time and leisure time and noted the confusion between ideas of *observed* and *intended* use of time (Betzig & Turke, 1985). For example, a task assumed by an observer to be work might instead be regarded by participants as an occasion to "pass the time of day" in the social activity accompanying the task.

Leisure as Activity

Leisure is defined as activity when pursued for its own sake and for enjoyment or fun. Leisure activities can be categorized into activity sets that share important characteristics (Goodale & Godbey, 1988). Examples of activity sets include competitive sports, cooperative games, outdoor endeavors, cultural pursuits, and socializing. Defining leisure as activity assumes that participants not only have free time for leisure activity, but also suitable environments. Historical evidence suggests that societies have consistently created both time and space for leisure activity.

We commonly study leisure activity by inventorying the distribution and frequency of participation in specific activities. Data on participants in leisure activity and the frequencies of their participation are important to recreation planners, programmers, and researchers. Local, state, and federal recreation agencies compile such information, as does the Bureau of the Census. Trade associations and business groups are often good sources of information on leisure activity patterns.

One of the problems with the conceptualization of leisure as activity is that not all traditionally identified activities are leisure for every person. For example, many people regard golf as a common leisure activity yet some individuals have tried golf and found it to be unenjoyable for a variety of reasons. Another problem with leisure as activity is that these activities are usually considered physically active in some way. An individual may really enjoy sitting on a park bench watching ducks swim on a lake, but one will not likely find this listed in activity checklists.

Leisure as Psychological Experiences or State of Mind

Even when defining leisure as activity or time, psychological themes such as motivation, fun, enjoyment, and freedom are present. Psychological definitions of leisure distinguish between leisure and nonleisure in at least three ways: (1) leisure is freely chosen and not compulsory; (2) leisure is done for its own sake (i.e., intrinsic motivation), not as a means to another goal (i.e., extrinsic motivation); and (3) leisure allows the participant a sense of control over its outcomes.

Neulinger's (1981) concept of *perceived freedom*, among the best-known psychological conceptualizations of leisure, states,

> Any activity carried out freely without constraint or compulsion may be associated with the experience of leisure. *To leisure* implies being engaged in an activity as a free agent and of one's own choice. (p. 16)

Leisure exists when people perceive themselves as having freely selected an activity. Neulinger added two qualifications. First, the individual always perceives degrees of freedom, not complete freedom. Second, the motivation for an individual's activity influences perceived freedom. Perceived freedom is more likely if one is intrinsically rather than extrinsically motivated.

Ellis (1973) suggested that another important psychological definition of leisure uses the concept of *optimal arousal*. Human beings seek stimulation in their environments. If arousal levels are too high (e.g., because of an inability to affect the outcome of an activity) or too low (e.g., because an activity's outcome is easily controlled), people experience unpleasant or uncomfortable psychological states. People attempt to achieve balanced or optimal arousal levels and to experience pleasant psychological states (Mannell & Kleiber, 1997). In other words, they seek to have fun. Optimal arousal levels vary from individual to individual and for the same person across different occasions and activities. Optimal levels also fluctuate based on the novelty of environmental stimuli and the individual's perceived competence, motivation, and sense of control (Crandall, 1980; Iso-Ahola, 1980; Kleiber, 1979; Mannell, Zuzanek & Larson, 1988).

Csikszentmihalyi (1975) described a flow or autotelic experience as one the individual is motivated to pursue by the experience itself even when other rewards are absent. Autotelic activities "give participants a sense of discovery, exploration, problem solution…a feeling of novelty and challenge" (p. 30). People are intrinsically motivated to engage in autotelic activities because they enjoy increasing their senses of competence and control. Familiar, routine, or unchallenging activity creates boredom, while strange, unusual, or demanding activity generates anxiety. The flow state occurs when a person engages in an activity with "total involvement" (p. 36) that moves beyond time and effort and when the individual feels merged with both activity and environment.

Leisure also has been characterized as a state of mind, perhaps better described as spiritual rather than psychological. The roots of a state of mind conceptualization lie in ideals often associated with the solitary, withdrawn, or contemplative life (O'Laughlin, 1978). Pieper (1963) described leisure as "a mental and spiritual attitude" (p. 40) independent of time or work. As the opposite of idleness, Pieper also described leisure as an "inward calm" or "silence," and a "receptive attitude of mind" (p. 41). Bregha (1991) suggested leisure is an end in itself requiring wisdom and self-mastery, and is a form of inward liberation culminating in "inner strength and independence" (p. 53). In this state of mind conceptualization, leisure provides a sense of peace within oneself and in connection to the world around. Many people find leisure in wilderness experiences that allow for these connections.

Leisure as a Cultural Construct

Each preceding approach to defining leisure—time, activity, and psychological experience—shares a tendency to separate leisure from other activity. Human activity is more complex than these definitions suggest. Many people, for example, find similar satisfactions in leisure and in work. The separation of modern leisure and work has never been as absolute as the previous discussion suggests. Contemporary leisure and work are currently undergoing several transformations that tend to integrate rather than separate them. Examples include flexible work schedules and the ways people can connect to their work through electronic communications. The outcomes of these transformations cannot yet be predicted, but people will likely need to reconsider the conceptualizations of leisure to take them into account.

A more integrated definition of leisure acknowledges that activity, time, or psychological experiences are not inherently either leisure or work. Kelly (1996) took an important step by gathering these dimensions together to define leisure as the quality of an activity occurring during unobligated time, characterized by a sense of relative freedom and intrinsic satisfaction. Kleiber (1999) went further, distinguishing between the context (preconditions) of leisure and the characteristics of leisure. In Kleiber's view, the context for leisure is established by freedom of choice, intrinsic motivation, and freedom from evaluation. People experience activities differently— activities that are boring or frightening for some people are fascinating or exhilarating for others. Even the prospect of several days of free time elicits different responses. Some people find free time enticing while others find it intimidating. To reflect differences in people's preferences for or reactions during leisure experiences, Kleiber defined leisure as "the combination of free time and the expectation of preferred experience" (p. 10). People engage in specific leisure activities during their free time because they anticipate certain outcomes.

Individual preferences are not independent of societal and cultural influences. Every society defines some activities as work, others as leisure. The outcomes anticipated in these activities are socially and culturally defined even before we begin to consider them. What is experienced as leisure, and how it is experienced, often depends on factors outside the individual's control, such as the structure and value of work (Parker, 1971). Further, leisure is not free from the influence of social and moral norms. Gist and Fava (1964) pointed out that social values and peer pressure limit choices of activity even during discretionary time. Therefore, the symbolic meanings of leisure generally come to us from our culture. Whether activities are regarded as work or leisure, what is preferred, and what is expected from the activities depend in significant part on customary behaviors within that culture. One should be open, however, to the diversity of meanings and values likely to be associated with leisure within different cultures.

Rojek (1989) made the point that "leisure time and space do not merely exist in society" but are in fact "continuously made and remade by the actions of people" (p. 203). People decide what constitutes leisure or work and how they are valued. Citizens and leisure professionals need to remember that when we reflect on leisure activity, time, and experience, we participate in making and remaking their symbolic meanings in our cultures. We must be sensitive to the definitions around which we organize our professional and personal lives. These definitions have consequences regarding our attitudes as well as our behaviors pertaining to important human activities like work and leisure.

Reflection Questions

1. Describe the contemporary views of leisure.

2. Which of the current conceptualizations of leisure most closely fits with your personal perspective on leisure?

3. Discuss the role of time in shaping our contemporary views of work and leisure.

4. How has a change from cyclical to linear time influenced work and leisure patterns?

5. What consequences do you think the different definitions of leisure might have for how leisure is studied and how recreation and leisure services are delivered?

1.4　Freedom and Leisure

Some people believe that to have leisure one must be free and to be free one must have leisure. The association with freedom is a primary source of leisure's enduring value, although the relationship has changed throughout history. Today freedom and leisure tend to be framed in individualist terms, obscuring the fact that neither exists independently of social context. Instead, both freedom and leisure are aspects of human activity in specific social contexts. Several components exist in a social context:

- Social structures (e.g., individuals, families, friendship groups, governments, corporations);

- Resources and their distribution (e.g., wealth, education, kinds of work, time, recreation facilities and programs); and

- Values (e.g., status of work, whether work or leisure is more important).

Thus, social contexts influence freedom and leisure in at least two important ways. First, they shape the meanings and structures of freedom and leisure. Second, they affect who has freedom and leisure, what kinds, and to what extent. Freedom cannot be fully understood without considering the social contexts where leisure occurs.

Freedom and leisure mirror the history of their social contexts. History may be understood as an ongoing discussion over the meanings of freedom and leisure and the people involved. Ignoring these issues fails to recognize how often the presence of freedom and leisure in the lives of some people has depended on the absence of freedom and leisure in the lives of others (Foner, 1994; Patterson, 1991). Denying some people freedom and leisure dilutes the human value of freedom and leisure for all.

Negative and Positive Freedom

By about 1800 freedom in England and the United States meant the sum of rights protecting the individual from unwarranted intrusion into her or his affairs. The individual was free to conceive and pursue aspirations in life without interference. *Negative freedom* or "freedom from" reflects the way in which rights were first established to protect individuals from being forced to act in ways that harmed their own interests. For example, people did not want to be compelled to practice a specific religion or to surrender property without compensation. Negative freedom is essentially the freedom to be let alone and not be hindered in activities by outside authority or force, whether by government or private individuals. It has been the prevailing definition of freedom in the European-American tradition from the late 17th century to today.

Whether an individual has the opportunity to carry out plans effectively lies outside the scope of negative freedom. If an individual's circumstances (e.g., distinguished from talents, abilities, or effort) deny her or him this opportunity, the individual's freedom is abstract and empty. No person interferes, but circumstances interfere with effective pursuit of aspirations and plans. Consider how often circumstances reflect preexisting distributions of resources or access to opportunities. How much freedom in leisure can a person experience without free time or access to recreation facilities and services? Negative freedom is not particularly helpful in answering this question.

Concern about the shortcomings of negative freedom and its tendency to reinforce existing patterns of social advantages and opportunities developed late in the 19th century. To a growing number of social reformers, religious leaders, politicians and academics, negative freedom seemed an incomplete freedom. Among them was Green (1964), an Oxford professor of moral philosophy who wrote that freedom was incomplete unless it included "a positive power or capacity of doing or enjoying something worth doing or enjoying" (p. 51). This notion became more commonly known as *positive freedom* or "freedom to."

Positive freedom was not meant to replace, but to build on negative freedom. Perhaps its greatest influence has been in expanding the definition of rights. As they do in negative freedom, rights establish an area of non-interference, but positive freedom also defines the effective use of rights. Rights establish entitlements to resources necessary for people "to make the best of themselves" (Green, 1964, p. 55). Freedom remains incomplete when an individual's rights are limited. Existing obstacles must also be removed. Even Berlin (1969), a strong critic of positive freedom, was moved to ask, "What are rights without the power to implement them?" (p. xvi).

Because of positive freedom, rights have become more grounded in people's daily lives. Greater attention is given to the importance of access to the resources that make rights concrete rather than abstract. In an analysis of freedom, MacCallum (1967) argued that negative and positive freedom should not be regarded as distinct types, but as two dimensions of freedom. He suggested that when asking about an individual's or group's freedom we ask one question with three parts: Who is to be free, from what they are to be free, and what are they free to do or become? Therefore, being free involves more than the absence of interference. It also means being able to expand beyond the limits of the present to experience different possibilities.

Implications for Freedom in Leisure

All definitions of leisure have at least some reference to freedom. Kelly (1987) referred to leisure as activity characterized by a sense of relative freedom, while Kleiber (1999) termed it "a context of relative freedom that presents opportunities for preferred experience" (p. 5). Freedom in leisure is clearly not absolute, but how does relative freedom occur? We can explore this question using the basic approaches to conceptualizing leisure identified in Chapter 1.3: time, activity, psychological experience, and cultural construct.

Time and Activity

Leisure is defined as time or activity when free from compulsion, necessity, or obligation. Time is free when it is at our disposal, available for us to use as we wish. Similarly, activity is free when we choose it ourselves; that is, when it is what we wish to do rather than what we must do.

Freedom in leisure time and activity requires individual and social resources. The kind of work we do, our family obligations, and other related factors affect how much time we have for leisure. How often we can engage in our preferred leisure activities, whether we must substitute other activities, and how much discretionary income we can spend on leisure are all influenced by individual factors. People have different levels of information about leisure and may or may not know how to get more. We develop or refine individual resources such as leisure interests and skills. Social resources include friends and acquaintances who might alert us to leisure opportunities, participate with us, and share knowledge, equipment, or cost. Other social resources consist of clubs, organizations, facilities, programs, and other services provided by public and not-for-profit agencies in our communities.

Distribution of individual and social resources does not occur by chance. Many influences shape resource distribution, including geography and climate, economic conditions, social diversity, public policy decisions, and social attitudes and opinions. When considering freedom in leisure we must always keep in mind not only the resources needed during leisure time and activity, but also the factors affecting their distribution in social contexts.

Psychological Experience

The source of freedom in leisure varies depending on how one defines the psychological experience of leisure. Neulinger (1981), for example, viewed the source of freedom in leisure as the structure of the individual's psychological perceptions and not the activity itself. Neulinger acknowledged that freedom of choice is never complete, but suggested that perceived freedom is greater when the individual's motivations are intrinsic and aimed at the activity itself.

Harper (1986) criticized the emphasis on free choice in psychological models of freedom in leisure because choice is not a unique feature of leisure. Instead, Harper proposed that two other features of psychological experience in leisure created its freedom. The first is "ongoing consent," or the reaffirmation of an initial choice to engage in a leisure activity by continued participation because it is fun or enjoyable. The second factor is "intensification of ordinary experience" when leisure seems to become richer or fuller. According to Harper, freedom in leisure exists when people commit to ongoing activity because it lifts them beyond their routine experience.

The definition of leisure as psychological experience has influenced implications for freedom in leisure. Each of us desires to experience some freedom in the leisure available to us now. To make a choice of leisure activities, however, does not create freedom in leisure. Choice does not create freedom in leisure because the alternatives we choose have already been filtered by the social contexts in which leisure occurs. Individual and social resources, our personal circumstances, our social identities, and social roles powerfully influence our choices. The range of available opportunities effectively establishes the amount of freedom of choice.

The illusion of freedom may be more important than its reality. Ellis and Witt suggested "perceiving oneself as 'free' from necessity is more important than actually being free" (1985, p. 106). Neulinger (1981) asserted that whether perceived freedom is true freedom or only an illusion is irrelevant, because even illusions have real consequences. The crucial consequence of the illusion of freedom is leisure. However much we enjoy moments of escape from the cares and tasks of daily life, those cares and tasks remain real. Freedom in leisure must also be real, even if partial and incomplete.

Cultural Construct

The cultural approach to defining leisure focuses most directly on leisure's social contexts. These contexts influence both people's expectations about leisure and how they structure their leisure to fulfill their expectations. As we noted in the previous chapter, the cultural meanings of activity, experience, and time all shape leisure expectations. Even individual leisure styles reveal the influence of the surrounding culture. Cultures provide characteristic repertoires of behaviors or actions that people use in deciding how to act in different situations. People may or may not think about why they made the decisions. Leisure does not escape these cultural influences that shape both the formation of leisure expectations and how they are pursued.

Social roles are among the ways that people order their actions. Social roles incorporate cultural values and culturally defined expectations that establish the ranges of behaviors acceptable for individuals. By structuring

activity in culturally acceptable ways, role expectations allow us to anticipate how people in specific social roles will act. Social interaction thus
becomes more predictable and less costly because there is less need to negotiate appropriate actions in any given situation. We seldom occupy only
one social role at a time. Role conflict occurs when circumstances arise in
which our different social roles impose differing expectations. The mediation of role conflict draws on values established by cultural and social
contexts, and on our own personal interpretations of them.

Cultural influences affect freedom in leisure. For example, Kelly (1978)
asked people why they had participated in specific leisure activities based
on issues of freedom and meanings of role expectations. He then used the
reasons people gave to classify leisure into four types (see Figure 1.4):
unconditional (i.e., high freedom, intrinsic meaning), compensatory or recuperative (i.e., low freedom, intrinsic meaning), relational (i.e., high
freedom, social meaning) and role-determined (i.e., low freedom, social
meaning). When the four types of leisure were analyzed for their relations
to social role expectations, only unconditional leisure was relatively independent of one's social role. Compensatory or recuperative leisure activities
contrasted deliberately with the demands imposed by social role expectations, such as relaxation to recuperate from the stresses of parenthood or
work. Relational leisure activities enhanced personal relationships as part
of expectations associated with social roles like being a friend or neighbor.

		Freedom	
		High	Low
Meaning	**Intrinsic**	Unconditional Leisure	Compensatory Leisure; Recuperative Leisure
	Social	Relational Leisure	Role-determined Leisure

Adapted from Kelly, J. R. (1983). *Leisure identities and interactions.*
London, UK: Unwin Hyman Limited.

Figure 1.4:   Leisure: A Revised Paradigm

Respondents did not experience these role expectations as constraints, but said the expectations guided them in making leisure choices. Role-determined leisure, as the term indicates, was directly constrained by social role expectations (e.g., parent, spouse). In contrast with relational leisure, social role expectations were experienced as leisure constraints rather than as sources of personal leisure satisfaction.

Based on Kelly's findings, freedom in leisure is relative to social roles and the cultural expectations about behavior that shape these roles. People organize their leisure activities in response to role expectations and in anticipation of the consequences of conforming or not conforming to them. How people prioritize competing role expectations and negotiate role conflicts is central to leisure in daily life. As Kelly (1978) concluded, leisure does not occur "in a completely separate life and space unrelated to other roles and meanings" (p. 326). Social roles embody culturally constructed expectations about people's activities. They are a fundamental aspect of the social contexts in which leisure, and thus freedom in leisure, occurs.

Two factors mediate the influence of social roles on leisure. The first factor, cultural diversity, often leads to ambiguous role expectations, especially in multicultural societies. Differences in role expectations affect leisure. The freedom that people expect from their leisure and how they structure their leisure activities to achieve it also varies across cultural contexts. All recreation and leisure professionals require sensitivity to cultural diversity and its implications.

The second mediating factor is the availability of resources such as income, education, or time. Although social roles differ in the nature of the resources they require, access to a broad variety of resources increases the likelihood that an individual will be able to meet her or his role expectations satisfactorily. The relative importance of different resources varies among cultures. The increased importance of commercial recreation and the trend toward market models for public services, for example, have made income a more fundamental leisure resource. Linder (1970) has also demonstrated that income may be substituted for other leisure resources, especially free time. Given these considerations, we must emphasize the persistent, unequal, and nonrandom distribution of resources in the United States. To the extent resources are required for leisure, inequality in resource distribution leads to inequity in the opportunity for freedom in leisure.

Thus, freedom and leisure are inextricably related. Freedom in leisure is part of overall freedom. The freedom of some people should not come at the expense of others' freedom. Freedom entails a certain basic equality, if not in outcomes then in genuine opportunities. Freedom and its rights are hollow if they are systematically or effectively denied to any person or group of people. Perhaps the best means to ensure one's own freedom is to help others achieve theirs. The opportunity to help others find freedom in leisure is a large part of what can make a career in leisure services so rewarding. Freedom and leisure are highly influenced by social contexts that shape the meanings and affect who has leisure.

Reflection Questions

1. Distinguish between *negative freedom* and *positive freedom*. To what aspects of leisure do you think each of them is most applicable?

2. How do social contexts affect freedom in leisure?

3. In what ways might you as a recreation and leisure professional assist people in creating more freedom in their leisure and in their daily lives?

4. What is the role of freedom in shaping individual and community leisure?

5. Are recreation and leisure fundamental human rights?

1.5   People and Play

Many attempts have been made to explain the meaning and purpose of play as related to leisure and recreation in the past 100 years. Play interests biologists, physiologists, psychologists, sociologists, and educators, as well as recreation and leisure professionals. The theoretical basis of recreation and leisure services stems from society's notions of play and the meanings of leisure. In a sense, recreation exists because people want and need to play; recreation professionals in all sectors provide the environments and opportunities for selected play, leisure, and recreation expressions. Approaches and theories of play and leisure have given direction to recreation programs, to the design and forms of facilities and equipment, and to the rationale for the importance of recreation and leisure in society.

The Descriptions of Play

The term play comes from the Anglo-Saxon *plegian* and *plega* and from the German *pfegen,* all meaning to take care of oneself. Play has been used to describe the free, natural, engaging, spontaneous, and satisfying activities of the young. People really never cease to play, but that play behavior may be refined and described by some other label such as "fooling around" or "chilling out" when adults are involved.

The term recreation emerges from the Latin *recreāre,* which means to re-create, restore, and renew. It frequently describes the play activities of adults, although some people define it as being distinct from play. Both are engaging forms of expression freely chosen without concern for external gain or achievement except for the satisfaction derived from playing. Both are self-contained experiences with intrinsic rewards. We generally think of recreation as being more formally organized and play being the spontaneity that occurs within that organization.

The understanding of play and recreation constantly changes. Because play, leisure, and recreation behaviors are part of the overall pattern of human expression, the theories offered as explanations for them rarely differ from the theories offered to explain behavior in general. Recreation and play theories should always be considered in the context of the history and culture in which they were formulated.

Theories of Play and Recreation

Prior to scientific research, most explanations for behavior were simple and direct. One played "when the spirit moved him or her." This view changed with the coming of scientific methods and the need to have testable hypotheses and ways to describe and predict action accurately. *Theories* offer a reason for observed behavior and stimulate questions about that behavior. According to Ellis (1973), many theories of play have been identified. These theories can be grouped into four major schools of thought: physiological, psychological, sociological, and contemporary theories.

Physiological Explanations

The earliest explanations of play stressed genetic and biological factors. Theories offered during the latter half of the 19th century reflected much of the thinking of the Darwinians, who ascribed all human behaviors to genetics. People thought children played because they were genetically programmed for that activity. Play developed the necessary skills for survival, and children would cease to play or modify their forms of play when it was no longer needed. These theories suggested that children had little to say about what they were going to play since those determinations were biologically and genetically set. Some of the modern notions of letting children play to drain off their energies, or thinking that all boys should play sports because "that is what males naturally do" emanated from these early explanations of play.

As the inadequacies of the biological explanations became apparent, new schools of thought developed. The first of these were the psychological-biological theories that suggested people had certain basic innate needs and drives that had to be met. These needs could be fulfilled in a variety of ways with play being one of them. Play was assumed to be a compensatory and cathartic activity and a way of releasing energies and psychic tensions, especially for adults. Work was tension producing and play was the opposite. Therefore, play provided an emotional balance. Workers needed the pleasures that came from recreation, and play was not an activity exclusive to children.

Psychological Explanations

With a growing awareness of the role played by the social environment in shaping behavior, new psychological explanations of the origin and function of play were offered. Sigmund Freud (1964) influenced many of the early psychological theorists. One of the more interesting Freudian analyses of play suggested that society had legitimized certain forms of play that allowed the individual to deal with internal conflicts and to express basic urges. For example, the death wish might be accommodated and released through automobile racing, whereas exhibitionist tendencies might be handled through acting and dramatic performances. Instead of attacking someone when frustrated, one can hit a ball.

Later psychological play theorists embraced the views of developmental psychologists such as Erik Erikson and Jean Piaget. Both schools of thought cited the relationship of play to growth and development (especially for children) and acknowledged the interaction between play motivated by inner drives and urges and the social control of society. Erikson (1968) stated that play was essential for the establishment of self and that certain types of play were critical to certain stages of development. He said that pleasures first came from being physically able to engage in activity. Later, as children develop, they derive pleasure from being able to manipulate physical objects. The child also learns to deal with social relationships through play. In all stages, the ability to master play satisfies and moves the process forward. For adults, Erikson suggested play provides an escape from work expectations and a means of continuing the developmental process. Piaget (1962) stated that children go from the random and symbolic stages of play to games as they move through their own developmental process. According to Piaget, play through games contributed to the intellectual development of the child. Through play children learn to assimilate ideas and behavior and accommodate the world by adjusting to the external order of things.

Sociological Explanations

Although some sociologists wrote about the role of play earlier in the 20th century, most sociologists did not devote much attention to it until George Herbert Mead discussed its role in the socialization of young children in 1932. Sociologists did not attempt to explain why people play, but focused upon the forms of play and its role in maintaining social groups and social organizations. They assumed that play was natural and useful, and served definite societal functions. According to sociological theory, play helps to maintain the social structure. Consequently, play reflects and perpetuates the values and controls of society.

Mead (1963) believed play to be second only to language in the development of the social self. In play, children explore social roles and learn the ethics and morals of a society. For example, through fantasy play the child assumes and acts out various roles such as father, mother, astronaut, or firefighter. Games reinforce social expectations since the nature of the game itself requires the player to play by the rules and recognize her or his role and the role of others playing the same game.

A recent concern is the difference in participation rates of males and females as well as individuals from various socioeconomic, ethnic, and racial backgrounds. The civil rights movement and the women's movement in the United States have emphasized the need to examine whether all individuals have equal opportunities for play and recreation participation.

Contemporary Explanations

The newer concepts of play and its relationships, particularly to recreation, blend the physiological, psychological, and sociological views into a single explanation. Today's theories suggest play is necessary for human development. We need play for the total functioning of the individual and to interact with the environment at an optimum level. Further, play and recreation are essential for contributing to the quality of life of individuals, communities, and societies. Through play, people express who they are and interact socially.

Social psychologists identify a variety of motives or satisfactions that drive leisure behaviors, including satisfactions that come from adventure, being a part of a group, learning something new, expressing one's creativity, engaging in fantasy, and/or experiencing solitude. Theorists argue that leisure, recreation, and play experiences are satisfying because of the qualities inherent in the experience.

Csikszentmihalyi's (1975, 1990) work with flow is another example of a social psychological response to the environment as a challenging set of relationships and elements. When the situation is no longer challenging (i.e., boring) or exceeds the skill level of the individual (i.e., produces anxiety), the response is either to discontinue the activity or to change the activity to become manageable. If the game becomes too complex, for example, an individual develops the skills necessary to play, does not play, or modifies its rules. Csikszentmihalyi cautions, however, that in play one does not always experience flow.

We have attempted to demonstrate the importance of theory to traditional and more recent understandings of play, recreation, and leisure. Although some differences exist among the theories, several points of agreement exist. For example, all of the theories conceive of play and recreation as action rather than inaction or idleness. Action does not necessarily mean vigorous physical action, but it does imply the expending of energies in the play pursuit, whether psychological, physical, or emotional. In addition, these theories suggest that play and recreation are pleasurable and somewhat motivated by the satisfactions derived from the experience. Since play activities are usually freely chosen, the activities generally are not continued if they are not satisfying and enjoyable. Play may assist or be a primary vehicle in the social development of individuals, allowing for learning and exploration in children as well as adults.

Through play and recreation, a person develops and tests his or her concepts of self and the world. Regardless of whether the descriptions of play relate to individual or social outcomes, children and adults experience leisure through play. The values and traditions of society ultimately shape play behavior and avenues of leisure fulfillment. Attitudes and behaviors regarding play and recreation are culturally molded.

Reflection Questions

1. How have the four broad explanations of why people play changed over time?

2. How are cultural norms and values conveyed through play?

3. Why is play critical for social understanding and social interaction?

4. What do you think are the values of play?

5. How is play related to recreation and leisure?

1.6 Approaches to Leisure

People sometimes snicker when someone says they are majoring in recreation or are taking a course in recreation and leisure studies at a university. We hope by now that you see that the study of recreation and leisure is not a trivial undertaking. Leisure and recreation have value in relation to work, time, freedom, culture, and a variety of life issues. This chapter will address the traditional philosophical views and emerging paradigms used to examine leisure.

Traditional Philosophical Approaches

Philosophers have always attempted to explain the nature of human beings and the universe. Many people who write about recreation have discussed philosophies of leisure and play. The study of leisure has been eclectic, with a combination of several traditional and contemporary paradigmatic approaches. Traditional philosophical positions that have influenced our understanding of leisure and recreation delivery systems over the years include idealism, realism, pragmatism, existentialism, and humanism.

Idealism

Idealism holds that an eternal set of goals or ideals govern human behavior and that one should seek to understand these truths and work for perfection. According to the idealist, individuals should be goal-directed and the means employed to achieve their goals should be equal to the ends. How one plays the game is just as important as the final score.

The earlier writers and thinkers in the park and recreation movements were idealists. Perhaps the most influential of these pioneers was Joseph Lee, one of the founders of the Playground Association of America. He believed all play should contribute to the wholesome development of the individual; consequently, play should teach discipline, sacrifice, and moral character as well as be pleasurable (Knapp & Hartsoe, 1979). Nash (1960) also supported this idealism philosophy of recreation by suggesting that participating in a creative way was the most preferred form of leisure expression, whereas spectatorism and vandalism were undesirable pastimes. To Nash and other idealists, being physically active was important and essential to creative participation.

Realism

The development of scientific thought, with the concomitant need to measure and test ideas, forced a modification of the idealistic philosophical position for some professionals. The school of realism emerged with the idea that people must constantly measure their performance against some standard to know what they have accomplished and what their objectives and plans should be. In the realist philosophy, leisure would be beneficial if positive changes could be measured in one's life. Many of the concepts of scientific management and administration in leisure services delivery also resulted from the realist position. Although realism is a viable philosophy, data must be continually generated to keep participants and professionals up to date with current standards.

Pragmatism

Pragmatism has had the greatest impact in the development of recreation and leisure systems. The pragmatist holds goal achievement to be the critical element; the method is secondary. A participant coming from a pragmatic position would be concerned about whether he or she reached goals in recreation such as becoming more proficient at playing a musical instrument or getting a T-shirt for finishing a race.

Pragmatism is a more flexible philosophy than idealism and stresses some of the functionalism of realist perspective. John Dewey, noted educator and pragmatic thinker, influenced the thoughts of early recreation providers. He stressed the importance of play and recreation in the learning process. He stated that one learns best by doing and that individuals should have freedom of choice and opportunities for self-expression rather than adhere to a set pattern of behavior imposed upon them by an "authority" (Dewey, 1916). He considered play spontaneous activity and an outlet for creative expression and creative development. Each player should find his or her own means for expression through individualized programs. Each community should also provide leisure services to its citizens based upon the needs and interests of that community. According to the pragmatist, each community should develop a unique approach to recreation and park services based upon the resources and traditions of the community and the skills and resources of staff.

To pragmatic recreation professionals, methods and techniques are important only as tools. Pragmatists use standards as guidelines, not as binding laws. They acknowledge that an ideal state exists toward which one should work, but the ideal is relative and subject to change depending upon the changing needs and views of people. Pragmatism's major shortcoming has been the expediency factor that sometimes causes goals to be sacrificed for the immediate situation. Individual needs often become secondary to group concerns and management approaches that focus on setting goals and getting things done.

Existentialism

Existentialism emerged after World War II. To the existentialist, the individual is all-important and the only absolute is life itself. It is the philosophy of "here and now." How one feels about life is more important than what one does.

Existentialism has impacted recreation and leisure services by returning the individual to the forefront. Existentialism is often evident in the foundations of therapeutic recreation. Further, existentialists challenge the policies of governmental bureaucracies that tend not to be responsive to individual needs. The biggest danger accompanying this philosophy is the tendency to underestimate the future and the consequences of the actions that people might take. The here and now has a way of becoming the past, and the decisions of yesterday do affect the present and the future.

Humanism

To the humanist, the human being is the supreme value. The humanist focuses on the individual's potential and advocates the elimination of all social, physical, economic, and psychological barriers that might hinder or restrict freedom as well as growth and development. Unlike existentialism, this philosophy is action-oriented. Recreation professionals find humanism attractive because it stresses purposeful living, higher functioning, and a sense of social consciousness. It forces us to consider the whole person, the interaction between the individual and the physical and social environment, and the limitations that those environments impose upon the individual. According to humanists, oppressive environments must be changed. Moreover, the failure to grow is the result of the environment, not the fault of the individual.

Humanism gained popularity in the late 1960s. Its advocates strongly support civil liberties, equal rights for women, cultural diversity, and broadening the scope and mission of leisure service systems. They promote a more individualistic approach to the provision of recreation opportunities, advocating that recreation professionals assume a more humanistic perspective in allowing for individual exploration and self-discovery.

These traditional philosophies provide a foundation for understanding recreation and leisure over the past 100 years and offer frameworks for examining recreation and leisure in the 21st century. A philosophy can serve as a base for some of our beliefs, but each of us will continue to develop our philosophy of leisure and of life. By shifting perspectives of our basic philosophy, we often see new understandings that we previously missed.

Contemporary Paradigms and Approaches

According to Babbie (1986), a *paradigm* is a "fundamental model or system for understanding things" (p. 29). Kuhn (1970) explained a paradigm as a model embraced by a group that emerges as a result of competing perspectives about what constitutes knowledge. Paradigms, similar to global philosophies, are frameworks for understanding how the world works. Like philosophies, paradigms help to explain what people see and experience in a way that helps us to make sense of the world. Various paradigms can help people think about historic and contemporary notions of leisure, the ways that researchers theorize and conceptualize leisure, and the ways that practitioners and professionals facilitate leisure experiences.

Perhaps the most important paradigm shifts in how Americans have thought about leisure occurred from the 19th to the 20th century. During these shifts, leisure began to emerge as a distinct institution within American society. Between 1880 and 1920, three events occurred that influenced the creation of leisure as an area to be studied and a profession to be cultivated. First, in the shift from farm life to urban living and from agrarian to industrialized economies, we moved toward a mechanistic society where people's lives were fragmented and controlled by the artificial rhythms of the clock. Second, this time period ushered in the contemporary construction of adolescence. This concept of adolescence contributed to the development of primary and secondary schools, the passage of child labor laws, and the professionalization of recreation and leisure services. The third important shift during this era was the evolution of sociology as the study of social groups.

People who have studied leisure have been educated in a variety of disciplinary paradigms including economics, history, psychology, anthropology, sociology, and education. Sociology, social psychology, and interdisciplinary emerging approaches have offered different paradigms that have affected the way we think about leisure theory.

Sociological Approaches

Sociology has been instrumental in understanding play, recreation, and leisure. *Middletown: A Study of American Culture* by Lynd and Lynd (1929) and *Leisure: A Suburban Study* by Lundberg, Komarovksy, and McInervy (1934) were the earliest formal social science studies of leisure in North America. These theorists viewed leisure as something objective that was a part of the community fabric but experienced apart from the individuals who engaged in a particular activity. Sociology focused on collective and group experiences of leisure rather than on how individuals experienced leisure subjectively and internally.

Sociological studies of leisure were the dominant paradigm used to understand leisure through the 1960s. According to Godbey (1988), the study of the sociology of leisure never fully developed because of a lack of theory building and linkage to mainstream sociology. Godbey further argued that it was difficult to pin down precisely what a sociological explanation of leisure would include. Ultimately, the sociology approach has produced what Godbey characterized as a "range of sociological concepts" (p. 41) that relate to leisure. Such concepts include:

- Historical trends and hours worked

- Lifetime allocations of work and nonwork time

- Time budgets of daily life

- Trends in holidays, vacations, and retirement

- Age of entry into and exit from the labor force in relation to life expectancy

- Monetary expenditures in relation to leisure

- Frequency of participation in leisure activities

- Characteristics of participants

- Social groups and formation of such groups in leisure settings

- Motivations, satisfactions from, and barriers to participation in leisure

- Leisure within families

- Changes in leisure interests, resources, and participation associated with life stages

- Relations between occupational status and type of leisure

- Use of leisure as social control and social agent

- Progression and specialization within leisure activity

- Impact of modernism on leisure

- Leisure subcultures

- Demographic predictions of leisure behaviors

- Value orientations expressed during leisure, tourism, and sports (adapted from Godbey, 1988, p. 38)

Sociology gave researchers and other professionals a way of conceptualizing leisure as a construct to be examined empirically through the process of social science research. Gathering data about what people did for leisure and what they might want to do and with whom has assisted leisure professionals in gaining a better understanding of leisure service program planning and implementation. Mannell and Kleiber (1997) argued that social science could provide tools for professionals in leisure services who are involved with human behavior and experiences during free time. Responding to this assertion, a new generation of researchers and theorists began to question dominant theories and develop alternative explanations for leisure behavior through another approach called social psychology.

Social Psychological Approaches

The sociological approach and the theories that emerged gave some understanding of what people did in their free time, how often people engaged in leisure, and with whom. Yet, these studies fell short of telling us what people thought, how they felt about leisure, and how it may have influenced how they saw themselves and their relationships with other people. Recognizing that sociological explanations of leisure were no longer satisfactory to many professionals, leisure researchers began to draw on social psychology in the late 1960s. Deliberate attempts to develop and promote a social psychology of leisure emerged in the late 1970s. The 1978 Leisure Research Symposium, sponsored by the National Recreation and Park Association, introduced social psychology as one of the categories for research presentations.

Social psychology focuses on the leisure experience and behavior of the individual within various contexts. Psychologists ask why people think and feel the ways they do and what forces influence thoughts and motivations. Social psychology broadens the focal point on the individual to understanding the individual within social contexts and environments. Social psychological studies include issues of freedom, motivation, boredom, constraints and barriers to leisure, and more recently, leisure's role in identity formation. Social psychologists ask what happens to the individual when placed in a variety of leisure contexts such as sports, arts, and the outdoors. They also ask questions about the impact on the individual when she or he cannot engage in leisure because of various constraints, and the benefits of participation in leisure. Although the social psychological paradigm continues to drive the research and theory building that takes place within North American leisure studies, some researchers have sought to broaden this framework by employing critical theory and cultural studies perspectives.

Emerging Approaches

Paradigms related to social psychology have focused on individuals within leisure contexts and on characteristics of identity such as race, gender, ability, and age. For example, in the late 1970s and early 1980s, researchers began to examine gender to determine differences in leisure patterns among women and men. Similar research has been conducted among individuals with disabilities and individuals who identify as lesbian, gay, or bisexual. Although some of this work employs various theoretical perspectives (e.g., feminism), the research and writing used the social psychological approach. In the 1990s, some leisure theorists began to shift their work away from social psychology explanations toward social and cultural analyses of leisure.

Feminism is an example of an approach that has influenced our understanding of leisure and the provision of leisure services. *Feminism* is a philosophical perspective that embodies equity, empowerment, and social change for women and men. It seeks to eliminate the invisibility and distortion of women's experiences (Henderson, Bialeschki, Shaw & Freysinger, 1996). Feminism looks at the role of oppression in women's lives and the way oppression plays a part in the social reality of our lives. Feminism is about the rights of women related to freedom of choice and the power to control their lives. Under this philosophy, women and men come together to resist gender-based oppression. Although many forms of feminism exist (e.g., liberal, socialist, radical, postmodern, cultural, poststructuralist), they all work toward a philosophical stance of equality and freedom from restrictive gender expectations and responsibilities. Gender has become a departure point for further discussion and explorations about leisure. Australian and European feminist theorists such as Wearing (1998) and Scraton (1994) have moved beyond identifying gender as a variable that influences leisure to employing critical theory and cultural studies analyses that examine the influence of power and politics that shape individual identity.

Critical paradigms also emerge as a useful way to understand the potential of leisure. If we are not critical then we accept the status quo. *Critical approaches* seek to empower people to make changes in their lives by examining the social structures that enable and constrain them. Hemingway (1996) employed a critical perspective when he discussed the ways that freedom and leisure do not exist independently of the context in which human beings find themselves. For example, people are free to engage in leisure, but they may have to pay for it. A critical perspective also addresses how leisure has the potential to be positive as well as detrimental to individuals and groups.

Many aspects influence philosophical and paradigmatic approaches to leisure. Knowledge of philosophies and paradigms and how they function can assist us in understanding leisure and the ways it manifests itself through leisure service delivery systems. Philosophies and paradigms change as new problems and approaches emerge. In leisure studies, social psychology continues to be the dominant approach and humanism seems to be the dominant philosophy, but these perspectives are always open to challenge. In addition, individuals need to determine what philosophies or world-views best fit with their beliefs and behaviors. Emerging new ideas make leisure interesting and provide excitement and new possibilities in our lives.

Reflection Questions

1. What are the primary philosophical beliefs about leisure?

2. Pick one philosophy and discuss how it does or does not explain your leisure behavior.

3. What is a primary approach used to explain the leisure behavior? What are the strengths and weakness of this approach?

4. What shapes your philosophy of leisure?

5. What are the differences between leisure philosophies and leisure approaches or paradigms?

1.7   Identities and Leisure

How we see ourselves, how others see us, and how we see ourselves connected with others capture the essence of identity. In addition to the physiological changes that accompany growing up and growing older, people also experience psychological changes in how they see themselves and their relationships with other people over time. Biological, cognitive, and social factors, as well as family, peer, work, and school contexts, influence how people construct themselves and their identities. This chapter examines the role of leisure in understanding identity formation. Identity formation is not a static process; identities are changeable and individuals have personal control over their identity. Each of us has the power to change how we see ourselves, how we respond to how we are seen, and how leisure plays a role in this process.

Roots of Identity

Early philosophers, writers, poets and religious thinkers—Aristotle, Plato, Shakespeare, Whitman, and Austen—have all dealt with issues of self. Not until the end of the 19th century, however, did people begin to scientifically examine what constitutes identity. Psychologists, sociologists, and anthropologists began to develop ways of empirically examining identity through case studies, interviews, and ethnographies. Writings by Sigmund Freud, Carl Jung, Margaret Mead, and others influenced how we in the 21st century think about identity. Today, we continue to embrace elements of these earlier theorists with notions that identity formation includes stages of development that begin in infancy and end in death. Developmental theorists assert that individuals become acutely aware of the process of identity formation during adolescence, and subsequently a "normative" path exists that most people are expected to take toward identity formation.

Virtually all of our knowledge about identity is a social construct. Something is a social construct when the world around us (e.g., what we see, what we hear, and the language that we use to communicate) has been artificially created by people in society. What we know factually and what we accept as truth in terms of how the world operates is based on the idea that people in society have created and constructed knowledge about everything, including our identities.

Personal and Social Identities

Researchers and theorists generally agree that identity formation is composed of two parts: personal identity and social identity (Deaux, 1992). *Personal identity* refers to the core characteristics of how an individual views oneself. For example, "I am a happy person. I am a funny person. I am a good person." The messages received from others, beginning in childhood, influence the extent to which people internalize core characteristics. *Social identity* refers to the social roles that individuals embrace and internalize that allow others to recognize the individual and collective roles played. Often, we embrace many social roles simultaneously, such as daughter, sister, student, or teacher.

The process of identity formation occurs largely during the period of adolescence (ages 13–23). Although people change and grow throughout their lives, the basic structure and core of our identities is formed during adolescence. Erikson (1968) stressed the importance of early family experiences and unconscious thought processes in identity formation. The underlying assumption of his theory is that the more successful the individual is at resolving problems during stages of development, the more psychologically well-adjusted and happy the individual will be.

Developmental theorists focus on how individuals embrace and internalize socially sanctioned roles and identities. These theorists describe what constitutes a psychologically "healthy" individual and have a powerful role in proscribing and reinforcing social norms and mores regarding social identity formation. A healthy individual in America contributes to his or her community through gainful employment, civic involvement, and participation in community life. Between the ages of 23 and 64, the bulk of most people's identity is inextricably linked to paid work. Society often devalues those who cannot work (e.g., people who are unable to work because of a disability). Therefore, leisure can provide a context for identity formation.

Leisure and Identity Formation

Biological, social, and cognitive factors as well as school, family, peers, and leisure contexts contribute to development. Typically, the intersection of personal and social identity occurs in adolescence because society gives permission to young people to experiment with different identities. Adolescence in America has been constructed such that allowances are made for young people to step outside of socially sanctioned expectations of how individuals should look and behave. During adolescence young people have opportunities to engage in a variety of structured and unstructured recreation and leisure opportunities (e.g., sports, music, dramatic arts). Whether the

activities contribute to identity development or whether identity occurs to
the extent that an individual is committed and engaged in the activities
varies. Both ideas are central to determining the impact of structured and
unstructured recreation and leisure upon a person's life.

Leisure can be instrumental and/or expressive. Instrumental leisure
suggests that an individual may be motivated to engage in a typical leisure
activity because it might assist in other areas of life that have nothing to do
with leisure. An individual might engage in a leisure activity in high school
(e.g., music) because she or he enjoys that activity, but that individual
might also do it because she or he hopes to get a scholarship to college
based on that activity. Because leisure is the context that is used to help
the individual facilitate access to some other area of life, instrumental leisure may be more externally motivated. Expressive leisure is pursued and
engaged in simply because of the enjoyment and meaning that an activity
provides in and of itself. It means doing something for the sake of doing it
because you enjoy it. For example, someone might like cross-country skiing and engage in it because it is enjoyable, not because it will assist with
developing physical fitness. Regardless of the motivation for engaging in
leisure, leisure may assist with identity formation in the following ways:

Leisure contexts are transitional. Adolescence as it has been constructed
in the 20th century assists with the transition from childhood to adulthood.
Many factors and contexts contribute to this transition, including leisure.
The activities coupled with the participant's level of commitment and engagement can provide numerous developmental benefits. For example,
think about the leisure activities you participated in while in high school.
Are there qualities of those experiences that assisted you in how you came
to see yourself while in high school and now? What skills are transferable
from leisure to other parts of your life? Some skills that can be learned
through leisure contexts include communication, cooperation, teamwork,
flexibility, negotiation, working with diverse people, and enhancing listening
skills. Such skills help make the transition from the world of childhood
play to the adult world of work.

*Leisure contexts provide opportunities to explore and try on different
leisure identities.* American society provides opportunities for a variety of
structured and unstructured recreation and leisure activities that have the
potential to contribute to how we see ourselves. Municipal agencies and
not-for-profit organizations offer numerous summer and after-school activities (e.g., music, sports, photography) for young people. According to
Haggard and Williams (1991, 1992), the more people engage in these activities, the more likely they will embrace the social identities that accompany these activities (e.g., musician, athlete, photographer). Alternatively,
what might it mean for our identities if we actively choose not to participate

in leisure activities? Is it possible that nonparticipation may have as much of an impact on our identities as participation? Would it be important to investigate why someone would choose to not participate?

Flow-producing activities contribute to intrinsic motivation. Larson (1994), using Csikszentmihalyi's (1975) theory, argued that the more that young people experience flow in various contexts, the more likely they will become intrinsically motivated. If you like something that provides you with a sense of enjoyment and accomplishment, then you are more likely to continue to pursue that activity. The more you pursue the activity, the more you will need to challenge yourself to avoid boredom. As you continually challenge yourself, you internalize a desire to continue with this activity. If you are internally motivated you probably also take responsibility for your actions and behaviors. Seeing ourselves as being responsible for our actions and behaviors leads us to feel competent and in control of our lives. Leisure contexts can assist with internalizing intrinsic motivation that can carry over into other parts of our lives.

Leisure activities across the life span assist with continuity in our lives. Developmental theorists Silbereisen and Todt (1994) argued that leisure contexts could assist with continuity across the life span. Leisure activities begun as young people and continued throughout life can provide stability and help people to manage difficult situations. Using leisure contexts to develop mechanisms for coping with stress and difficult situations can assist with strengthening one's identity. For example, someone who enjoys jogging may find that over time, running becomes the primary way to reduce stress, maintain fitness levels, and meet people. At this point, a person may acknowledge being a runner has become a part of one's identity.

The underlying assumption is that leisure is a positive developmental context for identity formation and identity change. Although leisure can lead to positive development, leisure contexts can also reinforce cultural identities that might not be positive. For example, even in American society today, girls and boys tend to be socialized to play with gender-specific toys and to engage in gender-appropriate recreational activities. Play is a powerful tool that teaches people how to communicate with one another, how to conform by following rules, how to negotiate in challenging situations, how to deal with conflict and work cooperatively, and how to internalize socially acceptable roles. No leisure context is free from values and cultural norms.

In the years after adolescence, people develop relationship identities (e.g., partnering with another person, marriage, children) and work identities. Typically, between the ages of 23 and 45, these two aspects of our identity take on increasing salience. As adults move into midlife, priorities may shift as children grow up and leave home, personal relationships are reevaluated, and the role of work is reexamined. Leisure has the potential to take on increasing importance as some people begin to end their formal work lives and move into semiretirement or trade in paid work for opportunities to volunteer.

Although the basic elements of who we are and how we see ourselves might change throughout our lives, the basic structure of our identities that emerged during adolescence remains intact. Understanding the role that leisure can play in identity formation can be helpful in knowing what activities can support positive youth development. In addition to providing developmentally useful leisure activities, leisure service providers must also work to cultivate commitment to and engagement with leisure.

Reflection Questions

1. What is the role of leisure in shaping our identities?

2. How have you used leisure to shape various aspects of your personal identities? Your social identities?

3. How do identities shape what people do in their leisure?

1.8 Social Values of Recreation and Leisure

What is important to you? Your family? Getting good grades? Finding a job that interests you? Enjoying life? We base our answers on values or patterns of beliefs held as important. Our values reflect the experiences we desire, our expressed preferences for what we do with our lives, and the courses of action we choose.

Each of us has different perceptions of what is important and what constitutes "the good life." These perceptions are the product of experience as well as cultural backgrounds. Individual recreation behaviors and priorities are modified by personal, social, and cultural beliefs about the benefits or outcomes of involvement as well as the constraints that prevent us from being involved. Thus, values influence what we believe is important and why we choose leisure pursuits.

Social Values

Social values play a critical role in shaping leisure behaviors and delivering community recreation services. Social values relate to action, vitality, individualism, materialism, and group identity. For example, people in Western society tend to favor goal-oriented action. They value time and keeping busy. Values are demonstrated in paid work and reflected in consumptive activities and destructive behaviors related to recreation and leisure. US society also tends to value vitality. Active individuals are more vital because they can probably produce and consume more goods and services.

American society values individualism. Recreation professionals have often experienced ambivalence in enforcing norms of behavior that inhibit self-expression yet may be necessary to protect the environment and the right of equal opportunity.

Materialism allows for individual worth to be judged in terms of material possessions. The value of materialism is supported by the desire for immediate gratification. Many individuals can enjoy immediate pleasures through deferred payment by charging goods against future income (i.e., using credit cards). The boom in recreation equipment and apparel, accompanied by an increased demand for recreation areas and facilities, has been one result of social values associated with materialism and consumptive behavior.

Group identity is another social value. Fitting in with others holds great importance for many people. Group identity may be the prime motivator behind the creation of private clubs, associations, and social groups that are so prominent in the United States. A diversity of groups, interests, and lifestyles exists within society. A complex leisure service delivery system including the public, not-for-profit, and private commercial sectors has been created to accommodate these many interests. People want to express their individuality, but feel most secure when others share that individuality.

Numerous shifts have occurred in the American value system. Some of the values formerly held to be important now seem to be less critical, as represented in the decline of involvement in organized religion in the past two decades (Smith, 1991). Old values are being replaced by other patterns and beliefs. Differing value patterns and expressions often exist between urban and rural groups. The priorities of upper and middle-income people are not necessarily the same as those held by lower-income individuals. Some people express their affluence through big houses or the most recent recreation equipment, while others enjoy flashy clothing and package tours. Both the activities pursued and the means by which they are pursued are a function of the value system.

The greatest shifts have not been in the values themselves, but in the way they are expressed. For example, advertisers provide constant encouragement to "pamper yourself," encouraging egocentric and immediate gratification behaviors. Problems arise when the search for pleasure as a value leaves in its wake pollution, a decline of quality, a loss of order, and an increasing number of legislative regimentations. If people in society are concerned about pollution and that concern increases the relative importance of the value of conservation, then recreation agencies tend to allocate more of their resources for maintenance and control in outdoor areas. If people are concerned about equal opportunity, then staff responsible for recreation programs should emphasize more program efforts and activities for people who are disadvantaged. Values concerning individual recreation behavior and program practices are intertwined; each affects the other.

Values of Recreation and Leisure Experiences

Social values influence our perceptions of recreation and leisure experiences. Imagine sitting on top a mountain after a three-hour hike or having just completed a 1,500-piece puzzle. The exhilaration felt is the experience of leisure and recreation. Some theorists analyze the value of the recreation experience in terms of its meanings and motives. Others value recreation as simply pleasurable and entertaining activity pursued for its own sake.

Recreation and leisure experiences can be planned or spontaneous, social or solitary, passive or active. These multiple opportunities within the recreation experience permit the meaning of the experience to be individually defined. Think of three friends who embark on a tour of area art museums with diverse expectations and meanings. One person wants to learn about new mediums, one enjoys the leisurely walk through the historic district to look at the old houses and architecture, and one wants to spend time with friends. Each person is experiencing leisure and the one activity has three meanings.

Recreation experiences are not one isolated activity. On the simplest level an individual might anticipate and plan a leisure or recreation experience, participate in the actual activity, and then reminisce about the experience. Although specifically discussing outdoor recreation, Clawson and Knetsch's (1966) explanation seems appropriate for recreation in general. They discussed outdoor recreation activities as a multifaceted experience with satisfactions coming from any one of a combination of its component parts. Five distinct stages or phases are involved in an outdoor recreation experience.

- *Planning*—preparing for the trip, planning activities, and anticipating satisfactions;

- *Travelling*—just going somewhere;

- *Doing*—intense involvement with the activity;

- *Returning*—anticipation of getting home; and

- *Reminiscing*—memory of the experience, thinking about the next trip, showing photographs.

All of these stages provide satisfaction and add to the motivation and enjoyment of the actual recreation or leisure experience. Involvement in a recreation experience consists of more than just the activity or the actual time spent in leisure as the following scenario represents:

> During dinner on Wednesday night, the Jones family decides to take a trip to the lake the next Saturday. For the remainder of the week, anticipation builds. They locate and organize the fishing tackle. They purchase new lures and bobbers and pack a picnic lunch. The night before the trip, the children can hardly get to sleep. On Saturday morning they get up at 5:00 a.m. instead of the planned 7:00 a.m. Driving to the lake includes multiple "Are we there yet?" questions and eventually, the family arrives. Dad, an experienced angler, foregoes a day of strategic competition with the fish and rather, sits in a lawn chair on the bank of the lake. Red worm affixed and bobber floating, he assists his child in pulling in the first sunfish she's ever caught. Although the fish is about four inches long, the little girl thinks that never before has

such a great feat been accomplished. The smiles, the joy,
and the bonding result in an experience that will last for years.
Cold fried chicken has never tasted so good. Leaving the lake
results in a wane in the excitement. However, 15 minutes
into the drive home stories of the biggest fish, when mom
slipped into the lake, and predictions for the next outing
are being shared. At home, everyone is both exhausted and
totally refreshed as they prepare for bedtime.

Therefore, many recreation experiences are a combination of both contemplating and doing an activity. Although recreation can occur spontaneously, many of us anticipate and relive the experiences beyond actually doing the activity itself.

Another concept related to social values is the idea of serious leisure. *Serious leisure* is the systematic pursuit of an amateur role, hobby, or volunteer activity that participants find so substantial and interesting that they often center their lives on the special skills, knowledge, and experience associated with the activity (Stebbins, 1982). People involved in serious leisure might be amateur musicians or volunteers who contribute many hours to social causes. Serious leisure can be contrasted with casual leisure, described as immediately intrinsically rewarding relatively short-lived pleasurable activity requiring little or no training to enjoy it. *Casual leisure* might include relaxation, passive entertainment such as television or recorded music, sociable conversation, or sensory stimulation such as eating or drinking (Stebbins, 1999). Both types of leisure have social values for individuals. Kleiber (2000) has argued that people have often neglected the value of relaxation as a means for appreciation, contemplation, and peacefulness. To do things "at your leisure" speaks to a slower and more relaxed way of doing things. Clearly many values are associated with leisure, and they result in a variety of experiences and benefits for individuals in their communities.

Benefits and Motivations for Recreation and Leisure

People seek recreation and leisure because of the values and benefits they perceive will be derived from their involvement. Benefits to involvement in leisure and recreation manifest a variety of positive outcomes. Further, the benefits that individuals seek are often closely related to their motivations for involvement. Motivations are those inner urges that prompt one to behave in a certain way, often based on what the individual expects. Some outcomes from recreation and leisure benefit the individual while others benefit the community, environment, or economy. Driver, Brown, and Peterson (1991) categorized these benefits under six headings:

- *Physiological*—Benefits of recreation embodied as regular exercise and physical activity are documented scientifically. For example, regular aerobic exercise reduces serum cholesterol, helps prevent hypertension, and offers other cardiovascular benefits.

- *Psychophysiological*—Many of the same physiological benefits result in stress management. These result in mental and physical relaxation as well as positive changes in mood.

- *Psychological*—Benefits of leisure can relate to enhanced self-competence, improved sense of self-worth and a better ability to relate to others.

- *Economic*—Economic benefits as a result of recreation occur in communities where tourism dollars are spent. The value of leisure and recreation involvement also may result in healthier lives that can result in saving money due to lack of absenteeism on the job.

- *Environmental*—Environmental protection has been an outgrowth of a commitment to saving outdoor recreation resources.

- *Sociocultural*—Benefits may result from recreation or leisure when one develops pride in one's community and in an ethnic heritage as a result of being involved in a recreation opportunity such as an ethnic festival.

Participants in leisure and recreation experiences should be able to identify the benefits evident in a recreation experience. From a leisure services perspective, professionals must be able to plan for the positive outcomes that individuals and society seek from recreation experiences and programs.

A new movement has emerged in the recreation and leisure profession in the past ten years called the *benefits-based movement*. This approach has three components: benefits-based awareness, programming, and management. The program strives to increase public awareness of the benefits of recreation and leisure through effective programming, management, and marketing strategies that create support for parks, recreation, and leisure services. For example, if the purpose of a camp program was to foster leadership skills in campers, then this benefit would become the goal of the program and plans would be implemented to address those outcomes. Parents and the general program would be informed of the benefit and the camp program would be evaluated to see if those changes really occurred. Much is yet to be learned about the benefits of recreation and leisure among different groups in society, what constrains people from realizing benefits, how much certain benefits are worth to people, and how benefits to recreation and leisure experiences can best be optimized.

Constraints to Recreation and Leisure

For benefits and outcomes to be realized, and for individuals to get the most social value from their leisure and recreation experiences, constraints must also be recognized. Individuals might be aware of the importance of leisure in their lives, but may be unable to experience leisure fully because of constraints that impede involvement or the full satisfaction from involvement. *Leisure constraints* include any factors that affect leisure participation negatively by preventing participation, reducing the frequency, intensity, or duration of participation, or reducing the quality of experience or satisfaction gained from the activity (Jackson & Scott, 1999). Therefore, constraints do not just affect what a person does, but also how an individual might feel about a leisure experience.

Various models have been developed to conceptualize and understand leisure constraints. One emerging model suggests that constraints can be classified into four categories: intrapersonal, interpersonal, intervening structural, and antecedent structural (Jackson & Scott, 1999).

Intrapersonal constraints may lead to a lack of interest in a particular activity. These factors relate to attitudes about leisure and personality factors that may make involvement less appealing. For example, an individual who is never exposed to some types of activities (e.g., sports) may never become interested.

Interpersonal constraints are associated with relationships with others. For example, some activities may require a partner. If someone is not available, an obvious constraint results. Some people, particularly some women, do not feel comfortable going out alone at night, which becomes a constraint to certain types of activities.

Intervening structural constraints mitigate between the expression of interest in an activity and one's ability to participate. For example, lack of time, lack of money, lack of transportation, or lack of facilities may influence how an individual participates in a recreation activity. These constraints can also lead to less than optimal participation and a reduced level of enjoyment. Although these structural constraints are influenced by society, they usually focus on what individuals can do to overcome them. If I am constrained by money and cannot go on a vacation to Europe, I might still go on vacation to a nearby city.

Antecedent structural constraints exist in society outside the individual's control and prevent an individual from experiencing leisure to the fullest. These include stereotyping of activities and a lack of funding for activities for some segments of the population. These antecedent structural constraints cannot be overcome by the individual himself or herself, but require a community effort. For example, an individual may not be able to walk for exercise because there are no sidewalks or trails in the neighborhood for walking. This constraint is not an issue that can be solved by the individual alone.

These four areas of constraints, while not mutually exclusive, provide a means for understanding why individuals may not be as involved in recreation and leisure as they would like to be. These constraints may also result in the social values of leisure being unappreciated by some individuals and some groups of people. An emerging area of research interest seeks to understand why some constraints are more salient to some people than to others. Understanding how people make leisure-based decisions and overcome obstacles they encounter may help leisure service providers better understand how to plan and program recreation and leisure experiences.

The benefits of recreation and leisure must outweigh the constraints if positive leisure experiences are to occur. In addition, adequate opportunities for participation and enjoyment of leisure must exist. A balance between benefits perceived, opportunities that exist and the ways that constraints can be negotiated, all combine to influence the social values associated with recreation and leisure experiences.

Reflection Questions

1. Which social values best describe your values system?

2. How do your values influence your leisure behavior?

3. What are the multiple stages of the recreation experience? Apply those stages to a recent leisure experience you have had.

4. What benefits can be gained from recreation and leisure?

5. What steps would you take to eliminate external/internal leisure constraints in your life?

6. Explain whether your leisure is more likely to be serious or casual.

1.9 Economic Values of Recreation and Leisure

You do not have to be an economist to appreciate the monetary value of leisure. The economic value of any product or service relates to the supply and demand for it. The nature of work, the acceptance of the importance of leisure, and the satisfaction from recreation experiences have created the demand. Governments, not-for-profit agencies, and private commercial businesses have responded by providing the desired areas, facilities, programs, goods, and services.

This chapter provides a more in-depth examination of why and how leisure has become big business. As citizens benefit from opportunities for personal growth, the economy is enhanced as jobs are created, goods are consumed, and tax revenues increase. This discussion of the economics of leisure relates to overall expenditures, participation, intangible benefits, and employment.

Expenditures

Examining the amount spent each year on selected activities dramatically illustrates the significance of recreation and leisure on the economy. While comprehensive statistics are difficult to obtain, expenditure studies are periodically conducted.

To measure a society's living standard, economists often consult income data. Some economists from the National Center for Public Analysis (1999), however, think that a better measure might be what people are spending on recreation. For example, a recent study showed that in the late 1880s, less than two percent of household expenditures were devoted to recreation. By the 1930s, this recreational budget share had risen to four percent and by 1991 it reached six percent. Even when income falls, recreation spending usually remains the same at about five to ten percent of family living expenses. Recreation has been described as recession and inflation resistant.

The category of arts, entertainment, and recreation is examined regularly by the US Bureau of the Census. This sector comprises establishments involved in producing, promoting, or participating in recreational activities and amusement, hobby, and leisure time interests. In 1997, this group of organizations and businesses that paid federal taxes included over 80,000 businesses in the United States, with 85 billion dollars of receipts and a payroll over 26 billion dollars. In addition, almost 20,000 establishments with revenues of approximately 20 billion dollars and a payroll over six billion dollars were exempted from federal taxes (US Bureau of the Census,

1999). Table 1.9 shows a breakdown of these services based on organizations and businesses that pay federal tax and those that do not.

Specialty retail sales also greatly influence the US economy. Consumers spend over 35 billion dollars annually on outdoor vehicles and equipment. The sports that produce the greatest revenues include hiking, camping, and backpacking, with mountain biking and in-line skating growing rapidly.

Table 1.9a: Summary of Statistics for Firms *Subject to* Federal Income Tax for the United States in 1997

Kind of Business	Number of Establishments	Receipts in Thousand $	Annual Payroll in Thousand $	Number of Paid Employees
Arts, Entertainment, and Recreation (Total)	79,637	85,129,350	26,115,034	1,207,943
Performing Arts Companies	5,883	5,271,542	1,452,152	51,802
Dance Companies	159	109,384	35,272	2,349
Musical Groups and Artists	3,369	2,172,497	635,040	16,354
Spectator Sports	3,881	13,656,033	6,151,215	92,393
Racetracks	807	4,142,020	797,261	44,880
Other Spectator Sports	2,591	1,705,329	431,564	14,183
Promoters of Performing Arts, Sports, and Similar Events	2,633	5,045,093	1,052,645	51,411
Museums, Historical Sites, and Similar Institutions	787	483,683	122,404	7,281
Amusement, Gambling, and Recreation Industries	52,908	51,902,081	13,158,268	964,736
Amusement Parks and Arcades	3,344	8,418,476	1,961,871	138,930
Gambling Industries	2,100	15,582,455	3,233,042	169,102
Skiing Facilities	379	1,340,813	431,147	58,513
Marinas	4,217	2,541,481	516,589	22,765
Fitness and Recreational Sports Centers	16,604	7,944,954	2,405,043	256,397
Bowling Centers	5,590	2,820,685	821,044	88,044

Source: *1997 Economic Census, US Bureau of the Census* (1999)

In addition to the obvious recreation expenditures, a host of related expenses exist. For example, what percent of the billions of dollars spent for telephone services can be attributed to social conversations? What percent of the billions of dollars spent for clothing, shoes, and accessories were used primarily in recreation behaviors?

A huge amount of money is infused into the economy indirectly because of leisure goods that are bought and consumed. This relationship may be illustrated best by examining the impact of one piece of equipment, the baseball bat. First, the timber for the bat must be cut. This procedure requires properly equipped lumberers, tree farmers and foresters to select the trees to be cut, and people to plan the reforestation of the cleared areas. The lumber must be transported to the sawmill and processed requiring labor and machinery. The finished lumber is then sent to the factory where it is manufactured into a baseball bat. Everyone working at that factory (e.g., the lathe operator, the polisher, the janitor, the bookkeeper, the typist, the

Table 1.9b:	Summary of Statistics for Firms *Exempt from* Federal Income Tax for the United States in 1997			
Kind of Business	Number of Establishments	Receipts in Thousand $	Annual Payroll in Thousand $	Number of Paid Employees
Arts, Entertainment, and Recreation (Total)	19,463	19,626,564	6,683,417	380,287
Performing Arts, Spectator Sports, and Related Industries	4,624	4,875,904	1,621,537	90,831
Performing Arts Companies	3,316	3,298,514	1,273,094	70,201
Dance Companies	371	323,306	131,019	6,821
Musical Groups and Artists	1,211	1,154,012	498,783	29,768
Museums, Historical Sites, and Similar Institutions	4,793	6,280,306	1,714,74	84,495
Amusement, Gambling, and Recreation Industries	10,046	8,470,354	3,347,131	204,961
Golf Courses and Country Clubs	3,212	5,582,855	2,291,482	115,960
Fitness and Recreational Sports Centers	4,679	2,217,294	858,762	75,706

Source: 1997 Economic Census, US Bureau of the Census (1999)

salespeople) depends upon the product for his or her living. The product is then advertised, distributed through a wholesaler to a retailer, and sold. Perhaps the bat will be sold to a major league baseball team where a professional athlete whose salary depends upon his effectiveness with the bat uses it. In that case, all people affected by the play of the professional team (e.g., the groundskeepers, sportswriters, team owners, television camera operators, concession personnel, parking lot attendants) become involved with the baseball bat.

As you can see, recreation is big money. Expenditures, however, include not only what individuals buy but also how the government spends money for recreation. Recreation and leisure services exist at all levels of government. In 1999 the Department of the Interior received a Congressional appropriation in excess of 1.7 billion dollars to operate the National Park Service (National Park Service, 2001). Various states expended over a billion dollars in support of their state park systems in that year. At the city and county level an estimated ten billion was spent for park and recreation facilities, programs, and services in the United States.

Revenue from recreation involvement is produced in a variety of ways. In 1997 revenue from the state park systems was about 600 million dollars while the National Park Service grossed 175 million. The revenue developed by both systems increased over 50 percent between 1990 and 1997. In addition, many millions of dollars were collected through the sale of hunting and fishing licenses, not to mention the billions from the sale of alcoholic beverages, pet licenses, and permits to contract home swimming pools.

Participation Rates

Analyzing the number of participants engaged in specific activities also measures the effect of recreation and leisure on the economy. Recent years are compared to earlier ones to see if interest in recreation activities increases or declines. If recreation involvement rates increase, then expenditures for recreation and recreation related items also increase (e.g., types of equipment, clothing, admission fees).

Recreation participation rates are up in almost every category and activity. In the United States in 1997, there were 60 million swimmers, 45 million bowlers, 26 million golfers, and 11 million tennis players. Both college and professional teams reported increased attendance. The figures for college football were in excess of 36 million fans while 65 million people attended a major league baseball game (Statistical Abstract of the United States, 1999). With few exceptions, growth has been spectacular and recreation expenditures have increased even in years of economic decline.

Intangible Benefits

The relationship of leisure to the economy is more than the number of dollars Americans spend for recreation. It also includes benefits such as the location of recreation and property values, the economic impact of the tourist dollar, and leisure goods and services.

Location and Property Values

In some communities, private commercial recreation businesses are a primary employer of the community's residents. Ski villages in the West, and beach communities along the Atlantic Coast depend almost entirely upon tourists for their financial existence. Imagine the consequences to the Orlando, Florida area if Walt Disney Enterprises terminated its operations. Thousands of employees would be without jobs and many of the industries such as hotels and restaurants depending upon tourists would be without clients. Property values would drop, unemployment would increase, and local government would find difficulty in continuing the level of services as tax revenues and property values fell.

Under certain conditions parks and greenways help increase land and property values, especially when the recreation areas are properly constructed, maintained, and operated. Realtors support the contention that the presence of recreation facilities frequently has a favorable influence on land and property values. Real estate developers know that when public improvements are made in a residential area, property value increases. These increases are reflected clearly in the records of the tax assessors. As the market value of the land increases, so does the amount of tax the owner pays. Waterfront lake properties generally have a higher value than do those lots without direct access to water. The presence of a community center, park, or swimming pool will generally enhance the overall property value of a neighborhood, although the property immediately adjacent to these facilities may be negatively affected by the facility's presence if the area is heavily used.

Economic Impact

Not all communities are as intimately involved in commercial recreation as are Orlando, Aspen, or Atlantic City. All communities, however, do have commercial recreation enterprises, such as bowling lanes, pool halls, and restaurants, and may benefit from local participation as well as recreation travel. Citizens recreate at home and tourists spend money in places they visit. Private commercial recreation businesses use public utilities, contribute to the tax rolls, and employ workers just as do public and not-for-profit agencies and organizations.

Measuring the total economic effects of recreation resources and leisure services is difficult. For example, a water reservoir may be constructed primarily for reasons such as flood control, irrigation, and electrical power. When fully developed, however, recreation use may become the more obvious generator and sustainer of the local economy. New subdivisions in communities may be developed because of the recreation potential of the lake. Marinas and other businesses depending upon water activity can be established. Motels and resorts accommodating tourists could be built and the public grows to depend upon the lake as a recreation and economic resource. Because planners now recognize the economic potential of natural resource development, they account for recreation as a part of the justification and cost of most projects.

Goods and Services

Recreation also has intangible benefits on larger economic development scales. For example, industries generally try to locate their plants near sources of raw materials, near expanding markets, in areas where taxes and costs will be kept to a minimum, where available skilled labor exists, and where employees will be happy (Decker & Crompton, 1990). Recreation contributes significantly to the last consideration. People usually want to do business and establish their homes where they can live comfortably and where they most enjoy themselves. Family satisfaction cannot be purchased through the paycheck alone. Something more than high pay, good working conditions, and fringe benefits are needed to attract and keep workers on the job. Recreation opportunities often can serve that function. They add to the quality of the social and personal environment and therefore to the economic life of that environment.

Realtors attempt to promote sales by focusing on the recreation features of a given neighborhood. The real estate sections of daily papers are full of advertisements trying to sell property on the basis of "leisure living." Thousands of retirement communities and real estate developments are sold in this manner. As one real estate sales agent said when asked about his promotion of a retirement community,

> This is not just a lot of tract homes. This is a recreational development. We are going to put in a small boat harbor, and later a golf course. There will be a beach club to which all lot holders may belong.

The literature advertising the subdivision was filled with pictures of sailing, power boating, and sunbathing by the lake. It spoke of the values of recreational living and the potential growth of property value as the result of the presence of the recreation facilities.

Recreation services also appear to reduce accident and medical expenses by helping to keep the population alert and healthy, although this is difficult to document. Further, law enforcement authorities and recreation professionals have argued that a dollar spent on recreation reduces the number of dollars the public has to spend on crime prevention and correctional rehabilitation.

Did You Know...?

It costs approximately $30,000 to incarcerate a juvenile offender for one year. If that money were available to the local Recreation and Park Department, we could:

Take him [or her] swimming twice a week for 24 weeks, and give him four tours of the zoo plus lunch, and enroll him in 50 community center programs, and visit Oxley Nature Center twice, and let him play league softball for a season, and tour the gardens at Woodward Park twice, and give him two weeks of tennis lessons, and enroll him in two weeks of Day Camp, and let him play three rounds of golf, and act in one play, and participate in one fishing clinic, and take a four-week pottery class, and play basketball eight hours a week for 40 weeks after which we could return to you $29,125 (of taxpayer money) and one much happier kid.

Adapted from National Recreation and Parks Association Brochure (2000)

Employment

The leisure service delivery system employs millions of persons. In the public sector alone, over 500,000 people work for park and recreation agencies as managers and supervisors, clerical workers, maintenance personnel, program specialists, and seasonal and part-time employees. The number of individuals working for the not-for-profit sector, which includes membership-based groups as well as youth-serving organizations, is equally as large. Consider the thousands employed as camp counselors, camp administrators, employee recreation workers, tennis pros, country club managers, aerobics instructors, and other similar positions. The travel and tourism industry alone employs more than nine million people in the United States (Academy of Leisure Sciences, 1993). Table 1.9 (p. 70–1) indicated that one and half million employees are involved in the arts, entertainment, and recreation. Perhaps as many as one-fourth of our nation's jobs are related in some way to recreation and leisure. Leisure services likely will continue to grow with our postindustrial emphasis on service economies (Begun, 2000).

The economic value of leisure is clearly significant. Hundreds of thousands of people earn their living from industries producing materials, equipment, clothing, and services designed to meet recreation and leisure interests. A National Park System, local community recreation and park departments, or therapeutic recreation services would not be needed if people had no leisure interests or time to pursue their recreational experiences. Each generation spends more time and money on recreation and leisure pursuits than did the previous one.

Reflection Questions

1. How does leisure *directly* influence the US economic situation?

2. How does leisure *indirectly* influence the US economic situation?

3. If leisure provides tremendous economic benefit in our society, why is it still so undervalued?

4. Some taxpayers in your community need to be convinced that recreation makes an economic contribution to the community. Describe four examples you would use to convince them of the importance of recreation to the economic health of the community.

1.10   The Problem with Leisure

A number of researchers (e.g., Driver & Bruns, 1999) have been conducting research to empirically identify the many benefits of leisure. Leisure is valuable, it plays an important role in American life, and it should have a legitimate place in our culture. Popular sentiment shaped by the legacy of Puritanism and its valuation of work over leisure, however, often views leisure as frivolous and not worthy of serious consideration. When students say they are taking a university course about recreation and leisure, parents sometimes wonder if it is a good use of tuition money, and friends often stifle their laughter as you patiently explain that this topic is a legitimate course of study.

In a society that values people for what they "do" relative to their gainful employment, there seems to be less tolerance for thinking about people in terms of the activities they engage in outside of paid work. If we were really honest with ourselves, however, we would acknowledge that the core of who we are is most likely to be found outside the realm of work. Because leisure is so vital to people's lives, recreation and leisure professionals advocate for its rightful place in American society.

Many years ago the Greek philosopher Socrates indicated that the unexamined life is not worth living. Unless we examine leisure critically, it may not be the useful concept that we have described so far in this text. Therefore, this chapter discusses how and why leisure might not always be positive, and how the provision of leisure services sometimes might be a problem. Additionally, we will explore how individuals can become critical consumers of leisure and not to fall prey to its potentially negative effects.

A Bit of History

Historically, leisure has not always been viewed as something positive, nor has it always been assumed that leisure is for everyone. As you will see in unit two, every society has had to figure out the role of leisure relative to cultural norms and values. For example, the ancient Greeks viewed leisure as a necessary component of becoming a citizen, but becoming a citizen was a privilege reserved only for free men. The ancient Romans used leisure as a means of social control and as a way to distract the masses from the poverty, despair, and powerlessness of their own lives. For example, bread and circuses provided entertainment along with food distribution.

The way people think about and use leisure has changed over time. For example, with the transition from an agrarian to an industrial economy, family-based and neighborhood-based leisure shifted toward more commercial leisure that could be purchased for the right price. As factory life became the center of people's lives in urban areas, public leisure and recreation services emerged. People who may have once relied upon their families and/or their neighbors for leisure began to look outward to meet their leisure needs. Such a change had long-lasting effects on the ways that individuals viewed leisure and the provision of leisure services.

Today people use services provided by public, not-for-profit, and private commercial sectors. Current demographic trends suggest that European-American baby boomers will be retiring at least ten years younger than the standard retirement age of 65. Similarly, the baby boomer generation will likely be the recipients of a large transference of wealth in this country. These trends will affect free time and disposable income. The trends also raise questions about whether recreation and leisure should be a context for the personal, social, and political liberation of individuals, or whether leisure should be associated with consumerism and maintaining the status quo.

Liberating and Constraining Leisure

No easy or clear-cut answers exist to what the 21st century holds regarding leisure. In the past five years, much has been written about constraints and barriers *to* leisure, yet little has been written that addresses constraints that emerge *within* various leisure contexts. The issue of how leisure can be both liberating and constraining is complex. Leisure contexts can be personally, socially, and economically beneficial. We can use leisure contexts to enhance self-esteem, to improve communication and negotiation skills, to promote physical health and mental well-being, and to empower ourselves. Personal empowerment, however, does little good if it exists within a larger exploitative work and economic system that renders some individuals powerless while others have opportunities for many of these benefits.

The benefits of leisure need to be viewed within the larger context of US society. For example, students are often asked to speculate on the number of weeks off they will have once they begin full-time work. Most people say two weeks. When asked the average number of hours they expect to work, they say 50–60 hours per week. These responses belie both an implicit and explicit attitude of resignation. When challenged about the length of their future workweek and the brevity of their vacations, most people have come to believe that they cannot change this situation. Their futility is illustrative of a larger sense of powerlessness that some people come to accept as a trade off for being lucky enough to have a job that they enjoy.

Attitudes about work invariably carry over into how people come to think about recreation and leisure. The message that many people get as they grow up is that one is only entitled to leisure once one has engaged in work. Puritanism advocated this message over 200 years ago: "Work first, play later." The fact that work and leisure are inextricably linked may constrain leisure.

Leisure and Mass Consumption

Over the past fifty years, the rise in technology has contributed to making recreation and leisure opportunities commodities. The mass consumption of movies, books, CDs, computer and video games, tourism and travel, and professional and college sports has displaced local-based recreation and leisure. For example, think about the rise in corporate book and music stores. Local independent bookstores and music stores cannot compete with the mega superstores such as Virgin Records, Blockbuster, Barnes & Noble, and amazon.com.

People seem not to get together in person as much now because many people think that it is easier to click on the computer and see each other over a webcam or engage in video conferencing. Ironically, the consumption of technology that claims to bring people closer together seems to have the opposite effect. High-tech products like web-mail, cellular phones, and pagers may actually distance us from one another and from our communities. For example, in our desire to communicate efficiently with one another, we write e-mail that is short and to the point. Technology can also make us more impatient with one another since we know we can get in touch with one another at a moment's notice. We expect others to respond immediately, and we often expect that the world around us will also speed up to keep pace with technology (including cars, traffic, and lines in stores).

Advertisers have played a central role in the making leisure a commodity to be bought and sold. They have effectively tied the consumption of products to our identities. They have created artificial needs and desires so that people feel "less than" or "not whole" if they do not own the most current clothing or equipment. This perceived void becomes the motivation for consumption, and the motivation for consumption reinforces our need to work so we have money to buy these products and identities. We charge these products until we get in debt, and we then find ourselves working more hours to pay off the debt. In the race to stay ahead, people might fail to see leisure time slowly slipping away. Ironically, the desire for the consumption of leisure products may have led to our inability to find time to enjoy the very items that we thought might make us happy in the first place.

Problems with Leisure Services

American society depends on others for enjoyment, entertainment, and leisure. Even the institutionalization of leisure services created a system whereby a small percentage of individuals are educated to become professional leisure services providers. These professionals have used their expertise to shape policies and programs that influence recreation and leisure services provision throughout the United States. Although the creation of professional national membership associations like the National Recreation and Park Association (NRPA) have lent credibility and legitimacy to this profession, a chasm between individual participants and leisure service professionals may have developed.

The advocacy of leisure services may have taught people to become dependent upon others to find meaningful leisure experiences. If recreation and leisure professionals help people try something new, help them to challenge themselves in positive ways, or provide opportunities for expression in various ways, then leisure services can be positive. If on the other hand people come to believe that they cannot really have leisure if they do not participate in a structured setting, or that they have to spend money or consume products, then we have encouraged the creation of leisure that fosters negative dependency. Hemingway and Parr (2000) argued,

> a professional paradigm constructed around self-referential claims (e.g., possession of unique expertise) can be fairly challenged as more likely to lead to dependency than to development and emancipation. (p. 158)

One way to counteract negative dependency is to teach participants how to become critical consumers of leisure. We can ask people to assess their knowledge, attitudes, and behaviors regarding leisure. We can also ask people how recreation professionals can be supportive of their leisure interests. Perhaps a local town council needs to provide a neighborhood with a sum of money so they can create a particular leisure program. Similarly, perhaps professionals need to work side-by-side with constituents to plan, implement, and evaluate programs. It is difficult to ascertain whether or not people would be interested or willing to provide leisure for themselves and their immediate neighborhoods given that people have gotten used to professionals typically providing a variety of services.

Leisure services professionals may want to consider moving away from solely service provision toward becoming facilitators of leisure services. Most individuals have the skills and abilities to become stewards of their own leisure. If recreation and leisure are valuable to people, recreation professionals should support individuals and their communities in self-identifying and meeting their own leisure needs and interests. At the same time, citizens will need to be challenged and empowered to take responsibility for their leisure with the support of recreation and leisure service professionals.

Leisure and Culturally Sanctioned Norms

As noted earlier in this unit, leisure is a context for identity formation. This includes reinforcing culturally appropriate sexual and gender identities. We learn how to be and behave as women and men through various leisure settings such as sports, dramatic arts, and dance. Although leisure settings can enhance positive attributes in terms of personal identities (e.g., smart, strong, funny, capable, cooperative), these same settings might be reinforcing culturally sanctioned norms and behaviors that may limit opportunities in different ways.

The types of leisure activities and opportunities provided through structured recreation and leisure contexts sometimes show gender bias. Although more girls engage in a variety of sports than ever before, the expectation still exists that they will not participate in aggressive and violent sporting contexts. Similarly, it is expected that boys will not participate in more cooperative and traditionally feminine leisure contexts such as dancing or cheerleading. Various messages about culturally appropriate behaviors get conveyed through leisure contexts, including music, videos, and movies. The images we see around us in the world influence how we see others. If images in films, television and videos consistently portray women and men in certain ways (e.g., women are thin, beautiful and emotional, and men are strong, reserved, and unable to talk about their feelings), then we begin to internalize some of the messages about what it means to become and be a woman or man in US society.

Leisure contexts also reinforce culturally appropriate sexual identities. The underlying presumption of heterosexuality in many mixed gender leisure settings such as dances, proms, and social gatherings sometimes renders lesbian, gay, or bisexual individuals as invisible. These social gatherings, especially for young people, are places where they learn how to socialize and interact with one another. Young people who identify as lesbian, gay, or bisexual, or who are questioning their sexual identities, may have trouble finding other young people like them or they may have trouble being accepted in mainstream venues. A recreation agency in Phoenix, Arizona, for example, turned away a group of young gay men who attempted to participate in a community dance because they were concerned about the safety of these young men. The message conveyed through this interaction was that young gay people are not welcome in public recreation and leisure settings and that community recreation agencies may not want to deal with the potential ramifications for violence as a result of intolerant people. Thus, while leisure can contribute to positive self-identity, it can also reinforce dominant stereotypes that may not hold true for all individuals.

A problem with leisure influencing identity is that if leisure is a context where people come to internalize beliefs about who they are, who they should be, and how they should behave in the world, then they may be limiting themselves. Recreation and leisure are not inherently good, and we must recognize their limitations along with the strengths. As mentioned in the next chapter on leisure and social justice, leisure has the potential to promote personal and social change. At the same time, without awareness of how to use and consume leisure, we might fall prey to its negative effects. Ultimately, the issue goes beyond whether or not leisure is beneficial to how to create opportunities that are empowering to all individuals.

Reflection Questions

1. What are the negative influences of recreation and leisure?

2. How can a leisure services professional combat the negative aspects of leisure?

3. Identify and discuss problems of leisure related to freedom and identity.

4. Describe how leisure has become a commodity in our society.

1.11   Leisure and Social Justice

Leisure can be a context for social justice as well as personal and social change. Social change influences individual and community aspects related to leisure. As we have seen throughout this unit, leisure can be of great value or a potential liability. Recreation and leisure, however, cannot be separated from the world in which we live. Thus, this chapter explores the relationship between leisure, change, and social justice. Consider the following parable:

> A Midwesterner was vacationing on the New England coast. One morning, very early, she was walking along the beach. The sun was still below the horizon, the rain had ended, the sea was calm and a rainbow bridged the blue Atlantic with the green shoreline.
>
> While enjoying the beauty about her, she glanced down the beach and saw a long figure of a young man silhouetted against the sea. He skipped and frolicked as if performing a ritual dance to celebrate the dawn. Fascinated, she moved closer.
>
> As she approached, she realized the young man was not dancing. He was with graceful and joyous movement, picking up objects and tossing them into the sea. Soon she realized the objects were starfish.
>
> "Why are you throwing starfish into the sea?" She asked him.
>
> "The tide is going out and if they are still here when the sun rises, they will die," he replied.
>
> And without breaking his rhythm he continued tossing them out to sea.
>
> "That's ridiculous!" she exclaimed. "There are thousands of miles of beach and millions of starfish. You can't really believe that what you are doing could possibly make a difference!"
>
> He smiled, bent over and picked up another starfish, paused thoughtfully, and remarked as he tossed it into the wave, "It makes a difference to this one." (*It makes a difference*, 1992)

Earlier we described some of the benefits of recreation and leisure. Those benefits can be examined in relation to social change and social justice.

Any individual committed to quality of life issues related to recreation and leisure should also be committed to the fundamental values of justice, equity, and empowerment (Henderson, 1997). Further, leisure should be an intentional act designed to bring about positive outcomes in individuals. If equity is to occur, then we must frame the ethics and aims of leisure and not leave matters to fate. As Singh (1989) suggested,

> to be a member of a community of moral persons is to be concerned as much with the actions of others as with one's own, and 'learning to act justly and fairly towards other people, races, sexes, etc., cannot be left to chance.' (p. 230)

Equity is embodied in demonstrating an interest in the protection, growth, health, and well-being of all people and environments.

Just Leisure

Just leisure relates to the notion that leisure and recreation contribute to social as well as environmental justice. Fain (1991) suggested, "every act of leisure has moral meaning" (p. 7). Therefore, recreation and leisure professionals should examine how leisure helps others make appropriate and ethical choices. Fairness, rather than sameness, is required to achieve justice. Further, justice includes aspects of social as well as environmental justice.

Social justice includes a vision of society with an equitable distribution and physically and psychologically safe and secure members. In this society, individuals are both self-determining and interdependent. It involves a sense of one's own agency and a sense of social responsibility toward and with others and for society as a whole (Adams, Bell & Griffin, 1997). Social justice refers to an understanding of present and historical social inequities and recognition of how these inequities continue to influence attitudes due to the pervasiveness of oppression in society. These definitions depend upon people thinking that they can make a difference in the world, as indicated in the starfish story above. Social justice focuses on historical (and current) power differences.

Environmental justice, an outgrowth of social justice, focuses on how the environment influences people's lives and vice versa. It goes beyond environmentalism that emphasizes species and land preservation (Warren, 1996). With its roots in problems resulting from environmental racism (i.e., a concern that people of color tend to be ignored regarding environmental problems), environmental justice proposes that individuals and communities practicing just leisure cannot abdicate their responsibility to examine the impact on the environment from ecological and social perspectives. The goals of both social and environmental justice are reflected in social movements and radical approaches that allow individuals and communities to go from best interests to choices, from paternalism to self-determination, and from invisibility to visibility (Rioux, 1993).

Ethical Fitness

Ethical fitness is defined as the capacity to recognize moral challenges and respond to them within the context of daily and community life. Recreation professionals need to examine how people make choices that reflect personal and professional ethics of caring about themselves, each other, and the environment. Personal and professional ethics help to enable a sense of right and just living in a complex world and to determine what the relationship between people and the environment should be. Leisure professionals have an obligation to analyze how people develop the sensitivity to recognize a situation as posing personal or professional ethical considerations. They also need knowledge of what responses are ethical, a willingness to act, judgment to weigh considerations, and humility to seek additional knowledge to guide actions (Quinnett, 1994). For example, when a leisure opportunity is proposed, people need to think how this behavior might affect the environment and others in the community.

Developing ethical fitness is similar metaphorically to developing physical fitness. It provides a basis for making sound choices about the personal, professional, or environmental dimensions of leisure. Kidder (1995) described ethical fitness as a capacity to recognize the nature of moral challenges and respond with a conscience, a perception of the difference between right and wrong, and an ability to choose what is right and live by it. Ethical fitness may be as important as physical fitness when the focus of the profession's work is on just leisure. Ethical people base their actions on reasoned knowledge and attitudes, and their actions reflect what is in their hearts. Further, ethical fitness is not only a dimension for individuals, but also for managers of leisure services.

Hierarchy of Leisure

Most individuals who have studied recreation note that it provides pleasure and renewal. Recreation often flows from a feeling of well-being and involves activity that takes on no one single form. To qualify as leisure, however, many people believe an experience must have some outcome for an individual (Jensen, 1977). Jensen described a hierarchy of leisure time uses arranged similarly to how Maslow arranged the hierarchy of needs (see Figure 1.11, p. 88). Jensen suggested that the bottom of the pyramid were acts destructive to society or self. Next was amusement and time-fillers (e.g., TV watching). At the third level was emotional involvement in another's performance (e.g., attending a symphony or football game). The next level was active participation (e.g., being physically active, sport), followed by creative endeavor (e.g., playing a musical instrument), and finally service to others (e.g., volunteering).

Jensen's hierarchy, although highly value laden, illustrates how leisure might contribute to personal and social change as an individual makes decisions about using leisure. The potential for social change and opportunities leading to social justice can occur in any of the levels on the hierarchy. This framework also illustrates how personal change and social change may occur together. As an individual moves up the hierarchy, she or he also contributes more to building a better community.

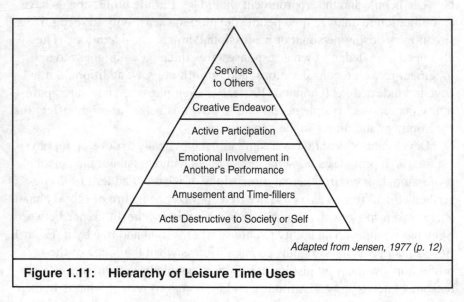

Adapted from Jensen, 1977 (p. 12)

Figure 1.11:   Hierarchy of Leisure Time Uses

Potential of Leisure

Leisure has been described by a number of scholars as having great potential for personal and social change. For example, Kelly (1983) noted how leisure provided a forum for self-identity, social interactions, and opportunities that could clearly lead to social change. Kaplan (1991) suggested that leisure was a context for individual and societal freedom. Implicit in Kaplan's message was that leisure might be a context for individual liberation and for building more democratically focused communities (Kivel & Kivel, 2000). Leisure has the potential, as Jensen also suggested above, for contributing to stronger communities. The value of leisure lies in finding the ways that it most appropriately contributes to social change and making the world a fairer place. Many avenues for change exist, but the change we seek should empower positive courses of action.

As Howe-Murphy and Charboneau (1987) suggested in their discussion of an ecological approach that therapeutic recreation specialists must be able to integrate the clinical model of individual change with the social reform/community development model of social change to be effective. Individuals influence their communities and communities shape individuals. Changing individual behavior is only possible with a supportive community.

Leisure can be a forum for personal growth as well as a context for promoting key values of equal opportunity, democratic participation, and social justice. In examining leisure, education and awareness are important. We must, however, move beyond personal pleasure toward recognizing how leisure contributes to personal development, quality of life, and social justice. For leisure to be a context for change and social justice individuals must ask how they can work toward personal and social change in their own lives as well as in the institutions where they work (Kivel & Kivel, 2000). By working for social change through leisure in our communities, we ourselves will also be changed.

Leisure and Critical Theory

Some of the criticism of leisure as being only "fun and games" lies in our inability to see the social change potential of leisure from a more critical point of view. Thinking about leisure as a process, and not a product, may be useful for this discussion.

Critical theory emphasizes the challenge of empowering individuals to make changes (Henderson, 1993a). It focuses not only on critique and dialogue, but also on action in addressing particular problems. Further, critical theorists assume that positive social change does not occur when current structures benefit only those people in power. This approach suggests that individuals wanting to understand leisure, and help others understand it, must examine the forms of power, experience, and identities for wider political and cultural significance. Leisure behavior, for example, requires that we analyze leisure for how it enhances the quality of life for all people (i.e., how it leads to inclusive recreation) and not just focusing on those individuals who can afford it (i.e., those who can pay, can play). Critical theorists interested in examining leisure note that change will not occur without conflict. If we believe that leisure ought to be an opportunity for all people, then we must examine it with critical, disciplined, and innovative attention.

Recreation and Leisure for Change

We do not intend to provide a specific road map for managing leisure in your personal life or as a professional. We hope, however, to raise issues for you regarding the value of leisure personally, as well as how the opportunities for leisure in communities can contribute to social justice and the overall quality of life. Several suggestions may help you to be better participants in recreation and leisure as well as reflective community members.

First, it may be useful to reexamine leisure within the context of social justice and its relationship to aspects of personal and social change. As indicated earlier, the notion of just leisure has potential for personal and social change—an important first step in an awareness of leisure's value. Further, as individuals and as professionals, we must recognize that leisure is value laden. Although these values can be problematic, they can also give us a direction regarding how leisure can be essential in people's personal lives as well as in communities.

Second, our awareness of leisure's significance must lead to some type of action. What we do as individuals reflects our view of the world whether we articulate this understanding explicitly or implicitly. We must examine leisure critically and then determine how to move forward in ways that will make recreation and leisure valuable to individuals and communities. The challenge lies in finding ways to try new things, take risks, and engage in activities that go beyond stereotypical or socially proscribed boundaries (Kivel & Kivel, 2000).

Third, as individuals and professionals we also might consider how to move away from our immediate community to examining the larger society. A great deal of misinformation and stereotyping continues to exist from the media, our families, our schools, our churches and synagogues, and community centers about people based on characteristics such as gender, race, class, sexuality, age, and disability. Part of using leisure as a tool for social justice relates to a process of realizing how people's views have been shaped and how leisure exists within the larger society. An examination of issues on a personal level can give a basis for a broader understanding of the organizations in which we work and play.

As the starfish story indicated, each action of our personal or professional lives can make a difference. Whether you are interested in a career in this field or just find the subject intriguing, the challenge of social justice will require further thinking, sensitivity to the process of change, and a willingness to take some risks. As Allison (1987) suggested,

> We have to confront ourselves not only with the challenge
> *of* change, but also the challenge *to* change. (p. 153) [our
> emphasis]

Reflection Questions

1. What is meant by *just leisure*?

2. What is the difference between *social justice* and *environmental justice*?

3. What are the levels of Jensen's hierarchy of leisure time? Do you agree with this hierarchy?

4. Discuss the ways that leisure can be a context for social justice and social change.

5. What is the relationship between personal change and social change as it relates to recreation and leisure?

6. Write a brief position statement describing your beliefs that leisure is or is not currently "just."

UNIT TWO: HISTORICAL BACKGROUNDS

Leisure has a long and fascinating history, serving as a testament to human creativity and inventiveness. No single history of leisure exists, so we refer to the written *histories* of leisure. Historical analyses of leisure provide insight into the forces shaping contemporary society. The better we understand these forces, the better prepared we will be to make our own contributions to leisure's present and future.

Suppose you have been hiking a trail in the mountains. As you gain elevation you note landmarks, like a distant peak that comes into view on your left and a waterfall deep in a ravine at a bend in the trail. Retracing your path as you walk down the same trail, the peak and the waterfall are still there but your relationship to them has changed. The peak is on your right now and disappears as you walk while the bend in the trail now hides the ravine from your view until you are past it. You had two distinct angles of vision on that trail, each shaped by your surroundings, activities, and expectations.

History is like that mountain walk. Landmarks catch our attention depending on the questions important to us and what we think counts as an answer. Both questions and answers change as our historical angle of vision changes. Each generation writes its own version of history because different dimensions of history become important at different times. How we evaluate leisure's history and the profession's origins and development influence how we regard contemporary leisure services. We must appreciate history if we are to understand contemporary leisure.

2.1   Early Histories of Leisure

Every society or culture reveals some evidence of leisure's presence, from the ball courts of Mesoamerica to the theaters and stadia of ancient Greece to the arenas of ancient Rome. Toys, sports equipment, and game pieces have been found at many archeological sites. Examining ancient leisure reveals more than similarities and differences with modern leisure. It also demonstrates the universality of leisure.

Egypt

The Egyptian civilization, one of the most highly developed cultures in the ancient world, endured for thousands of years from approximately 5000 BCE (Before Common Era) into the Roman era. Ancient Egyptian society was extremely hierarchical. Citizens regarded the pharaoh as a god, indicating close ties between religion and government. Wealth, status, and privilege were largely hereditary and concentrated in a relatively small elite. Below this social stratum were people engaged in crafts, trade, and agriculture.

Archeological evidence allows historians to develop general ideas about Egyptian leisure. Tomb walls were decorated with intricate images that offer important clues about customary leisure activities. Dancing, singing, and musical performances appear to have been frequent forms of entertainment along with dramatic presentations. Bullfights and gymnastic exhibitions are also depicted. Board games like chess and backgammon were common. We also know the pharaoh's court moved according to the season or the pharaoh's mood, seeking relief from the intense Egyptian summers. The Egyptians were aware of the restorative benefits of travel to more pleasant climates and environments.

Little is known about Egyptian attitudes toward leisure and work. Most likely the elite had much free time at their disposal, especially when they participated in activities appropriate to their status. For centuries the Egyptians were a powerful military as well as cultural force. Some vigorous leisure activity was necessary to maintain their fitness for warfare. Nonetheless, a sense of pleasure seeking appears to have prevailed among the elite. Hunting preserves, gardens, and even animal parks (first created by the Assyrians) were created for their enjoyment (Ceram, 1971). As for the vast majority of Egyptians, however, we know less about what leisure they had and how they used it.

Ancient Athens

What we call ancient Greece was actually a collection of small city-states near the sea and generally surrounded by small agricultural villages. Although a sense of common Greek identity existed based on a shared language and religious beliefs, people thought of themselves as citizens of their city-state. Ancient Greece was never a single political entity in the modern sense. This discussion focuses on Athens since historians know the most about this city-state.

Athenian Society

Definitions of citizenship varied among the city-states, but all established sharp distinctions between citizens and noncitizens. Citizens were full members of the city-state, and noncitizens were excluded. Athens citizenship was restricted to adult native-born males legitimately descended from a citizen father and native-born mother (Manville, 1990). Women had an ambiguous place in Athens as members of the community but not citizens. They had important public roles in the community, particularly in religious and civic ceremonies and rites (Patterson, 1994), but were barred from the political arena.

Slavery was widespread in ancient Greece. Martin (1996) estimated that by 600 BCE slaves comprised one-third of the population in some city-states, but whether the average citizen owned slaves is hotly debated by historians. The expense, not the immorality, probably prevented average citizens from owning slaves. Reprehensible as slavery is to us, to the ancient Greeks "the freedom of some could not be imagined without the servitude of others and the two extremes were not thought of as contradictory, but as complementary and interdependent" (Austin & Vidal-Naquet, 1977, p. 19).

Athenian Leisure

Social distinctions were evident in Athenian leisure. Among aristocrats, traditional competitive values emphasized the cultivation and display of excellence. Excellence depended on a careful balance of the virtues of mind, body, and character. Aristocratic leisure consisted of intellectual (e.g., philosophy, mathematics) and cultural (e.g., poetry, music) activities, physical exercise, and politics. For many, Athenian politics was an important arena for demonstrating their virtuous character through action informed by thought and experience (Hemingway, 1988). The wealthiest Athenians were also liable to special tax assessments to finance public cultural or religious events.

Aristocratic leisure took place in the home, the public square, the gymnasium, public buildings, meeting places, and theaters. Food and drink were involved and professional entertainers hired. Plato's great dialogue,

The Symposium, recounts a supper and drinking party where revelers competed by making speeches on the meanings of love. The latest scandals, cultural trends, and political issues were topics of conversation with wit highly valued. Aristocrats engaged in impromptu poetry contests or composed and sang songs, sometimes while dancing. These friendly competitions had important consequences for individual reputations. Some aristocrats residing on rural estates or fearing political and legal attacks, however, preferred secluded lives (Carter, 1986). They are often forgotten in discussions of Athenian leisure.

We know less about the leisure of Athenian common citizens. In the agricultural area surrounding Athens, many farmers had small plots of land to support their families, but they were never far from sliding into poverty. Except for major religious festivals and public events, these small holders were less likely to visit Athens proper. Their public lives focused on local affairs, festivals, and rites. Other leisure time they had was spent in the household. In the city itself the largest number of citizens were members of the least wealthy property classes. Desperate poverty was rare during times of peace, but most citizens lived simple lives. The city of Athens provided entertainment enough. All citizens could attend and speak during meetings of the assembly and many people served in public office at some point in their lives. Admission to public theatrical and musical performances was free for citizens, women, and noncitizens. Common citizens passed time in public areas, gathered in taverns, and visited the market. The modest size of common citizens' residences generally discouraged socializing at home.

Greek Games and Festivals

Religious dimensions existed in almost all activity in ancient Greece to the extent that Hansen (1991) suggested the city-state is best understood as both a religious and a political association. Ancient Greek games and festivals illustrated this connection. In Athens 600 BCE, about sixty days were devoted to festivals annually (Snodgrass, 1980).

The most famous games, dedicated to Zeus, chief of the Greek gods, were held every four years during midsummer at Zeus's shrine in Olympia (Chamoux, 1965). The Olympian Games began the quadrennial cycle of Panhellenic games known as an Olympiad. Founded in 776 BCE, the Olympian Games contributed to and were evidence of a growing Panhellenic identity in Greece. Safe passage was guaranteed to all competitors and spectators on their ways to and from Olympia. In addition to being free citizens of a Greek city-state, competitors had to satisfy religious requirements since the games were a religious festival that would be profaned if someone unfit participated. No team events were in the Olympian Games. Athletes competed as individuals in foot races, wrestling, field events, and boxing. The premier event, by all accounts, was a foot race of some two hundred yards. Early competitors were wealthy young men with time and energy to develop their athletic skills. Although a garland of olive leaves from a tree at Zeus's shrine was the only prize awarded at Olympia, an Olympic victory was often lucrative once the winner returned home. Statues and plaques were erected and victory odes written to honor the winner. Some city-states awarded stipends to Olympic winners while others allowed them to dine at public expense for life. Eventually, professional athletes and prize money weakened the games (Martin, 1996).

Spectators came from across Greece. Men were admitted as spectators apparently without fees, but sources differ on whether women were admitted. Interestingly, unmarried women were allowed entrance as spectators but married women were barred "under pain of death" (Martin, 1996, p. 46). Religious ceremonies and athletic contests were not the only attractions at Olympia. Outside the sacred area people enjoyed dramatic and musical entertainments, listened to orators and debaters, and attended public lectures by scholars who came to gain fame and perhaps a patron. The Olympian Games were more a religious and cultural festival than an athletic competition. Three other Panhellenic games completed the quadrennial cycle: the Isthmian Games, the Pythian Games, and the Nemean Games.

Interestingly, women apparently had their own games at Olympia. Pausanias (1918), a Greek traveler active in the late second century, reported that during a visit to Olympia he learned about the Heraea Games held every four years to honor Hera, the consort of Zeus. Pausanias described a number of the associated religious rites. During the Heraea unmarried women competed in three age groups in foot races approximately five-sixths the distance of those in the Olympian Games. Victors received the Olympic garland and, according to Pausanias, part of the cow sacrificed to Hera.

Athenian Attitudes toward Leisure and Work

In *Politics*, Aristotle wrote that the correct use of leisure is the first principle of human activity. He condemned the hunger for wealth that distracted people from the excellences of character developed only in leisure. The ancient Greeks did not regard work as inherently virtuous or ennobling, nor did they understand it as a distinct category of human activity (Austin & Vidal-Naquet, 1977). The ancient Greeks did not see work as part of a larger economic system, but thought in terms of the moral effects of specific occupations. Character was revealed by one's occupation and the conditions associated with it. Because they valued independence, the ancient Greeks viewed dependence on someone else for one's livelihood as a character flaw. Agriculture, for example, was widely regarded as the occupation most suitable for a citizen. Retail trade, commerce, and manufacturing on the other hand were at the bottom of the scale. Not only did one depend on others, but also these occupations tempted one to lust after excessive wealth. They considered wealth a fatal character weakness, and regarded such occupations as most suitable for foreigners or slaves.

Athenian citizens were wealthy if they could live without working. Once the modest needs of an average Athenian citizen were met, citizens fulfilled their religious and civic obligations and offered appropriate hospitality to relatives and friends. Citizens were expected to turn their energies to activities more important than work. Leisure was not a consequence of being wealthy, but rather an intrinsic component of wealth itself. Wealth is different than how we think of it today. Materially, it is closer to sufficiency than to plenitude or abundance. True wealth was achieved in leisure by participating in the intellectual, cultural, and political life of Athens.

By this definition, the majority of Athenian citizens were poor. The Athenians, and ancient Greeks generally, valued leisure more than work. We must, however, distinguish between a cultural ideal and its social reality. The ideal was always largely aristocratic in content, and only the aristocrats and a few wealthy citizens ever managed to achieve something like it. Much work was regarded as a sign of a flawed character, and leisure was valued as part of true wealth. The vast majority of ancient Greeks worked by necessity. Many, despite being citizens, worked alongside slaves to earn their bread. Unlike slaves, citizens found relief in the knowledge that they retained their freedom, but their freedom was reduced by their need to work. Plato, Aristotle, Xenophon, and others glorified the ancient Greek aristocratic ideal of leisure, but as Martin concluded, work "was the most abiding continuity in ancient Greek history" (1996, p. 221).

Thus, the early history showed leisure as a phenomenon that influenced people for centuries. An understanding of the histories of different groups of people and different times gives us a foundation for understanding recreation and leisure in the present. Leisure was highly valued in many cultures and reflected the values of the time. The Greek ideals of leisure, in particular, have provided a model for valuing leisure today.

Reflection Questions

1. How might an understanding of the early history of leisure influence our current/contemporary understandings of leisure?

2. What is the relationship between the Greek concepts of work, leisure, and citizenship?

3. For the Greek historical period, identify the general meaning of leisure, some common leisure activities, some constraints to leisure involvement, and the power structures that influenced leisure behavior.

2.2   The Roman Empire and Medieval Europe

Rome's history as an empire and the medieval period that followed are also part of the early history of Western culture. We will describe these periods as they related to leisure and show how the events during these times influenced our thoughts about work and leisure today.

Roman Empire

Rome's history is one of steady expansion from a small hilltop village (conventionally dated to 750 BCE) into an immense empire followed by spectacular collapse. The empire's strength was greatest in the period up to AD 150, but by AD 200 it was already being weakened by internal decay and foreign enemies. The division of the empire into western and eastern parts by the emperor Constantine fatally weakened Rome's central imperial authority. The empire had to be secure at its center in Rome, or whatever happened on its frontiers would be irrelevant. Therefore, the emperors' first priority was to ensure their popularity in Rome. This focus led to the famous policy of bread and circuses as the monthly distributions of food and entertainment. Indulgence spread to private leisure as the Romans poured their wealth into food, drink, and amusement. Internal rot weakened the empire until it could not stand against its enemies. The Romans suffered a significant defeat by the Goths in AD 378, who overran the city of Rome itself in AD 410.

Roman Society

The following discussion focuses on the city of Rome itself, around the years AD 100 to 150. During this period, the empire was near the peak of its power and prosperity. Two broad classes of citizens existed in Rome: the patricians and the plebeians. Social distinctions between these classes further elaborated status distinctions in the patrician class. The Romans often extended citizenship status to inhabitants of conquered territories, however, resulting in regular infusions of new ideas and personalities into Rome. Ideas circulated surprisingly easily in Roman society and an element of egalitarianism remained, allowing merit to be recognized and rewarded.

The gap between the Roman elite and the rest of Roman society, nonetheless, grew larger over time. At its height, imperial Rome was first and foremost an administrative center—taxes flowed in from provinces to support it. This wealth was concentrated in the hands of an elite group. The middle class shrunk to almost nothing in Rome. The vast majority of the population lived in or on the edge of poverty. At least a third of the people relied on charity. Slave owning became more widespread in Rome during the empire. Around 200 BCE households owning more than one slave were unusual, but four hundred years later it was unusual to find a household owning *only* one. The wealthy often owned hundreds of slaves.

Roman Leisure

The Romans regarded work as the negation of leisure. To Roman citizens, work was an indignity to be avoided. Many people did not work and Toner (1995) concluded that "regular paid employment was not the norm" (p. 73). Various doles and allowances of food were available, along with a well-developed system of social patronage. Citizens could rely on both public and private support. Work was there for citizens who wanted it, but even they did not spend much time at it. Workers usually had all or most of their afternoons free. Merchants and shopkeepers had organized themselves so well that they worked only six or seven hours a day. The Romans clearly preferred leisure to work.

In Rome daylight regulated most activity. Patricians and plebeians alike generally rose with the sun and retired not long after darkness. Only the young and the sturdy stayed out late. Only those needing to recover from late nights lingered in bed.

The patrician's first task was attention to personal appearance and wardrobe. Men often visited the barber to have their hair done and to collect the latest news and scandal. The rounds of social visits were a significant practice in Roman society. Depending on social rank, one received callers at home or called on others, especially one's patron, who was an individual of generally higher status. Patrons dispensed gifts and put in a good word when and where necessary. Calling on one's patrons was required not only to keep their favor, but also so the patrons could display their status. Patrons assembled their followers before setting off on their own visits to make a grander impression. Business transactions were usually completed by early afternoon. Citizens holding public office, however, might devote more time to their tasks. Once business was out of the way, the remainder of the day was devoted to leisure.

Plebeians imitated the wealthy to the extent their own needs and limited means permitted. Those plebeians who worked left home early after a modest breakfast. They could usually count on quitting by midday or slightly later. Plebeians who did not work visited the houses of patricians where they might receive food or small sums of money. This widespread practice of depending on handouts for survival was socially degrading and caused resentment among those forced to do so. Whether employed or not, by midafternoon the plebeians also turned to leisure.

Rome was like an amusement center (McDaniel, 1924). All classes enjoyed Rome's attractions, but social distinctions were evident. People strolled in public squares or gardens and conversed or watched the many street entertainers. They exercised at gymnasiums, ball courts, or athletic fields. In the theaters Romans preferred comedies to dramas, but the theaters' popularity waned as the circuses became more elaborate. Scholars and authors gave lectures and readings in public halls hoping to find patrons and a demand for their works. Games of chance were highly popular in the street and taverns, particularly guessing games or dice games. The baths were wildly popular among the Romans, with facilities to match all tastes and incomes. Dinner itself was frequently a social occasion. Guests appeared trailing their often-uninvited retinues, but this practice was accepted in the social status game reflected in Roman leisure. In wealthy patrician households dinners could be extravagant with entertainment between courses, much talk, and lots of wine.

Games and the Circus

The Romans had an extraordinary number of public holidays devoted to festivals and games. By McDaniel's (1924) estimate, there were 175 holidays per year in the fourth century. Some emperors attempted to reduce the number of holidays, but with little success. In fact, it has been argued that between AD 100 and 150 the citizens of Rome "enjoyed one day of holiday for every working day" (Carcopino, 1940, p. 206)

The circus or chariot races were the most glamorous of all Roman games. Large arenas—the largest one holding 385,000 people—enclosed a large rectangular course rounded at one end. Competitors entered from separate gates below the stands and raced seven laps around the pylons at each end of the course. The frequent collisions were highly dangerous. Charioteers braced themselves with special footholds and wrapped the reins around their wrists and forearms. To avoid being dragged by their horses if thrown, charioteers carried a small knife to slash the reins. With luck they might scramble to safety before being trampled by the other chariots. Charioteers often leaped on the horse's backs and even did handstands as they raced. These showmen were celebrities in Rome, particularly among the plebeians.

Animal and gladiator games became more sinister as a response to the need for more sensational entertainment. Wild animal shows were especially popular because exotic species could be sent to Rome from the empire's distant provinces. Lions were a particular favorite and on occasions hundreds were present at one time. As this novelty wore off, human beings were forced into the arena with the wild animals, sometimes armed to fight for their lives and sometimes unarmed just to be mauled. In the gladiator games men killed and were killed for the amusement of onlookers who bonded in their common bloodlust. As the dead were dragged out of the arena, groundskeepers spread sand on the blood, not to hide it, but to ensure the next combatants had firm footing.

The original religious meanings of Roman festivals and games were obscured when their political uses became more important than the activities. As Toner (1995) noted, leisure was the "synthetic agent that bound together Roman society as it developed from Republic to empire" (p. 117). Games and festivals contributed to social stability in Rome by entertaining the citizens. They also allowed the emperor and other members of the elite to establish a degree of contact with the public. When the emperor appeared in the imperial box at the arena, he was seen as the people's benefactor, the source of bread and circuses, and a symbol of Roman power. In turn, the people cheered him if times and the show were good, or expressed dissatisfaction in bad times. Wise emperors used games and circuses to gauge and influence people's moods. The spectators themselves were a major attraction. All classes of Roman society filled the stands along with visitors from throughout Italy, the empire, and beyond.

Medieval Europe

The fall of Rome in AD 410 shocked the Mediterranean world. Because it was cut off from intellectual and commercial centers in the Mediterranean and Near East, western Europe was the weakest and least prosperous region in the empire. Under the combined pressures of migrations and invasions from eastern Europe (Le Goff, 1989) and the unwillingness of its citizens to muster the effort to save it (Strayer, 1955), the western empire disintegrated.

By AD 700 conditions deteriorated throughout western Europe. Agriculture, the dominant occupation, lost ground. Commerce, trade, and industry almost disappeared. Technology remained primitive. Craftspeople produced only for local markets and innovation was stifled. Travel and communication were difficult and roads were little more than paths. Most people remained close to their manors throughout their relatively short lives. Early medieval European society was "dominated by a spirit of resignation, suspicion, and fear of the outside world" (Cipolla, 1994, p. 117). Two of the most powerful elements in medieval Europe emerged, the feudal system and the church (Ferguson, 1940, 1968).

Feudal Society

Feudal society consisted of three basic social orders: the peasantry (concentrated on and around the manors), the nobility (including landowning manorial lords and royalty), and the clergy. Once the cities began to grow again after AD 1100, artisans, craftspeople, and merchants achieved a distinct social status in medieval society. The manors were the center of early feudal society with at least 90% of the population living in rural areas (Goetz, 1993). Medieval Europe labor time was measured by sunrise and sunset (Le Goff, 1980). The day's work was determined by season and climate. Neither tenant peasants nor serfs had much free time. Free time occurred when agricultural work was slack, mostly in the winter months. We have little reliable information about peasants' leisure, which was probably confined to the family or the tiny manorial village. Some festivals were celebrated according to the church calendar such as Lenten holidays. Other festivals were common to rural life particularly at the end of the harvest, the start of the seasons, and May Day. Entire villages joined in celebrating personal events like weddings.

The most characteristic aspect of the medieval nobility was the growth of the courts consisting of the king, a prince or other nobleman of high rank, his family, and members of the nobility. Many attendants and servants supported this assembly. Routine duties that were part of court life included managing estates and manors, resolving competing claims of land ownership or rights, and maintaining relations with neighboring courts. Knights engaged in regular training to maintain their fighting skills. Even if the nobility did not live altogether in idleness and ease, court life was considerably more pleasant than manor life and offered more opportunities for leisure. Festivals occurred on established religious holidays and to celebrate special events. Banqueting and socializing followed religious observances. Food and drink were important aspects of all medieval festivals for both nobility and peasantry. Court banquets were accompanied by music and theatrical performances and dancing was popular. Tournaments, the grandest festivals, included elaborate banquets and entertainments with the contests among knights as the main attractions. Tournaments helped define knighthood as a distinct social and professional status. Only larger courts accommodated the numbers of participants and spectators attracted to tournaments.

Other courtly leisure included the favorite activity of hunting because it allowed the display of skill, courage, and social status. Only the nobility hunted since they retained exclusive rights to game on their lands. Indoor leisure included board games like chess, backgammon, dice games, music, dancing, and versions of blind man's bluff that tested skill and quickness.

Substantial differences existed within the feudal order of the clergy. Preparation for eternal salvation motivated the creation of the monasteries as self-sufficient communities. Many monks and lay brothers came from poor families. They lived simple lives working in the fields or workshops. Monks able to read and write served as copyists. Their transcriptions of collections of ancient scrolls and manuscripts were often magnificently illustrated and bound. A few monks were also active scholars and allowed to devote themselves to theology, philosophy, and the study of ancient languages. Monastic life was organized around the cycles of religious observances. Work and contemplative leisure had their places in these cycles and both were offered up to God.

Outside the monasteries, the clergy lived different lives. Village priests were figures of local importance and often participated in village and manor festivals. Bishops had courts in larger towns that occasionally rivaled or even surpassed the local nobility. The bishops had considerable regional power, had access to church revenue, and were active in local society. Finally, as splendid as any royal court, the papal court sat amidst the ruins of Rome. Leisure in courts of the pope and many bishops resembled leisure in royal and noble courts more than leisure in the monasteries.

Late Medieval Society

Between AD 1000 and 1300, western Europe changed significantly. The growing population became more urban. Medieval cities were small (few having more than 20,000 inhabitants), but to people from manor villages (fewer than 500 residents) they were large enough. Advancement remained blocked by feudal social structures. People found more opportunities in cities, but late medieval cities were not egalitarian. The difference between the cities and the manors was the openness of urban economic and social hierarchies to individuals willing to try new ideas, work hard, and take risks. Commerce was revived and new manufacturing techniques were developed as a money economy emerged. In the growing cities, an increasing demand for goods occurred and the supplying them provided an opportunity to become wealthy. A distinctly urban social class called the *burghers*, who had no place in the traditional feudal social orders, also developed. Free by birth, burghers engaged in commerce and manufacturing or worked as craftspeople and artisans. To accommodate this new social class, new social structures appeared in the cities, including occupational guilds, fraternal organizations, and the commune as a form of civic association.

Changes in leisure followed these developments in the economy and social structure. Cities became more diverse as they grew larger. Urban markets and fairs attracted a wider variety of people and goods than could be found in any manor village. Taverns and public spaces were livelier. The new wealth in the cities slowly began to attract entertainers, artists, and scholars who would previously have sought patrons at the noble courts. The burghers acquired interests in the learning and culture that had been the prerogative of the clergy and nobility. Fellowship and mutual support were available in the occupational guilds and fraternal organizations and became new venues for leisure activity. Life in late medieval cities remained difficult and squalid for many. Nonetheless, urban leisure began to reflect economic and social forces that pointed toward new vitality in western Europe (Ferguson, 1940).

A number of differences existed between the eras of the Roman Empire and the medieval period. Leisure was important in the Roman Empire and had mass appeal. The corruption of leisure and the focus on amusements, however, were also elements leading to the downfall of Rome. The medieval societies of Europe defined leisure in relation to the feudal system. Although the wealthy had access to many leisure opportunities, leisure was simple for most of the people living in European cities and manors during this time.

Reflection Questions

1. For the Roman Empire, identify the general meaning of leisure, some common leisure activities, some constraints to leisure involvement, and the power structures that influenced leisure behavior.

2. What purposes did festivals and games serve in ancient Greece and imperial Rome? Are there any similarities between them and festivals and athletic events in contemporary society?

3. How did the ancient Romans use leisure to maintain social order?

4. How did the concept of leisure differ between the Greek and Roman cultures?

5. In what ways did medieval leisure reflect social status?

6. What characteristics of leisure were apparent during medieval times?

2.3   Renaissance and Reformation

We begin with a sketch of Renaissance Europe (about AD 1300 to 1600) and then turn to the Reformation (about AD 1500 to 1700). Modern ideas about leisure, work, and wealth are intimately tied to the business system known as capitalism. During the Renaissance capitalist business practices were established and refined in northern Italy. They quickly spread across Europe. The Protestant Reformation accelerated the spread of capitalist business practices by providing a moral justification for them. These occurrences had implications for leisure in Europe and beyond.

Renaissance

Although the word *renaissance* means rebirth or renewal, this period was more a time of transition. Some regions in Europe changed more quickly and thoroughly than others. Important continuities existed between the late medieval and early Renaissance periods.

Renaissance Society and Economy

Two major difficulties persisted as the transition from the medieval era to the Renaissance got underway: agricultural technology remained inadequate to support the steadily increasing population, and existing business practices limited economic expansion. A limit on economic expansion was dependence on human labor rather than machines. Hiring more workers could increase production, but the additional wage costs for employees with less than reliable work habits often ate up potential returns. The absence of widely established standardized principles for accounting, finance, and contracts imposed another limit.

Distinctively Western capitalism emerged only once entrepreneurs moved beyond the simple profit motive and began reinvesting current profits to expand capital to generate still larger future profits. The resulting growth in commerce, finance, and manufacturing stimulated artistic, intellectual, political, and social energies. Renaissance artists and scholars restored much of the classical learning, created distinctive styles in the arts and architecture, and conducted groundbreaking scientific and technological investigations. In larger cities, advancement through talent and ambition allowed burghers, craftspeople, and even a few artisans to claim places beside the hereditary aristocracy.

Burke's (1987) warning against the "myth of the Renaissance" (p. 5) must be heeded, however. Change began in Italy but spread unevenly

through Europe. Life continued in many regions as it had in the medieval
era, with unreliable food supplies and fluctuating economic conditions. For
the majority of people, life was difficult even in the most advanced cities.
Nothing demonstrated the uncertainty of life more tragically than the Black
Death, the devastating plague. Repeated outbreaks occurred into the next
century, and in AD 1420 the population of Europe was about one-third what
it had been in AD 1320.

The plague's human costs were catastrophic, but its other effects were
more ambiguous. Italy never fully recovered, but in northern Europe development actually accelerated. Demand for food decreased as the population
collapsed, allowing land exhausted by overcultivation to lie fallow or be
turned to pasture and other uses. Mill owners were forced to adapt equipment to other applications that improved mechanized manufacturing.
Soaring labor costs spurred interest in less expensive machines and tools
to replace workers. Gutenberg's invention of moveable metal type was one
example of technological innovation. Other technical advances occurred
in shipbuilding, construction, and metallurgy.

Renaissance Attitudes toward Leisure and Work

The emergence of Western capitalism involved more than the availability of
the necessary business practices. It also depended on the social meanings
attached to work, wealth, leisure, and time. For example, Florentine diaries
and letters were filled with references to gaining and holding on to wealth
(Brucker, 1971). Business affairs were a common topic and even family
relationships and friendships were subject to economic calculations. As
Pullan (1973) commented, "The ethic of worldly success and failure was
beginning to replace the conventional Christian ethic" (p. 171). Work was
celebrated because it enabled human beings to develop their physical and
mental faculties (Garin, 1965).

Wealth enabled entrepreneurs to engage in forms of leisure previously
open only to the aristocracy and high clergy. Much of leisure involved the
display of wealth and status along with a sense of obligation to the community. Sometimes merchants and manufacturers simply imitated the tastes
of the aristocracy, but more often they sought outlets for their own interests
and preferences. They helped create a distinctive Renaissance Italian urban culture (Ferguson, 1940) whose influence extended throughout Europe.
They financed many public buildings, churches, and squares, and were patrons of the arts and of learning while pursuing their own creative and intellectual projects. Consumer goods were valued in daily life and leisure,
as was evident in the home furnishings, clothing, and diets of wealthy
Florentines (Jardine, 1996). The aristocrats and high clergy continued to regard leisure as a prerogative of their hereditary social rank as the medieval

nobility and clergy had. For the merchants and manufacturers leisure was an opportunity to secure the new social status conferred by wealth.

Meanings of time also changed during the Renaissance. Florentine financiers recognized that time had economic value. They understood how to calculate interest and structure loan repayments to maximize profits and also maintain their flow of capital. In commercial and manufacturing cities life was increasingly structured around the daily hours of work. The change regarding work was gradual and did not occur everywhere. Traditional religious and agricultural rhythms continued to be important for many years. As Le Goff (1980) noted, time structured around traditional (e.g., festivals, Sabbath days) or memorable (e.g., military victories, births, deaths) events was being replaced by "regular, normal time" (p. 48), measured in definite intervals throughout the day. Regular, normal time was not welcomed by all, with conflicts sometimes arising between workers and employers over the regulation of time. Special bells were sometimes installed in church steeples and public towers and used to ring work hours and curfews.

A final piece of evidence for increased sensitivity to time's economic value during the Renaissance was the presence of *time thrift*. Prosperity required knowing how to make time one's own because "time well used belongs to him who knows how to use it" (Alberti, 1969, p. 166). Centuries before Franklin wrote that "time is money" Alberti described a simple formula for success: "make as good use as possible of time" on "praiseworthy pursuits" (but no more than necessary), "avoid sleep," and "never remain idle" (pp. 171–172). Many contemporary advice books are filled with the same sentiments.

Reformation

The Reformation was an era of economic, political, social, and religious change. In the decades around AD 1500, Europe was not a peaceful place. Peasant uprisings occurred in the country and workers rioted in the cities. Large and small wars were fought everywhere. This turmoil was evidence of three fundamental changes occurring in Europe. First, the power of the Catholic Church weakened. The extravagances of the papal courts alienated many believers. The church compounded this problem by selling indulgences and imposing taxes to raise money. These secular practices continued to trouble many in the clergy, including a monk named Martin Luther. Second, political power became increasingly centralized. Europe's political geography reflected its feudal heritage including a bewildering array of fiefdoms, baronies, duchies, and principalities ruled by the nobility. Everyone had wearied of the disruptions caused by repeated outbreaks of violence among the nobles. Monarchial kings began to assert their influence over the nobles to stop the violence. Third, the nature of economic activity changed. Larger and more complex business organizations appeared. Merchants and entrepreneurs found the values of their property and other fixed capital increasing along with sales prices for their goods. Manorial lords, other nobility, and wage earners were seriously threatened. The nobility depended on fixed payments whose purchasing power was decreased by inflation. Many minor nobles and younger sons in noble families were forced to abandon family estates. Wage earners were particularly hard hit. Without other sources of income, they faced impoverishment as wages failed to keep pace with inflationary prices.

The Protestant Ethic

The Reformation unfolded in the turmoil and uncertainty created by these changes. One particular concern is with what Max Weber (1930) termed the Protestant ethic. Weber sought answers to two questions: How did work, once limited to satisfying material needs, become instead an end in itself? Why did this happen particularly in England and the United States? Weber thought the answer lay in the fusion of ideas from two Reformation thinkers, Martin Luther and John Calvin. While not entirely correct, Weber's analysis remains important for its depth and influence.

Diligent work is praised as a virtue in several Biblical passages. We are admonished in 1 Thessalonians 4:11 to tend to our business and in 2 Thessalonians 3:10 that "If any would not work, neither shall he eat." It was through Luther and Calvin that the moral value of work became a central theme in early modern European history. Work was within most people's experience. They understood a community of workers more easily than they did many other kinds of communities.

Luther (1483–1546) had been profoundly moved by a phrase in the Bible, "the just shall live by faith" (Romans 1:17). He interpreted this passage to mean eternal salvation was granted only through God's grace, not earned by virtue of good works in the church or in the world. He thought that a believer's faith was an inner sign of grace, and a relationship between God and the believer needing no mediation by a priesthood or church.

Calvin (1509–1564), however, differed with Luther on several important points (Palmer & Colton, 1965). Calvin's doctrine of predestination was more severe than Luther's doctrine of justification through faith. Calvin believed God decides everything in advance, including the course of people's lives and whether they are among the elect to be saved. People cannot know in advance, and cannot earn salvation through earthly works. Calvin also rejected any relationship between political and religious authority. The church was an independent community of believers who regulated their own affairs. For Calvin, the community of believers was the model for a reformation of society.

Work had an important role in Luther's doctrine of the calling and Calvin's doctrine of predestination. Since work was necessary as a result of humankind's sinful nature, diligent work was evidence that one accepted God's will and that one had faith. Work glorified God while allowing believers to trust in their salvation. Success in work, including wealth, could be taken as a sign of God's grace and of faith. Converting this success into worldly social or political status, however, was a lapse into earthly glory. Luther and Calvin did not exalt work as an end in itself. Their contribution to modern ideas about leisure, work, and wealth was to translate an ascetic religious ideal into an ascetic justification for disciplined work. Rather than withdrawing from the earthly city to contemplate God, the moral internalization of work discipline allowed one to work in the world, yet not be of it. The priesthood of believers became the priesthood of workers as long as work was understood as evidence of faith. Leisure was at best an occasion to restore one's energies for this work, and leisure was at worst a snare for one's soul (Weber, 1930).

As the history of the Renaissance and Reformation shows, understandings of work and leisure of today were bound with the emergence of capitalism and a focus on time use. These periods of time contributed to the development of attitudes toward work and leisure that continue today. The Reformation led to the Protestant work ethic that made work a virtue. This attitude remains prevalent in US society today.

Reflection Questions

1. Discuss the newly emergent relationship between work and leisure during the Renaissance and the Reformation.

2. What developments during the Renaissance contributed to the emergence of modern capitalism? How have those developments influenced leisure?

3. Describe the contributions of Luther and Calvin to changing ideas about work and leisure.

4. How has the Reformation affected our leisure life today?

2.4   Industrialization

Industrialization was more a process than an event, occurring differently and not linearly in Europe and in North America. Some economic sectors, such as the English textile industry, industrialized before others. Other industries, particularly those requiring extensive craft or detail work, remained only partially industrialized into the 20th century. No society became completely industrialized. Further, industrialization occurred episodically and was accelerated and delayed by the state of technology, political events, economic cycles, and social changes.

Reform and Reason

The energies released by the Reformation stirred up religious and political turmoil across Europe until around 1700. Religious refugees (Puritans) from England immigrated to New England during the 1630s and 1640s. Oceanic and land explorations yielded discoveries with economic significance that intensified competition among European governments. In the 18th century, European wars reached across the Atlantic for the first time to involve English and French traders and colonists and their Native American allies.

The 17th and 18th centuries were also periods of European intellectual discovery. Modern scientific inquiry owes much to Galileo's use of experiments and Newton's rigorous mathematical reasoning. Francis Bacon developed the experimental method as the basis of scientific research. The theme that ties the work of these thinkers together is the power of human reason to understand the structure of the world. This conviction broadened during the Enlightenment, lasting from about the last quarter of the 17th century through the end of the 18th century. The Enlightenment—a period of intense intellectual activity and cultural secularization—centered in France but influenced all of Europe and North America. Franklin, Jefferson, and other colonial leaders saw themselves as part of it.

Society and Economy

Aside from wars and other conflict, daily life in Europe was influenced by four ongoing trends that began in late medieval Europe and continued through the Renaissance into the early modern period. The origins of industrialization lie in these trends (de Vries, 1994). First, there was a growth in agricultural productivity and increased economic activity in rural areas. Second, the dynamic population reflected migrations and disruptions in traditional marriage patterns. Third, there were significant economic and commercial connections among European cities, including established regions of economic growth in which industrialization was able to gain secure footing. Fourth, economic activity involved a growing level of domestic manufacturing generally occurring in rural areas and often involving a second job, seasonal employment, and child and women laborers. Society and economy in Europe were neither traditional nor static.

Historians debate whether industrialization occurred because of technological advances in production resulting in a greater supply of goods, or because of an increase in demand for manufactured goods. The question is difficult to answer because the evidence is contradictory. On the one hand, increases in real wages leading to more purchasing power did not occur until later. On the other hand, more material goods seem to have been in circulation even among some of the less well off. If wages did not increase, how were these additional goods obtained?

The answers lie in changing economic behavior at the household level (de Vries, 1994). Families faced the choice of devoting resources either to production of goods for consumption in the household, or to production of goods for sale outside the family. These goods could be the same (e.g., vegetables from gardens, honey, or wool). What governed a family's choice was whether these goods were more useful to them for their own consumption or whether by selling them, they would then be able to purchase manufactured goods. As tastes and fashions changed, manufactured goods became more attractive and families were more willing to shift their resources to production of marketable commodities.

Leisure was replaced by work to produce the goods necessary to enhance the family's purchasing power. Women and children were increasingly involved in household economic activity, primarily because they had more existing disposable time that could be turned to profit. At first their increased activity occurred in the household, but women and children also began to take employment outside the home. Families were able to acquire material goods without a growth in wages earned, but the cost to the family was reducing the leisure available. This change in household economic behavior begins to explain the increased labor force involvement of women and children characteristic of industrialization, as well as the existence of a demand for manufactured goods at an early stage of industrialization.

The supplies of manufactured goods also began to expand and were produced in a range of settings that included workshops of various sizes and large, highly organized factories. Factories were among the economic innovations characteristic of industrialization and made possible by technological advances and strict worker discipline. Factory discipline entailed fines, suspensions, or dismissals for even minor infractions, such as being a few minutes late, talking or singing at work, socializing or horseplay, and any number of other seemingly trivial offenses. The hours and pace of work were set by the employer and were often physically exhausting. In workshops, on the other hand, workers were freer to set their own hours and pace or even to skip work altogether. Many workers, despite intense dislike of factory work and discipline, chose to work in factories because of the higher wages paid.

The structure of factory work had both economic and social implications. Above all it created new senses of time and place. Time truly became money in the factories. From the employer's perspective, the worker was hired to work for a specific period of time at a pace specified by the employer. The more the worker could be made to produce during this time, the better the bargain was for the employer. For the worker, on the other hand, factory work created both temporal and spatial distinctions that disrupted traditional patterns of life. Workers experienced a separation between time sold to the employer and time that remained their own. Having lost control over the hours and pace of their work, the necessity to work arose from the external discipline of the clock and not the tasks performed. The casual social activity that had accompanied preindustrial work, and that still existed in the workshops, could now occur only away from the workplace during nonwork time. With the advent of work under factory discipline, daily life began to separate into distinct spheres. These distinctions between work time and one's own time, and between the work place and nonwork places, are at the heart of the modern organization of work and leisure.

Considerable conflict existed in England as workers in the factory system initially resisted the elimination of the traditional organization of work with its greater flexibility in work hours and pace. One reason for their resistance was, as Thompson (1967) noted, uncertainty about how the workers might benefit from these changes. They knew what they were giving up, but not always what they were getting in return. Another reason, according to Walvin (1978), was that the reduction of workers' free time left them with few appealing leisure opportunities. Sunday was their only free day, but considerable social and religious pressures existed to keep public and commercial recreation closed in order not to detract from the day of worship. The unintended side effect was increasing business in the pubs and taverns because they were the only establishments likely to be open. Eventually younger workers began to accept factory work because of the wages offered and the level of conflict over work was reduced. Conflicts generated by attempts to control or even outlaw traditional forms of workers' leisure continued for some time, however.

Industrialization in the United States

As indicated earlier, no single model of industrialization existed and the process varied not only by industry but also by country. In the United States several factors affected industrialization, including the largely rural nature of the early settlements, the vast extent of its territory and natural resources, the steady influx of immigrants, and the existence of slavery.

Herbert Gutman (1977) suggested that industrialization in the United States was an ongoing process that could be divided into three periods. From 1815 to 1843 US society was largely preindustrial and the workers in the few existing factories generally came from "rural and village preindustrial culture" (p. 13). From 1843 to 1893, the United States underwent a major transformation with significant tensions existing between traditional, preindustrial patterns of work and the parallel development of modern industrial work and capitalist financial practices. After 1893, the United States had a mature industrial economy.

Each period was characterized by specific conflicts over the expansion of industrial patterns of work, leisure, and time. Early resistance to modern work patterns arose among workers in smaller artisan and craft workshops (Roediger & Foner, 1989), because they had enjoyed flexibility similar to that in the English workshops. Between 1860 and 1900 workers struggled to cope with workweeks of more than 60 hours (Hunnicutt, 1985). US workers experienced sharp declines in free time and growing separation between their work and nonwork lives. As the United States became a mature industrial economy and society, resistance to industrial work patterns became more organized as unions sought to win support by advocating the reduction of work hours along with wage increases. During the Great Depression, from 1929 until 1941, US workers shifted from challenging the industrial organization of work and seeking shorter hours toward concentrating on job and wage security (Hunnicutt, 1988). This emphasis generally continues today. Just as in England, US workers had accommodated to industrial work by learning that time is money.

A number of factors created industrialization and the resultant influence not only on work but also on leisure. This industrialization occurred at different rates in Europe as well as in the United States. Its impact has been felt around the world and continues today. The changes that occurred from ancient times to industrialization set the stage for activity involvement and the development of the leisure services profession through the 20th century.

Reflection Questions

1. How did industrialization in the United States differ from industrialization in Europe?

2. Discuss some of the impacts of industrialization on leisure.

3. Discuss how leisure changed during America's shift from an agrarian to an industrial economy.

4. Provide three ways that society moved from a household economic focus to a market focus. What were the repercussions for leisure?

2.5   Leisure in the United States in the 19th and 20th Centuries

Recreation activities in early America were common but not held in high esteem. People associated idleness with evil, loose morals and personal degeneration. Opportunities for leisure were available when "earned," but leisure was usually meant for constructive purposes. Blue laws attempted to control such undesirable practices as gambling and drinking by prohibiting these behaviors during certain hours and certain days of the week.

Since people came to North America, however, they have recreated and played. Social life was important to the aristocracy of the South, the industrialists of the North, workers in factories, farmers in rural areas, and residents of small towns. Workers and slaves had their folk and ethnic games. Free-time expressions were controlled but permitted. This chapter gives an overview of leisure in the United States during the late 19th and the 20th centuries and describes how leisure activities emerged and changed over that time.

Late 19th Century Recreation and Leisure

With the opening of frontiers and the rise of urban centers in the 19th century, recreation activities took many interesting forms. Social dancing was popular in the East; square dancing flourished in the West. The waltz, polka, and quadrille emerged as popular dances. Other forms of leisure included sleigh rides, ice skating, and trips to the beach for the daring experience of public bathing. Travel to Europe and to resorts in wilderness areas (for those who could afford it) increased during this period (Dulles, 1965).

The intellectuals and avant-garde educators of the times openly discussed the issue of the "new leisure." Horace Greeley spoke of the need for the wise use of leisure. This new, wise use of leisure meant activities had some specific purpose—whether to recuperate so one could work harder or to enhance one's social status. The prestigious *Atlantic Monthly* magazine carried articles on leisure's significance in making social connections. Gentlemen's clubs such as the New York Athletic Club were organized in the larger cities. Billiard rooms and pool halls were opened and well-patronized by middle and upper class males. Workers were being freed from long hours of labor, and with the shorter workweek came time for recreation pursuits. Private enterprise responded to the opportunity by encouraging sports, arts, and entertainment opportunities.

Outdoor sports increased in popularity. Turkey shoots, buffalo hunts, and sport fishing were promoted. Professional sports were being organized, particularly boxing, racing, and baseball. Americans were enjoying bicycling, bowling, softball, basketball, and volleyball. The Young Men's Christian Association (YMCA) was involved in the promotion of the latter two sports.

Church leaders, who had been critical of organized play and entertainment, began encouraging and supporting specific recreation activities during the latter half of the 19th century. Church members cited the importance of play for proper growth and development of young people. The healthy body was viewed as a living testament. Popularly known as the muscular Christian movement, the trend toward melding church and leisure activities reached its height during the late 19th century. By 1895, there were 1,400 YMCA branches in the United States (Knapp & Hartsoe, 1979).

Theatrical and literary activities also increased in popularity during the nineteenth century. The newly created theaters in Boston, Philadelphia, and New York competed for popular support. Minstrel and variety shows were small town favorites; lecture series were also popular. Band concerts in the park, huge holiday celebrations, taffy pulls, and quilting bees were found in most towns throughout the nation. Thanks to the railroad industry and P. T. Barnum, the circus could come to every city, and by 1872 Barnum's circus train had 61 cars and was touring 16 states annually.

Entertainment went to the people. The traveling medicine and Wild West shows were second in spectator appeal only to the circus. Amusement parks and penny arcades, forerunners of theme parks and video game arcades, sprang up across the country. America learned to play, to relax, and to spend money on its pursuit of pleasure. Resort areas such as Saratoga Springs and White Sulphur Springs prospered, as did a fledgling tourist industry. A popular culture emerged; it was believed that all Americans could share the same forms of entertainment (Dulles, 1965).

Parks also enjoyed a similar degree of attention and recognition. Although Boston had established its commons in 1634, and the town of Newton, New Hampshire had acquired a community forest in 1710, the first major urban parks did not come into being until the mid-1800s. Central Park became the cornerstone for the development of large urban park and parkway systems. The park concept rapidly spread throughout the eastern seaboard and Great Lakes regions. Fairmount Park (Philadelphia) was established in 1867; Washington Park (Chicago) was created nine years later. These new parks broke with the tradition of simply providing green areas and forest; the new parks accommodated a variety of activities including horseback riding, pleasure walking, concerts, and floral gardens. Frederick Olmsted provided the basis upon which modern landscape architecture and park planning was founded.

Regards for conservation paralleled the growth of urban areas in the late 1800s. For example, the potential development of spas as commercial areas prompted the United States government to reserve the land around Hot Springs, Arkansas, in 1832 for public use. This area later became the Hot Springs National Park. In 1864, the United States Congress gave land grants within the Yosemite Valley to the state of California to operate the area as a state park, and eight years later established Yellowstone as the first national park. In 1885, New York made a significant contribution to the conservation movement by acquiring the lands around the Niagara Falls as a preserve. One year later, the Ontario, Canada government approved the establishment of a provincial park at Niagara Falls. Both of these purchases of land resulted from an active campaign by leading citizens in the United States and Canada for the preservation of these areas.

The Turn to the 20th Century

The 20th century began on an optimistic note in the United States. A genuine feeling existed that the quality of life could be enhanced and the problems in society minimized through social reform. It was an era of philanthropy with dedicated citizens concerned about the future. The provision of a proper environment for play and the wise use of leisure were major concerns. The activities of wealthy philanthropists and social reformers led to the growth of recreation opportunities for the urban poor. Although not eliminated, Victorian concepts and ideas were giving way to views of liberalism and humanism. Structured leisure opportunities, however, were not as developed in rural areas where people were isolated, had limited discretionary money, and the church maintained a powerful influence (Braden, 1988). This period also marked the beginning of the professionalization of recreation and leisure services that will be discussed in greater detail later in this unit.

Interest in the outdoors grew in the early part of the 20th century. President Teddy Roosevelt strongly supported the outdoors. When a newspaper published a picture of him on a Rocky Mountain hunting expedition with a brown bear dead at his feet, the Ideal Toy Corporation contacted the president for permission to use his name on a new toy, the Teddy Bear (Fraser, 1966).

Manufactured toys were a luxury of the wealthy class but they also reflected life in America at the time. A Humpty Dumpty Greatest Show on Earth set cost from $1 to $4. Rocking horses and tea sets were popular children's toys. Dean's Rag Books, introduced in 1903 as an indestructible book for children, still exist today (Fraser, 1966). As the First World War become imminent, toy manufacturers increased production of war toys. Soldiers and guns were typical and Milton Bradley produced a war game, At the Front. Instructions on the box stated,

> The box contains soldiers which are to be taken out and fired
> at, for which deadly purpose there are pistols enough for
> considerable execution. Each soldier stands till he is shot
> and then falls like a man and takes no more part in the game.
> The uniforms are the latest and most correct styles, repre-
> senting armies of different countries. (Fraser, 1966, p. 184)

The invention of moving pictures, automobiles, and the telegraph laid the technological groundwork for the future. The Nickelodeon, one of the first theaters for mass showings, soon spread to cities throughout the country. Movies were cheap and popular diversions. Chase movies involving cowboys, bankrobbers, and villains had the greatest appeal (Dulles, 1965). The automobile initially served as a plaything for the wealthy because only they could afford to own one. The growing profit of mass production allowed people, regardless of their social class, to have new leisure options and time.

The Jazz Age (1920–1929)

The jazz age introduced issues such as women's rights, political scandal, and economic upheaval. The years following World War I resulted in extensive expansion of all types of recreation opportunities. Stimulated by an era of unparalleled prosperity, Americans sought to enjoy the new freedom of a somewhat shorter workweek (about 60 hours), the benefit of mass production, and the expansion of new technology. Whereas there were only 5,000 radios in 1920, by 1924 there were over one million (Chubb & Chubb, 1981). The first "talkie," *The Jazz Singer*, boosted the movie industry. During this time, Babe Ruth hit 60 home runs for the New York Yankees. Racing automobiles, horses, and dogs had a phenomenal growth and became big spectator activities.

More people had larger incomes and more opportunity for leisure. Commercial recreation pursuits grew with the discretionary money that people had. In addition, commercial enterprises reported large profits and sought to promote themselves in a variety of ways. For example, as a promotional campaign, a New York hotel owner offered $25,000 to the first aviator who crossed the Atlantic from New York to Paris. Over the next eight years, six aviators died in the attempt and others were injured. Newspaper reporters reveled in the popularity of this endeavor and kept the fire growing. The media hype ended only after Charles Lindbergh and the *Spirit of St. Louis* accomplished the feat in 1927.

In 1920, the skirt was ankle length but by 1922 the hemline had steadily risen, just covering the knee. Female emancipation took off and the flapper was the heroine of the Jazz Age. Short hair, short skirts, turned down hose, and eyes peering out from under a pulled down hat marked the fast and brazen modern woman of the twenties. Thin was in, and women who did not conform dieted.

The film industry blossomed during the twenties. MGM, Warner Brothers, Paramount, and Universal ruled Hollywood. Sid Grauman built movie theatres in Los Angeles and established the tradition of stars placing their handprints in cement outside the theatre as a tourist attraction. This period saw the first Mickey Mouse film made by Walt Disney in 1928. The Motion Picture Academy awarded the first awards in 1927.

The focus on entertainment of the period also fueled the acceptance of African-American art forms. The Harlem Renaissance resulted in the Lindy Hop, literature, art, and social commentary about the plight of the African-American culture. Jazz and ragtime blues were lasting contributions to leisure made by African-American performers.

Spectator sports grew during the 1920s, as did active participation. Parks had swimming pools, tennis courts, and baseball diamonds. Universities built new stadiums to house the growing attendees at athletic events (Braden, 1988). Prize fighting and horse racing both attracted large crowds.

Crossword puzzles, miniature golf, dance marathons, bathing beauty contests, and contract bridge were activities of the day. Train companies provided dictionaries to riders who passed the time completing crossword puzzles. Free street dances drew young people away from the popular dance halls, which were generally considered disreputable places. Fraternal clubs had existed for many years, but during this period the Rotary, Kiwanis, and Lions Clubs were founded for men to maintain business associations and provide service to their communities (Braden, 1988).

Not everything was wonderful during the decade of the 1920s. The Red Scare infiltrated the United States. The government responded to a fear that Russia was attempting to take over the United States. Over 10,000 American citizens were unlawfully arrested and questioned about communist behavior. The government established the Anti-Radical Division led by J. Edgar Hoover to stifle the efforts. Government further affected the lives of citizens with the enactment of the 18th amendment, National Prohibition Act, leading to crime and an illegal alcohol market. Black Tuesday collapsed the "slap-happy" period of the Roaring 20s and triggered the Great Depression.

The Great Depression (1929–1940)

The Great Depression of the 1930s was a time of unemployment lines, personal tragedies, and economic collapse. It was also a decade of changing philosophies of economics and government. The New Deal approach of Franklin Roosevelt was a radical departure from dependence on philanthropy. The New Deal programs reflected the belief that any work was better than idleness of unemployment, and that it was the duty of the government to furnish work when private enterprise was incapable of doing so. Varieties of public work projects provided jobs for millions. Many of those jobs benefited the recreation participants in the United States as public swimming pools, bandstands, and picnic shelters were built in many communities. New Deal money supported unemployed artists through the Federal Arts Project and the Federal Theatre. Artists created museum exhibits, taught art fundamentals, and captured the culture of the country through photographs and paintings. They produced art for government buildings, schools, and hospitals with many paintings highlighting regional and small town life or "American Scenes," the unofficial style of the period. Many community orchestras began with funding from the Works Progress Administration (WPA). The theatre was the largest of the WPA projects. At its peak, the WPA employed 13,000 people in 31 states. Over 30 million people attended theatre project productions during this time (Bolino, 1998).

Many Americans took respite from economic worries through baseball. Two professional organizations existed separately, the Major Leagues and the Negro Leagues. The Major Leagues played in public stadiums with large crowds coming to see stars like Joe Dimaggio and Lou Gehrig. The Negro Leagues played in small town fields with small crowds (Marasco, n.d.).

Women were also making a place in sports. In 1932, Babe Didrikson set three world records at the Los Angeles Summer Olympics in the javelin, hurdles, and high jump. Also common during this time was the involvement of women in team sports, particularly through industrial sports programs organized by manufacturing companies. During the 1920s, a "play for all" era arose that included girls in many aspects of physical activity, but in the 1930s, an era of social control emerged suggesting that girls and women should not be placed under the pressures of sport (Henderson, 1993b).

Motels catered to motor travel by the late 1930s, as car travel was a favored vacation and leisure option. The automobile trailer also debuted and vacation trailer parks followed. Closer to home, young people often drove to "roadhouses" located along highways for entertainment, dining, and socializing (Braden, 1988).

Outdoor sports were generally expensive and thus available only to the wealthy. Skiing was season-limited and expensive, and the resorts that surrounded the ski industry provided other luxury accommodations such as heated swimming pools, lounges, and restaurants to expand the attraction. Miniature golf and softball were favorite outdoor activities for the lower economic class.

During the Depression, movies provided an escape from economic realities. The neighborhood theater offered solace from the heat or cold of the weather as well as a Hollywood fantasy. Many theaters gave away dinnerware with the purchase of a ticket. By 1939 there were over 15,000 movie theatres with a $700,000,000 annual income (Bolino, 1998). In 1939 *Time* magazine named Shirley Temple, Clark Gable, Sonja Henie, Mickey Rooney, and Spencer Tracy among the top movie stars in America (Bolini, 1998).

Music of the period was often different based on geographic region. Kansas City jazz, New Orleans Dixieland, Appalachia country, and New York City Broadway hits were enjoyed by Americans. African Americans had great influence on the development of American musical entertainment with Duke Ellington, Louis Armstrong, and Billie Holiday among its leaders.

World War II and the Decade After (1941–1959)

The economy of the Depression rebounded with the start of WWII. After the bombing of Pearl Harbor in December 1941, the concerns of the United States focused on preparation and maintenance of war efforts. As during WWI, industrial centers grew. Material goods were rationed to provide the necessary supplies and equipment for the war effort.

A host of social changes resulting from World War II altered the face of the United States. The changes resulted in a focus on consumerism, higher education, increased births, consumptive behavior, and civil rights. Returning servicemen had grown accustomed to the recreation services of the American Red Cross and United Service Organization. Upon return, they demanded similar services in their communities. This attitude, coupled with the GI bill, eventually lead to people attending college in greater numbers than ever before. People also had more money and discretion in its use for education and for leisure.

Television became a household fixture in the 1950s. Shows like *Howdy Doody*, *Candid Camera*, and *I Love Lucy* were popular. In 1957, *American Bandstand* broadcasted nationally and Perry Mason made his first appearance. *The Nat King Cole Show* was the first variety TV series with a black star. Television's growth also was spurred by the birth of cablevision. A television retailer in the mountains of Pennsylvania found it difficult to sell the new gadget to residents in the mountainous valleys. There were few stations and reception in the mountains was dismal. He posted a tall antenna on a nearby mountain ridge and wired the reception to his store. Sales increased and Community Antenna Television was born (Pennsylvania Cable and Telecommunications Association, n.d.). Frank Sinatra and Bing Crosby popularized movies (Jenkins, 1977). American war movies featured the heroic efforts of young men, and Humphrey Bogart starred in classics like *The Maltese Falcon* and *Casablanca*. *Citizen Kane* emulated the American dream of being rich and famous.

Baseball remained a national pastime through the 1940s and 1950s. The largest paid crowd of that time for any single baseball game in Wrigley

Field history occurred in 1947. The excitement was for Jackie Robinson, the first baseball appearance of a "Negro" athlete as a big leaguer. Over 30,000 of those fans were women who came for the free Ladies Day (Marasco, n.d.). Football was also becoming the fastest growing spectator sport.

By the 1950s, Americans were moving to the suburbs. The culture was turning to convenience as demonstrated by more labor saving appliances such as the electric clothes washer, telephone, and flush toilets. Packaged cake mixes, Oreo cookies, boxed cereal, M&M candies, and TV dinners appeared on the scene to changing eating habits and to give people more free time. In 1948, McDonald's opened their first fast-food stand and drive-ins proliferated. Eat fast (in your car) and keep going was the subliminal message. Diners also became a common social gathering place where teenage boys in jeans, loafers, button-down shirts, and manicured hair danced with girls with ponytails and poodle skirts. The Wurlitzer jukebox and bopping at the diner became prevalent (Sherlock, 1999).

Cars, now a part of everyday society, grew "fins" in the 1950s. The emphasis on stylish, not just practical, automobiles flourished. Competition ensued to create the fastest or wildest looking car. Gadgets like cigar lighters, clocks, and power windows evolved. To address the trends, *Hot Rod* magazine debuted in 1948. Fuzzy dice hanging from the rearview mirror and eight-ball gearshifts characterized the period. Air transportation also changed. Prior to World War II, fewer than 2% of all travelers went by air. By the mid-1950s, air traffic equaled rail passenger traffic.

During World War II children were toy-deprived. A picture frame workshop located in a garage was the birthplace of Mattel, where scraps of picture frames were used to make dollhouse furniture. As the war ended, manufacturing returned to making new toys with new materials, such as Silly Putty in 1949. Lithographed tin, die-cast metal, and plastic toys emerged. Plastic Hula Hoops and Frisbees became popular in the mid-1950s, and in 1959 the first Barbie doll appeared. Toy manufacturers also attended to the needs of children with disabilities. Magnetized or permanently affixed toys were developed to hold toys within reach of children with visual or orthopedic problems.

Technology became more important daily in US society. Microwave technology increased the reception of stations across the country. Radios had long been popular, but with the faster and more mobile society, the transistor was the first step toward electronic mobilization for the mass of society.

Rebel art emerged in the 1950s, including "Folkniks," musicians for social change who were against racial segregation, military draft, McCarthyism, nuclear research, and the Cold War. The invention of the electric guitar gave birth to the rock-n-roll era. Chuck Berry, Elvis Presley, and Bill Haley and the Comets pushed rock-n-roll forward. In 1959, the

BBC banned the Coaster's "Charlie Brown" because of the socially unacceptable reference to spitballs. African-American artists were supported
by the development of Motown recording label.

Life was good for the dominant White culture in the United States during
the 1950s. This time also spurred the efforts of marginalized groups to seek
out their rights. The 1954 Supreme Court ruling of *Brown vs. Board of
Education of Topeka* led to the desegregation of schools. African Americans
across the country became active in protests to end racial discrimination and
to increase opportunities for community membership. Access to leisure was
one of the issues that emerged indirectly in the emerging equal rights focus
for people of color as well as women.

The Sixties (1960–1969)

The complacency of the fifties would come to a screeching halt with the
assassination of President Kennedy in 1963. Until that time Americans felt
safe, except for the outside chance that we would die together in a nuclear
war. Similar to the 1920s, the 1960s were a decade of tremendous economic
expansion. Commercial and outdoor recreation became popular and service
agencies increased programs for postwar baby boomers that were now
reaching their adolescence. Advances in technology provided climate-
controlled homes, home entertainment centers, and a multitude of gadgets
to increase quality of life. Alan Shepard became the first American to fly
into space and nearly every radio in the country tuned to the coverage.

Gasoline prices were relatively inexpensive so Americans took to the
road. Car camping was propelled by guidebooks listing camping areas in
state and national parks. Boats and camping equipment were becoming
common. Americans were looking beyond the developed cities for escapes
in the outdoors. To enhance this outdoor recreation, artificial snow and
icemakers became useful to extend the skiing season.

Toward the end of the 1960s, prosperity took a negative turn. The
Vietnam War and the assassination of Martin Luther King, Jr. resulted in
serious questioning of what was happening in American society. Many
people spent their time advocating for issues of social justice. The antiwar
movement was significant, as were the efforts to expand racial equity. Civil
unrest heightened when the National Guard oversaw the integration of the
University of Mississippi by the first black student in 1962, and when 41
people died in the Detroit race riot (Sugrue, 1996). Protestors disrupted the
1968 Democratic nominating convention in Chicago to make their voices
heard about the Vietnam War and other issues of social unrest.

The social changes facing the United States led to conflicting lifestyles
and aspirations between generations. Environmental concerns related to

potential damage done by new outdoor recreational activities such as snowmobiling, dune buggies, and trail bikes increased. Environmentalists made dire predictions that at the present rate of pollution saying the earth would not support life by the beginning of the 21st century. On the other hand, consumer leisure was increasing as evidenced by attendance at athletic events, longer vacations, and international air travel. The 1960s showed that great divisions existed in American society.

The Seventies (1970–1979)

The seventies was a transitional decade in which liberalism of the sixties gave way to conservatism in the eighties. The early years were a continuation of the feelings and actions of the later sixties, but with the Watergate scandal and the subsequent resignation of President Nixon, changes occurred in our national culture. Concerns in the early 1970s such as enforcing civil rights, taking care of the urban poor, rights for women, and concerns for the environment and endangered species gave rise to numerous causes and special interests groups. Many of these concerns resulted in legislative actions that restricted or regulated the national political, social, and economic behaviors. Federal bureaucracies grew as the government attempted to enforce regulations that would guarantee the rights of all, protect the environment, and assure a continued rate of economic growth and prosperity. To accomplish these goals, taxes were increased.

In 1974, the Congress passed the Education for All Handicapped Children's Act to guarantee equal educational opportunity for youth with disabilities. Further legislation reduced architectural barriers to public buildings for access by people with disabilities. The large institutions that had warehoused people with disabilities began to downsize and people with disabilities began to move back into the community. Community opportunities like the Special Olympics, which had begun in the 1960s, became commonplace. Leisure for people with disabilities became an issue for the first time.

Electronic gaming was on the rise. *Pong*, a computerized tennis game, became a huge success as a bar game. In response, Magnavox marketed *Odyssey*, a similar computer game for home use. Hand-held games such as *Simon* and stand-alone games like *Space Invaders* soon followed.

The music of the 1970s was varied from psychedelic to disco. Artists such as Fleetwood Mac, Bob Seger and the Silver Bullet Band, Pink Floyd, the Eagles, Elton John, and Bob Marley and the Wailers were popular. Bubblegum music like *Jam Up and Jelly Tight* became popular, and disco music, represented by John Travolta and *Saturday Night Fever*, dominated the music fads of the end of the decade. Psychedelic music dominated the early part of the decade, followed by disco toward the end. Music became portable with the eight-track tape players in cars and eventually even more convenient with the cassette tape. To get the most of the music at home, people built component stereo systems where "bigger was better."

Television in the 1970s was comedic with shows like *Gilligan's Island* and *The Brady Bunch*, and serious with mini-series such as *Roots*. Gender battles were fought vicariously through the Billie Jean King–Bobby Riggs tennis match. Popular movies of the decade included *Star Wars*, *The Godfather*, and *Rocky*.

The divisions in American society in the 1960s became recognized as differences in the 1970s. Everyone did not always understand the differences, but the variety of public tastes resulted in recreation becoming more important as reflected in the number of public, not-for-profit, and commercial providers emerging to meet the growing and diversified leisure interests of the American public.

Conservatism in the Eighties (1980–1989)

By the end of the 1970s, Americans grew weary of big government, big corporations, and big automobiles. In response to the new conservatism, Ronald Reagan was elected President on a platform to downsize and deregulate government. The federal government reduced spending for support of outdoor and recreational facilities. Entrepreneurialism took the place of large government programs. The deregulation of airlines and banking industries helped to stimulate the growth of commercial ventures, including leisure opportunities such as malls and resorts. Social concerns were passé and making money was in vogue during the 1980s.

During Reagan's administration, the federal mandatory retirement age was eliminated, while services for retired persons grew. Residential communities geared at older adults proliferated, and Airstreams and Winnebago's caravanned in the southern migration of retirees each winter.

World politics and violence continued to infiltrate the Olympics as well as other sports. Sports spectatorship grew and women entered the sports arena as a result of the passage of Title IX in the 1970s that became enforced in the 1980s. Concerns began to emerge, however, related to the growing commercialization of sport. Sports were further scrutinized by the British soccer stadium riot where 95 fans were killed and 2,000 more injured in the mayhem.

Computers continued to grow in popularity. The introduction of Pac Man catapulted the industry. The invention of personal computers resulted in the technology available for work in the home as well as for recreation.

The End of the Century (1990–1999)

The conservatism of the eighties was modified into the 1990s. The emphasis on material consumption, however, decreased to some extent. New age spirituality and back to nature aspects intrigued the aging baby boomers who still continued to be concerned with making money. Social liberalism was popular concerning children, homeless people, and immigrants (Sessoms & Orthner, 1992; Kunstler, 1993). Concerns for health and welfare became more important than national defense.

Theme restaurants popped up across the country. Martha Stewart was the diva of home decorating, and "do-it-yourself" home improvement was popular. Casual Fridays became typical in US corporations. Tae-bo, salsa dancing, in-line skating, Beanie Babies, and body piercing were options for showing one's individuality. Women's sports continued to grow and the Women's National Basketball Association provided women a professional culture to support. Tiger Woods swept the athletic industry on the heels of Michael Jordan and Nike. Electronic games, personal fitness equipment, and vacations remained popular expenditures.

The Americans with Disabilities Act in 1990 furthered the rights of people with disabilities and established Universal Standards for new construction of all facilities. More so than ever before in this country, people with disabilities had access to freely chosen and appropriate leisure opportunities. The Paralympics established itself as an elite sporting event, held every four years at the same site as the Olympics.

Satellite television, personal computers, and the Internet connected ordinary citizens with information, people, and globalized the world. The majority of homes had cable television and many homes had Internet access. The 1990s saw the introduction of CD-ROMS and DVDs for personal use. Home and hand-held video games went to a new height of sophistication. Sega reported earning $98 million within the first 24 hours of launching the new game platform *Dreamcast* in the United States.

The last decade of the 20th century brought prosperity for many Americans, but a growing number of people did not have the same options for meaningful work and leisure. Throughout all the decades of the 20th century, social trends influenced consumerism, work and family life, and leisure. Economic prosperity and decline, wars, and rapidly advancing technology have influenced popular culture and the ways that people view leisure. These changes also greatly influenced the ways that recreation and leisure services were provided in the United States, as we will explore in the next chapter.

Reflection Questions

1. What role did popular leisure play in relation to social events of each time period?

2. What was the role of the church in providing leisure in American society?

3. How has war influenced leisure behavior?

4. What technological advances have changed leisure behavior?

5. How have historical events influenced leisure in the 20th century?

6. Discuss the influence of late 20th century technology on leisure attitudes and behaviors.

2.6 Roots of Recreation and Leisure Services

The model for recreation and leisure services, particularly in the public and not-for-profit sectors, began in the United States over a century ago. Recreation and leisure services emanated from a concern for the quality of life and the social and educational needs of all the people. That model has changed over time, but it continues to serve as a format that provides many opportunities for recreation and leisure for individuals in communities. This chapter builds on what we know about recreation and leisure in the United States and explores how the roots of recreation services evolved within the context of the cultural, social, and political aspects of this country.

The growth of recreation and leisure services in the United States over the past 100 years was the result of a number of developments, including advances in science and medicine, the growth of public education, industrial and technological progress, and the changing of social and political attitudes. During the 19th century, the United States moved from a pioneering, agricultural nation to an industrialized society with large centers of population. Urbanization occurred as people moved from farms and small towns to the cities and suburbs. Mass production of convenience items benefited many Americans, freeing them from the routines of daily activity. These changes, in combination with growing affluence and better healthcare, allowed Americans to enjoy leisure in ways previously unknown.

Public and not-for-profit recreation in cities, particularly the large metropolitan areas, also began to take shape at the end of the 19th century. The movement started with the sand gardens as an idea brought to America from Europe in 1885. By 1893, the Massachusetts Emergency and Hygiene Association, a Boston charity, was operating ten summer playgrounds utilizing both volunteer and paid leadership. Joseph Lee was one of the pioneers in this effort. Lee believed that every child had a right to play. Playgrounds resulted because of the settlement house movement, the social concerns of religious reformers, and concerns about the effects of urbanization on youth.

As the 19th century came to a close, small parks dotted the landscape of many communities, public libraries and community centers were being established, and America entered a new era of social consciousness. Concerns for the less fortunate, for the young, and for the preservation of the environment were a part of this consciousness. These concerns had a significant effect on the park and recreation movement.

Twentieth Century Highlights

The first decade of the century was an era of expansion and new beginnings for recreation services. The first playground commission within a municipal government was established in 1904 by the city of Los Angeles. Luther Gulick, an early pioneer in youth activity and the first president of the Camp Fire Girls, organized the first public school athletic leagues in New York in 1903. Psychologists such as Carl Groos and G. Stanley Hall were citing the importance of play in the development of children. Several youth-serving agencies, including the Boy Scouts, began during this decade.

The year 1906 marked the beginning of the Playground Association of America (PAA), later was known as the Playground and Recreation Association of America (PRAA), then the National Recreation Association (NRA), and ultimately as the National Recreation and Park Association (NRPA). As a service organization supported by voluntary contributions, the PAA promoted community recreation for more than half a century (Dickason, 1985). It grew out of the work of Joseph Lee, Henry Curtis, Luther Gulick, and Jane Addams, who were the first officers. PAA was established as an association comprised largely of volunteer and interested citizens.

PAA served both volunteers and professionals through its field staff and national office. Many of these volunteers were women who wanted to use their talents in a society that tended to view women's roles narrowly and often rendered women invisible. Henderson (1992) described how an ethic of caring defined many women's lives and opened the door for these volunteers and professionals to address social justice issues pertaining to leisure. The contributions of groups of women, particularly through club activities in both the White and Black communities, was significant. Without the tireless efforts of many unheralded women, the quality of national and local recreation services would have been greatly diminished.

The enactment of the Antiquities Act in 1906 gave the federal government a tool for protecting scientific and historic areas. This act gave the President the power to designate national monuments and to protect these areas from destruction. Devils Tower and the Lassen Peak (Lassen Volcanic National Park) were among the earlier designated monuments. The growing number of national parks and national monuments led to the establishment of the National Park Service ten years later.

The public schools were also involved in the development of early organized recreation services. In 1907 staff in Rochester, New York, embarked on a program of making school facilities available as community facilities. This beginning had far-reaching effects on the general use of schools for community purposes. The National Education Association in 1911 recommended the use of school buildings and grounds for recreation, and the

community school program emerged. As one successful example, the recreation program of the Milwaukee School System, led by Dorothy Enderis,
was nationally acclaimed for its "lighted school houses," which offered
programs for children and adults.

The early years of the 20th century were characterized by a marked
expansion in the voluntary agency and camping movements. Without the
efforts of wealthy philanthropists and social reformers, the growth of recreation opportunities for the urban poor would have been impeded. The
settlement houses, established in the slum sections in large cities in the East
and Midwest, were the first neighborhood service centers. Hull House was
built in Chicago in 1889 and operated by Jane Addams, who felt that recreation could be a powerful force in the prevention of delinquency and antisocial behavior. Youth-serving agency and private camps also increased in
number. Frederick William Gunn and Dr. Joseph T. Rothrock are credited
with having established the first school camp (1861) and private camp (1876)
before the turn of the century. By 1900 over 100 camps were in operation.
By 1916, the camping movement was large enough that those involved had
organized the Camp Directors Association, later to become the American
Camping Association.

Government interest in outdoor recreation increased during this period.
In 1903 the voters of Chicago approved the nation's first five-million-dollar
bond issue to acquire and develop recreational parks. One year later Los
Angeles established the first Municipal Recreation Commission, an appointed
board to oversee its playgrounds as an independently governed unit separate
from both the school and park boards. Although unpopular for politicians
to speak on behalf of such trivia as recreation a few years earlier, by 1906
it was expedient to be in favor of recreation and conservation. In 1908,
President Theodore Roosevelt convened a White House conference with the
governors of various states to kick off his public conservation program.
The National Park Service was established in 1916 to

> promote and regulate the use of the federal areas known as
> national parks, monuments and reservations . . . to conserve
> the scenery and national historic objects of the wildlife
> therein and to provide for the enjoyment of the same and
> by such manner and by such means as will leave them un-
> impaired for the enjoyment of the future generation...(Act
> of August 25, 1916)

The early pioneers viewed the natural environment as a dangerous unknown that needed to be tamed with resources thought to be limitless. They
believed in Manifest Destiny (that lands abounded for use in any way
needed) and the God-given right to dominate nature and to use it for society's

benefit. By the mid-1800s, however, the transcendentalist movement was underway. This movement viewed nature as the vehicle to inspire intuitive thought, to lift the consciousness to greater spiritual wisdom, and to learn to relate rather than exploit. The great transcendentalist writers such as Emerson and Thoreau inspired future naturalists as well as the general public to respect and preserve the natural world.

By the early 1900s, naturalism emerged. In keeping with the philosophy of realism, these naturalists-scientists observed nature and recorded their observations in ways that promoted a reverence for the natural world based on scientific fact. Their efforts spearheaded a preservation movement that gained momentum in the mid-1900s and still exists in the mainstream of today's society. A number of important conservation groups also were created around the turn of the century: the Sierra Club (1892), the Scenic and Historic Preservation Society (1895), and the National Audubon Society (1905). Professionals concerned with the management of resources were also working during this period. These pioneers put into practice the concepts gained from the transcendentalists and the naturalists-scientists. Practitioners such as Frederick Olmsted, Aldo Leopold, Gifford Pinchot, and Stephen Mather laid the foundations for such institutions as the National Park Service and the US Forest Service and shaped the roles of park and recreation practitioners.

The conservation movement became a major social focus at the turn of the 20th century. This movement grew from a concern over commercial development opening up natural resources to support expanding industries. For the first time, power tools were being used heavily in the lumbering and mining industries with little concern by businesses for conservation. Land erosion, droughts, and floods were natural consequences of these exploitative patterns. These wanton acts of destruction incensed many citizens, who banded together, developed political muscle, and became the first lobbyists for conservation. They advocated for legislation that continues to influence our ability to enjoy outdoor recreation pursuits today. A new concept of parks emerged as active organized recreation programs began to appear. To some extent, the concepts of conservation and preservation gave way to the people's recreation desires. Distinctions were made between parks and playgrounds, with the former emphasizing design and the latter stressing places for play.

The expansion of parks and recreation agencies required the development of professional leadership. The first training program for professional directors of play services, later to be known as recreation leaders, was published in 1909 under the title, *The Normal Course in Play*. Several universities, including Harvard, Columbia, Northwestern, and the University of California at Berkley, offered courses in play and summer playground institutes. Among the earliest educators were Luther Gulick (1905, New York

University), Neva Boyd (1911, Chicago Training Institute, later a part of Northwestern) and George E. Johnson (1915, Harvard). In 1912, the New York State College of Forestry at Syracuse University established the nation's first program to train for park administration and city forestry (Sessoms, 1993).

Influence of Wars on Leisure Services

The events preceding and surrounding World War I affected the growth of municipal recreation and park services. Organized recreation took on a community focus. Rainwater (1922) referred to 1915–1918 as the "neighborhood organization" stage of the playground movement in the United States. He said these years were characterized by the development of self-supported, self-governed, decentralized play activities in neighborhoods with funds being solicited for the operation of community recreation facilities. Much of this growth directly related to the activities of the Playground and Recreation Association of America (PRAA).

With the entrance of the United States into World War I and the establishment of a universal draft system, community life underwent upheaval. Communities adjacent to military installations and training centers that boomed as "war" towns were particularly affected. Suddenly, hundreds of thousands of servicepeople and transient workers found themselves in new settings without traditional support systems. To provide some continuity, communities during this time established recreation programs that would accommodate their new citizens and allow for the wholesome use of leisure. Under the leadership of the PRAA, the War Camp Community Service (WCCS) was organized. In two years of its operations the Association raised over 2.2 million dollars to aid local communities in developing recreation opportunities and services for the military and defense workers. In those states where racial segregation was legal, the WCCS operated over 100 clubs specifically for the Black military (Knapp & Hartsoe, 1979).

In addition to the activities of the war camp program, several religious organizations and the YMCA established recreation programs on military posts. These programs were approved by the War and Navy departments and emphasized both religious and social welfare activities as well as recreation services. They were forerunners of the special programs now provided by the military branches for their service personnel. With the coming of peace, these special war-effort programs terminated, but their effects were long-lasting. They stimulated the interest of many communities in organized recreation services and ushered in the dynamic 1920s.

The years following World War I resulted in extensive expansion of all types of recreation services, including commercial recreation. Organized parks and recreation grew rapidly, as did the demand for paid leadership.

Whereas only 400 communities offered organized recreation services at the beginning of the 1920s, over a thousand offered them as the decade came to an end. The PRAA responded to this leadership need by establishing a series of training programs.

The Great Depression brought bad times for many people, but it was not an era of decline for organized park and recreation services. The Federal Emergency Relief Administration (FERA), the Works Project Administration (WPA), and the Civilian Conservation Corps (CCC) made major contributions to recreation services and facilities. FERA assumed two approaches to recreation services: (1) to employ workers through the construction of facilities; and (2) to employ program and activity leadership. For example, writers, musicians, and actors were given jobs through the federal theater. The Division of Recreation Projects, as a part of the organizational structure of the WPA, also became a major employer of recreation personnel. WPA leaders worked under the general supervision of such local tax-supported units as recreation departments, park boards, school boards, and welfare departments. The CCC was created to give employment and vocational training to unemployed young men. It helped several states to establish their state park systems. The CCC built roads, picnic areas, campgrounds, cabins, and hiking and riding trails for local, state, and federal park and recreation areas programs. It also constructed swimming and boating facilities and upgraded the specialized recreation facilities required by the National Park Service, the US Forest Service, and the Work Projects Administration. Meyer and Brightbill (1964) estimated that these "make work programs of the federal government during the Depression advanced organized parks and recreation by twenty-five years" (p. 17). These programs stimulated organized recreation services at every level of governmental responsibility. In 1930 there were less than 25,000 volunteers and professionals engaged in the field of recreation, with only 2,500 of these employed full-time. By 1935 that number had increased to 45,000 full-time workers and the number of communities offering recreation services had doubled.

The United States was slowly recovering from the Depression when war broke out in Europe in 1939. By 1941 it seemed inevitable that the entire world would be at war. As during World War I, industrial centers expanded, small towns adjacent to military installations were inundated with the arrival of new recruits, and the federal government assumed a greater responsibility for the social behaviors of all US residents. Among those programs that had a direct bearing upon the lives of the military were the activities of the various branches of the armed forces and the United Service Organization. Each of the armed forces was encouraged to establish recreation programs. Facilities and services for recreation and entertainment were provided at the various military installations. As Meyer and Brightbill (1964) cited,

> Never in the history of the armed forces was so much at-
> tention given to recreation as a functional part of the total
> military operation. (p. 20)

Private organizations combined efforts and formed the United Service Organization (USO). It organized camp shows and provided a range of social
and recreation services, primarily for the off-duty military.

Another private voluntary association that contributed significantly to the
war effort was the American Red Cross. It operated approximately 750 clubs
and 250 mobile units throughout the world. Through these programs, hundreds of thousands of servicemen and servicewomen were able to escape,
however briefly, the events of war. Whereas the special service programs
stressed athletics and theatrical activities, the American Red Cross effort
emphasized social programming. Possibly the most significant contribution to
the recreation movement at this point was the Red Cross workers in military
hospitals who were concerned about recreation activity with therapeutic value.

During World War II, the Federal Security Agency established a Division
of Recreation within the Office of Community War Services. The Division
helped communities to organize, develop, and maintain adequate recreation
programs, especially in those areas affected by the war effort. The Division
strongly advocated the establishment of state and federal recreation services
by providing technical assistance.

The war years also resulted in more opportunities for women in many
areas, including recreation. For a short time during World War II, more
women than men were employed as professionals in the field of recreation
(Henderson, 1992). Many of the functional roles as volunteers and as paid
workers in the profession related to caring and support roles, programming,
and advocacy. Nevertheless, women representing a diversity of backgrounds
(Henderson et al., 1996) were involved and continued this involvement as
leaders and advocates in local communities into the postwar years.

The Post–World War II Years

Recreation and leisure services grew more after mid-century. Following the
war, hundreds of towns and cities constructed community centers, swimming
pools, playgrounds, and athletic facilities as "living war memorials." Tax-
supported public recreation systems increased in number, and states gave
greater attention to their responsibility in organizing recreation and youth
services. Hospitals established therapeutic recreation services, universities
created degree programs in parks and recreation, and tourism became a major
industry. Americans were on the go, seeking pleasure and enjoying newfound
leisure. The workday and workweek shortened; vacation periods lengthened.
Not even the disruptive years of the Korean War could delay these changes.

Examples of some of the events that occurred after World War II that helped establish current patterns of behavior and organizational approaches for recreation and leisure services included:

- In 1951 the White House Conference on Aging emphasized the role of recreation for a growing population of older citizens.

- The National Association of Recreation Therapists was created as a separate professional body and joined with the Hospital Section of the American Recreation Society to establish the Council for the Advancement of Hospital Recreation.

- The Supreme Court decision made racial segregation in public schools unconstitutional and thereby opened the system to all citizens, regardless of race. This law also affected many community recreation programs that had previously been segregated as well.

- The growth of international recreation services resulted in the establishment of the International Recreation Association (now the World Leisure and Recreation Association).

- Disneyland was established in 1955 on 150 acres in Anaheim, California. It was the first major theme park and became the model for subsequent theme parks.

- The public's discovery and use of natural resources for recreation purposes quickly resulted in overcrowding in public parks and outdoor recreation areas. In response the National Park Service and the US Forest Service began to upgrade and expand federal recreation and park areas.

- The US Congress established the Outdoor Recreation Resources Review Commission in 1958. The Commission provided estimates of the need for outdoor recreation areas for the years 1976–2000.

- The Federal Aid Highway Act in 1958 created the interstate highway system. This network of superhighways encouraged travel and stimulated the growth of an already expanding motel/ franchise quick food industry. In a sense, the highways became the playgrounds for millions; vacation travel became synonymous with recreation.

- The establishment of the President's Council on Youth Fitness and the authorization of the National Cultural Center for Performing Arts (Kennedy Center) furthered the nation's interest in physical fitness and the performing arts.

During the 1960s and 1970s a great expansion of commercial and outdoor recreation facilities and youth-serving programs occurred as the children of the postwar baby boom years entered adolescence. Governmental involvement in parks and recreation also expanded during this period. The Bureau of Outdoor Recreation (BOR) was established in 1962. Three years later, Congress established the Land and Water Conservation Fund (LWCF), which provided matching funds to enable local recreation units to acquire and develop land for outdoor recreation purposes.

By 1966 several major recreation and park organizations had merged to form the National Recreation and Park Association (NRPA). One of NRPA's first undertakings was to assess the recreation and park employment situation. According to the 1967–68 personnel analysis, about 200 universities and colleges were preparing recreation and park specialists (National Recreation and Park Association, 1968). Enrollments in these programs exceeded 15,000 students. The projected need for annual new personnel in 1980 was twice that figure. Although critics of this report questioned its research methodology and validity, all agreed it did accurately reflect the growing importance of parks and recreation as an area of professional service.

The Last Quarter of the 20th Century

During the 1970s, several significant governmental actions affected recreation and leisure services. In response to the recreation interests of urban residents, the National Park Service established two urban parks, Golden Gate in San Francisco and Gateway in New York City. The national park system embarked on an urban parks program, intensified in 1978 when Congress appropriated 1.2 billion dollars to improve urban and national park systems. Some conservationists responded with alarm to the establishment of the urban parks program that took money away from traditional national parks. Other believed that urban parks would take the pressure off the overuse of many of the national parks.

In matters concerning human rights, governmental action was equally pronounced. Congress passed the Education for All Handicapped Act in the mid-1970s, which guaranteed equal educational opportunity for handicapped youth in the least restrictive environment. The field of therapeutic recreation services expanded, particularly at the local level where hundreds of park and recreation departments created program divisions to serve these populations. The Bureau for the Education of the Handicapped stimulated the growth of these programs through its financial support of the training of therapeutic recreation personnel.

The focus of recreation and leisure studies in the 1980s and 1990s evolved toward entrepreneurialism. Reflecting the general attitudes towards business and government, the private commercial and not-for-profit sectors of the leisure service delivery system prospered. The public sector became more businesslike by developing programs and services that were self-supporting or assured the agency some recovery costs. Pricing and marketing concepts became a part of the leisure studies curricula, as did specializations in commercial recreation/resort and tourism management. Some curricula even changed their names to reflect the trend, becoming Departments of Parks, Recreation, and Tourism.

In the 1980s student interest in recreation and other human service fields declined. Enrollments in park and recreation curricula dropped, except for those specialties embracing entrepreneurialism and therapeutic recreation. Therapeutic recreation was aided considerably by the focus on the American Disability Act and the creation of the American Therapeutic Recreation Association and the National Council on Therapeutic Recreation Certification. Furthermore, for the first time in the history of the profession, more females than males were choosing parks and recreation as a major. By the end of the decade, the ratio was two females for every male (Bialeschki, 1992).

At the end of the 20th century, the growth in public recreation and not-for-profit sectors stabilized. After some decline in university programs in recreation, the numbers of students remains relatively constant. Private commercial recreation and tourism continue to offer opportunities for a variety of leisure services. Environmental protection is important but weighed against sustainable economic activities like tourism. Efforts focus on youth from high-risk communities and underserved and disadvantaged populations. The leisure service delivery system, however, still faces a number of challenges.

A Century of Recreation and Leisure Services

In the United States when there has been a social need people have organized themselves for action. Less complex societies handled their educational, religious, and recreation behaviors through the activities and structures of the family and other immediate peer group units. Complex societies developed delivery systems to meet these needs. The leisure service delivery system comprises public, not-for-profit, and private commercial interests. Table 2.6 summarizes the stages of development that led to the recreation and leisure systems that exist today: services to youth, diversionary activity, outdoor recreation and the environment, and entrepreneurialism and public policy.

Stage One: Services to Youth (1890–1916)

The desire to serve underprivileged children characterized the earliest stage of recreation and leisure services. Voluntary youth organizations such as the Boy and Girl Scouts, the Playground Association of America (later the National Recreation Association), and the YMCA and YWCA dominated the movement and provided the basic programs. They relied heavily upon private and voluntary financial support and utilized the methods and techniques most frequently associated with today's social group work programs. Recreation experiences were seen as a means to an end for building character and developing better communities.

Stage Two: Diversionary Activity (1917–1955)

The second stage of development emerged during the Great Depression and reached its peak in the late 1940s. Recreation services became a government responsibility; recreation was seen as an activity needed to break the monotony of poverty and relieve the tensions of war. During this period local communities developed park and recreation commissions and charged them with the responsibility of providing diversionary recreation opportunities. The number of community recreation buildings, athletic fields, and other sports facilities increased. Organized recreation took a mass approach, and sports became synonymous with recreation. Commercial enterprises strived to please spectators through entertainment.

Stage Three: Outdoor Recreation and the Environment (1956–1976)

The third period began with the expansion of outdoor recreation interests in the late 1950s. Private investments coupled with expanding federal and

Table 2.6:	Stages of Development of Organized Recreation and Leisure Services			
	Stage One (1890–1916) *Services to Youth*	**Stage Two (1917–1955)** *Diversionary Activity*	**Stage Three (1956–1976)** *Outdoor Recreation and the Environment*	**Stage Four (1977–present)** *Entrepreneurialism and Public Policy*
Program Focus	Conservationist and youth services	Parks and diversionary activity	Outdoor recreation and environmental concerns	Entrepreneurial approach to local services and public policy issues
Leadership	Volunteers	Professionals and volunteers	Professionals	Professionals and volunteers
Major Provider of Services	Not-for-profit	Federal and local governments	All governments	Governments, not-for-profit agencies, and commercial businesses

state programs had an impact on leisure behaviors. Camping, water sports, winter sports, and vacation travel grew significantly. The nurturing and development of natural resources to accommodate these interests, and the need for recreation and park professionals with managerial and planning skills to manage these efforts, characterized this era. During this stage federal and state governments assumed greater responsibility in providing opportunities for individual recreation pursuits. Businesses offered the equipment and clothing necessary to make these experiences pleasurable. During this era a host of public policy issues began to emerge.

Stage Four: Entrepreneurialism and Public Policy (1977–Present)

Initially, public policy concerns were largely restricted to the role of government as a regulatory agency in the protection of the environment. The affluence of the 1960s and 1970s placed great demands upon natural resource agencies. They were pushed to their limit to accommodate the growing outdoor recreation interests while also trying to protect the environment from overuse. Partially in response to the demand for accommodations and a growing service economy, private entrepreneurs recognized the potentials of leisure as a market. Entrepreneurship was furthered by the tax revolt of the late 1970s that considerably reduced the ability of the public sector to provide programs without seeking some recovery costs from the participants. Public park and recreation agencies also had to become more entrepreneurial, offering more programs that were self-sustaining or recovering costs. They also began to contract some of their operations, such as maintenance to private contractors. Political actions and debate characterized the public policy/entrepreneurial era.

In 1980 the issue became whether private interest or government was responsible for providing basic recreation services. With cutbacks in federal appropriations for the acquisition of land, the burden of providing capital for recreation developments shifted from the federal to state and local governments. Rather than be a direct supplier, some government agencies assumed a facilitator role. They provided the facility and technical assistance but let others do the programming. Commercial and private providers were expected to become more active as suppliers. This shift influenced programs of professional preparation of recreation and parks personnel. Courses in marketing strategies, economic theory, and management were included in many undergraduate curricula, while activity courses and the social sciences took a back seat. Some park and recreation educators say that recreation has moved away from its humanistic approach to services to a more businesslike or entrepreneurial approach. As the 21st century begins, a focus on inclusion again emerges in all of the sectors providing recreation and leisure services.

Reflection Questions

1. What key legislation influenced the development of the leisure profession?

2. What social and cultural norms have been conveyed through recreation in the 20th century?

3. Discuss the role of the federal government in creating recreation opportunities at the beginning of the 20th century.

4. Provide an example of a social trend related to leisure that led to the establishment of some type of leisure services organization.

5. How have the stages of recreation evolved over the past 100 years?

2.7 The Professionalization of Recreation and Leisure Services

One of the characteristics of a social movement is its evolution toward professional status. The early stages of social movements, like recreation, are often directed and administered by volunteers and interested lay persons. These movements often result in formal organizations and professionally trained personnel. Those individuals employed in the movement seek to establish their identity as professionals and to the criteria of a profession (Sessoms, 1990). This chapter further describes the history of the recreation profession and leisure services as evidenced in the development of professional status.

Recreation and leisure studies is an emerging profession. Professions differ from trades and other classifications of occupations in a variety of ways. Not every field of work becomes a profession, although professionals are in nearly every area of service. A professional is a person who is paid for his or her work and whose identity is tied to an occupation. Professionals apply the techniques of performance of specific trades and the theories of selected disciplines to some specific social problem or concern. Professions also develop their own theories and methods to deal with the social concerns that they address. Those theories and practices become a part of the body of knowledge that guides their work.

Components of a Profession

When a social movement becomes established within a culture, professional status occurs. Six criteria must be met before an area of service is considered a profession:

- Develop an alliance with a social concern;

- Develop professional societies and associations;

- Establish a code of ethics;

- Develop a specialized body of knowledge and practical skills;

- Establish programs of professional education and training; and

- Develop professional standards of accreditation, certification, and licensing. (Sessoms, 1990)

The recreation and leisure profession has satisfied these criteria. The recreation profession addresses quality of life for individuals, the benefits from recreation, and the interest in inclusion and diversity. Therefore, the first aspect of being a profession has been met. The following sections address the remaining aspects to becoming a profession.

Develop Professional Recreation and Park Associations

Recreation and park professionals have established several organizations dedicated to the advancement and improvement of recreation and parks as a profession. These groups have given individuals in the profession a chance to pool their common interests for their own benefit and that of society. Mutual concerns and experiences are shared through professional organizations. They provide a means for establishing and developing standards, exchanging information and ideas, and influencing public action.

National Recreation and Park Association

The largest professional park and recreation organization, the National Recreation and Park Association (NRPA), came into existence in 1966 as the result of the merger of five smaller organizations:

- *American Institute of Park Executives* (AIPE) evolved from the New England Association of Park Superintendents, later known as the American Association of Park Superintendents. The American Institute of Park Executives members were drawn from executive positions in public parks throughout the United States and Canada.

- *National Recreation Association* (NRA) was organized in 1906 originally as the Playground Association of America. As the first organization to address recreation specifically, this group served as a major force in the development of the recreation movement for sixty years. The NRA membership included both professional and private citizens concerned with providing recreation opportunities for all people.

- *National Conference on State Parks* (NCSP) was founded in 1921 as a professional and service organization for those employed by federal and state natural resource agencies. This organization provided information to the public on the values and functions of state parks, historic sites, monuments, and recreation preserves.

- *American Association of Zoological Parks and Aquariums* (AAZPA) was established in 1924 as an affiliate of the American Institute of Park Executives. The AAZPA provided a professional association for zoo and aquarium directors, curators, and other professionals concerned with the preservation of wildlife and its display for the general public.

• *American Recreation Society* (ARS) was established in 1938 as the Society of Recreation Workers of America. The primary objective was to unite all recreation professionals in the United States in one organization. The American Recreation Society, opened primarily to those employed in the field of parks and recreation, viewed itself as a professional rather than a service association.

The first national meeting of the newly formed NRPA was held in Washington, DC in October 1966. As recognition of the significance of merger and the nation's concern for adequate recreation and park resources, President Lyndon B. Johnson, along with the Secretary of the Interior, the Secretary of Agriculture, and the Secretary of Housing and Urban Development addressed the first national meeting of NRPA.

Professional branches and special interest sections have been established within NRPA since its first years of operation, including:

• American Park and Recreation Society (APRS)

• National Society of Park Resources (NSPR)

• Armed Forces Recreation Society (AFRS)

• National Therapeutic Recreation Society (NTRS)

• Citizen and/or Board Members Branch (CBM)

• Society of Park and Recreation Educators (SPRE)

• National Recreation Student Branch (NRSB)

• National Aquatics Section (NAS)

• Leisure and Aging Section (LAS)

• Commercial Recreation and Tourism Section (CRTS)

• Ethnic and Minority Section (EMS)

The National Recreation and Park Association promotes professionalism through its branches. Each branch has its own officers, board of directors, and staff liaison with NRPA. The branch organizational structure allows identity with special areas of service such as education, government, and therapeutic recreation. Service to the profession is done primarily through branch activity, while the NRPA staff functions primarily to promote recreation and parks on a national level.

The goals of the National Recreation and Park Association are to promote awareness of and support for the values of recreation and parks in the lives of individuals and to provide services that contribute to the development of NRPA members. The organization is financially supported through membership fees, public contributions, self-generated revenue, endowments, and grants. The NRPA national headquarters are in Ashburn, Virginia with five regional service centers around the country. In 2000, NRPA consisted of approximately 22,000 members.

Additional Professional Organizations

An exhaustive list of professional organization activity concerned with recreation and leisure would fill many pages. Consequently, just a few of them are described with respect to their purpose and function.

- *The Academy of Leisure Science* (ALS). Formed in 1980, the Academy of Leisure Sciences is an honorary group with elected members. ALS recognizes members for their exceptional scholarly and intellectual contribution to the growth and development of the understanding of leisure in contemporary society. ALS promotes the understanding of leisure through discussion, debate, and exchange of ideas. It is an interdisciplinary body with membership representation from the fields of business, the natural and social sciences, the humanities, and parks and recreation.

- *American Academy for Park and Recreation Administration* (AAPRA). Also established in 1980, AAPRA comprises distinguished practitioners and scholars committed to the advancement of park and recreation administration. This organization encourages the development and enhancement of excellence in administration practices and publishes the *Journal of Park and Recreation Administration*.

- *American Association for Leisure and Recreation* (AALR) of the *American Alliance for Health, Physical Education, Recreation and Dance* (AAHPERD). The American Association for Leisure and Recreation is one of the major divisions of the American Alliance for Health, Physical Education, Recreation and Dance. The Alliance, a member organization of the National Education Association, is dedicated to the improvement of health education, physical education, recreation education, and dance education throughout the United States. Professionals primarily interested in recreation education and leisure studies identify with AALR.

A number of other allied professional groups such as the National Girls and Women in Sports, and the Coalition for Outdoor Education are also affiliated with the Alliance. The Alliance contributes significantly to recreation through its publications and sponsorship efforts. The publications include the *Journal of Physical Education, Recreation and Dance* (including the special articles within the journal entitled *Leisure Today*) and *Research Quarterly for Exercise and Sport.*

• *American Camping Association* (ACA). This association, incorporated in 1910, comprises representatives of agencies and institutions interested in the development of organized camping in the United States. The ACA membership consists of camp directors, members of camp staffs, educators, and others directly associated with the operation of camps or interested in the camping movement. ACA represents camping of all types: church, school, public, independent, and nonprofit. The ACA furthers the interests and welfare of children and adults through camping as an educative and recreation experience. ACA assumes leadership in developing new camping areas and acts as a channel through which new trends in camping are disseminated to members and the public. Standards for the improvement of camp practices are implemented through a voluntary accreditation program. The official publication of the Association is *Camping Magazine.*

• *American Therapeutic Recreation Association* (ATRA). Formed in 1984, ATRA has assumed a major leadership role in promoting therapeutic recreation services through its advocacy of certification and professional development for recreation therapists. ATRA members view therapeutic recreation as an appropriate intervention to promote independent functioning through the development of a healthy leisure lifestyle. ATRA has worked with the NTRS branch of NRPA in upgrading standards for therapeutic recreation practitioners, and publishes the *Annual in Therapeutic Recreation.*

• *National Employee Services and Recreation Association* (NESRA). The National Employee Services and Recreation Association is dedicated to the development and improvement of employee recreation services. The membership comprises companies that have employee recreation programs. NESRA is a clearinghouse through which information and ideas related to the planning, organization, and operation of recreation programs serving employees and their families are exchanged. NESRA provides technical assistance and consulting services for its members, aids in the placement and training of recreation personnel, conducts surveys and research activities, and publishes guides, reports, and *Employee Services Management* magazine.

- *Resort and Commercial Recreation Association* (RCRA). Formed in 1982 to serve the emerging specialty of resort and commercial recreation, this membership organization promotes career opportunities in this area of service through its national meetings and job bulletins. RCRA is a primary voice for those professionals administering and directing leisure services in resort communities and similar recreation developments. One of its major contributions has been the development of internship opportunities for students interested in seeking employment in a commercial recreation setting.

- *World Leisure and Recreation Association* (WLRA). The World Leisure and Recreation Association promotes recreation and leisure interests throughout the world. WLRA has worked cooperatively with various national organizations, such as NRPA and United Nations programs. WLRA has become the voice of international recreation concerns. Its program efforts include publishing *World Leisure*, offering consulting services to recreation professionals, and conducting various study tour groups, exhibitions, symposia, and world congresses on leisure and recreation.

Recreation Interest Groups

In addition to the professional service organizations described, countless groups promote or represent specific recreation activity interests, including:

Academy of Model Aeronautics

Amateur Athletic Union of the United States

Amateur Badminton Association

Amateur Softball Association of America

American Baseball Congress

American Bowling Congress

American Canoe Association

American Contract Bridge League

American Federation of Arts

American Iris Society

American Lawn Bowling Association

American Library Association

American Power Boat Association

American Rose Society

American Shuffleboard Leagues

American Theater Wing

American Water Ski Association

American Youth Hostels

Hobby Guild of America

Izaak Walton League of America

Little League Baseball, Inc.

Model Yacht Racing Association of America

National Archery Association of the United States

National Association of Angling and Casting Clubs

National Association of Senior Citizens Softball

National Audubon Society

National Council of State Garden Clubs

National Federation of Music Clubs

National Field Archery Association

National Horseshoe Pitchers Association of America

National Shuffleboard Association

National Skeet Shooting Association

National Ski Association of America

National Softball Congress of America

National Wildlife Federation

Nature Conservancy

North American Youth Sports Institute

Outboard Boating Club of America

Professional Golfers Association of America

Professional Lawn Tennis Association of the United States

United States Amateur Confederation of Roller Skating

United States Fencing Association

United States Handball Association

United States Karate Federation

United States Lawn Tennis Association

United States Ski Association

United States Table Tennis Association

United States Tennis Association

United States Volleyball Association

Establish a Code of Ethics

Another step in the process to becoming a profession is to establish a code of professional ethics. Ethics are the part of philosophy that considers moral issues and judgments. This discussion centers on appropriate standards of conduct that will guide behavior. For recreation professionals, this focus on ethics provides a framework for distinguishing between right and wrong conduct, and a way to rationally critique beliefs and practices that become the foundation for the profession.

The code of ethics established by a profession acts as a contract with society. This code acts as a pledge between the professional and the people served that duties performed will be conducted within an acceptable moral frame. The types of ethical situations can involve individuals (e.g., guarding the welfare of the participants), the community (e.g., following the laws), or the environment where recreation occurs (e.g., promoting stewardship of the environment).

For most professionals, a code of ethics is compiled and promoted through the efforts of professional associations. For example, the American Camping Association (ACA) has a code of ethics for all members of the association as well as a statement of exemplary ethical practices for camp owners, directors, and executives (see Table 2.7). Each member must agree to abide by this code to maintain a professional affiliation with the ACA. The code of ethics can also be linked to certification of the professional, where a standard of behavior has been predetermined. If the recreation professional does not meet the ethical expectations set by the credentialing organization, she or he may lose credentialed status.

Develop a Specialized Body of Knowledge and Practical Skills

The fourth mark of a profession is the existence of a specialized body of knowledge. This knowledge is built over time as information is gathered through research and evaluation of practice and theory. Theory provides the basic principles that serve as the foundation upon which to conceptualize key aspects of the field. These principles guide ongoing research as well as the development of professional leadership and practices of recreation professionals. For example, the basis for this textbook is the body of knowledge (including information emanating from research and best practices) related to recreation and leisure services.

Recreation and leisure service professionals master a unique body of knowledge that enables them to provide a valuable service to society. While recreation professionals often are knowledgeable about information from other disciplines (e.g., sociology, psychology, business, natural resources) the profession is built upon specific research and literature. This knowledge serves as the basis for professional preparation programs, continued research and evaluation efforts, the revision of ethical practices, and the development of institutionalized programs of accreditation and certification.

Common ways to keep one's skills current after going through a professional preparation program as an undergraduate or graduate student is to read the recreation research journals (e.g., *Journal of Leisure Research, Journal of Park and Recreation Administration, Therapeutic Recreation Journal*), attend professional meetings and conferences, and engage in continuing education opportunities.

Establish Programs of Professional Education and Training

The search for identity and the professionalization of parks and recreation has also been influenced by programs of professional preparation for recreation and park personnel. The need for professionally educated persons to administer and operate leisure service systems was recognized during the formative years of the movement. As early as 1911, short courses and training manuals for instruction of playground workers were prepared.

Table 2.7:   Code of Ethics for All Members of the American Camping Association

1. I shall conduct myself in a manner consistent with the Association's mission to serve organized camps, affiliated programs, and the public by promoting better camping for all.

To accomplish this mission, ACA:
   • Educates camp personnel to create positive growth experiences for children, teens, and adults, using the outdoors responsibly as a program environment;
   • Protects the public by promoting health and safety practices and effective management through accreditation, certification, and education programs;
   • Promotes advocacy of issues affecting camps; and
   • Communicates the value of camp experiences to the public and encourages camp opportunities for all.

2. I shall recognize my responsibility for the welfare of others in my care.
3. I shall abide by and comply with the relevant laws of the community.
4. I shall be a member of the proper ACA classification as currently defined by the ACA National Board of Directors, and I shall disclose my affiliation with ACA only in a manner specifically permitted by the association.
5. I shall make a clear distinction of any statement or action as to whether I speak as an individual member or a representative of this association.
6. I shall respect the confidences of ACA members, camps, and other constituents within the camp community; however, I shall accept responsibility to pass on to the appropriate ACA official, information I deem reliable that will help protect the camp community against unethical practices by any individual.
7. I shall be truthful and fair to all in representations I make regarding any camp.

Exemplary Ethical Practices for Camp Owners, Directors, and Executives

The association recognizes the camp owner, director, and executive as the primary professional persons assuming the greatest responsibility for actual camp practices. Therefore, in addition to the Code of Ethics for all members, any member or nonmember operating a camp accredited by the American Camping Association agrees to subscribe to the following *Exemplary Ethical Practices for Camp Owners, Directors and Executives.*

8. I shall endeavor to provide an environment conducive to promoting and protecting the physical and emotional well-being of the campers and staff.
9. I shall seek to instill in my staff and campers a reverence for the land and its waters and all living things, and an ecological conscience that reflects the conviction of individual responsibility for the health of that environment.
10. I shall follow equal opportunity practices in employment and camper enrollment.
11. I shall endeavor to employ persons based upon factors necessary to the performance of the job and the operation of the camp.
12. I shall be truthful and fair in securing and dealing with campers, parents/guardians, and staff.
13. I shall provide a written enrollment policy for all camper/family applicants including fees, payment schedules, discounts, dates of arrival and departure, together with clearly stated refund policy.
14. I shall provide for each staff member a written job description and employment agreement including period of employment, compensation, benefits, and exceptions.
15. I shall promptly consult with parents or guardians of any camper or minor staff member as to the advisability of removing him/her from camp should it be clear that he/she is not benefiting from the camp experience or the camper's or minor staff member's actions have created this need.
16. I shall make arrangements with the parents or guardians for the return of their camper(s) or minor-age staff member(s).
17. I shall pay the correct national and section service fees as established by the ACA National Board of Directors and the ACA Section Board of Directors.

Adopted in April 1995 by the ACA Council of Delegates. Revised March 1997 by the ACA Council of Delegates. American Camping Association 2001 (http://www.acacamps.org)

The growth of parks and recreation parallels the acceptance of recreation and leisure services as a career field. Prior to the expansion of the outdoor recreation interest in 1960, only 62 colleges and universities offered instruction in parks and recreation, and the majority of these programs were housed in departments of physical education or education (Sessoms, 1993). With the growth of the recreation and leisure field, and the expanded involvement of governmental agencies at all levels of recreation and park services, the number of positions in parks and recreation grew more rapidly than did the supply of professionally prepared graduates. In the late 1960s two-year and four-year institutions began developing curricula for the preparation of parks and recreation technicians and professionals. Currently, almost 300 schools offer degrees in parks, recreation, tourism, and leisure services. These degrees range from technical associate-level degrees at community colleges to Ph.D. programs at some of the major research universities in the country.

Develop Professional Standards

Establishing professional standards of practice for parks and recreation has resulted in the establishment of several programs for accreditation and certification by professional organizations. Agencies are accredited; individuals are certified.

Accreditation symbolizes a professional concern for meeting the criteria of a specified set of "best practices" by a recreation provider system. For example, the American Camping Association has a long-standing voluntary accreditation program for any camp that wants to go through the process. Based upon the body of knowledge and current research, the ACA standards address particular areas deemed important to providing a high-quality camp experience, including health and wellness, programming, personnel, transportation, administration, and site and facilities. If the camp meets the standards in the opinion of the visitation team, they can advertise that they are an accredited camp.

In the early 1960s a major effort on the part of professional recreation organizations was to have recreation accepted as a field through two accreditation programs focused on universities and on public agencies. The Council on Accreditation—jointly sponsored between the National Recreation and Park Association (NRPA) and the American Association of Leisure and Recreation (AALR)—administers the accreditation of university programs of study related to recreation and leisure. North Carolina State University was the first institution to be accredited in 1977. Today over 100 colleges and universities throughout the United States have accredited recreation programs. In the 1990s an accreditation program, the Council on Park and Recreation Accreditation, was initiated for public park and recreation programs. A number of cities in the United States have gone through the extensive self-study and visitation by peers that comprise this accreditation. Accreditation is usually for a set period (3–5 years) and then the process is repeated to assure continued compliance.

Certification is similar to accreditation in that the concern is for best practice, but it focuses on the individual professional. The individual completes professional development training (e.g., academic professional preparation program or continuing education) and meets selected baseline criteria that indicate individual competence and skill. For example, NRPA offers certification of professionals through the Certified Park and Recreation Professional (CPRP) program, formerly known as Certified Leisure Professional (CLP) program. More information on certification will be discussed in the chapter on careers in unit three.

Both certification and accreditation are based on selected standards important to the continued development of the profession. They indicate to the public that the profession has carefully developed standards of practice for the individual as well as for the larger organization. When choosing programs, the public can be assured that staff and faculty in community recreation programs, as well as university programs, have adopted a specified standard of practice, and that certified individuals have made efforts to keep their professional skills at a high level.

Reflection Questions

1. Explain how recreation and leisure services have fully or partially met each of the six criteria of being a profession.

2. What is the role of professional organizations?

3. What has led to the proliferation of professional and interest organizations related to recreation in the 20th century?

2.8 Religions and Leisure

The role of religion and spirituality cannot be overestimated when we contemplate leisure meanings and quality of life. The preceding chapters have mentioned religion primarily related to the Reformation and the Protestant work ethic. This chapter provides some additional discussions of the history and philosophy of various religions and how they relate to leisure. Although people in the United States have been primarily influenced by the Judeo-Christian tradition, the history and philosophies of Eastern religions, as well as other Western religions, can serve as a basis for understanding more about leisure.

Religion and Spirituality

Religion and spirituality have differing connotations. For purposes of this discussion, religion is described as an organized and institutional group experience with accepted beliefs. Spirituality is a personal belief in something greater than oneself (Henderson, 1993c). People's involvement in organized religion in the United States decreased somewhat until the early 1990s when this decrease seemed to level off. The interest in spirituality, however, has increased as many people seek to nourish their souls amidst the complex lives they lead.

Leisure is sometimes described as having spiritual dimensions and benefits (Zuefle, 1999). For example, Pieper (1963) described leisure as a gift from God. Csikszentmihalyi (1975) noted how the concept of "flow" could be connected to a spiritual experience. The Sabbath as a day of rest from work has been prominent in the lives of many Americans since the early settlers came to the country. Religion has an impact on people's values and beliefs that raises ethical issues about play as well as the natural environment.

The United States is becoming more religiously pluralistic. People studying the meanings of recreation and leisure find that religious beliefs both enhance and constrain recreation and play involvement. Religious doctrines, practices, and philosophies have played a role in determining cultural attitudes and behaviors towards the natural world and toward leisure (Kaza, 1996).

When discussing religions, however, we must be careful to note four important considerations. First, no one religious belief is better than another. Each person must decide what religion, if any, works for herself or himself. Each person's ethics and behavior evolve from his or her belief systems. Second, many differences exist within religions. For example, within the

Christian religion, differences exist between Roman Catholics, Eastern Orthodox, and Protestants. Even among Protestant denominations, great differences exist. Third, all religions fall short of their professed ideals (Kaza, 1996). The philosophy of a religion and how it is actually practiced may not always be consistent. Humans do not always live consistently with their religious beliefs. Finally, although we have tried to interpret the meanings of religions, it is often difficult to fully capture the meanings as experienced by those who actively practice a religion. While the meanings of these religions are generalized for this short discussion, we do not mean to oversimplify the importance that the religions hold for the believers.

According to Smith (1991), all traditional religions share some common attributes. For example, all have some authority of a divine nature. Each religion has rituals (e.g., prayers, Sabbath, pilgrimages) that people value in their daily lives and in times of anxiety. All religions are based on mystery and speculation about trying to find answers to questions about the meanings of life. Most religions have history and traditions that serve as templates for action. Each religion also contributes to particular perceptions about leisure and recreation. Collectively, religion helps us understand the nature of reality and gives people a basis for how they should live their lives.

This chapter describes eight major religions and some of the implications that these religions have to recreation and leisure historically and culturally. These selected religions were chosen because of their influence in the world and the numbers of people involved. This discussion of religions will include a brief examination of primal religions, Western religions, and Eastern religions.

Primal Religions

Traditional religions only cover 4,000 years, yet people have always practiced forms of spirituality. Religion and spirituality existed among primitive people, and they exist among tribal people of today. Among primal or tribal people, the ordinary or regular life was intertwined with the religious life—one's entire life was ritual.

The primal religions, such as those embodied in American Indian cultures and Aboriginal groups, share features. For example, they pass traditions by word of mouth and not by written texts. The value of the environment also was evident in daily living as in all aspects of spirituality. Further, the sense of external time is boundless as people live within their own world with the afterlife occurring in conjunction with the present.

A major trend has been to convert these groups to organized religions as evidenced by the predominance of missionary work occurring among people who live in the so-called primitive cultures. Although those efforts have been diminished, a tendency now exists to romanticize some of these primal people due to the dominant society's disenchantment with the industrialized world. To understand these primal religions, we need to put both prejudice and idealization behind.

Leisure for primal people is lived as part of their religion. Life is not segmented into work, leisure, or family but is interrelated with all components as equally important. The "oneness" between the world and humans and the lack of compartmentalization in these cultures make living a holistic experience.

Western Religions

Judaism, Christianity, and Islam are considered Western religions (Smith, 1991). Since they evolved from the same part of the world, they share commonalities. Collective action is evident in these religions. Followers believe in the importance of performing good works, humanitarianism, and social service. These three religions also share a focus on the physical body and the notion of nature as a host for the Divine with the belief that the kingdom of God is on earth.

Judaism

Judaism began almost 5,000 years ago in Israel. Judaism is a way of life as well as a religion with strong emphasis on family and the study of religious texts. Many individuals identify as cultural and/or religious Jews. Some people embrace the culture but are not necessarily involved in religious rituals.

Jewish people believe that God created the world and that the world is filled with meaning. Jews believe that they were put on earth to have dominion over it while maintaining respect for nature and God's creations. Taking care of the environment is valued, but people are perceived to be at the top of the hierarchy. Further, people are given the opportunity to make the world better. Jewish people are instructed to care for each other and for the world.

A theme in Judaism is that people should enjoy life's goodness and at the same time augment the joy by sharing it with God (Smith, 1991). A leisure ethic seems important. Jewish law sanctions all good things like eating, marriage, children and nature, and considers them holy. This goodness is manifested through tradition, with history and holiness inseparable. Jewish ceremonies and observations are important because Jewish culture defines a way of life including mores, art forms, styles of humor, philosophy, and literature.

Fundamental to Judaism is a practice of self-restraint where one is rewarded for being good. The laws of the Ten Commandments are a foundation. Jews are also commanded to do good deeds. Caring for one's body as God's creation and maintaining good health are also aspects of religious practice. Dietary customs are important, as is keeping the Sabbath (from sunset on Friday to sunset on Saturday). Work has a sacred meaning, but leisure is valuable for meditation and self-expression. In the Old Testament, the reader is reminded to have leisure and to use it to know God (Psalm 65:11)—to celebrate the Sabbath as a day of "gratitude and thanksgiving," and as "a gift of grace. . .rather than a reward for work" (Goodale & Godbey, 1988). From Judaism we might heed the concept of Sabbath and let our bodies as well as our land rest.

Christianity

The Christian faith, which began about 2,000 years ago, is made up of followers of Jesus Christ. Christianity is the most widespread religion and has the largest number of believers in the world (Smith, 1991). Christian thought is closely related to the philosophical traditions of Europe. Christianity was not founded on abstract principles, but concrete events. All the teachings of Christ found in the Bible's New Testament as stories about moral living can be recited in about two hours. Religious historians have noted, however, that the impressive thing about the teachings was that Jesus lived them (Smith, 1991). His life was one of humility, self-giving, and love. Christians' belief in the resurrection of Christ's earthly body, however, was what made Jesus different than just being a good teacher and role model. Within the Christian religion, however, is astonishing diversity.

In the United States, Christianity has strongly influenced the way Americans live and the meanings they hold for leisure. The Bible says little in the New Testament about work. Followers were warned by their teachers to "take no heed of tomorrow" and not to be concerned with the gaining of wealth and material things. Duties were to be performed, but making a profit was not the ultimate goal. Early Christians held that beyond sustaining oneself, work had little value. The Protestant work ethic, as one interpretation of Christianity in the past 400 years, continues to influence Western civilization today and generally offers no support for frivolity and amusement. This ethic has implied something sinful in seeking pleasure for pleasure's sake or in associating with those who take time out for pleasure. Recreation was acceptable only if it promoted the virtues of work. Some of these interpretations have changed, yet Christianity generally does not presume to support notions of leisure.

Further, although separation of church and state is a fundamental right in the United States, Christian influence on governmental actions are obvious. Christian holidays impact the secular work schedule. For example, Christmas and Good Friday are legal holidays with many businesses and most governmental agencies closed on those days. Further, recent legislation efforts to legitimize prayer in schools have a strong Christian influence. Seeking truth through prayer and contemplation as well as service to others seems to be the preferred use of free time among many Christians today. Christians operating out of love have a sense of right action for whatever they do in their leisure.

Islam

Islam means the peace that comes when one's life is surrendered to God (Smith, 1991). The religion is named after the attribute it seeks to cultivate (i.e., life's total surrender to God). Moslems believe that to be a slave to Allah is to be free from other kinds of slavery like greed, society, or personal status (Smith, 1991).

Islam is a Western revealed religion that came through the prophet Muhammad. Moslems believe that other great prophets, like Jesus, also lived. The sacred text of Islam, the *Koran*, is among the most recited and read books in the world (Smith, 1991). The theological concepts of Islam are similar to Judaism and Christianity with beliefs in God, creation, human self, and the Day of Judgment. The charge to the followers of Islam is to practice good and prohibit evil.

This Islam religion, however, is often misunderstood because of the complexity of religion, culture, and geography. Similar to Judaism, culture and religion are intertwined. Moslems spend time daily in prayer and also have religious holidays that are shared with family and friends. Islam is very specific about how one ought to live and remember life on a daily basis (Smith, 1991). The social teachings include dignity and courtesy towards others with material goods widely and appropriately distributed. Islam says little about leisure directly but does encourage people to do what is good for them. Moslems believe that the protection of nature is a spiritual duty. They believe both work and play are important if they are lived within the moral laws. Leisure is good as it embodies a duty toward others. Islam focuses on the enjoyment within life through worship and sharing with others.

Eastern Religions

Eastern religions share the commonality of an Asian heritage. They relate to one another in some of their belief systems, but offer alternative ways to view the world. The four religions discussed here are Hinduism, Confucianism, Taoism, and Buddhism.

Hinduism

Hinduism, among the oldest of the recognized world religions, originated in India over 3,000 years ago. Hinduism is more than a religion; it is a way of life reflecting the development of Indian culture over centuries. Hindus believe in one Supreme Being, but they also believe that divinity exists in many forms, including gods and goddesses. They also believe in the sanctity of life and that God may take form in a variety of ways, including as an animal. Reincarnation means that all souls move through different forms and one never knows what form the soul will take in future lives. Therefore, all forms of life are to be respected and protected and this idea relates to the dignity of individuals and to the earth in all activities including recreation and leisure.

The Hindu tradition encourages three principles: sacrifice, giving, and penance. Adhering to these principles provides a means of replenishing the earth, society, and the soul. People are taught to replenish what has been given to them. Individuals also focus on a strong healthy body that lives in spiritual harmony with the world. Followers of Hinduism believe that God and nature are one and the same. People following this religion have a strong sense of place and they often make pilgrimages to sacred rivers and mountains. Hindus appreciate sustainable land measures and follow a principle of nonharming.

The value of leisure is implicit in Hinduism's four aims of life: (1) joy in sensual, sexual, artistic, and aesthetic forms of expression; (2) economic and social fulfillment; (3) morality as a duty to people, animals and plants; and (4) union with God through the spiritual paths, including knowledge, love and devotion, selfless action, and meditation. Hindus believe that as long as morality is obeyed, an individual should seek the sensuous and pleasurable.

According to Smith (1991), each Hindu believes he or she is wholly responsible for his or her present condition and will have the future that he or she is creating. Karma suggests that every decision will have its determinate consequences. Hindus believe it is a just world where everyone gets what he or she deserves and creates his or her own future. Karma is never suspended and people live in a world of infinite vitality. Play, leisure, pleasure, and relaxation are interrelated and necessary for healthy living.

Confucianism

Confucianism is a philosophy, religion, and way of life for many Chinese, Korean, and Japanese people. It was named after the teacher, Confucius. Confucius's philosophy is a blend of common sense and practical wisdom. Examples of Confucian sayings that give people focus include:

> Feel kindly toward everyone, but be intimate only with the virtuous.

> To go too far is as bad as to fall short.

Nobler persons first practice what they preach and afterwards preach according to their practice.

When you know a thing, to recognize that you know it; and when you do not, to know that you do not know—that is knowledge. (Smith, 1991, p. 159)

Central to the beliefs of Confucians is the notion of the universe as constantly changing, unfolding, and filling with vital force or power called *chi*. Life is not cyclic nor spiral, but transformational. No single personification of good and evil exists. Creativity is transforming something that already exists. Thus, all life is a form of chi and it is influenced by tension between yin and yang (i.e., the contrasts that exist in our world such as day and night or man and woman). Confucians believe that the world is a concentric circle with self in center, encircled by family, teachers, friends, government, and then the universe. People are seen as inherently good and the concern is for social harmony. The environment is not as important as how people live together. Leisure is important as it contributes to chi and to social harmony. Leisure and play have significance as they help people relate better to one another.

Confucianism suggests that the good man or woman always tries to become better in all that he or she does in both work and leisure. Life is a process of continual self-cultivation toward the end of becoming more fully human. As a social philosophy, this transformation occurs in relation to others.

Taoism

Followers of Taoism have different approaches ranging from religious to philosophical Tao. Tao refers to "path" or "way." Taoism is the way of ultimate reality, way of the universe, and way of human life. It became popular as a religion in the 6th century BCE by Lao Tzu and Chuang Tzu, who wrote a small book of verse describing a way of harmony with nature. Taoism is sometimes viewed as more of a philosophy than an organized religion. For example, environmentalists, naturalists, and alternative health practitioners are influenced by it (Kaza, 1996).

Followers of Taoism believe nature is the self-existent source of all things. Taoists believe the environment determines the condition for one's own actualization or enlightenment. Taoists also value simplicity and spontaneity in anything undertaken, including leisure. The notion of yin and yang provides a sense of energy, direction, and balance. For example, people do not need institutions because they create a superficial and artificial separation between people and the natural world. Taoists would not want to disrupt anything in the landscape. This preference for naturalness and simplicity

most separates a Taoist from a Confucian. While Confucians focus on social responsibility, Taoism focuses on naturalness and spontaneity.

Taoists view leisure as a natural part of living. People following Taoism avoid being strident and aggressive towards others or nature. Taoists
argue that a reflective approach is a way to conserve life's vitality by not
expending energy in useless, draining ways like friction and conflict. Taoists also go beyond conserving life to increase the Tao that they have. *Chi*
means vital energy. Tai chi chuan is one example of a leisure activity that
combines calisthenics, dance, meditation, yin-yang philosophy and mar-
tial arts into a synthesis destined to draw chi from the cosmos and dislodge
blocked energy flows. Taoism emphasizes action in harmony with nature
with implications with what we do during leisure.

Buddhism

Buddhism means to become enlightened or to become awakened (Smith,
1991). It is considered "the Path of the Middle Way" with a focus on avoiding
the extremes of asceticism and hedonism. Buddhists believe multiple causes
exist for everything. The Buddhist law of karma, or cause and effect, states
that today's thoughts, words, and deeds shape the experiences of the future.
For example, what we do today to the earth affects its ability to regenerate
its vitality. What an individual does to take care of himself or herself will
have a long-term effect on happiness and the quality of life as well as an
immediate effect.

Buddhists base their ethics on three practices: morality, meditation, and
wisdom. The ethics are those of self-restraint to avoid greed, anger, and
delusion. They focus on decreased needs and desires and increased spiritual
satisfaction. Followers of Buddhism ask questions regarding the path to
enlightenment and may find this path through many avenues including
leisure. The highest destiny is nirvana, or the boundless life, where one is
in connection with everyone and everything around oneself. Buddhists believe that if people could really understand life and understand themselves,
nothing would be a problem. Leisure and recreation might be viewed as a
means and an end for self-understanding.

Zen, as a form of Buddhism, is not concerned with theories of enlightenment but wants people to know the good life that focuses on one's relationship to others. Zen Buddhists find the meaning of life in simple acts (like
doing the dishes or watching a butterfly float). Leisure would, thus, be
embodied in a variety of activities and events that one might have in his or
her life. Buddhism teaches interdependence and how to seek happiness by
taking care of one another and the land.

Meanings of Religions

We must be cautious against lifting pieces of religions out of their cultural context. An interpretation of any religion and the meanings it portrays for leisure is much more complex than it may appear on the surface. Knowing something about what people from different religions believe about living, however, may help us understand some aspects of leisure better.

These ideas about world religions can be a starting point in stimulating conversation and understanding how all religions, not just the dominant Judeo-Christian influences in the United States, can influence people's lives and leisure. They also point to how people who follow the religions experience their lives and their leisure. Listening to the values described as the bases for religions can help us learn deeper meanings of living and respect for life. Relative to leisure services, these religions may also help us understand more about the history and diversity of people who live in our communities.

Reflection Questions

1. What is the importance of understanding a variety of religious beliefs/customs?

2. How might the recreation professional use this information to better serve its constituency?

3. How do religious beliefs influence leisure practices?

4. What is the difference between spirituality and religion?

5. Select three types of religious practice and describe each one's influence on and relationship to leisure.

UNIT THREE:
PROFESSIONAL OPPORTUNITIES

Professional opportunities in recreation and leisure services encompass an array of services. This unit focuses on the areas of service and employment opportunities available to people interested in this profession. Generally, these services are categorized into public, not-for-profit, and private commercial sectors.

In the most general sense, public leisure services are those available to all citizens and supported by public tax dollars. Typically, public services are not committed to make a profit from their services. A city, however, might operate a golf course at a profit so that the municipality can provide services that are not self-supporting such as an after-school program. A not-for-profit agency such as the Girl Scouts, which relies on membership fees and donations for its operating budget, may utilize the public recreation center for meetings. A commercial agency operates for a profit, but a commercial tour company might provide a free class about a foreign country to the older adults gathered at a tax-supported congregate meal site. The future of the leisure services profession will bring new and different interrelationships between and within service providers. This unit provides an overview of the various venues.

3.1   Career Opportunities in Recreation and Leisure Services

When people employed in recreation and leisure services tell others what they do, they sometimes get a quizzical look with a remark like "that must be fun." Many people choose the recreation field because they get pleasure from facilitating opportunities for others to experience joy and to find what they love to do. The field of recreation and leisure is a serious occupation with many career opportunities now and in the future.

The Job Market

Since the 1980s the field of recreation has grown steadily. Jobs in leisure and tourism are expected to comprise almost half of the job opportunities in the 21st century (Begun, 2000). The jobs will exist in the three sectors of public, not-for-profit, and private commercial recreation and have a variety of job titles and descriptions.

The public sector offers opportunities in city, county, state, and national government. The majority of public recreation spending comes from government taxes. Therefore, the person employed in public recreation works for the government and the citizens of the community, state, or nation. Numerous jobs exist in local parks and recreation departments including opportunities such as recreation director, recreation supervisor, older adult programs supervisor, aquatics specialist, athletic director, naturalist, park planner, community center supervisor, recreation inclusion supervisor, and youth outreach director. In the state and federal governments, most jobs are related to natural resources and might include park ranger, park planner, campground manager, or outdoor education interpreter. Opportunities in state government also exist for therapeutic recreation specialists in state institutions and correctional facilities. Campus recreation positions exist in most public and private universities in the country. The US military also has a number of civilian employees who work in recreation services around the world.

The not-for-profit sector addresses specific social issues through organizations that raise money primarily through memberships or fundraising. Many not-for-profit organizations do not have recreation as a mission, but use recreation as a primary tool. The Boy/Girl Scouts and YMCA are common groups that fall into this sector. In the past, many of the groups have been concerned primarily with youth issues, but the field of not-for-profit management related to recreation has expanded to all age and ability groups, as well as environmental groups. The jobs in these organizations might include center director, youth leader, church ministries leader, camp director, adventure programmer, recreation therapist, or program leader. Professionals working in this sector might be employed by organizations such as the Boy Scouts, Girl Scouts, Boys and Girls Clubs, Salvation Army, Easter Seals, Sierra Club, or local charitable foundations.

The private commercial sector includes for-profit organizations and many aspects of tourism. These groups provide recreation opportunities that generate a profit for the owners or the corporation. This sector is rapidly growing throughout the world. Commercial recreation includes opportunities within a community such as golf course manager, bowling lanes manager, miniature golf manager, restaurant operator, and employee recreation manager. Tourism opportunities include jobs such as a cruise line recreation director, theme park manager, fitness center director, marketing specialist for sports teams, or resort manager.

In all these sectors, numerous part-time jobs and volunteer opportunities exist. Many students interested in exploring careers in recreation and leisure services gain valuable experience and insight through volunteer, part-time, and seasonal jobs. They then have the opportunity to move into professional positions as they gain more experience.

Curricula in Recreation and Leisure

An individual interested in a career in recreation must obtain the appropriate education and experience to pursue desired job opportunities. Changes have occurred in the past century regarding the ways students have been educated for careers in recreation. Historically four organizational patterns have characterized the development of recreation and park education. The first pattern was evident during the early curriculum development years of the recreation movement (1920–1940) when recreation education and park education were separate and distinct. Those students moving toward a career in recreation services were equipped to be program leaders or activity specialists. Their education involved courses in the social sciences and physical activity. Park-oriented students were prepared to be resource managers and administrators of large land holdings, preserves, and municipal park systems. Their preparation involved coursework in design, landscaping, architecture, horticulture, and the plant sciences.

After World War II, the focus on physical activity intensified. Whereas recreation had been seen primarily as a means to an end by the developers of the earlier professional programs of preparation, the emerging curricula of that time emphasized a second pattern where recreation was an end in itself. The courses were largely activity-oriented and were administered by departments of physical education and/or education. With the growth of outdoor recreation interest in the late 1950s, other changes occurred. Public departments of parks and recreation merged. New programs of professional preparation in universities were established, frequently as separate departments of parks and recreation that were no longer connected to physical education. Typically they were more concerned about management and administrative practices than the preparation of activity leaders or park rangers. The technical training of professionals was left to community colleges and technical schools. Programs in schools of forestry and natural resources took on a more behavioral orientation while those curricula housed in departments of sociology, physical education, and education became policy-oriented and program-oriented.

The third pattern was the growth of therapeutic recreation and recreation management as the dominant course of study and interest. Therapeutic recreation professionals associated themselves with health consciousness and the growth of allied health professions. Therapeutic recreation focuses on rehabilitation and prevention of secondary illnesses as emerging trends. Accompanying this shift in focus has been the incorporation of more coursework in business, the health sciences, assessment and evaluation methodology, marketing, and leisure theory. A few universities with a major focus on therapeutic recreation have chosen to locate the programs within allied health fields. A focus on recreation management and programming has been the standard general emphasis for the field in community settings. This includes specialties related to the sector where individuals would like to work as well as the activity or age interest that they have.

The most recent pattern in recreation education programs in higher education is the direction of hospitality, travel, and tourism. Because of the projected growth of these areas, along with the related area of commercial recreation, universities have focused on the private for-profit sector. Some university programs in travel and tourism have been merged with hospitality services or business management. Sports management is another emerging area aligned in some universities with recreation in some universities with sport sciences. This field of study encompasses local community sport management, campus recreation, and professional sports administration. The principles of management apply to this area just as they apply to recreation administration in general.

Ideally, programs of professional preparation in recreation at the baccalaureate level should: (1) provide students with a broad general education; (2) equip them with the skills and methodologies of the profession; and (3) provide them with practical experience through internships and supervised field practicum. At the graduate level, most recreation programs offer one or more specializations such as recreation and park administration, recreation resource management, or therapeutic recreation services. Most recreation educators agree that graduate study should be distinctly different from undergraduate study. The development of research and problem-solving skills at the graduate level characterizes that difference.

The stabilizing of programs of professional preparation in recreation reflects maturity within the profession. Curricula also reflect a shifting interest on the part of students. Rather than attempting to prepare students for a wide range of positions within the park and recreation field, universities and colleges now emphasize the entry-level positions that have a definitive professional orientation. Possibly the most significant force in stabilizing curricula content and in defining the entry-level position of the professional has been the enactment of programs of accreditation and certification.

Certification and Accreditation

Recreation specialists, like other professionals, increase the quality of service through the type of education received. Developing strong programs of certification and accreditation ensures quality. Institutions and programs are accredited; individuals are certified or registered. *Accreditation* is a process whereby an institution such as a camp, recreation department, or university curriculum is judged to have met the minimum requirements and standards for the conduct of a program or course of study. *Certification* is the act of documenting that someone has met the minimum standards required for the practice of one's skill or profession. Many types of certification exist ranging from being a certified lifeguard to a certified aerobics instructor. At present, professional recreation certification programs are largely voluntary, although some states have enacted legislation of a permissive nature that allows communities and institutions to include the certification of recreation personnel as a prerequisite for employment. North Carolina, for example, now has a legal requirement that one must be a certified therapeutic recreation specialist to use that title.

Most professionals advocate certification and licensing as acts of public protection. When certification is required, the public is assured that employees have achieved a certain level of education, training, and/or experience. Certification says nothing, however, about the quality of the individual's experience or ability to perform. Opponents to certification argue that it is an act of exclusion because the field of parks and recreation may be closing out some individuals who could make a significant contribution to the profession simply on the basis of their failure to meet an educational or some other experience requirement. Furthermore, they argue that until the recreation profession has defined which positions are professional positions, certification lacks validity.

The National Recreation and Park Association (NRPA) and the National Council of Therapeutic Recreation Certification (NCTRC) have been the primary promoters and supervising agencies of professional certification. Certification titles given include the Certified Park and Recreation Professional (CPRP) through NRPA, and the Certified Therapeutic Recreation Specialist (CTRS) administered through the National Council on Therapeutic Recreation Certification (NCTRC). Both have developed certification examinations that began in 1990. Both organizations also require continuing professional education in the form of continuing education units (CEUs) for continued certification. NRPA also certifies paraprofessionals as Certified Park and Recreation Associates (CPRA).

Accreditation and certification are interwoven processes. For certification to exist, recognition of education is necessary. This recognition is best achieved when applicants can demonstrate that they are graduates of accredited programs. When accreditation exists, graduates from these programs are automatically assumed to have obtained the basic preparation for the profession, and are therefore qualified to practice it. In both instances, the public is protected because minimum levels of quality are assured through experience and training.

Professional Competencies

Individuals seeking careers in recreation and leisure services generally possess professional competencies. Being aware of some of the competencies that professionals need to exhibit may help to determine whether a career in recreation is what one wants. We might think of the skills needed as people, conceptual, and technical skills.

Most individuals going into positions in recreation and leisure will be working directly with *people*. Therefore, recreation professionals must have a compassion for people. They must possess communications skills including speaking, listening, writing, presenting information clearly and concisely, and working one-on-one as well as in groups. Many of these skills can be developed and learned in classes, but really liking people is an important prerequisite. Further, the more practice an individual has in working with others, the better the human skills can become.

Recreation professionals also need *conceptual* skills in terms of understanding how groups work and how organizations and communities function. These individuals need to be creative problem solvers able to plan, implement, and evaluate recreation programs and processes. They also need to be people who understand how such disciplines as psychology, sociology, economics, philosophy, and political science come together to create the interventions and services provided. These individuals need to be aware of how society changes and the implications those changes have for programs and services.

Technical skills include the ability to do such job requirements as activity analysis, planning a budget, doing a risk management plan, promoting and advertising a program, and maintaining a swimming pool. Many of these skills are learned in recreation courses as well as through internships, on-the-job training, and continuing education opportunities.

Other Related Professional Issues

Careers in recreation and leisure have also been aided by the actions of various civil service systems and the demands of the profession for more programs of continuing education and professional development. In many states civil service systems and their counterparts determine the procedures to be used in the selection and employment of personnel for recreation occupations. These systems generally include specific eligibility requirements such as residence requirements, examination scores, educational and experience requirements, and other personal and skill requirements consistent with the rules of affirmative action. Some personnel systems have included graduation from accredited curricula and/or certification or registration with the professional recreation agency as an eligibility requirement for specific position titles.

Career opportunities within the profession of recreation and leisure continue to grow. All opportunities share a common commitment of assuring that people's leisure needs and interests are addressed. People should have many choices in their recreational pursuits if they are to experience the meanings of leisure. Recreation professionals learn through their education and training how to offer people those choices.

Reflection Questions

1. Describe the differences among the three categories of leisure services.

2. What is the role of certification and/or accreditation in the professionalization of a particular field?

3. What are the most important skills needed by a leisure professional?

3.2   Public Recreation and Government Involvement

Concern for citizens' health and welfare and the necessity to use natural resources carefully has led to the US government's involvement in recreation and parks. For example, the federal government is a major supplier of outdoor recreation opportunities through the programs of the Department of the Interior (e.g., National Park Service) and the Department of Agriculture (e.g., US Forest Service). Government also stimulates cultural and creative interests, advocates cultural heritage, and influences public opinion on matters pertaining to leisure, recreation, and conservation.

Each state government draws its power from the US constitution and provides those activities that citizens deem vital to their well-being. The state pattern of services of recreation and parks has been similar to that of the federal government. Management of natural resource areas, the establishment of natural resource policy, and the distribution of information about various recreation and leisure opportunities within the state boundaries have been the primary activities, although some states have also established zoos, symphony orchestras, and performing arts centers. The influence of the state or federal government on local government-sponsored park and recreation services has been primarily through the controls established to deal with such issues as employment practices, environmental protection, and civil rights. This chapter introduces public recreation and the overall roles that government has played in the United States. In the chapters that follow, we will describe the specific roles of federal, state, and local governments.

Justifying Government Involvement

Many reasons to justify government involvement in the delivery of recreation and leisure services exist. Several support a social ethic of responsibility for the quality of life of all members of society. Some of the most commonly accepted rationales include:

- Government is the only agency supported by and for all people.

- Government has financial resources to acquire, establish, improve, and operate facilities.

- Government has the authority of eminent domain that allows acquisition of private lands for a greater public good.

• Government provides a source of continuity and permanency.

• Legal precedent has been set over the years.

The government also has various resources to support public recreation and leisure services. As a government body, public parks and recreation can use compulsory resources such as income tax and sales tax. For every tax dollar paid to a governmental body, a small portion of it can be earmarked for recreation purposes.

Although the government provides money for public recreation in the form of tax receipts, most government agencies also generate earned income. This income is a result of fees to the users of the programs and/or facilities. Another source of income for public recreation is from contractual receipts such as rentals and concessions. For example, when you buy a souvenir from a shop in a national park, that operator has paid a certain fee to the government for the privilege of setting up business in the park. Lastly, other financial assistance in the form of donations, gifts, or grant money is available to certain public recreation entities.

Government carries out societal functions in an orderly fashion. Without government, anarchy and chaos likely would engulf us. The United States has chosen a democratic form of government to meet the needs of its people. Although the patterns of governing have varied from time to time and among government levels, ultimately government does for people collectively what they are unable to do individually. Since democratic governments are concerned with the well-being of their citizens, and since recreation experiences contribute to that well-being, it is not surprising that recreation and leisure services are a responsibility of government.

The mission of government is to serve the public without excluding anyone from its programs. The government is the only agency that can serve all segments of the population without discriminating according the age, sex, race, and economic condition of those served. It alone has the financial resources to acquire, establish, improve, and operate recreation facilities to meet the public's need. Government also has the power of eminent domain, which means it is the only agency that has the right to take, or authorize the taking of, private property for public use when such action is in the best interest of the public. Furthermore, government is continuous and permanent. It is in the best position to develop the basic policies upon which effective recreation services depend, and it can do so at a minimum unit cost.

Recreation Functions of Government

The government provides myriad functions related to public recreation. Some of these functions vary by level of government or particular branch of government. Five functions, however, seem to be common to all:

- Management of land and natural resources

- Provision of technical assistance

- Financial assistance

- Direct service delivery

- Enactment and enforcement of regulations

Management of Land and Natural Resources

One of the most widely recognized functions of public recreation is the management of natural resources. The creation of the National Park Service and the formation of the National Conference on State Parks in 1921 established the legitimacy of government in outdoor recreation. At the federal level, the United States has over a hundred national parks and other outdoor recreation sites with millions of acres of publicly managed lands. In addition to federally operated public lands within a state are the state's own network of parks and other outdoor recreation facilities and resources.

Outdoor recreation has been used to describe those activities of a recreational nature that normally take place in a natural environment and depend primarily upon that environment for satisfaction. Distinctions in outdoor recreation activities are based on the degree to which the environment is the focus of the activity. Outdoor recreation activities that depend on the use of natural resources for the activity are usually classified as *resource-oriented* outdoor recreation. Within this category are further divisions of outdoor recreation. For example, primitive resource-oriented activities use basic outdoor skills, are nonmotorized, and are generally perceived as isolated close-to-nature activities such as backpacking and mountaineering. *Activity-oriented* outdoor recreation emphasizes the pursuit of certain activities (e.g., softball, golf, tennis) where the environment is of secondary concern.

Federal and state governments have been primarily concerned with resource-oriented outdoor recreation, while local governments have focused on both resource-oriented and activity-oriented recreation. Activities range from the more urban forms of walking for pleasure and picnicking to the more traditional wilderness experiences of backpacking and primitive camping. These activities may involve minimum equipment as for bird-watching and gardening or expensive and highly specialized equipment such as powerboats or snowmobiles.

Management of natural resources has been influenced by political trends, intergovernmental and intragovernmental relationships, historical events, and current management concepts. For example, during the 1960s a number of states began to modify their philosophy of operation and management of state parks. Some states (such as Kentucky, West Virginia, and Oklahoma) developed extensive accommodations for tourists with lodging and dining facilities comparable to commercial motels and restaurants. Policymakers in these states hoped their state park systems would add to the economy of their regions. The parks took on a resort quality with golf and tennis facilities constructed along with the more conventional picnic and aquatic facilities. Initially this pattern was most prevalent in the Appalachian region but with public entrepreneurialism and an emphasis on private/public partnerships, it has became common nationwide (Meyer, 1990).

Provision of Technical Assistance

Technical assistance is a function of federal and state recreation providers. Because of the need to acquire and develop outdoor recreation resources, many state park agencies provide technical assistance and consulting. The best approach to assure interagency cooperation and a systematic development of recreation resources on all levels and among all sectors is to combine the resource management and technical assistance functions. Organizations that provide technical assistance have helped to stimulate the expansion of public park and recreation services. Regional and state planning has been enhanced through the efforts of these agencies, especially if connected to travel and tourism. They influence the legislative process, provide both government departments with needed data, and increase the public's awareness of recreation and parks as a profession.

Financial Assistance

Financial assistance is provided by and to public recreation services, often in the form of grants. These monies are available for land acquisition, facility development, restoration of historic areas, trail development, staff training programs, and program services (e.g., artistic efforts) that benefit the public. These grants often are established as a component of legislation or regulatory actions. For example, the Land and Water Conservation Fund (LWCF) was established in the 1960s as a way to offset the development of outdoor spaces. The LWCF monies primarily came from three sources: entrance or user fees at federal recreation areas, receipts from the sale of surplus federal real property and offshore drilling leases, and taxes from the sale of motorboat fuels. A portion of the money generated through these charges was earmarked for recreation enhancements. The federal government gave each state a percentage of the revenue generated. The state could use a certain portion of the money for needed state-supported recreation efforts. The remainder of the money was then available to community parks and recreation through a matching grant program. The community proposed a needed recreation development project and showed a commitment to fund half the project with local money. If awarded a grant, the state would match the money needed for the project. In the 1980s, Congress stopped appropriating the full amount of money for the fund, even though the original legislation dictated the spending of the offshore drilling money for recreation. Over the past two decades LWCF slowly became defunct. Renewed interest was resurrected in 2000, however, with a bill considered in Congress for a new fund called Conservation and Reinvestment Act (CARA) to provide the same type of support as LWCF did in the 1970s. Many other examples of financial assistance for parks and recreation efforts come from the federal government, as will be described in more detail in the next chapter.

Direct Service Delivery

The fourth major responsibility of government in recreation and leisure services includes a variety of direct service activities. Many of these services are cultural and social while others involve health and higher educational systems. The primary purpose of most local parks and recreation departments is to provide direct services to the people of the community.

Several examples exist to illustrate the wide range of direct services provided by states. For example, some states operate fair or exhibition centers used year round to accommodate commercial shows and exhibitions such as boat shows, horse shows, and music concerts. Additional examples include major sports areas, zoos, aquariums, performing arts centers, and museums. The other major direct service component at the state and federal level involves the provision of recreation at various institutions. For example, therapeutic recreation programs are offered at veterans' hospitals or within state hospitals and training centers. Recreation has been accepted as a legitimate responsibility of the government for individuals incarcerated or who have voluntarily sought treatment and rehabilitation.

One other example of direct service at the state level is offering a parks and recreation major at state-supported institution of higher education. These university curricula not only engage in the preparation of students for the park and recreation profession, but also frequently contribute to the state's responsibility for technical assistance. In addition to providing recreation services for students and faculty, the university system also provides entertainment and recreation for citizens through various athletic, cultural, and entertainment programs.

Enactment and Enforcement of Regulations

The final role of the government is to provide and enforce regulations. Some of these regulations are made directly by the various recreation governmental departments and divisions. For example, regulations regarding grazing on national forest lands would be regulated and enforced by professionals in the US Forest Service. Other regulations may be enacted by nonrecreation governmental units but applied to recreation situations. For example, the Americans with Disabilities Act requires that people with disabilities have access to recreation facilities and experiences without necessarily being segregated or asked to pay more for services. This legislation is translated into practice when facilities are made accessible, when program support staff is knowledgeable about special needs, when assistance is automatically available, and when people with disabilities have the same opportunities as everyone else.

State governments in particular influence recreation services through the legislative process. All local recreation and park programs, services, and facilities supported with tax monies have their foundation of authority in state laws and local ordinances. Recreation services, whether under governmental auspices or not, are influenced by state laws. For example, a commercial recreation facility such as a theme park must adhere to the health and sanitation laws of the state. Likewise, the seating capacity of a theater must conform to state or local laws and ordinances such as fire regulations and hours of operation. The function and operation of tax-supported public recreation and park systems are specifically defined and authorized by law. An understanding of the relationship between law and recreation and park services is essential because the legislative process affects all recreation programs.

Four general types of laws enacted at the state level have bearing on recreation systems. *Enabling laws* are found in the State Park Code of Laws, the State School Code of Laws, and/or in the State Recreation Enabling Legislation. All states have such laws, and efforts are being made to broaden and liberalize them. Enabling legislation grants the local community the right to establish, organize, administer, and conduct recreation and park programs under any one of several authorities. These enabling acts are permissive and not mandatory. They do not require the establishment of a recreation and park system but allow local governments the right to expend public monies for parks and recreation purposes. In some states, local park and recreation systems function under local ordinances that result from the enactment of municipal charters. In those instances, the municipal charter serves as the document that directs and defines the power of the municipality. Regardless of the enabling or charter law, the authority, the geographic jurisdiction of the managing authority, and the responsibilities and functions of that authority are detailed.

Service laws authorize state agencies and departments to provide and operate services and facilities. They determine the scope and focus of state agencies. For example, they may assign the function of recreation services to an agency such as a Youth Commission or a Governor's Commission on Physical Fitness. Service laws detail the authority and structure of an agency established for the provision of park and recreation services, such as a state department of parks, recreation, and tourism.

A third set of laws, *regulatory laws,* regulate, control, license, censor, or supervise recreation activities in the best interest of the public's health, safety, and welfare. A primary example of this type of legislation includes establishing the dates for hunting and fishing and setting limits on the number of species killed or caught. Health and sanitation codes are also types of regulatory acts.

Finally, some laws authorize actions or the expenditure of funds for projects of interest to a given locality that statewide authority is neither requested nor required. These *special project laws* give local groups the right to act on a specific matter that is of no interest or consequence to other communities in the state. For example, if a community wanted to receive a special dispensation of a use permit from the state for certain public lands, it would need to have a special projects law enacted.

Government Roles

People are demanding more recreation opportunities and the government (along with the other sectors) has a role to perform. The federal government is reassessing its responsibility for recreation and is likely to offer greater expenditures in the future, especially by providing new grant monies. State governments recognize the impact of economic development through tourism and other outdoor opportunities and support recreation through financing, legislation, and direct services. Local governments are increasing their capabilities through seeking bond issues and increased tax sources. Government aid also comes in the form of grants funded by lotteries or through special park and recreation funds. New enabling legislation may be required to give local government the right to create special recreation districts or to expend public funds to assist private developers and nonprofit agencies with expansion of recreation services and opportunities. Regardless of the role that governments assume in recreation and leisure, their involvement and acceptance is a necessary ingredient in the recreation and leisure system that has been established.

Reflection Questions

1. What is the government's justification for supporting and providing leisure services?

2. Describe the role of legislation in the provision of recreation and leisure services.

3. Justify the spending of tax dollars for support of recreation and leisure services.

3.3   Recreation in the Federal and State Governments

Federal and state government involvement in recreation and leisure began in the 19th century with the establishment of Yellowstone as the first national park. Around this time, states were also setting aside land for parks. Questions concerning policy and the relationship between federal and state government roles, however, remain unanswered today. For example, some people advocate a policy of federal and state financial involvement with recreation while promoting the rights and autonomy of local agencies. Some people suggest that the federal government should be setting standards and monitoring the quality of local services. Other individuals do not believe that state or federal government should be involved with local recreation programs. They believe recreation and parks is a highly individualized service and should respond directly to local needs, resources, and demands. These differing opinions reflect the public's view of recreation and leisure as a governmental responsibility and the growing concern for environmental and consumer protection. As discussed in the previous chapter, government has specific responsibilities regarding recreation and leisure. This chapter explores the ways that federal and state agencies have been responsible for managing land, providing technical assistance, offering financial assistance, providing direct services, and enacting and enforcing regulations.

Federal Services

The role of the federal government has been dynamic and ever changing. For example, in earlier years (1916–1926) government promoted preservation and encouraged states to establish their own park systems. During the Depression and war years, government actively developed recreation programs and services for youth. In the 1960s and 1970s it became involved in grant activities and financial support for outdoor recreation and programs for people with disabilities. Prior to 1960, few federal programs had a direct relationship to local recreation and park services. The federal government's involvement greatly decreased during the 1980s, but rebounded through the 1990s. In 2000 over 70 federal agencies had programs that dealt with some aspect of recreation and park systems. The following descriptions summarize the scope of services and the federal agencies associated with recreation and leisure.

Department of the Interior

Without question, the Department of the Interior is the primary federal agency concerned with parks and recreation. The Department's responsibilities include protection of natural resources, regulation of hunting and fishing activity, care of cultural and historic sites, and management of facilities designed primarily for recreational purposes. The Department of the Interior also offers technical assistance to local and state governments, conducts research investigations, and stimulates the development of recreation resources through various grant programs. The most visible role that the Department of the Interior plays related to recreation is the administration of the National Park Service.

National Park Service (NPS). The *National Park Service*, established in 1916, has played a prominent role in providing outdoor recreation opportunities. The system includes national parks and monuments; national historic areas and memorials; national seashores and lake shores, parkways, river ways, and recreation areas; the National Capital Park System; the Wolf Trap Farm Park for the Performing Arts; and the John F. Kennedy Center for the Performing Arts. In 2000, the National Park Service was managing some 380 units, encompassing more than 83 million acres with over 287 million daily visitations. The mission of NPS is to

> promote and regulate the use of the federal areas known as national parks, monuments, and reservations . . . by such means and measures as to conform to the fundamental purpose of the said park, monument and reservation, which purpose is to conserve the scenery and natural and historic objects and the wildlife therein and to provide for the enjoyment of the scene in such manner and by such means as will leave them unimpaired for the enjoyment of future generations. (National Park Service, 2001)

This mandate preserves and interprets our national areas while making them available to the public for enjoyment. The NPS system is organized according to five essential functions:

1. *Resource management responsibilities* include the management of land, water, and wildlife resources within a given administrative unit and its surroundings, the general ecology of a park area and its surroundings, and the relationship of use to capacity of the resources.

2. *Visitor services* include those activities that insure the comfort and protection of the user while visiting the park. Among the services are concession (such as food and lodging), safety, and traffic control operations.

3. One of the major responsibilities of the national park system has been to stimulate the public's interest in the historical, geological, biological, and cultural aspects of a given area or resource through *interpretation services*. These take many forms including tours, exhibits, film presentations, publications, museums, websites, and demonstrations.

4. Over half of the financial resources of the National Park Service are devoted to the *maintenance and development functions*. Trail systems, roads, visitor and information centers, and historic buildings must be maintained in a reasonable manner if they are to provide the visitor with a safe, positive outdoor experience. The quality of the national park experience directly relates to the quality of its maintenance operations.

5. *Administrative services* include managing personnel, planning, budgeting, interagency cooperation, public relations, and developing and disseminating data.

For the past several years, the National Park Service has vigorously attempted to upgrade and expand its facilities, camping areas, and resources. The NPS staff has encountered resistance, however, from some people who feel that users are inundating the park areas. These concerned citizens want NPS to restrict admissions and use. On the other hand, the NPS has received criticism from other concerned citizens who feel the facilities are not as accessible to the public as they should be. The latter group has demanded the development of more urban recreation areas and urban parks as well as more development and ease of access to more remote parks.

The National Park Service is also concerned with areas other than the national parks. Only Congress can establish a national park, whereas the President or the Secretary of the Interior may designate national recreation areas. Because of the power and the actions of recent presidential administrations, a new controversy has arisen. In response to the demands for recreation areas, various presidents and/or secretaries have increased the number of areas within the NPS system. Unfortunately, appropriations for NPS have not kept pace with expansion and demand. Consequently, some of the resources that might have been used for maintenance and development of our national parks have been expended for the development and operations of national recreation areas. Despite the general feeling that the services provided by the National Park Service are important, not enough money has been allocated to the continued maintenance and operation of park areas. As a consequence, some national parks have restricted access due to the lack of personnel available to supervise and control park operations.

These public concerns over the use of national park areas illustrate the tension involved in meeting the dictates of the original act and the roles that government ought to have regarding recreation and environmental issues. NPS personnel are in a continual struggle to protect these park areas and yet allow use by all interested citizens. The dilemma is where to draw the line between saving an area and meeting the public demand for access and use. For example, the policy of support for urban outdoor developments and areas has come under attack from such groups as the Conservation Foundation, whose members have called for the Park Service to return to its traditional role of administrator and preserver of our unique natural areas and get out of the recreation business. In another example, the Sierra Club has asked the National Park Service to close certain sections of the national parks to motorized vehicles and to restrict the number and type of camping units permitted in the parks in an effort to save these precious areas.

At the same time that these demands are being heard, the Park Service is being urged to modernize its camping program and provide more lighted areas to reduce vandalism and related crime. During peak periods of activity, national park and recreation areas exhibit most of the characteristics of urban America, including concerns for convenience and security. Added to these concerns is the pressure of the concessionaires who wish to add to their sales potential by expanding their line of goods and services, thereby making the parks a more urban environment.

The role of the national parks will continue to be debated in the coming decades as conservationists, concessionaires, and the manufacturers of recreation equipment advocate their positions. Debates about funding and future outdoor recreation acquisitions and operations will be discussed further in unit four when we describe some of the environmental issues influencing recreation.

Other Department of Interior Roles. The *Bureau of Indian Affairs* (BIA) was established at the turn of the century primarily to oversee Indian reservations and maintain a positive relationship between American Indians and non-Indians. The BIA has developed and operated various recreation facilities such as campgrounds, ski resorts, museums, restaurants, hunting, and fishing areas on Indian reservations. These services are primarily for tourists who happen to be visiting Native American lands. It also operates a more typical community recreation program for Native Americans with community centers, playground facilities, and programs for special populations.

In 1946, the *Bureau of Land Management* (BLM) was established to oversee all federally managed public lands not under the jurisdiction of other agencies such as the National Park Service, the US Forest Service, and the Army Corps of Engineers. The Department of the Interior empowered the BLM to sell unreserved, nonmineral lands to other political subdivisions for recreation and park purposes. It also leases or sells small tracts of land to individuals for camps, cabins, and other recreational use. Prior to the enactment of the Alaska Land Bill, which designated the National Park Service as the caretaker of much of the Alaska area, the Bureau of Land Management was responsible for those Alaskan holdings. Like the US Forest Service, the BLM has a multiple-use philosophy that suggests the simultaneous development and utilization of areas for recreation, mining, and resource exploration. The BLM seeks a balance between conservation and controlled development.

The *Bureau of Reclamation* was established primarily to oversee the development of water resources in the western states. This Bureau has encouraged the recreational use and development of its resources for many years. Active participation in outdoor recreation activities, especially those related to water sports such as boating, fishing, and swimming, are encouraged. The Bureau works closely with other federal agencies since its policy is to transfer reservoir areas that qualify as national recreation areas to the Park Service for operation. It also works jointly with the National Park Service and various states in planning, developing, and promoting outdoor recreation facilities. State or local government organizations may administer or develop recreation resources on Bureau lands.

The *Fish and Wildlife Service* (FWS) is both a regulatory and a resource management agency. It has two major responsibilities: (1) the protection and development of fish and wildlife resources, which includes the enforcement of federal game laws, and (2) the management of recreation areas associated with national wildlife refuges and national fish hatcheries. The refuges protect a variety of wildlife, including migratory waterfowl and other migratory birds; the fish hatcheries are devoted almost entirely to the preservation and development of fresh water game fish and salmon. These refuges and fisheries are open to visitors primarily for photography, picnicking and sightseeing. The FWS also gives financial assistance to state fish and game departments for projects to restore, conserve, and manage fish and wildlife resources. Excise taxes from the sale of firearms, ammunition, and fishing equipment support these programs. In 2000, the Fish and Wildlife Service operated over 400 nature preserves encompassing some 53 million acres of land and water.

Department of Agriculture

The US Department of Agriculture (USDA) has been one of the federal government's major providers of recreation services, primarily through the Forest Service, Federal Extension Service, and Soil Conservation Service. This department has provided technical and educational assistance, outdoor recreation resources, and encouraged and enacted regulatory policies to protect the quality of the environment and the recreation experience.

Although established to serve rural America, the USDA has many urban program thrusts. In 1997, the *US Forest Service* operated a 192 million acre system that included forestlands in 42 states (Statistical Abstract of the United States, 1999). The philosophy of the US Forest Service has been on multiple use with compatible activities occurring simultaneously at the same resource. These national forest lands are open for recreation, grazing, hunting, and mining. Recreation is an important use and the Forest Service has developed areas for picnicking, camping, hiking, and boating. Millions of persons visit the national forests each year to engage in their favorite outdoor recreation activities. Private investors are able to develop resorts on public lands. Many of the better-known winter ski and sports resorts are located in national forests. Hunting and fishing in national forests, except in a few areas, are controlled by state laws.

The *Federal Extension Service* (FES) provides a wide range of technical and educational assistance programs, including information on designing and developing recreation areas, converting croplands to recreation use, and operating tourist attractions. The Extension Service functions only in an advisory and consultative role. Much of its activities are implemented through its 4-H clubs, the work of county agents, and the activity of the extension programs of land-grant colleges and universities. The Extension Service of some states includes the employment of full-time recreation specialists.

The major purpose of the *Soil Conservation Service* (SCS) is the conserving of land, but this federal organization also encourages camping, picnicking, hunting, fishing, and other forms of outdoor recreation. Most of its service facilities are for public day use. Under the provisions of the Watershed Protection and Flood Prevention Act, the Soil Conservation Service entered into cost-sharing arrangements with local organizations for the development of certain lands for public recreation or fish and wildlife usage. SCS was one of the earlier federal programs offering direct financial assistance to local organizations for the development of recreation resources.

In addition to those services mentioned above, the USDA has conducted a variety of research activities directly related to outdoor recreation behavior and natural resource management of recreation agencies through its agricultural experiment station network. The US Forest Service operates comprehensive recreation research programs. The findings have influenced the design, maintenance, and construction of various recreation sites and have offered direction for recreation resource management.

Department of Defense

The Department of Defense is one of the few federal agencies that provides direct recreation services. The recreation programs operated by the military branches are similar to those normally found in a local recreation and park department or an employee recreation service. Recreation professionals employed by the Department of Defense experience many of the same issues confronting staff in local recreation agencies.

Since World War I the military has been concerned with morale, welfare, and recreation programs needed to promote the physical, social, and mental well-being of military personnel and their families. Each branch of the service (i.e., Army, Navy, Air Force, Marines) has its own pattern of recreation administration. All branches attempt to serve the military personnel and their families with sports, library services, arts and crafts centers, musical and theatrical programs, and youth and family services. All rely heavily upon monies appropriated by Congress and self-generated revenue (nonappropriated funds) resulting from the operation of post exchanges and on-base clubs.

Recreation programs exist in the military because they serve as inducements for enlistment, provide increased levels of productivity, encourage sustained morale, and allay the loneliness associated with military service. The branches employ civilian personnel as recreation specialists to run recreation programs on their base or to work cooperatively with adjacent communities. Recreation programs exist on almost all military bases in the United States and around the world.

The *Corps of Engineers*, a branch of the Army, has functions similar to the US Forest Service and National Park Service. The Corps is a provider of outdoor recreation opportunities through the development and maintenance of recreation areas. Although the primary responsibility is to develop and maintain rivers and waterways in the interest of flood control, the Corps of Engineers has built picnic areas, hiking trails, public boat launching and docking facilities, campgrounds, and other recreation facilities for public use. Federal legislation in the 1940s and 1960s authorized the Army Chief of Engineers to construct and maintain public park and recreation facilities at Corps water resource and development projects. The laws also provided that the Corps financially assist local groups and governments in the development, operation, and maintenance of project land and water areas for recreation, fish, and wildlife enhancement.

Department of Education

The Department of Education promotes the cause of education throughout the nation by collecting and disseminating information, awarding grants, and providing consulting services. Recreation and play are recognized as a significant part of education, and the involvement of the public school system in the provision of adequate recreation opportunities is encouraged.

The Department of Education has had a special influence on park and recreation services for people with disabilities. The *Office of Special Education and Rehabilitation Services* (OSERS) supports personnel training, program development, and efficacy research. The *Office of Special Education Programs* has offered training grants since 1969 for the preparation of recreation personnel to work with youth with disabilities related to free and appropriate public education.

Associated directly with OSERS is the *Rehabilitation Services Administration* (RSA), one of the first federal agencies to offer financial support for the development of graduate study in the field of therapeutic recreation. RSA has supported recreation demonstration projects by recreation departments, schools, hospitals, and residential providers to improve the provision of recreation and treatment opportunities of people with disabling conditions. RSA maintains close liaison with federal counterpart agencies such as the Social Security Administration, the Department of Labor, National Institute of Mental Health, the President's Committee on the Employment of Persons with Disabilities, the Office of Special Education Programs, the Office of Adult and Vocational Education, and the National Institute on Disability and Rehabilitation Research.

Department of Health and Human Services

Several bureaus and programs within the Department of Health and Human Services influence the recreation and leisure services system. The most prominent are the Administration on Aging, the Children's Bureau, and the Public Health Service.

The *Administration on Aging* was established in 1965 as part of the Older Americans Act to encourage and financially assist with the establishment of comprehensive program services for older persons. The provision of recreation opportunities has been a prime element of that effort. Under the Older Americans Act, funds have been expended for recreation-related purposes such as the renovation and repair of facilities, payment of salaries, and the operation of continuing education, recreation, and outreach programs.

The *Children's Bureau*, established in 1912, is one of the oldest federal agencies involved in recreation. The Bureau has largely concentrated efforts in the development of literature pertaining to the play and play environments of children and has worked cooperatively with state, federal, and private not-for-profit national agencies and organizations to promote services for youth.

The *Public Health Service* addresses recreation that involves matters of health. Funds for research and training through the various national institutes of health are another service provided by this program. The major contribution to recreation is in the areas of safety and environmental care. Any federal or state agency may call upon the Public Health Service for technical assistance concerning the development, planning, operations, or maintenance of a recreation facility if communicable diseases might be transmitted and where sanitary services are needed.

Department of Housing and Urban Development

The Department of Housing and Urban Development (HUD) is primarily concerned with the comprehensive planning and development of American cities. Recreation concerns are part of the planning process. HUD has encouraged the development and use of planning standards for recreation and parks and the necessity for effective evaluation of park and recreation delivery systems. HUD has made efforts to include space for recreation in public housing areas, but has not assumed responsibility for administering recreation programs within these areas. Those programs generally have been retained by local public and not-for-profit recreation agencies.

Other Federal Programs

In addition to the previously mentioned federal departments, several other agencies and activities have programs impacting recreation and leisure.

The *National Endowment for the Arts* assists individuals and nonprofit, tax-exempt organizations in the development and promotion of arts, dance, literature, music, and theater. This program was created in 1965 to aid local communities in the creation and support of performing arts activities. Although funding was reduced by recent administrations, the program remains vital with private philanthropic support. Its efforts to stimulate cultural arts programs in the inner city and correctional facilities merit special mention.

The *President's Council on Physical Fitness* was established in 1956 as a result of a concern for the lack of fitness of American youth. Since then, the President's Council has aggressively promoted the cause of fitness and sports in the United States. It disseminates information on the importance of fitness to general well-being, sponsors various national forums, and encourages the development of fitness programs throughout the school system. It works primarily through existing agencies and organizations rather than by providing direct services.

The *Tennessee Valley Authority* (TVA) was established in 1933 to oversee the development of hydroelectric power in the Tennessee Valley and to monitor the flood control and navigation aspects of the Tennessee River. Even though recreation was not a major concern initially, the TVA has been a significant force in the development of recreation resources and activities in that region. It has created a wide range of recreation facilities including boat docks, fishing camps, resort sites, and lots for vacation cottages. Within the TVA region, the Fish and Wildlife Service maintains more than 100,000 acres of game refuges. Since its creation, the TVA has transferred over 200,000 acres to various governmental authorities for recreation use.

The *Department of Veterans Affairs* operates therapeutic recreation programs at each Veterans Administration Hospital and Home. Programs include a wide range of activities and services directed by a professional staff of therapeutic recreation specialists. The objectives for these thera-peutic recreation programs are to aid patients in adjusting to hospitalization and treatment, to contribute to the morale of the patient during hospital-ization, to facilitate the patient's recovery and rehabilitation, and to aid in the patient's return to life in the community.

Despite the numerous programs and services that currently exist, no single federal agency is uniquely concerned with recreation and leisure. Some people feel that a federal agency primarily concerned with recreation and leisure activities and services should be established to coordinate the overall effort of the federal government. Furthermore, these individuals argue that this new agency should have cabinet rank. Since we have a De-partment of Labor, we should have a Department of Recreation. Others argue that the present system of many federal agencies involved in recreation, parks, and leisure is ideal because of the variety of options and support.

State Government Involvement in Recreation

The role of state governments in recreation and leisure varies. States directly provide program services when they operate fairs, parks, and museums. State governments also influence recreation behaviors through the regula-tory legislation enacted and administered by state governmental units. Overall, state involvement is more similar than dissimilar to the federal government in organizational structures and policy statements.

The initial role in recreation and leisure services assumed by most states was that of protecting the natural resources. The state park move-ment began in 1864, several years before Yellowstone was established as a national park. Concerns within states for game regulations, forestry management, and state fair operations were also shown before the turn of the century. In general state involvements in parks and recreation have followed or been patterned after federal actions. Possibly the most signifi-cant development of state governments in recent years has been the ex-pansion of public services, including recreation, parks, and tourism.

The range of recreation services provided vary from state to state but generally include the following activities:

• Acquiring, developing, and managing land and water resources for conservation and outdoor recreation purposes

• Advertising and promoting recreation resources and attractions by state tourist bureaus and development commissions

• Enacting permissive legislation that enables communities and districts to mobilize their resources for recreation services

- Establishing state recreation commissions, boards, departments, or divisions as a unit of state government to coordinate the development and management of state recreation and park services and opportunities

- Employing recreation and park personnel in such state departments and agencies as state youth commissions, departments of public instruction, departments of natural resources, state hospitals, and training schools where responsibilities are broader than that of providing recreation services

- Enacting laws and establishing policies designed to protect natural resources and wildlife and to regulate certain individual recreation behaviors

- Developing technical assistance programs to aid local communities in establishing, improving, and developing their park and recreation facilities and services

- Appropriating public funds for managing a state recreation and park system and granting funds to local communities for the supplemental support of their park and recreation system

The future role that states play will depend largely upon the role played by the local and federal governments. No governmental subdivision alone can address the problems of urban planning and recreation resources. The growing concern with the preservation of natural and cultural resources, the acceptance of leisure as a major economic and social force, and the expansion of tourism ensure further discussion of the appropriateness of federal and state involvement.

Many direct services can be offered in local communities, but federal and state governments will have a continuing role regarding technical assistance, resource preservation, planning, applied research, and information dissemination. Governmental support for recreation at all levels and with multiple functions is likely to remain a viable option in the future, but the challenge will be for staff to show efficiency and quality in meeting the varied needs of a diverse constituency and the changing natural environment.

Reflection Questions

1. List five federal agencies involved in recreation and leisure and explain their scope.

2. Briefly describe three social issues that are being addressed by federal recreation programs.

3. Why do you believe we need or do not need state provided recreation services?

3.4　Local Government Involvement in Recreation

Local parks and recreation agencies, comprising both community and county departments and schools, have been important providers of leisure services for almost a century in many parts of the country. Organized recreation and leisure services are largely an urban phenomenon. As cities grew, so did the need for recreation services. Today people living in rural areas and small towns as well as cities enjoy being entertained and having opportunities for leisure expression. Although local government services do not meet the recreation interests of every facet of public life, they do guarantee a basic level of support and opportunity. The public expects government entities to provide certain types of facilities, opportunities, and services where people can meet and play.

For the most part local public recreation departments are financed by the general fund of the community (e.g., monies that come from taxes levied on property) or from a special recreation tax. State and local laws and ordinances determine the funding sources. Revenue derived from user fees, grants, gifts, and special assessments supplement these monies. In addition to these sources of support for daily operation, departments generally rely upon bond issues to fund their capital development projects (e.g., facility and land acquisition).

Professionals in communities create recreation systems with a variety of organizational structures. The organizational structures reflect the historical origins of the recreation and park movement, the attitudes of the profession, and the experience and traditions of each community. No single pattern for administering local recreation systems exists. Each local program is determined by the legislation that allowed the community to become an incorporated body. These charter or enabling acts permit municipalities, counties, or other local units of government (such as a park district) to decide how recreation and leisure and other public services are to be provided.

Local Recreation Providers

Public recreation systems are administered in a number of ways by different types of governments. Local recreation services are provided primarily through the offices of municipal government. Municipalities draw their power from their state constitutions. In most instances, enabling legislation by state governments makes recreation services a local government responsibility.

A second local government approach to the provision of recreation services is through a special recreation and/or park district (Toalson, 1980). These districts function as separate governmental units with the power to levy taxes for recreation and park services. The amount of the tax money varies from state to state and is usually determined by state law. Illinois and Missouri have used the district approach extensively in the development of their local recreation and park services. These districts function like municipalities except that they have only the one responsibility: to provide recreation and park services.

A third approach to the provision of local recreation and park services is the county recreation and park approach. Counties, like municipalities, draw their power from the state legislature and constitutional documents. With the growth of suburbia and urban sprawl, recreation and leisure services have become an accepted function of county government. Although similar in structure to municipal recreation services, county recreation and park systems have a slightly different orientation because the geographic area served is much greater and the population density is generally less than that of a municipality. Some of the administrative patterns for providing recreation and park services to rural and suburban areas through county governments include:

- Establishing separate county recreation and park departments or independent recreation or park districts;

- Creating a quasi-public recreation and park council with representatives from various communities; and

- Using a contract system whereby a community or political subdivision enters into a contract with a legal recreation authority of another political subdivision or private recreation agency to provide recreation and park services to the community for an annual fixed sum.

A fourth approach is to administer local recreation services through the public school system. In rural areas, the school unit is sometimes the basic provider of public recreation services. School districts function much like recreation and other special districts with the power to tax and administer services. Because the school is an essential and influential institution in every community, school officials and authorities cannot avoid dealing with the issue of leisure. They provide direct services for the millions of children and adults who spend a major portion of their lives each day within the confines of school facilities. Because schools have so many possibilities for addressing leisure in their possible structure as well as their mission, we will discuss schools in a bit more depth.

Schools and Leisure

Schools deal with the issue of leisure and prepare students for that aspect of life whether they are directly responsible for recreation provision in the community or not. The roles of schools involve shaping attitudes, developing leisure skills, and providing opportunities for practicing those skills. The public school system is a significant owner of public property and facilities. Most schools have gymnasiums, arts and music facilities, playgrounds, park areas, and/or athletic fields. Some have swimming pools, stadiums, and well-equipped industrial arts areas. Most of these facilities can and should be made available for recreation pursuits. Essentially, the school has five major responsibilities related to recreation:

1. *To educate for leisure.* This responsibility includes developing leisure attitudes and values, teaching activity skills, sharing knowledge of community resources available for leisure expression, and promoting an understanding by the individual of his or her interests, motivations, and leisure aptitudes.

2. *To provide recreation opportunities and services.* The school has the responsibility to provide recreation opportunities for the school population and where feasible recreation services to the entire community. It may provide services through direct programming or by opening its facilities for after-school and weekend use.

3. *To advise, counsel, and guide leisure behaviors.* Just as the schools make available counseling services on academic, vocational, and personal matters, the school should advise on matters related to the use of leisure.

4. *To prepare individuals for serving in recreation leadership capacities.* The school is the institution to which society turns for training in any field of service. Opportunities for leadership development and practice and curricula for the preparation of park and recreation professionals are essential.

5. *To be an advocate of leisure.* School officials and administrators play a critical role in the support of community recreation and park services. They can demonstrate concern for quality living through joint planning and development. Whenever possible, the school system should be represented on recreation advisory boards and vice versa. Two-way communication is essential.

Schools fulfill these roles with three basic methods: community school and school-park programs, contractual agreements with counties and municipalities, and extracurricular activities. The community school component suggests that school buildings should be available to the public. The school-park concept is a situation where a school is built in or immediately adjacent to a park and where the school as well as the community has access to using the park. Schools and other community groups, including local parks and recreation departments, sometimes enter into partnerships or contractual agreements to provide a variety of recreation opportunities for children and adults. Recess and extracurricular activities, including interscholastic sports, music, and dramatic activities are other ways that schools address issues of recreation on a local level.

Regardless of the whether the local government agency is a municipality, special district, county, or school district, the services and management patterns for recreation services are basically the same. Local governments, however, have organized the structures they use for providing public recreation in different ways.

Types of Operating Structures

Communities structure their leisure service systems in a variety of ways. The most dominant pattern of local organization is the combined park and recreation department. It has been the structure of choice since the early 1960s. The type of structure employed, however, has no specific relationship to the political subdivision responsible for parks and recreation services. Municipal or county governments, special park districts, or school districts may administer recreation services.

Combined Single Administrative Unit

Combined leisure services authorities are characterized by a focus on parks and recreation as an integrated function. In this structure parks and recreation services are seen as interrelated and equally important. This structure is usually thought to be the best approach to maximize the natural relationship that exists between programs and facilities. Proponents of this structure argue that when park and recreation services are administered jointly, coordination of maintenance and program schedules is enhanced. The combination broadens the base of political support since each facet of parks and recreation has its own constituent groups (e.g., conservationists, naturalists, sports enthusiasts, social advocates). The combined approach also allows for a more effective utilization of specialists. For example, recreation practitioners are typically prepared to create programming services, whereas park planners and administrators know how to design and maintain resources and facilitate their use.

Single Function

This type of structure has as its single function the provision of either a recreation service or a park service. The two functions operate independently of each other and are not administratively related. Both a department of parks and a department of recreation are maintained. When recreation services are being provided as a single function, they emphasize programs and leadership rather than acquisition and maintenance or property. The independent recreation unit generally will attempt to use the resources of other governmental units, such as those managed by the park department or the school system, to expand its services. It is not unusual for the school board and park commission to have representatives on the local recreation board or advisory committee and vice versa.

In those instances where the park system is operated by a separate park unit, the focus is generally on land acquisition, development, and maintenance rather than on program services and activities. Landscaping and environmental protection receive more attention than do programs of human services, since resource management and conservation are major concerns of independent park units.

Schools (Boards of Education, School Districts)

In some states, school laws make it possible for boards of education to administer public recreation services. When schools provide recreation services, a separate park board or park department generally administers the parks. Joint planning of parks and recreation may occur, but the recreation program is viewed as a function of the school system (not local government) and the recreation professionals are school employees. Recreation professionals generally recognize that the formal school system plays an important role in providing recreation services to a community. This role is undertaken whether the school administers the recreation system or not.

Community Responsibilities

In recent years, the need for more coordination of government services at the local level has stimulated interest in a new design for administering recreation and park services. This approach brings together various units concerned with cultural programs, social services, information, education, and related free-time activity. Such agencies are frequently known as departments of community services or departments of leisure and cultural services. They typically administer the libraries, park system, cultural arts programs, senior citizen programs, community buildings, and recreation programs. The primary function of these agencies is to provide leisure services; the term *recreation* is generally not a part of their title. The advantages of this structure are largely economical and political. The viability of this trend toward the merger of related services is unknown. The concept has support, but the uncertainty of the future and the tendency toward the bureaucratic nature of this structure may discourage some communities.

Regardless of the structure, the input that local governments and citizens have to public recreation varies depending on the local policy structures and traditions. All public park, recreation, and leisure service agencies are either under the direction of an independent commission with policy responsibilities or within a department of local government where the director is responsible to the mayor or city manager.

Local Policy and Advisory Boards and Commissions

Local boards or commissions are usually described as policymaking or advisory in nature. In the first half of this century, independent recreation or park units with board and commission members appointed or elected to office were popular. Recreation districts, park districts, and municipal recreation and park services followed this pattern. Administrators viewed recreation as a service similar to public education, and therefore modeled the administration of park and recreation services after the educational system. Since the school boards governed the school system, it was believed that policy boards should guide recreation and park units.

The arguments for the policy board approach are straightforward. By having citizens elected or appointed to direct the public recreation services, citizen input and control is assured. The recreation and park system is directly responsible to the community. Citizens, not professional administrators, set the direction for the recreation and park service. Having several persons involved in the determination of policy tends to make policy decisions more acceptable and politically appealing than when policies are formulated by a single individual (e.g., the director) or by a group (e.g., a city council) that may not have recreation and parks as its primary concern.

The arguments against the commission/board approach to managing recreation and park systems have been stronger, however, since most local recreation departments now function with advisory rather than policy boards. Opponents to these independent boards argue that parks and recreation units rely heavily upon the cooperation of other units of municipal government, such as public works, personnel, and accounting. These units are under the general direction of the town's chief executive officer, usually the city manager. When the city manager is able to coordinate the functions of the recreation and park department with those of other city departments, a better administration is perceived.

Regardless of the administrative structure, professionals employed in public recreation universally accept the need for some type of citizen representation. Because recreation is often viewed as an important but not essential governmental function, advocates are needed. This advocacy is often achieved through advisory boards and committees. They interpret the value of parks and recreation to the political structure as well as influence the programming views and thinking of professional park and recreation staff.

Recreation boards and commissions, both policy and advisory, are political entities with members who are appointed or elected. Consequently, they should be involved in the political process. Recreation professionals assist in the determination of policy and the development of program strategies, and they need to be politically astute and aware of how politics affect policies and public interests. Commission and board members, however, need to be politically involved with the decisions made in their communities.

Local Responsibilities

A variety of structures and a range of services are offered at the local governmental level. They vary from elaborate park systems, such as those in New York or Portland, to the direct involvement of local municipalities in professional athletics. For example, Durham, North Carolina, owns the athletic park where professional baseball teams play. In Phoenix, Arizona, the library system is administered by the Recreation and Park Department. In other cities, community theater is a function of local recreation agencies. The type of programs and services offered to the public locally depends upon factors such as tradition, other service providers, public expectations, and the philosophy and preferences of the professional recreation staff.

Professional leadership for recreation and leisure services is essential in communities. Although most people who direct public parks and recreation programs have professional backgrounds, some do not. In 1999, the National Recreation and Park Association passed a statement advocating for the hiring of professional leadership (see Table 3.4, p. 208).

Recreation programming is the heart of any local public recreation provider. The scope and content of the leisure programs depend on the facilities available, the mandate of the agency, and the interest and philosophy of the leadership. Through research and experience programming principles have evolved, including:

- Involve citizens in planning and conducting recreation programs whenever possible

- State objectives clearly so everyone knows what is to be done and how

- Realize that no one program or approach will be accepted by all

- Know the limits of appeal and the demands for a given service or program

- Provide sound leadership, adequate financial support, and have an appreciation of the forces such as local traditions that condition effective programming

- Assure that recreation is inclusive so that all citizens in the community have opportunities to experience leisure and play in a welcoming and accessible environment

---

Table 3.4:   Statement of Need for Professional Leadership for Public Park and Recreation Agencies

Quality of life is important to individuals. For this reason, many communities invest significantly in park, recreation and cultural services. The result is citizens who are content with where they live, work and play. They enjoy activities that renew them both physically and emotionally. Other benefits are also derived beyond that of the individual citizen. Quality park and recreation services aid the economy by sales of recreational equipment and clothing, by improving property values, and by attracting visitors, retirees, and new business and industry. Recreational programs provide a setting for ethnic and cultural diversity, and alternative to delinquent behavior, and opportunities for socialization. Parks provide a comfortable area for the enjoyment and appreciation of the natural environment.

Throughout the United States, significant portions of local tax dollars are invested in park and recreation programs, areas, and facilities. To maximize the return on this investment, there is a need for professional leadership in the provision of leisure services.

The responsibilities of a park and recreation administrator at the start of the 21st century are far greater than the administrative ability to plan and design facilities, to develop programs, and to operate these. The ability to work with personnel, citizens groups, and volunteers through partnerships and building consensus is essential to success. An understanding of politics is also important. The park and recreation administrator must possess knowledge of funding methods for leisure services, such as program fees, taxation, grants, and rental charges, while augmenting this with innovative funding strategies beyond those typical of a governmental entity. Other desirable qualities include marketing skills, entrepreneurial thinking, creativity, and other skills similar to those needed to manage a business.

A park and recreation professional should be academically prepared to undertake the unique tasks of administering park, recreation and cultural services. He/she should remain current on trends, issues, and technology that affect the quality of these services by engaging in professional continuing education programs, attending professional conferences and seminars, and reading appropriate professional publications. Those individuals who commit themselves to improving their community through park and recreation leadership should be professionally certified through their appropriate certification board.

Because of the specific professional skills required for park and recreation leadership in the 21st century, the National Recreation and Park Association recommends that cities, towns, counties, and special districts entrust the administration of their leisure service investment in those persons who are properly educated, professionally trained, and certified.

Adopted by the National Recreation and Park Association Board of Trustees in October 1999. Available at http://www.activeparks.org

The relationship between private commercial, not-for-profit, and public recreation service agencies is dynamic. In some communities, these relationships are cooperative while in others they are more adversarial. Some recreation professionals believe it is their responsibility to provide a cafeteria of activities and services to the public without much regard for possible competition with the programs and actions of the other sectors. Other professionals say their mission is to complement those sectors. Other local government providers approach the issue in a more supplemental way by only providing those programs not being offered by the other sectors.

With the growth of a business approach to the provision of public leisure services, the relationship between the local government provider and other recreation providers has become more complementary. Public leisure service agencies have developed market strategies to assure program success. Operating stables, marinas, golf courses, and fitness centers with a middle and upper middle class appeal can provide public recreation units with some recovery costs, be totally self-sufficient, or make a profit. Those revenues might be applied toward other activities that are not self-sustaining, such as programs for youth from high-risk communities. Local public providers have also contracted with the other recreation entities to develop and operate concessions or provide outdoor adventure activities. These arrangements expand the offerings of the local department without adding to the operational costs or liability of the unit.

Most people are influenced by recreation and leisure services at the local level. Regardless of the varied arrangements structured to provide public recreation opportunities, most cities and counties have focused on making their services available to everyone. If we believe that recreation is the right of all people, then the local government must be instrumental in assuring that those opportunities exist.

Reflection Questions

1. How are local governments authorized to provide recreation services?

2. What are the four primary structures for delivering local leisure services?

3. How is the school responsible for educating for leisure?

4. What are the roles of local citizens in the administration of local public recreation?

3.5 Not-for-profit Recreation and Leisure Services

Alexis de Tocqueville (1945), in his classic work *Democracy in America*, argued that voluntary associations were the backbone of American society and that the future of this country would depend upon these associations. Economist Jeremy Rifkin (1995) asserted that in the new millennium we will likely see a workforce dominated by white-collar individuals working in not-for-profit organizations. Today, such associations continue to be an integral part of American society. They have played an important role in the contemporary recreation movement in this country. Virtually every industrial country has a cluster of agencies that fill a gap in services not provided for by government or the private commercial market sector.

This chapter focuses on the not-for-profit sector related to agencies that address recreation and leisure services. Agencies that make up this grouping are also referred to as not-for-profits, voluntary associations, third sector, or independent sector agencies. As of 1999, there were more than 1.6 million registered not-for-profit organizations in the United States (Salamon, 1999).

Myths about Not-for-profit Organizations

Three common myths about not-for-profit organizations influence the way people think about this segment of the workplace:

Myth #1: Not-for-profit organizations do not make a profit, hence the name "not-for-profit." Many people mistakenly assume that not-for-profit or nonprofit means that an agency or organization cannot make an actual profit. Not-for-profit organizations can and do make a profit. What distinguishes this type of agency from a commercial for profit venture, however, is that these agencies may not distribute profits to individual stockholders. Not-for-profit agencies must put any profits gained at the end of the fiscal year back into the organization.

Myth #2: People who work for a not-for-profit organization do not make any money. This rationale is sometimes used by people who say they philosophically like the idea of a not-for-profit, but are financially concerned they cannot survive on the pay. Although working in the private commercial sector may result in a higher salary, individuals who work in not-for-profit agencies can and do make a living wage. As in other sectors, salary is primarily influenced by location. People who live in urban areas will likely earn what others in comparable positions make based on the cost of living for a particular region of the country.

Myth #3: All not-for-profit organizations are tax-exempt. Many people believe that one of the advantages about being associated with a not-for-profit organization is that the organization does not pay taxes and that people can make tax-deductible contributions to their organization. This statement is partially true. The Internal Revenue Service has developed 27 different tax codes for a variety of not-for-profit agencies and organizations such as farmers' cooperatives and political parties. These types of agencies are exempt from paying taxes. Unless a not-for-profit formally applies to receive tax-exempt status, however, the agency will not automatically receive this designation. The vast majority of not-for-profit organizations apply for a tax exemption, but some do not. Only one tax code, 501(c)(3), allows an agency to not pay taxes and to receive tax-deductible contributions from individuals and corporations.

Commonalities among Not-for-profit Recreation Providers

These myths begin to clarify what a not-for-profit organization is, but we also need to address what distinguishes these types of agencies from other providers. Most not-for-profit organizations receive community support in a variety of ways (e.g., United Way, community foundation grants, individual donations, funds solicited through special events, membership fees). Many of the elements of these services are like public agencies in the way that they approach recreation and leisure services for all.

The contributions of not-for-profit organizations in communities are varied and extensive. In some communities, not-for-profit recreation providers supplement the public recreation offerings. In other areas, not-for-profit agencies may be the basic provider of the community's organized recreation service. Among the many community organizations and groups comprising this system are the youth-serving voluntary agencies, employee recreation groups, special interest groups (e.g., Sierra Club, Audubon Society), religious organizations (e.g., churches and synagogues), specialized recreation associations (e.g., neighborhood clubs, soccer clubs, running clubs), education institutions, and those facilities and services provided by families and/or individuals for their own recreation pursuits. Nearly all not-for-profit groups focus on their participants, generally members and volunteers.

Justifications for Not-for-profit Organizations

Salamon (1999) identified several reasons why not-for-profit organizations were established. First, groups formed to meet the needs of their communities long before states started formally governing. For example, playgrounds, voluntary fire departments, schools, and adoption agencies were informal not-for-profit associations before they became functions of government. Another reason was due to market failure. The private market is good at providing individual consumable goods and products, but less effective at providing collective goods and services such as clean air and safe neighborhoods. Not-for-profit agencies provide a context in which groups of individuals pool resources to produce collective goods they desire but cannot convince a majority of society to support. The government also has limitations in funding and cannot provide directly for all of the needs of different groups of individuals. By granting not-for-profit status to agencies through the Internal Revenue Service, the government assists nongovernmental organizations in meeting a variety of community needs. Not-for-profit groups support ideals of freedom and pluralism and encourage individual initiative for the public good. Most major social reforms in American society have emanated from the voluntary, not-for-profit sector. Finally, we create not-for-profit organizations for the possibility of joint, collective action. Not-for-profit organizations emerged as a result of public need and public willingness to volunteer to work together to meet a need. Not-for-profit organizations played a pivotal role in the development of services and the entire profession of recreation and leisure.

Not-for-profit organizations fall into two major categories: *member-serving organizations* and *public-serving organizations* (Salamon, 1999). Member-serving organizations (e.g., Girl Scouts, YMCA) have some public benefit, but their primary purpose is to "provide a benefit to the members of the organization rather than to the public at large" (p. 23). Public-serving organizations (e.g., Sierra Club, MADD)

> exist primarily to serve the public at large rather than primarily the members of the organizations. They may do so [by] providing health and education services, sponsoring cultural or religious activities, advocating for certain causes, aiding the poor, financing other not-for-profits . . ." (p. 23)

Not-for-profit Operations

Not-for-profit organizations may operate like public agencies or private businesses, but they are unique in several ways (Salamon, 1999). These organizations are institutionally separate from government but may receive government support. They are self-governing and are not controlled by outside entities. In addition, not-for-profit organizations are noncompulsory and involve some meaningful degree of voluntary participation, either in the actual conduct of the agency's activities or in the management of its affairs. Typically, this takes the form of a voluntary board of directors. Extensive use of volunteers to supplement the work of paid staff is also common.

Any group of individuals interested in joining together to solve a community problem or meet a community need can gather together and consider forming a not-for-profit organization and apply to receive tax-exempt status. A typical structure would include a Board of Directors, Executive Director, paid staff, and volunteers. Not-for-profit organizations may have no full-time paid employees, as few as one or two paid employees, or as many as hundreds of paid employees. The size of the organization and the purpose will depend on the scope of the agency's mission. A neighborhood association with 100 residences would obviously be different than the American Alliance of Health, Education, Recreation, and Dance with its 40,000 members.

Funding for not-for-profit organizations comes from several sources. The United Way of America is one primary source of income for many agencies. The United Way—also referred to as the Community Chest, United Fund, or United Campaign—provides a way for individual donors to make contributions through their local or state employer to a United Way agency. Local boards determine how the money will be spent in their community. United Way identifies organizations that they fund on a continual basis. Various not-for-profit organizations can apply to receive these funds. In most communities, an organized fundraising effort is the most effective way of raising money for social service agencies. Billions of dollars are raised through these united campaigns annually. Although most of the groups that constitute membership in the United Way are not-for-profit agencies, public agencies sometimes participate.

Not-for-profit agencies may supplement their United Way monies by charging fees for services. These fees are typically moderate and scholarships are often available for persons unable to afford the fee. Other funds may be obtained through structured fundraising efforts such as direct mail, phone and face-to-face solicitations, events such as golf tournaments, or grants from corporations, foundations, and the government. A shift has occurred in the past decade in terms of sources of funding of not-for-profit organizations. These agencies have seen an increase in fees and government support and a decrease in private giving. Funding for not-for-profit arts, culture, recreation, and leisure organizations was comprised of approximately 26% fees, 14% government, and 63% private giving in 1999 (Salamon, 1999).

Volunteers in Not-for-profit Organizations

Just as the not-for-profit organizations rely primarily upon the United Way and other local coordinating councils to assist them in the developing and financing their efforts, they also rely heavily upon volunteers for the operation of their programs. The spirit of volunteerism is a longstanding hallmark of America's national identity. Recent estimates indicate that 95 million Americans of all ages volunteered an average of 4.2 hours per week to various charitable and other organizations in 1995 (Salamon, 1999, p. 38). The not-for-profit sector comprises agencies and organizations of all sizes throughout the United States that use many volunteers to provide leadership and labor in the provision of direct services to members and participants.

Two major types of volunteerism can be found in not-for-profit and public recreation programs: structured and unstructured. These types might also be classified as "regular" versus "lend-a-hand" volunteers, or long-term versus short-term (single event) volunteers (Tedrick & Henderson, 1989). These descriptions refer to the amount of training that might be required and how many hours a volunteer commitment might entail. People are generally looking for volunteer positions that meet their personal needs as well as contribute to an organization or a cause that interests them. They may be seeking to change the system or keep it intact, to work for their special interests or for others, to give monetary gifts or help solicit from others, or to work occasionally or to seek some type of continuous volunteering. Volunteers can assist leisure service systems in a variety of ways including teaching activities and skill classes, serving on policy or advisory boards or commissions, advocating through education or fundraising for certain causes, assisting in the carrying out of office routines such as distribution of pamphlets and other informational materials, serving as sponsors or advisors of recreation clubs, or providing transportation for people in special recreation services to and from recreation centers.

The Retired Senior Volunteer Program (RSVP) is an example of a volunteer program that involves thousands of adults over 60 in a variety of human service programs in over 800 locations throughout the United States. RSVP creates meaningful opportunities for persons of retirement age to participate more fully in the life of their communities through volunteer service. To this end, RSVP matches senior volunteers with volunteer assignments, provides insurance for volunteers, provides transportation/meal reimbursement, and provides recognition and social events for volunteers. The volunteers provide expertise and experience to meet community needs and determine the activity and time commitment that is compatible with their interests. Local RSVP programs receive money from the federal government as well as from state governments and local United Ways.

Examples of Not-for-profit Recreation Providers

In addition to youth-serving agencies that are discussed in the next chapter, three examples of not-for-profit groups that offer opportunities for recreation will be discussed. These include organized religions, employee recreation services, and advocacy organizations.

Organized Religion

With over 400 separate denominational organizations and sects, membership in excess of well over 100 million people and a corporate wealth in the billions, organized religion in the United States is a powerful social institution. Religion shapes people's values and attitudes and is a critical force in the lives of millions of people. Organized religions are a major element of the not-for-profit sector because they are a primary provider of recreation and fellowship experiences for many of their members. Three major coordinating organizations of religious bodies in the United States—the National Council of Churches of Christ in the United States, the National Catholic Welfare Conference, and the Jewish Welfare Board—have proclaimed recreation to be an important part of the church members' concern and service.

Churches have assumed three basic responsibilities in relationship to leisure services. First, they have aided and shaped the development of the public recreation and park agencies through the positions they have taken on recreation issues and their attitude toward specific recreation experiences. The blue laws that limit what activities can be done on Sundays is one example of how churches have influenced recreation in some communities.

Second, they provide direct recreation services for their members with their recreation centers, recreation activities, and recreation programs. Church officials often combine recreation with their education and worship programs. Further, the religious environment lends itself to the promotion of certain types of recreation pursuits. Probably no group in the community is more involved in music and drama than are church groups. Likewise, religious holiday celebrations are fundamental to recreation in many communities.

Finally, religions also provide a community service and a variety of programs for the public at large, especially by making their facilities available for youth and civic groups and through the public availability of many of their programs. Although primarily concerned with the recreation opportunities provided for its members, the church's involvement in recreation services goes beyond the individual member's interests. Church facilities are meeting places for the many youth-serving groups such as Boy Scouts, Girl Scouts, and Camp Fire Boys and Girls. In some communities, churches are active in providing day-care facilities for elderly and individuals with disabilities. They may operate programs for preschoolers such as childcare services. They may join with secular groups to offer adult education and senior citizen programs. Further, they often operate conference groups, camps, and other outdoor recreation facilities. Many local churches have constructed gymnasiums as part of the church facility and have operated youth sport leagues and teen clubs. Some employ full-time recreation professionals or youth ministers to direct their programs. Cooperation between leisure service providers and religious organizations benefits all. As leisure service providers, churches and synagogues tends to add to the quality of life in the community and assure the relationship among spirituality, play, and recreation.

Employee Recreation and Corporate Services

Numerous American industries and businesses provide recreation services for their employees. Employee recreation is the application of recreation services to a particular clientele (e.g., employees of a particular company and their families) sponsored by the corporation itself. Employee recreation may be provided by the employer and/or by the workers themselves. Although private companies and corporations generally conduct these services, many of the employee recreation services run as not-for-profit entities. For many employees and their families, employee programs are the key providers of organized recreation services and fitness opportunities. Employee recreation occurs in large industries and manufacturing plants as well as commercial enterprises such as banks, insurance companies, department stores, private utilities, transportation lines, and service firms. Many businesses sponsor athletic teams, operate camping and resort facilities, stage dramatic and musical productions, provide preretirement and leisure counseling, and offer tours or special travel arrangements for their employees. In recent years, the trend has been toward the development of fitness centers and a focus on wellness. Today, it is estimated that American companies and labor organizations spend billions of dollars annually on employee recreation services.

Corporation executives, labor unions, and industrial sociologists generally agree that recreation activities contribute to worker productivity and well-being. If employee recreation and fitness programs reduce absenteeism, worker turnover, and industrial accidents, then it is a benefit to the company and a good business investment. If these services add to the life of the worker, enhance the quality of the environment, and provide opportunity for personal fulfillment, then it is profitable both to business and to the community. Some advocates of employee recreation claim it does all of this; others are less charitable in their assessment of its contribution and see it as only fun and games. Nevertheless, many workers agree that recreation is of value and should be a concern of industry (Finney, 1984).

Advocacy Organizations

Most not-for-profit organizations and agencies exist to provide a direct service for their membership. The provision of opportunities for recreation is a major reason for why some organizations exist. Some organizations, however, impact recreation and leisure through their advocacy mission. Examples include environmental organizations such as the Nature Conservancy, which purchases ecologically significant lands and holds them in escrow until those lands can be acquired by governmental organizations as parks and preserves. The National Trust for Historic Preservation operates museums and advocates the acquisition and preservation of historical areas. The National Audubon Society also offers educational programs, lecture series, and support for wildlife sanctuaries. The National Easter Seals Society with its camping program; the Joseph P. Kennedy, Jr. Foundation known for its work with people with mental retardation through Special Olympics; and the American Association of Retired Persons (AARP) that advocates for the needs and interests of the aging population all provide advocacy services. The list of not-for-profit advocacy organizations is huge and many of these organizations have a tie directly or indirectly to recreation and leisure.

Careers in Not-for-profit Recreation and Leisure Services

The not-for-profit sector, with a focus on membership interest and an ability to respond to special interest groups, is a critical element in the leisure services delivery system. The role of this sector regarding recreation and leisure has varied depending upon public attitudes, fads, leisure interests, and patterns of governmental involvement. In general, the sector has not considered itself a part of the leisure services profession even though the methods for addressing issues often involves recreation programming and policy. In addition, the benefactors of the services often receive recreation opportunities that lead to a higher quality of leisure life. The more traditional groups such as the youth-serving organizations have identified with the social welfare movement. Generally they have relied upon their own programs of professional preparation or have sought graduates with a background from one of the social or behavioral sciences as well as from among recreation majors.

Administrative staff interested in careers in not-for-profit organizations require management, fundraising, and public relations skills. These organizations also need professionals and volunteers with leadership and programming skills. Regardless of whether these not-for-profit organizations associate directly with the recreation movement, they enhance leisure in communities in a variety of ways. In the coming decade these organizations will continue to be major employers of recreation graduates as well as individuals interests in other areas of human services. Further, their identification with leisure services will likely become stronger. The role of not-for-profit organizations in delivering recreation and related services will not diminish in the near future.

Not-for-profit organizations facilitate recreation experiences for individuals in numerous ways. Some of these organizations provide direct services while others offer opportunities for people to volunteer during their free time. Most not-for-profit organizations employ paid staff to supervise and coordinate the efforts of the agency. The recreation and leisure services system in the United States would be very different if this myriad of organizations did not advocate for people's recreation and offer opportunities for involvement in a variety of ways.

Reflection Questions

1. What is the funding structure of not-for-profit organizations?

2. What are the roles of volunteers in not-for-profit organizations?

3. What has been the role in providing recreation and leisure for not-for-profit service organizations in the United States?

4. What are three distinctions between public recreation providers and not-for-profit providers?

5. Why are both public and not-for-profit recreation systems needed?

3.6   Youth Services and Leisure

Issues concerning youth have always been central in the recreation movement. As we discussed in unit two, recreation services were initiated over a
century ago largely because of a concern for youth. The social welfare movement of the late 19th and early 20th centuries served as an impetus for
recreation development in both the public and not-for-profit sectors. Sensitive philanthropists responded to the needs of urban workers by creating
agencies and services for children and youth. Although recreation was not
the central reason for the development of many of these programs, it was an
essential ingredient and has remained a major thrust for hundreds of national
youth-oriented organizations in the United States. This chapter describes
some of the meanings of recreation for youth and how various organizations
have addressed the needs and interests of youth.

The Nature of Youth Organizations

Voluntary youth-serving agencies, also known as youth services, are a major
part of the not-for-profit sector. They join with public agencies in serving
an age group that society has deemed a primary target for recreation programming. Educational groups, family life agencies, fraternal and patriotic
orders, and religious bodies have youth programs. Probably the best known
of these are the YMCA and YWCA, the Boy and Girl Scouts, Youth
Councils, Camp Fire Boys and Girls, and the Young Men's and Young
Women's Hebrew Associations.

A large proportion of the youth movement is primarily directed by
youths themselves with organizational support from public school and
public recreation agencies. Thousands of teen centers and youth-directed
programs exist throughout North America. Most of these appeal to the older
teenager, whereas the programs of the more established national organizations have a younger youth constituency.

Some organizations stress services to minority groups, the urban poor,
and youth from high-risk communities. Not-for-profit organizations such as
the Police Athletic League and the Children's Aid Society are found primarily in metropolitan areas working almost exclusively with these children.
Recreation activities are generally used as a means for preventing delinquency and enriching the lives of these young people. Recreation and leisure
activities are important to all age groups, but youth generally have an
abundance of time and energies available to pursue recreation interests.

Characteristics of Youth

Today most people take for granted what being young means in America. The idea of adolescence as a separate developmental phase of life, however, is a relatively new idea formed through the writings of philosophers beginning in the 18th century. Rousseau was one of the first thinkers and writers to influence how societies began to think about and view adolescents. His view was tempered, at least in America, by the reality that children and youth of all ages were needed to carry out the work necessary for living in an agrarian culture. With the emergence of social and school reformers in the late 19th century, the lives of children and youth in America dramatically changed.

Social reformers of this time, who included many of the early proponents of the recreation movement, were concerned about child labor as well as the reality that children and youth had nowhere to play and nothing to do. These reformers also believed in the value of structured recreational opportunities, as did educators who believed that schools should provide education and recreation. The work of the social reformers coincided with the work of educators and youth workers interested in legal reform that would require children to attend school and limit their participation in the workforce. A convergence of many issues led to how America constructed adolescence in the 20th century, including increased mechanization during the industrial revolution, separation of work and home, changes in family structure, the movement to provide children and youth with opportunities for free play and structured recreation, and the institutionalization of education for all children at the federal level (Santrock, 1990). These issues led to interest in youth development and coincided with the creation of the contemporary recreation movement in the United States.

The history of adolescence in America provides some insight into how society has viewed adolescents and how leisure services for young people have been and continue to be offered. History generally depicts young people as being largely conformist except for a few brief periods of resistance. Such conformity is reinforced through school where young people are taught to follow the rules and do what is expected of them. For example, many communities have curfews for when young people should be off the streets and convenience stores often limit the number of young people who can be in the store at one time.

In addition to tight controls over young people, society has also constructed a phrase to categorize problem youth and/or youth who are considered to be delinquent in some way. At-risk youth has permeated our national consciousness and spurred a large-scale movement of people and products to respond to this segment of the youth population. Educators, social workers, youth workers and recreation professionals have developed curricula, videos, workbooks and handbooks on how to deal with young people who have been identified as being at risk for drug abuse, teen pregnancy, violence, and generally not making a successful transition from childhood to adulthood. This focus has made youth a problem while ignoring some of the other issues that might contribute to the negative situations that young people often face. Examples of these issues that make youth a problem include poverty, inadequate educational opportunities, institutionalized racism and sexism, physical and sexual abuse, and a culture that devalues children and youth by underfunding education, after-school programs, and other government programs that can help young people (Males, 1996).

Emerging Youth Services

Because American society has tended to hold particular views toward young people, structured recreation opportunities for young people have been planned through a variety of municipal and not-for-profit organizations. Youth services such as Boys and Girls Clubs, Boy and Girl Scouts, Big Brother/ Big Sister and Camp Fire Boys and Girls focus on character education and character development among young people. Most youth-based organizations, regardless of their stated mission, tend to convey and reinforce traditional values around gender, sexuality, and other aspects of identity.

The original goal of many of youth programs was to be diversionary and give young people something positive and structured to do to get them off the streets after school. Over the years, however, these programs have changed their focus toward developmental outcomes such as physical, cognitive, and emotional growth. Thus, many youth programs during the late 1970s and early 1980s focused on building and enhancing self-esteem in young people. During the 1980s, with the downsizing of government programs, not-for-profit agencies focused more than before on programs for young people. These agencies received financial support by broadening their agency mission to focus on youth-related health promotions such as teen pregnancy prevention, drug/alcohol prevention, and some HIV/AIDS prevention education, in addition to structured recreation programs.

In the mid-1980s, after-school programs for elementary school children and some middle-school-age children began to emerge throughout the United States. Typical after-school programs offered components such as homework assistance, tutoring, free play, and structured recreation opportunities. In the 1990s, agencies began to market their programs differently to attract a wider audience. Agencies advertised by suggesting their programs promoted overall health and well-being. Personal empowerment was the goal and agencies developed new advertising campaigns and created new curricula to respond to the expanding youth market.

One of the new curricula in the 1990s centered on the idea of developmental assets. A group of youth researchers at the Search Institute in Minnesota focused on the idea that young people need to cultivate their developmental assets and that communities need to assist them in this process. According to the Search Institute, about 40 developmental assets such as honesty, good communication skills, and ethical decision-making will help young people make a successful transition from childhood to adulthood. The idea with this approach as well as others is that if recreation professionals know what structured activities might be most developmentally beneficial, they can plan and implement programs that will assist young people in reaching adulthood successfully.

As the 21st century begins, new trends emerge in regard to youth services. First, there has been an increase in the number of mentoring programs throughout the United States. Mentoring also assists young people in learning how to communicate, negotiate, and trust adults who are not part of their immediate family or school contexts. Typically, the main organization for mentoring has been Big Brothers/Big Sisters, but over the past five years more programs in municipal and other not-for-profit agencies are adding a mentoring component. Part of this trend is due to an increased interest in volunteerism. Corporations provide more leeway for employees to volunteer with community agencies and individuals find more personal satisfaction by participating in volunteer opportunities.

Second, recreation professionals working with young people have begun to include youth in the planning process and have actively sought their feedback through focus groups and/or participation on advisory or teen boards that oversee many youth programs. Heath and McLaughlin (1993) discovered that successful youth programs that had a long-term positive impact on young people's attitudes and behaviors had passionate and committed leaders and programs that integrated young people into the planning and implementation process.

Third, research in the past ten years (e.g., Hendry, 1993) has identified that leisure (along with school, family, work, and religious affiliation) is an important context for identity development and formation. The more committed and engaged a young person becomes through participation in recreation and leisure activities, the more likely that young person will be to internalize the leisure social identity associated with that activity. For example, someone who participates in sports or music might consider himself or herself to be an athlete or a musician. Such identification has been found to be a positive developmental benefit for young people who use adolescence as a period of experimentation with various identities. If program planners understand how to structure various leisure contexts so that young people will internalize the most beneficial developmental aspects, then recreation and leisure will have an important impact in the lives of young people. Recreation professionals have always believed that recreation programs and services have the potential to assist young people with becoming capable, strong, independent, and creative adults. We had little scientific proof, however, that recreation mattered. Today, with growing research evidence and more support for structured recreation and leisure opportunities for young people, recreation professionals can demonstrate an important contribution to positive youth development.

Youth services are an important component of recreation and leisure services. We must continue, however, to be mindful of some of the issues that exist. Today many parents, educators, and youth workers are concerned about overscheduling young people. Further, with the proliferation of video games, computers, and other gadgets, youth are slowly beginning to lose their ability to be spontaneous and creative. Perhaps a message has also been conveyed to youth through the provision of some programs and services that a young person cannot have recreation and leisure without the leisure services professional. Finding a balance between the need for structured services and programs and the need for young people to learn how to play on their own with one another and without the aid of high-tech devices is a challenge.

One way to support future generations of young people as they begin to use and consume various recreation and leisure contexts is to provide them with the skills necessary to become critical consumers. For example, art and photography classes might include a component that asks young people to create images of how they see themselves and how they think society sees them. Clearly, recreation and leisure contexts have an impact on the lives of young people in this country, and many questions about how successful youth services occur need to be explored.

Youth Service Organizations

Numerous ways can be used to analyze and describe the youth recreation system. Youth-serving groups can be viewed in terms of their service focus (e.g., outdoors-oriented, social service-oriented, church-oriented, educational-oriented), appeal to one sex or the other or to both, organizational structure (e.g., national affiliation, local autonomy), management approach (e.g., group work-oriented, facility-based), or leadership structure (volunteers, professional staff, adult-directed, youth-directed). The leadership factor provides the basis for grouping the following major types of youth-serving agencies currently providing recreation and leisure services into adult-directed and youth-directed.

Adult-directed Organizations

A number of youth-serving agencies have policies and organizations established by adults, programming decisions ultimately made by adults, and employed professional staff to administer the program services. These groups are the older organizations and the best known by the public. They have a general appeal, often operate their own facilities, and have a character-building focus. Some of the groups that have large memberships and visibility in the United States are described in this section.

Boys and Girls Clubs of America. The Boys and Girls Clubs of America is currently a national federation of over a thousand clubs serving over two million youth. Originally two organizations, the Boys Clubs of America and the Girls Clubs of America merged in 1990 to become the Boys and Girls Clubs of America (BGCA). The organization guides urban boys and girls in their physical, intellectual, emotional, and social development. The national organization advises individual clubs on matters pertaining to the organization, administration, and operation of the club facility. The BGCA are largely urban-oriented, offering a wide range of services including tutorial programs, family counseling, and the more conventional athletic and crafts programs.

Camp Fire Boys and Girls. Although traditionally the oldest of the organized youth programs for girls, the Camp Fire program is less well known than are its Girl Scouts and YWCA cousins. Camp Fire was established to promote the spiritual ideals of the home and stimulate the development of good health and character for girls. Camp Fire programs now have a more outdoor recreation and community service focus for both boys and girls. The name was changed and "boys" were incorporated into the name and the program in the late 1970s.

Catholic Youth Organization. Established as a national organization in 1951, the Catholic Youth Organization (CYO) emphasizes programs for Catholic youth that have social, physical, and spiritual value. The parish priest and adult volunteers provide leadership. It is designed to attract and involve young people in the life of the parish. Athletics is regarded as a basic program to achieve that end.

4-H Clubs. 4-H leadership comes primarily from Cooperative Extension Service staff employed in virtually every county in the United States through cooperative agreements between the US Department of Agriculture, the state land-grant university, and county governments. On the local and county level, volunteers provide club and event leadership. The four Hs stand for Head, Heart, Hands, and Health, and the association was founded as a self-improvement group for rural young people at the turn of the century. Today, it is no longer restricted to rural environments. Camping and social activities are as much of a part of 4-H as are horses and sewing. The 4-H program is basically a group-centered approach to youth services.

Girl Scouts of the United States of America. The largest of the voluntary organizations serving only girls, the Girl Scouts of the USA has several million members. Established in 1912, it is primarily a group-oriented program with emphasis on nature, outdoor recreation, and community service activities. Leaders are both professionals and volunteers. The organization aims through a series of developmental experiences to provide a program to make members useful, responsible citizens. Like the Boy Scouts, the Girl Scouts operate day camp and residential camp facilities sponsored by local councils or troops throughout the United States. One of the differences of this organization from other established youth organizations is its focus on what Girl Scouts call "girl planning." Although adult professionals and volunteers exert leadership, the girls themselves undertake much of the programming and planning, especially within the older troops.

Boy Scouts of America. The Boy Scouts of America, the largest organization for boys in the United States, was established in 1910. The original intent was to promote character building and citizenship training for young males through a variety of outdoor recreation and nature activities under trained, professional and volunteer leadership. Today, Boy Scouts has broadened its base and now provides urban-oriented programs and activities. Some programs and troops for older youth accept female members. It is basically a group-oriented program as opposed to a facility-based one. The program focused on preparing the scout for adult life through various outdoor living experiences and service opportunities. Basic leadership comes from parents and other interested adult volunteers, and this leadership is coordinated through the efforts of the professional scout executives.

The Ys (Young Men's/Women's Christian Association, and the Young Men's/Women's Hebrew Association). These organizations are similar but vary by location concerning structure and approach. Most are facility-based and rely heavily upon a professional staff to operate their services. They have traditionally served primarily as general youth-serving and family organizations, not as recreation agencies, although the provision of recreation services and activities is a major component of their programs. Most have some religious orientation and often address family activities as well as services to youth.

The Young Men's Christian Association (YMCA) is one of the oldest youth-serving organizations, having been established in England in the 1840s. The first US operation was in Boston in 1851. Each YMCA functions autonomously but with a strong relationship with its national council. Although YMCAs were established as Christian groups, primarily Protestant, with a restricted membership based upon one's sex and age, they no longer function in that capacity. The range of services includes educational programs, opportunities for recreation, and physical fitness and aquatic programs.

The Young Women's Christian Association (YWCA) emerged in the United States shortly after the YMCA. It was originally designed to meet the needs of young women working in urban environments. Today the YWCA is the world's largest multiracial women's movement and the major goal is the empowerment of women and the elimination of racism. The program promotes the good health, education, and social awareness of its members. YWCA facilities vary greatly from community to community but may include housing opportunities, multipurpose recreation centers, camps, and social activity areas. Both the YMCA and the YWCA regard professional leadership as essential for their success.

Apart from their strong Jewish culture component, the Young Hebrew Associations are similar in approach and structure to the YMCA and YWCA. They do not consider themselves recreation agencies, but service agencies with a strong religious component. Social group work concepts and educational concerns are traditional with these groups. A typical YMHA/YWHA operates social, cultural, and athletic programs for all age groups. Culture and performing arts activities are also stressed, as are programs for teens designed to strengthen their religious and cultural heritage. These groups are frequently associated with Jewish Community Centers.

Other Groups. A variety of other youth services sponsored by adult organizations merit mentioning. Many of these are auxiliary groups and are directed by volunteers who are members of the parent organization. Typical among them are fraternal and patriotic societies and national civic organizations. Examples are the Junior Order of Elk, the Order of DeMolay of the Masons, branch organizations of labor unions, the Junior American Red Cross, the Junior Legion of the American Legion, and the Key Club of Kiwanis International. These programs range from sponsoring a youth recognition day to actively supporting a comprehensive youth service organization. Although recreation is not the basis of these programs, it is a key element. The parent organizations have found their youth programs to be a way to promote citizenship and introduce to youth the values and benefits of the parent organization. Few, if any, of these groups employ recreation professionals to administer their youth services.

Youth-directed Groups

Some youth programs and organizations are planned and directed by youth. These groups might be a program of the community parks and recreation department, a program established by the mayor or county commission, a private community-based not-for-profit organization, or autonomous. All emphasize the self-directed aspects of the program, with youth providing their own leadership with a minimum of adult advice and supervision. They are known by a variety of names, most frequently Teen Centers and Youth Councils (Bennett, 1980). No single national federation exists for these groups. They generally operate in a church, school facility, neighborhood recreation center, their own clubhouse, or an agency facility. There may or may not be an adult advisory board and they may or may not have adult supervisors or leaders. They rely heavily upon contributions and membership fees. Their programs are varied but always with a strong social and community awareness function. They may sponsor their own radio and television shows, have their own newspapers, or operate community service programs. Youth often respond positively to the challenge of having their organizations. Adult support may be necessary to provide some continuity, but the program must reflect the interests of youth.

Organized Camping

Organized camping has focused primarily on youth over the years. Since so many young people are involved in a variety of camping opportunities, we would like to discuss camping as one particular type of youth service. This area is also growing with the number of jobs that exist in independent (i.e., private market-driven) camps as well as in not-for-profit and religious camps. More than 10,000 camps are operated in the United States and many of these camps operate year-round as well as in the traditional camping season of summer.

Like many aspects of recreation and leisure services, the organized camping movement began in the late 1800s. It has gone through several emphases ranging from an earlier concern for physical fitness and activity to a more recent concern for environmental awareness. Today, camps take many forms and offer a wide range of experiences and benefits. The American Camping Association (ACA), the professional association for people involved with organized camping, defines camping as:

> A sustained experience which provides a creative, educational opportunity in group living in the out-of-doors. It utilizes trained leadership and the resource of natural surroundings to contribute to each camper's mental, physical, social, and spiritual growth.

This definition of organized camping requires an interaction with the natural environment, but some contemporary organized camps ignore this element. Activity camps that stress the pursuit of a specific activity such as basketball, music, dance, or cheerleading camps generally do not meet the definition associated with traditional camp programs, even though the living arrangements may be similar.

Organized camping encompasses a vast array of organizational structures and programs. Sponsors can include governmental organizations, private and voluntary agencies, civic and fraternal organizations, churches and synagogues, corporations and labor unions, and private enterprise. Some camps operate for profit and others do not. Certain organized camps are only for boys and men, others are only for girls and women, while still others operate a coed system or have a family orientation. Some camps offer day camping (where the camper leaves the site to return home each evening) while others offer resident or travel camps. Some camps offer sessions that last a few days while others may offer eight-week sessions. Some camps offer trip programs or extended outdoor experiences. Some camps have programmed specifically for people without disabilities, but with the implementation of the Americans with Disabilities Act, more camps are responding to the needs of people with disabilities and focusing on inclusive camping. Concerns for access and safety are two of the aspects considered by the ACA when it offers camp accreditation.

Camps, as all forms of recreation and leisure services, depend on leadership, facilities, programs, and finances. The success of the camp program depends on the quality of its leadership. Leaders range in experience and backgrounds from high-school students who may serve as junior counselors to experienced professional camp administrators. Program emphases and camp philosophy dictate the number and characteristics of facilities desired. Effective programming involves the careful planning, execution, and evaluation of activities and experiences. The program is also a reflection of the camp philosophy and is conditioned by the camp leadership, facilities, clientele, and organizational and administrative structures. Camp programmers generally acknowledge the dynamic interaction between the camper and the environment, the need for rules and regulations, the need for opportunities to enjoy both organized and unorganized activity, and the need for personal reflection and exploration. The final element of a successful camping program is its financial structure. Most camps operate on agency appropriations, camper fees, and to some extent, grants.

Youth Services Issues

A variety of issues and concerns confront youth service organizations. Several of the programming issues were mentioned earlier in this chapter. Structural issues such as funding and duplication of services influence youth services. Funding for services comes from a variety of sources and those sources vary among groups. Further, funding often dictates the programs offered, especially when staff depend on United Way or grant funding. Providing high quality services with adequate funding, particularly for programs that are adult led, will continue to be a challenge in the future. Although some concern has been expressed about duplication of services for youth, it is unlikely that too many services will ever exist. In addition, many opportunities now exist for partnerships so that several agencies in different sectors might come together to address the needs and interests of youth.

Program viability is also a persistent issue for youth agencies, particularly traditional adult-led youth-serving organizations. The needs of families and youth are constant, but the means to address those needs and interests change. It is difficult to establish a meaningful continuity of service when the clients continually perceive themselves to be different from those who came before them. In addition, the values of the young are not necessarily in agreement with those of their parents or recreation professionals. Thus, providing programs that meet the interests of young people are always a challenge.

All trends suggest that youth service organizations are seeking a broader base of support. In addition to working with youth from high-risk communities, more attention focuses on coed recreational activities, family activities, nonathletic activities, and short-term projects and activities rather than long-term club membership. Youth are becoming more involved in planning and conducting those programs and services designed for them. The issues facing youth in the United States related to drugs, peer pressure, gang activity, and sexual behavior create the need for a continued dialogue among the many youth service providers regarding recreation and other areas of young people's lives.

Youth services offer educational and recreational opportunities to young people. Youth organizations were one of the first ways that recreation was provided to young people over a hundred years ago. In many of these youth organizations, recreation was a means of developing character in youth. The goals of those original programs are similar today with youth programs aimed at helping young people develop life skills, providing outlets for energy, and giving a supportive environment for growing up. Many professionals seeking careers in recreation become involved with youth through a variety of activities including youth organizations, public recreation programs, and organized camping.

Reflection Questions

1. What are the current trends in youth services?

2. Describe a youth who is at risk.

3. How have youth services evolved in this country?

4. How has adolescence changed historically?

5. What is the contemporary view of adolescence in America?

6. What challenges do recreation organizations face when trying to meet the needs of youth in their communities?

3.7   Leisure Services for Marginalized Groups

The recreation and leisure services profession supported from its beginning over 100 years ago that services should exist for all people. The values of recreation experiences are well-documented and the right to leisure is constitutionally guaranteed to all. Unfortunately, not all citizens have had equal opportunity to participate in recreation and leisure services. Although any label has problems, for lack of a better description we refer to groups of people who have not necessarily had the same access to opportunities as others as marginalized groups. A variety of conditions, such as limited economic resources, racial and ethnic prejudices, transportation difficulties, age and gender biases, and disability can create discrimination resulting in groups becoming marginalized and lacking access to the benefits of recreation and leisure. Professionals in leisure services recognize this situation and respond by addressing the needs and facilitating services for these groups. The focus of recreation services as we enter the 21st century must be on inclusion, social justice, and recreation for all.

Everyone in the leisure service profession has the responsibility to increase opportunities for persons with marginalized status to participate in recreational activities. Several marginalized groups are described in this chapter, but it is important to note that these descriptions by no means cover all the diverse groups that might exist in any given community nor all the barriers these individuals face. Further, although we describe each of these groups specifically, the ideal leisure service programs in the future are not necessarily those that are planned for these specific groups, but rather programs that are inclusive with many different individuals having access, support, and opportunities to play together.

People with Disabilities

People with disabilities make up approximately 17% of the US population. With the growing older adult population, this percentage will likely increase. Disability is the inability to perform one or more major life activities of self-care, range of motion, manipulation, communication, learning, working, cognitive processing, or maintaining relationships. Disability may interfere with the ability to experience leisure opportunities to the fullest extent possible.

Several misconceptions result in barriers to the development and expansion of recreation services for people with disabilities. These include beliefs that programs for people with disabilities must be provided by specially trained professionals or that only people with a particular type of disability can recreate together and have satisfying leisure experiences. Although individuals who focus on inclusion no longer support the use of the term *special recreation*, a number of specialized recreation services exist in the United States. With the passage of the Americans with Disabilities Act, the movement in recent years has been toward inclusion.

Specialized Recreation Services for People with Disabilities

Although it is a misconception that recreation services for people with disabilities can only be provided by specialized staff or segregated by disability type, some services are managed that way. These programs can be highly useful, but it is important to note that specialized programs are not sufficient as the *only* option for people with disabilities.

Many park and recreation departments offer special recreation services for people with disabilities. These programs often have a training or skill acquisition focus to help participants gain abilities deemed necessary to pursue inclusive recreation. Such programs might include wheelchair tennis clinics or ballet for people with mental retardation. Social clubs or Friday night dances are popular leisure programs often marketed to persons with a particular disability. Special recreation centers increased in existence during the 1970s and 1980s. Today, public recreation departments also employ specialists to coordinate or provide special programs at general recreation centers located within communities. Other organizations such as Special Olympics, Wheelchair Sports, and the National Sports Center for the Disabled offer recreation programs.

Special Olympics (SO) is an international program of year-round sports training and athletic competition for more than one million children and adults with mental retardation. SO began in 1968 when Eunice Kennedy Shriver organized the first international SO Games at Soldier Field in Chicago. Today, athletes from all 50 states and over 150 countries compete with those of similar ability. The intent of SO participation is for athletes to have an avenue to test their skills and be motivated to continue to grow and develop. The competition is only one benefit of participation. Athletes travel to games across town, the state, nation, or abroad. Along the way, friendships and experiences are shared.

Wheelchair Sports, USA began in 1956 to provide competitive opportunities for wheelchair users, many of whom were WWII veterans. Today, Wheelchair Sports, USA coordinates sports programs for beginner to elite wheelchair users. Approximately 30% of the members are youth ages 5–18. Elite athletes compete to qualify for events like the Paralympics or the Wheelchair Basketball Final Four.

The *National Sports Center for the Disabled (NSCD)* began with a one-time ski lesson for children who had amputations. This organization is now one of the largest programs in the world. NSCD serves thousands of people each year with lessons and competition in skiing, biking, in-line skating, horseback riding, whitewater rafting, fishing, and rock climbing. No impairment is too great in the eyes of NSCD employees and volunteers across the country.

Specialized programs serve a unique function within the total leisure service delivery system. One benefit has been to increase the presence of people with disabilities in community recreation programs. Leisure opportunities for people with disabilities have steadily increased over the past century. Specialized programs led to mainstreaming and then to goals of inclusion. The improvement, however, has not come easily. Over the past 30 years researchers have queried recreation professionals about why recreation programs are not more accessible and available. The barriers described remain relatively consistent and include money, transportation, awareness of need, and inadequately trained staff (Hayes, 1969; Devine & Kotowski, 1999). The Americans with Disabilities Act of 1990 has been the most powerful piece of federal legislation to affect recreation services for people with disabilities in the community and to address some of the problems with barriers and attitudes about special programs.

The Americans with Disabilities Act

The ADA specifies that no one shall be denied opportunities, segregated, or otherwise discriminated against based on their disabilities. Along with housing, employment, and transportation, the law specifically identifies recreation (public, not-for-profit, and private commercial) as an area of potential discrimination. Public services (state and local, such as city and county parks and recreation programs) and public accommodations (restaurants, hotels, movie theaters, museums, zoos) must assure that people with disabilities are not unnecessarily separated, omitted, or discriminated against. As a result, programs that previously separated people with disabilities from those without disabilities have had to reevaluate their services to assure equity of opportunity and establish that they are not separating solely based on disability.

The enactment of the Americans with Disabilities Act requires that agencies evaluate their facilities and services before renovating, and plan proactively about architectural changes and modifications to include people with disabilities. Architectural (human-made) and ecological (natural) barriers can pose severe restrictions to the pursuit of leisure for individuals with disabilities. Providing ramps, doors large enough to accommodate wheelchairs, and smooth, well-defined walking areas improve access. The avoidance of architectural barriers deprives no one of the recreation experience, yet it enhances the opportunity for all people, including people without disabilities as well as parents with strollers. These open design features require little or no additional cost in construction and they benefit everyone.

Many communities have major investments in recreation areas and facilities. Although many of these facilities are not barrier-free, the problem is not insurmountable. For example, many recreation programs such as arts-and-crafts classes, and card and game tournaments do not have to take place in a recreation center. Public buildings in the community that are barrier-free can be used for these programs. Proprietary feelings about facilities should not block the recreation and park department's program efforts for equal access for people with disabilities.

Inclusion

Recreation opportunities for persons with disabilities can occur in either segregated or inclusive environments. Inclusive programs provide people with disabilities with the same opportunities for involvement in meaningful and satisfying recreation and leisure experiences as afforded people without disabilities. *Inclusion* is associated with programs for people with disabilities, but it could pertain to any marginalized group that does not have equal access to recreation.

Rather than offering special programs as the only option for people with disabilities, today the trend is moving toward providing supports within all recreation programs to increase inclusive leisure opportunities. For most individuals, providing program accessibility through the elimination of the economic, physical, and social barriers reduces the need for special programs. Inclusion is more than placing people with disabilities in a group of people without disabilities. Inclusion involves social interaction as well as physical integration. Providing support expresses an acceptance of a person and their abilities and attempts to enhance participation at the individual's desired level of independence.

Professionals enhance inclusion when they look for ways to alter the environment, rather than change the person. For example, Montgomery, Maryland, County Parks and Recreation Department created Mainstream Initiative, a program that focuses on integrating rather than separating people with disabilities in recreation programs. For those participants who might have difficulty participating in activities alone, the program offers recreation buddies, volunteers participating with and assisting the person with a disability with their specific needs. As another example, The Easter Seals Society of North Carolina disbanded its segregated camp programs for people with disabilities after 25 years of operation to adopt an integrated approach. Rather than spend the money to operate a segregated camp, staff at camps across the state receive training in ways to include campers with disabilities. After training, camp staff receives further consultation from Easter Seals throughout the summer if additional assistance is needed. In addition, a registry of camps with trained staff provides referral information for families with youth with disabilities seeking summer placements.

Other exemplary inclusive programs also exist. For example, Mammoth Cave and National Park in Kentucky allows wheelchairs users or others who need aid to descend to the caves by elevator and then take a two-hour trip via a dry passageway through the gypsum and crystalline formations. In the Everglades National Park, hard-surfaced interpretive trails allow visitors to go into the park and experience the Mango groves and native wildlife. In addition, multisensory art museums and gardens stimulate more than one sense so that a visitor can fully appreciate the displays. Having fragrant flowers and plants of different textures that may be touched as well as seen addresses the needs of people with and without disabilities.

When providing accommodations to recreation and leisure services, people with disabilities should not be singled out. For example, the National Park Service observed that people with visual impairments were sometimes offended when interpretative trails were created solely for them. They did not wish to be singled out by having special attention called to their disability and they wanted the park service to treat them as they would any other segment of the population. Having both Braille and printed characters placed on the stands where people normally went to receive instruction eliminated the problem. Further, having cassette tape recordings available to all visitors at various sites reduced stigma. The information presented through these recordings was of a general informative nature beneficial to all, and did not call attention to those with visual impairments (Seven, 1979). Another example was posted on the NRPA website (www.activeparks.org). The tour path of a national monument took the stairs to the right of the entryway to reach the second floor attraction. Unfortunately the elevator was to the left. A person who required the elevator to reach the second floor had to leave the group, take the elevator, and then cross the long hallway upstairs to rejoin the group. A simple accommodation was to take the tour group up the left stairs.

Not only has the public sector responded to increase leisure opportunities for people with disabilities, but also today many private commercial services are available. Persons receiving kidney dialysis, for example, have typically been restricted from traveling due to their medical needs. Today, a person can receive dialysis while on a cruise. Resource guides are beginning to explain accommodations and access for people with disabilities seeking air travel, cruises, auto rental, and admittance to theme parks. Museums and theaters have headphones and tapes that describe the objects of art in a gallery or the movements of dancers on the stage for those with visual impairments. Ski resorts now rent pull sleds, outriggers, and monoskis (ski equipment that does not require the use of legs) for skiers with orthopedic impairments such as amputations and paralysis. Wheelchair designers have streamlined and adapted chairs to facilitate wheelchair activities such as tennis, basketball, and marathon racing. A marathon wheelchair weighs only 14 pounds as opposed to the hospital chair that weighs more than 30 pounds. A bowling ball ramp can help anyone from small children to those with temporary back problems, to continue bowling. It is a small investment for the operator, but a big benefit to the community.

The continuum of leisure opportunities for people with disabilities cannot be easily dichotomized into specialized or inclusive programs. People may be anywhere along the continuum and offering either special or inclusive may not be best. People choose and are ready for differing degrees of inclusive participation. Some people, while choosing to participate in inclusive activities, require support. Thinking about how support can be provided, and not necessarily how to provide specific activities, is key to understanding the difference between special and inclusive recreation. Choice, however, is the core of both approaches. The following story of Alex helps to demonstrate the use of both special and inclusive options:

> Alex uses both special and general leisure services. He participates on the Special Olympic basketball and softball teams. Between the two sports, he works out two nights each week all year. He has competed at the local, state, and national levels and his room at the group home displays his many medals and awards. Alex is also an active member of the community theatre. He had a role in at least one play each of the past five years. He does not read well, so to memorize his lines he uses the support of a reader. Once his lines are memorized, he needs no additional support. He also contributes to productions when he is not performing. Alex has worked the concessions, built sets, and ushered.

Alex provides an example of how choice works for a person. He chooses to compete in Special Olympics with other athletes who have mental retardation. He also chooses to contribute to his community theatre where he is included and supported so he can recreate with persons without disabilities.

The National Recreation and Park Association adopted a Position Statement on Inclusion in 1999 that was written by the National Therapeutic Recreation Society (see Table 3.7). As a sign of the growing interest in inclusive options, the National Institute on Recreation Inclusion conference began to provide information, techniques, and strategies for general and therapeutic recreation professionals to support inclusive options.

**Table 3.7a: National Therapeutic Recreation Society Position
Statement on Inclusion**

Diversity is a cornerstone of our society and culture and thus should be celebrated. Including
people with disabilities in the fabric of society strengthens the community and its individual
members. The value of inclusive leisure experiences in enhancing the quality of life for all
people, with and without disabilities, cannot be overstated. As we broaden our understanding
and acceptance for differences among people through shared leisure experiences, we
empower future generations to build a better place for all to live and thrive.

Inclusive leisure experiences encourage and enhance opportunities for people of varying
abilities to participate and interact in life's activities together with dignity. It also provides an
environment that promotes and fosters physical, social, and psychological inclusion of people
with diverse experiences and skill levels. Inclusion enhances individuals' potential for full
and active participation in leisure activities and experiences. Additionally, the benefits of
this participation may include:

• Providing positive recreation experiences to contribute to the physical, mental, social,
  emotional, and spiritual growth and development of every individual;
• Fostering peer and intergenerational relationships that allow one to share affection,
  support, companionship, and assistance; and
• Developing community support and encouraging additional changes to reflect dignity,
  self-respect and involvement within the community.

Purpose
The purpose of the National Therapeutic Recreation Society's (NTRS) Position Statement on
Inclusion is to encourage all staff in park, recreation, and leisure services to provide
opportunities in settings where people of all abilities can recreate and interact together.

This document articulates a commitment to the leisure process and the desired outcomes.
Accordingly, the NTRS Position Statement on Inclusion encompasses these broad concepts
and beliefs:

Right to Leisure
• The pursuit of leisure is a condition necessary for human dignity and well-being.
• Leisure is a part of a healthy lifestyle and a productive life.
• Every individual is entitled to the opportunity to express unique interests and pursue,
  develop, and improve talents and abilities.
• People are entitled to opportunities and services in the most inclusive setting.
• The right to choose from the full array of recreation opportunities offered in diverse settings
  and environments and requiring different levels of competency should be provided.

continued on Table 3.7b, page 240...

People of Color (Ethnic Minorities)

The United States has taken great pride in its melting pot tradition and its
ability to mold immigrants into Americans. During the 1920s, Americaniza-
tion programs were quite prevalent in most big cities, with organized recreation services playing an important socialization role. Children, for example,
were taught to play the games of their new country and to sing patriotic
songs. To a great extent, the national policy of the United States was to
discourage minority and ethnic identification. All citizens were expected to

Table 3.7b: **National Therapeutic Recreation Society Position Statement on Inclusion (continued)**

Quality of Life
• People grow and develop throughout the life span.
• Through leisure an individual gains an enhanced sense of competence and self-direction.
• A healthy leisure lifestyle can prevent illness and promote wellness.
• The social connection with one's peers plays a major role in his/her life satisfaction.
• The opportunity to choose is an important component in one's quality of life; individual choices will be respected.

Support, Assistance and Accommodations
• Inclusion is most effective when support, assistance and accommodations are provided.
• Support, assistance and accommodations can and should be responsive to people's needs and preferences.
• Support, assistance and accommodations should create a safe and fun environment, remove real and artificial barriers to participation, and maximize not only the independence but also the interdependence of the individual. People want to be self-sufficient.
• Support, assistance and accommodations may often vary and are typically individualized. Types of support, assistance and accommodations include, but are not limited to: qualified staff, adaptive equipment, alternative formats for printed or audio materials, trained volunteers, or flexibility in policies and program rules.

Barrier Removal
• Environments should be designed to encourage social interaction, "risk-taking," fun, choices and acceptance that allow for personal accomplishment in a cooperative context.
• Physical barriers should be eliminated to facilitate full participation by individuals with disabilities.
• Attitudinal barriers in all existing and future recreation services should be removed or minimized through education and training of personnel (e.g., staff, volunteers, students, and/or community at-large).

The National Recreation and Park Association is dedicated to the four inclusion concepts of:
• Right to Leisure (for all individuals)
• Quality of Life (enhancements through leisure experiences)
• Support, Assistance and Accommodations
• Barrier Removal

in all park, recreation and leisure services. Properly fostered, inclusion will happen naturally. Over time, inclusion will occur with little effort and with the priceless reward of an enlightened community. Encouraged in the right way, inclusion is the right thing to plan for, implement and celebrate.

Approved by the NRPA Board of Trustees as NRPA Policy October 1999. Available at http://www.activeparks.org

accept the same ideals as the American way of life. Regardless of one's ethnic background, the basic program of services was the same for all citizens, although the concept of "separate but equal" also existed. Racial segregation was openly accepted with public recreation and park departments in many areas of the South who essentially operated two systems: one for Whites and one for Blacks. The National Recreation Association maintained a special program, a Bureau of Colored Works, from 1919 to the early 1940s. In communities where few minorities existed, recreation services were generally not available to most citizens of color.

The enactment of the Civil Rights Act (1964) ended the dual approach of providing recreation services. With the demise of the segregated system, a variety of social changes occurred. Minority groups and people of color began to proclaim their identity and uniqueness. New criteria were applied to measure program success and effectiveness as various groups demanded more participation in the decision-making process. America became aware that its citizens were not alike and did not want to be treated alike.

By 1980 a philosophy of programs for diverse groups had become an accepted part of the public recreation mission. The success in translating the philosophy into action, however, largely depended upon the approach taken by the local community. The key to success was that community members were mobilized with a sense of ownership, partnership, and social responsibility. In many communities, recreation administrators were asked to establish unique services for minority citizens. For example, they opened Black Cultural Centers, introduced Native American programs, and hired bilingual staff. Because populations of people of color grew at a faster rate than other population groups, their concentration in the inner city encouraged the maintenance of their cultural identity. Recreation programs were often inadequate in addressing their interests. Therefore, new systems and understandings were required to serve all racial and ethnic groups adequately (Dwyer & Gobster, 1992).

As we enter the 21st century, a philosophy of inclusion is starting within many leisure service agencies. Americans are redrawing the color lines and redefining what race means. People once thought of race as black or white but today it has nuances of brown, yellow, and red. In fact, three categories of race existed in the Census data in 1980, but today there are 30 categories with eleven Hispanic subsets (Meacham, 2000). Differences are important as people seek to establish their identity. On the other hand, the ethnic differences may mean less when other social influences such as socioeconomic level, language, education, and work and leisure opportunities are considered. Although discrimination continues to exist in US society, often much more implicitly than explicitly, the law requires equal opportunity in work and leisure. Recreation providers must assure that programs provide inclusion for all racial and ethnic groups, not just because of the law but because of the influence leisure can have on social justice. Some groups may prefer to participate separately, but all recreation services offered must focus on inclusion and welcoming environments for all groups.

People Who Are Incarcerated

Recreation and leisure professionals have had a longstanding interest in providing recreation services to prevent criminal behavior, to rehabilitate people guilty of criminal behavior, and to advocate for leisure as a right of inmates. Rehabilitative recreation for persons incarcerated in the criminal justice system mirrors therapeutic recreation in many other settings. In this section, we will discuss leisure services as a preventive measure and as a basic human right for people incarcerated for criminal behavior.

Recreation professionals hold that as prevention, participation in socially acceptable forms of recreation tends to negate deviant behavior. Through participation, individuals receive positive reinforcement, develop a healthy self-image, and have less need for antisocial acts. Munson (1991) suggested that the application of an ecological approach to recreation with adjudicated youth was useful. Social ecological approaches relate to how many different community groups have a responsibility for addressing social issues (e.g., teen pregnancy is not only the focus of health providers, but also schools, recreation agencies, churches, and social workers). Further, ecological perspectives may be useful in prevention efforts. An effective prevention program requires the cooperative effort of the home, school, judicial system, and the community. Today, many programs exist to deter crime. Police basketball leagues and gang intervention programs are examples of how recreation organizations have addressed prevention.

A major controversy about recreation in correctional facilities is whether recreation should be a right or a reward. When recreation is restricted as a form of punishment, the value of leisure as a basic human right is ignored. Similarly, the use of recreation privileges as a reward reinforces the notion that leisure must be earned, and again refutes the idea that leisure is a human right. The American Correctional Association and the National Correctional Recreation Association have worked to increase awareness and acceptance of the view that recreation is a human right. The courts have upheld the view that leisure is a human right by ruling that withholding recreation is a cruel and unusual punishment and is in violation of the Eighth Amendment (Barbee & Calloway, 1979).

Thus, recreation as a right is justified for persons who are incarcerated just as it is for persons in the general society. Recreation participation allows inmates to maintain their physical and mental health and provides an avenue for choice. Since many crimes occur during "free time," finding meaningful recreation pursuits can be important in rehabilitation. For example, rather than simply providing a daily hour in the recreation yard, a Miami correctional facility initiated an opera program. Performers from the community opera troupe came into the prison and cooperated with inmates on an in-house production. The program benefited the community and the inmates (Dustin & McKenney, 1999).

People Who Are Economically Disadvantaged

During the late 1960s and early 1970s, public and not-for-profit recreation agencies implemented a variety of programs designed to improve the quality of life for the urban poor and economically disadvantaged. Many of these programs were funded by grants from the federal government as a part of its "war on poverty" effort. Unfortunately, when federal support decreased most public recreation programs for the urban poor were discontinued or dramatically reduced. The economically disadvantaged continue to be marginal participants in the "good life" enjoyed by many Americans. Their recreation behaviors have been affected by their lack of resources. A lack of understanding of their needs has negatively affected many program efforts.

Kunstler (1993) suggested that leisure services providers should take the lead in collaborative comprehensive planning to positively influence the quality of life of these persons. To accomplish this goal, she proposed that recreation, medical, and social services agencies work cooperatively to develop referral networks for identification and placement of individuals who are economically disadvantaged or homeless, and create programs to address the issues of self-esteem, illiteracy, and lack of independent living skills. Among the most successful programs for people who are economically deprived have been those that utilize the leadership within their community. Portable pools and other mobile recreation units have helped reduce some recreation facility deficiencies. Busing programs to transport large numbers of urban children and youth to municipal and county parks have also been successful.

Like other populations, great diversity exists among people with limited economic means. Some are alone while others are in family units. Some have physical, social, and/or mental disabilities and could benefit from ongoing assistance while others find themselves only in short-term crisis situations. Unfortunately, people in the United States today with lower economic means continue to be overrepresented by racial minorities, and over half of individuals in poverty are women and children (Spigner & Havitz, 1993).

Regardless of the cause, a lack of economic resources and the stigma it brings is a difficult situation. People have low social status, lack power, and are treated as if their problems are solely their fault. They also often suffer from low self-esteem, poor social skills, the inability to enjoy life, fear of intimacy, and avoidant behavior that may result in social isolation (Krinsky, 1992). Society often acts as if impoverished people do not exist and believe that by ignoring them, they will just go away. In the booming economy of the United States at the end of the 1990s, while many people became richer, many people also became poorer due to a lack of education and jobs that paid a living wage. The gap has become wider rather than narrower despite the strong economy. Recreation professionals must keep these disparities in mind when a tendency exists to make people "pay to play."

Addressing the problems of people who are economically disadvantaged will take community-wide efforts. Leisure services has no less of a role in addressing the social problems associated with homelessness than it does with other groups experiencing deprivation and unequal opportunities. Although recreation is certainly no panacea for social ills, recreation and leisure services have been used throughout history to maintain social order. Empowering people aids in the development of self-esteem, gives a sense of community, and enhances one's coping skills (Fryer & Payne, 1984). Recreation and leisure can be an important element of a social ecological approach to addressing the needs and interests of people who are economically disadvantaged.

Older Adults

Regardless of where you work or play, you will probably interact with older adults. The aging and changing ethnic composition of America's population will challenge leisure service providers in the future. Typically we think of senior citizen status beginning at 65 years. Age, however, is not the sole determinate. Many people are "old" when they reach 60, whereas others are "young" at 80 years. Physical characteristics like gray hair and wrinkles may indicate the aging process, but the mind and spirit may suggest something much different.

Older adults do not suddenly begin to participate in recreation activities focused on seniors. Rather, people tend to continue activities developed during earlier adulthood although they may become more selective in their activities over the years. Today, many older adults place a high value on productivity and work because they lived through the depression and world wars. The US population is getting older as the large number of baby boomers turn 50 years old and continue to be healthier than any generation before them.

A number of barriers influence the leisure enjoyment of older adults. Barriers frequently cited include transportation, money, lack of previous experience, lack of a companion, and scheduling conflicts. Caregiving of a spouse or being the primary caregiver of grandchildren also contributes to lessened leisure participation. Older people of color sometimes face additional factors that influence community leisure participation. For example, some economically disadvantaged minority seniors are more likely to live with family members and maintain social roles within that unit. For African Americans, Hispanics, and American Indians, the family and the church are central. Further, about 40% of older Hispanics speak only Spanish and have significantly lower education levels than other groups. American Indian elders, while holding respected social and tribal roles, are at the greatest risk of living below poverty level (Hooyman & Kiyak, 1999).

In recent years, many communities have assumed that leisure services agencies should provide organized recreation opportunities for older persons. These programs have been largely facility-oriented and are an extension of the traditional community recreation center. Centralized senior centers have become commonplace in public recreation departments. Only about 15% of older adults, however, attend community senior centers and most recreate in their own neighborhoods (National Recreation and Park Association, 1994). Given this fact, services for older adults logically should be decentralized and offered where the older adults live.

Many community recreation departments employ senior specialists to coordinate programming with older adults. Through the efforts of these employees many opportunities have developed. In addition, associations for older adults only continue to grow. For example, *Senior Games* is an Olympic-like program for persons over the age of 55. In addition to athletics events, Senior Games activities include contests in art, dance, and music in competitions held locally, regionally, and nationally. The "Ms. Senior" pageant is another national program that encourages the expressive outlets of older women. Other local programs have included spelling bees, dance contests, and holiday celebrations.

Recreation agencies are not the only providers of services to meet the interests and needs of older adults. Many other jobs exist in long-term care facilities, retirement villages, travel and tourism support, and rehabilitation programs. Agencies such as the National Council on Aging and the American Association of Retired Persons are valuable partners in increasing the quality of life of older citizens. Many recreation opportunities are offered in cooperation with other service providers in centers that address a full spectrum of needs. Combined services might include counseling, healthcare screening, legal aid, or hot meals.

Many of these programs focus on the dominant culture of active older adults. There is also a need to increase services to the wide range of older adults living in our communities, such as the people living into their 90s, frail adults, and minority seniors. Services most used by minority older adults are located in the neighborhood, provide transportation, maintain cultural integrity, have bilingual and culturally sensitive staff, and involve seniors in planning (Hooyman & Kiyak, 1999). Further, many people continue to reside in the community as their health and abilities deteriorate. Some of these people live with family members who provide assistance with daily living tasks such as dressing, eating, and money management. For those unable to stay in their homes unattended, adult day care facilities provide an option for family caregivers. Older adults attend these facilities during the day when no one is home to assist them. Adult day care facilities combine leisure with daily living assistance. These programs also give caregivers a respite from the demands of their roles.

Many other groups of people might be discussed as marginalized. The groups discussed in this chapter were selected to show how a recreation services approach that assumes everyone is alike might not be the best approach to meeting the needs of a diverse society. Inclusion, rather than special services, is the emerging trend of the field. Recreation and leisure professionals meet a great diversity of people in the programs they facilitate in communities and in institutions. As discussed in the next chapter, a variety of programs and specialized services can be offered to meet the needs of these diverse groups.

Reflection Questions

1. Define a marginalized group.

2. What is the difference between specialized and inclusive recreation?

3. What legislation has impacted leisure for persons with disabilities?

4. Justify "leisure is a right" in regard to persons incarcerated for criminal behavior.

5. Describe how you believe inclusive recreation services relates to "just recreation."

6. What are the greatest challenges to inclusion that face recreation professionals?

3.8   Therapeutic Recreation Services

As our world changes, recreation and leisure providers will continue to alter the ways services are planned and delivered. Meeting the multitude of needs and interests requires strategies to stretch our understanding and acceptance of differences. In this chapter we describe how recreation and leisure service organizations might improve leisure opportunities for marginalized groups including people with disabilities. We also address the specialized area of therapeutic recreation and how it is used as an intervention strategy to help individuals with disabilities function more fully in society.

Improving Leisure Options for Marginalized Persons

Improved technology has increased leisure options for many people. The Internet, cable TV, and home recreation equipment allow people to meet many of their leisure needs at home. Similarly, adaptations exist for computers that allow people with upper body amputations to type and people with communication disorders communicate or translate materials into their preferred language. The growth of the Internet community has opened new leisure opportunities and resources for leisure providers. Further, as advertising moves to a web-based platform, leisure service providers must assure that websites are accessible to all users. Graphics, photos, and scrolling messages add flare to a website, but can be problematic for people with disabilities. English only versions also inhibit access by non-English speaking citizens.

Attitudes can be a strong barrier to opportunity and equity. Western societies tend to place great emphasis on the appearance of things. When things are attractive and unblemished, we feel we must be doing something right. Our society tends not to value wrinkles, gray hair, sagging waistlines, distorted features, or anything that suggests any imperfections. Huge industries aid in covering up these natural processes and other industries glorify a world where these conditions do not exist. Labeling people based on one characteristic or another is problematic. Labels can lead to preconceived ideas about what a person wants, needs, or is capable of. Many of these stereotypes have led to programs that either attempt to assimilate the person into, or segregate them from, the dominant culture. Therefore, as recreation specialists in all sectors seek to attract marginalized groups to recreation activities, preexisting attitudes must be continually challenged.

Recreation programs should be based upon the behaviors and constraints of the potential participants. If people are economically disadvantaged, or if older adults cannot come to the recreation site, then recreation professionals should outreach to them. If the users do not speak English, staff interaction and instructional materials should be in their native language. By having some swimming periods available to all free of charge, while also having at the same location some swimming sessions for which there is an admission fee, recreation departments can accommodate both those who want a degree of exclusiveness and those who cannot afford such an economic luxury. A trend in the past has been to automatically reduce fees for older adults or people with disabilities. Just because an individual has a disability or is older, however, does not mean that he or she lacks economic resources.

An outreach effort may include mobile recreation units or employ roving leaders. The mobile unit concept is not new; public health and public library officials have used it for years. When used by recreation departments, it requires equipping a trailer or mobile vehicle with necessary recreation facilities and supplies. The unit may be driven to those neighborhoods lacking recreation resources, where the recreation specialist can program directly from the mobile unit to conduct art, music, and related skill classes as well as bring recreation equipment to those who do not possess it. Although the mobile unit concept has been most successful when working with economically disadvantaged groups, this concept is effective with older adults or people with disabilities who are limited because of a lack of transportation or health-related barriers.

The use of roving leaders may be programmed in conjunction with, or independent of, mobile unit schedules. This approach has been effective in working with youth from high-risk communities. These outreach workers are recreation specialists who do not have a central recreation facility that they must supervise. They go to the citizens and utilize the resources available in those neighborhoods, often developing peer education programs and working cooperatively with police and social service personnel. They are to recreation and leisure services what a visiting nurse is to public health.

Program accessibility involves both access and omission. Smith, Austin, and Kennedy (2001) explained that most barriers to recreation participation for people with disabilities result from professional actions that encourage exclusion, often because of professional insensitivity. This statement also might be made for other marginalized groups. For example, by using only written advertisements for programs, persons with visual impairments are omitted. Likewise, when programs are scheduled some distance from residential areas, transportation problems are created for participants who may be economically disadvantaged. Without realizing it, the location of programs and financial policies become a great barrier. One of the reasons leisure service agencies may not see marginalized individuals in their programs is because they have not made their programs accessible to them. Accessibility involves more than just physical access.

Sensitive leadership is the key to successful programming for all people. Able-bodied, college graduates with middle-class value orientations staff many leisure services and tend to program for people like themselves. Consequently, potential participants who want activities more akin to their own interests and traditions have not accepted many program offerings. This is particularly true when people who are economically disadvantaged also happen to be members of an ethnic or racial minority group. Professionals must be sensitive to differences and be able to effect positive programs and approaches to services.

When a leisure service organization embarks on a program to make their services inclusive and available to all, questions of individual choice, program philosophy, and staffing arise. Some people choose to participate in activities specific to their group membership, such as Chinese New Year or Saint Patrick's Day. People who are not identified members of the group are not excluded, but at these events the predominate cultural perspective is that of the typically marginalized group. Fortunately, leisure services can facilitate equal opportunities in recreation for all individuals when a clear philosophy of choice underlying services, facilities, and staff exists. In some cases specialists are needed, but in other cases a recreation staff member can be trained to work with individuals who might be considered marginalized by society. Successful programming requires sensitivity to people's interests, removal of barriers that prohibit them from participation, and cooperative strategies that increase choice and opportunity for full living.

Goals of Therapeutic Recreation

All recreation and leisure can be therapeutic. When you think about the benefits obtained from leisure and recreation in general, one might wonder why one group of recreation specialists claims the right to therapeutic gains. Some people, however, are unable to access the opportunities or need support to gain the most from these activities. In addition, not all activities provide the same benefits. Therapeutic recreation, sometimes called recreation therapy, is a process where activities and experiences are chosen and implemented toward a specific, purposeful goal. Therapeutic recreation may occur in public agencies in communities, not-for-profit agencies and hospitals, and in private businesses and clinical settings.

Therapeutic recreation services involve the use of recreational activities, education, and personal support to enhance the lives of people. Services may support the improvement or maintenance of functional daily living skills, social skill development, or health and wellness. Professionals involved in offering recreation therapy attempt to modify or reinforce behaviors through recreation and play experiences.

The goals addressed in therapeutic recreation are as varied as the participants or clients involved. Goals depend upon the philosophy and function of the agency and the importance of these goals to individual needs and desires. The therapeutic recreation specialist must assume a variety of roles to carry out each of these tasks effectively. These goals usually address the four domains of function: cognitive, social, emotional, and physical.

An outing to the mall is an example of how these goals might be reached. Goals for the outing could be cognitive, such as to successfully count out and pay for a purchased item with cash. A physical goal might be to maneuver one's wheelchair through the mall. A social goal might be reached in cooperating with others in deciding where to eat lunch. An emotional goal might be to cope with a stressful situation if incurred while at the mall. Further, goals generally relate to enhancing functioning in life or leisure skills, increasing personal choice, gaining control over one's own life and community membership, and the maintenance or improvement of optimal health and quality of life. Goals for the prevention of illness and the promotion of health are seeing a resurgence of interest within the therapeutic recreation area (Austin, 1998; Wilhite, Keller & Caldwell, 1999).

Therapeutic recreation started as diversional recreation programming for children in pediatric units of hospitals in the 1920s. In the late 1940s providers of therapeutic recreation type services united through organizations such as the American Recreation Society and the National Association of Recreation Therapists to advance the field, especially after men returned from the war with many different types of disabilities. Today, the National Therapeutic Recreation Society (NTRS) and the American Therapeutic Recreation Association (ATRA) are the primary professional organizations supporting therapeutic recreation specialists. To become a certified therapeutic recreation specialist (CTRS), you must successfully complete certain educational requirements, including a supervised internship under a certified therapist, and pass the therapeutic recreation certification examination.

The Scope of Therapeutic Recreation

The CTRS wears many hats depending on the needs of the individual and the mission of the employing agency. The CTRS educates by assisting individuals in increasing their knowledge about leisure options, personal interests, barriers, needs, resources, and/or acquisition of functional skills. The CTRS may also facilitate recreation experiences conducive to the individual making choices, applying knowledge, or practicing newly acquired skills. A growing task of the CTRS is to intervene with the real world of the individual by providing education, securing resources, being a communication link to leisure providers, or serving as a liaison between an individual attempting to integrate and the community.

Some assumptions exist about therapeutic recreation. First, individuals needing therapeutic recreation services generally have some barrier (i.e., physical, mental, emotional, or social) to life fulfillment. Second, the individual population addressed through therapeutic recreation is not homogeneous. A variety of impairments, levels of functioning, and needs for intervention exist. Although most therapeutic recreation specialists work with people with disabilities, services might also be appropriate for people confronting life-span transitions such as divorce or retirement, or as a preventive intervention for persons who are workaholics. Peterson and Stumbo (2000) suggested:

> Most individuals experience barriers to full and satisfying leisure. For example, some individuals may view leisure as wasteful; some may not know how to access information about leisure opportunities; some may lack skills in meeting new people or establishing meaningful relationships. (p. 83)

Just as individuals vary, so do settings where therapeutic recreation occurs. Changes in healthcare such as reduced length of stay in hospitals and emphasis on services in the community result in more jobs for therapeutic recreation specialists outside of traditional hospital settings. Therapeutic recreation occurring outside hospital settings is not new. Meyer wrote in 1977 about the origins of therapeutic recreation services and argued that therapeutic recreation had little to do with the setting in which it was practiced. He suggested that therapeutic recreation is clinical by nature and therapeutic in intent. A recreation therapist in the community recreation center providing a program for postcardiac patients to assist them with their recovery to health is just as much therapeutic recreation service as is the recreation therapist leading an anger management group in psychiatric hospital. The majority of certified therapeutic recreation specialists, nevertheless, work in hospital type settings (45%). However, one of the fastest growing areas of employment (where 18% of the jobs exist) is with older adults in long-term care and skilled nursing facilities. Other CTRS's work in residential centers, community agencies, schools, corrections, and other treatment type programs and agencies (Connolly & Finegan, 1996).

Inpatient facilities in hospitals, rehabilitation centers, healthcare centers, and correctional institutions exist because community services do not meet the needs of people with disabilities. In these facilities and settings, the CTRS works as a member of a team as recognized by accrediting bodies such as the Commission on Accreditation of Rehabilitation Facilities (CARF) or the Joint Commission on Accreditation of Healthcare Organizations (JCAHO). Team members include doctors, nurses, physical therapists, occupational therapists, social workers, and nutritionists. Together these professionals provide a wide range of both group and individual interventions that address the functioning of the individual.

Most people do not reside in an inpatient setting. Less than five percent of the population resides in an institution at any given time. Thus, many persons are receiving therapeutic recreation services in agencies based in the community. These agencies include local mental health centers, outpatient clinics, municipal recreation departments, schools, and home-based care providers. The CTRS may work collaboratively with school personnel, family members, or providers of generic leisure services.

Therapeutic Recreation Processes

Therapeutic recreation is more than a place or an individual profile—it is a *process* of working with an individual to determine strategies for accomplishing goals. Therapeutic recreation specialists assess individual needs and desires, design individualized treatment plans, implement plans using various techniques and activities, and evaluate and monitor progress to document efficacy of services and readiness for discharge.

The first step in the therapeutic recreation process is to assess the strengths, needs, behavior, desires, social support, and resources of the individual. Assessment may concentrate on functioning abilities in physical, social, emotional, and cognitive domains, or on leisure skills. This information is gained through interviews with the individual, caregivers, or other medical providers or standardized evaluations used to ascertain abilities specific to a particular skill area.

Based on the data collected through assessment, the CTRS and the individual develop mutually agreed upon goals and strategies to accomplish the goals. Goals are outcome-oriented and a variety of activities may be selected to address those goals. Goal development with the individual is central to therapeutic recreation. When the CTRS does not include the individual in setting goals and planning a strategy, it is easy for the individual to consider the activity as diversion and not understand the therapeutic benefit of the experience.

Using the established plan, the CTRS may then employ a multitude of techniques or activities to accomplish goals. She or he selects activities based on the individual strengths and interests of the individual. A few of the prevalent techniques include relaxation skills, assertiveness training, physical activity, preoperative play, animal-assisted therapy, educational groups, aquatics, and community outings.

Leisure education is one of the components of therapeutic recreation services initiated to facilitate a person's discharge and transition back home. It exists in the majority of therapeutic recreation programs (Bedini, 1990).

Within the framework of therapeutic recreation services, leisure education includes helping individuals increase their leisure awareness, identifying leisure attitudes and values, developing decision-making and problem-solving skills, and becoming knowledgeable of the leisure resources of the community.

Accountability is vital in therapeutic recreation services. The CTRS documents the individual's progress toward the established measurable goals. Documentation is monitored to determine the effectiveness of the intervention, efficiency of services, and appropriateness of goals to meet individual needs. Monitoring can result in interventions being altered, continued, or terminated.

All recreation can have benefits. Therapeutic recreation is the use of the inherent and structured benefits of a recreation activity to address functional deficits. The predetermined goals and the individual interests and abilities direct what activities are chosen to ultimately increase a person's quality of life. Both community and facility-based recreation activities are necessary to provide a full range of options for people who may have a variety of physical, social, mental, or cognitive disadvantages.

Reflection Questions

1. How can professionals increase leisure options for people with various differences?

2. Define therapeutic recreation. How is this approach different from special recreation?

3. Where do therapeutic recreation services occur?

4. What are the goals of therapeutic recreation? How are they applied in practice?

5. How is a therapeutic recreation professional similar to or different from any other recreation professional?

3.9   Commercial Recreation

Commercial recreation is booming in the private sector with new markets, services, and products appearing constantly. In 1990 consumers in the United States spent $282 billion on recreation—about 7% of total personal consumption. By 1996 these figures had risen to $431 billion—over 8% of total personal consumption (US Bureau of the Census, 1999).

Commercial recreation is market-driven. Unlike the public and not-for-profit sectors, the mission of a private commercial recreation business or enterprise is explicitly to generate a desired rate of profit. Commercial recreation also has a bit of a split personality. Owners of and investors in commercial recreation enterprises do not often identify themselves with the leisure and recreation profession. Instead, they see themselves as business people who provide goods and services to customers at prices determined by market factors. Owners and investors often have business backgrounds, attend their own specialized trade meetings, read specialized trade publications, and evaluate the performance of their enterprises using criteria like rate of return on investments, market growth potential, and profit margins. Many front-line commercial recreation employees, however, see themselves as leisure and recreation professionals who provide goods and services that people want during leisure. The goal of commercial recreation employees is happy, satisfied customers who will come back again and tell friends about their good experience. Commercial recreation employees have a variety of backgrounds, including recreation and leisure studies, hotel and hospitality management, business, and on-the-job experience. Some have college degrees, but many do not. Many part-time jobs also exist in commercial recreation businesses in local communities.

The Structure of Commercial Recreation

Commercial recreation is a collection of industries that provides a wide range of recreation, entertainment, or amusement services. Commercial recreation enterprises vary in size from local mom-and-pop enterprises to huge multinational corporations (Crossley, 1990). Commercial recreation includes amusement and theme parks, professional sports, show business (e.g., movies, TV, theater), the tourist industry, manufacturers of recreation apparel and equipment, health spas and sports clubs, and elements of the transportation and food industries.

To describe and classify the components of commercial recreation, Bullaro and Edginton (1986) developed a scheme with five service domains: entertainment services, natural environment-based services, retail outlets, hospitality and food services, and travel and tourism services. Examples of businesses in each of these domains are shown in Table 3.9. Although this classification scheme is helpful in illustrating the scope of commercial recreation, these five service domains are not mutually exclusive. When people go to see a movie, for example, they may also often have dinner at a restaurant. Tourists patronize local businesses and not just travel and tourism businesses. Tourism provides a good example of the overlap not just of the five service domains in the commercial recreation sector, but also the overlap of commercial recreation with other sectors of the leisure and recreation industry (Gunn, 1988). Not all tourist enterprises are commercial. Many components of tourist services (e.g., parks, campgrounds, historical sites, cultural facilities) are provided by the public and not-for-profit sectors. The following sections discuss four of the five service domains. Travel and tourism services are discussed in the next chapter.

Entertainment Services

Entertainment services intend primarily to entertain or amuse people and include amusement and theme parks, special events, and spectator sports. Among organizations serving professionals in this service domain are the

---

Table 3.9:   Commercial Recreation Classification Scheme (Illustrative List)

Entertainment Services
Amusement/Theme parks
Bowling alleys
Carnivals
Circuses
Entertainment bureaus
Movie theaters
Nightclubs
Pool parlors
Professional athletics
Racetracks (e.g., horse, dog, auto)
Rodeos
Special events and festivals
Ticket agencies
Waterparks

Natural Environment-based Services
Beach/Waterfront
Campgrounds
Hunting preserves
Liveries
Marinas
Resident camps
Ski resorts
Zoo/Aquarium/Wildlife parks

Retail Outlets

Products:
Catalog showrooms
Full-line discount stores
Home shopping network
Specialty stores (e.g, recreational vehicles, athletic equipment, specialized boutiques, video rentals)
Shopping malls
Variety/Department stores

Services:
Aquatic center
Dance studios
Equestrian centers
Fitness clubs
Golf clubs
Ice rinks
Racquet clubs
Roller rinks

Hospitality and Food Services
Catering services
Convention centers
Guest houses/Inns
Hotels
Motels
Resorts
Restaurants

Travel and Tourism Services
Airlines
Tour promoters/operators
Tour boats (cruises)
Tour buses
Travel agencies

Adapted from Bullaro and Edginton (1986)

International Association of Amusement Parks, the International Association of Fairs and Expositions, and the North American Society for Sports Management.

Amusement parks began in England in the late 1800s and appeared in the United States shortly thereafter (Kasson, 1978; Snow, 1984; Wilson & Wilson, 1994). Coney Island was among the earliest amusement parks in the United States. To stimulate both sensory and psychological pleasures, they featured lights, moving objects, rides, and games of competition. By 1950, however, most amusement parks were in disrepair, suffered from poor public images, and faced financial difficulties.

The amusement park industry was revitalized in 1956 when Disneyland, America's first theme park, opened in Anaheim, CA. Careful planning of the physical and interior layout of the park and its component parts created a specific atmosphere. Even the dress and attitude of employees reflected the park's theme. Theme parks are successful because they offer more than amusement. They invite guests of all ages to escape by immersing themselves in the fantasy. Amusement and theme parks are enormously popular. In 1997 almost 111.5 million people, 57 percent of the population, went to US amusement parks, spending approximately $7 billion (US Bureau of the Census, 1999).

Theme and amusement park developers apply the concept of *clustering* to increase the attractiveness of their facilities. Developers encourage rather than discourage adjacent recreation developments. With a variety of opportunities available to them, visitors are more likely to prolong their stays in an area or to return for repeat visits, in both cases increasing the amount of spending they do. The theory behind clustering is that the more opportunities that are available, the more the customer is stimulated and drawn into the experience. When these opportunities are multidimensional and supported by attractive food service and accommodations, return visits are more likely. Clustering requires thorough planning and close cooperation, especially between the public and commercial sectors. The many successful examples of the clustering technique include Orlando, FL, Branson, MO, and Myrtle Beach, SC where many entertainment services exist in close proximity to each other. The clustering technique is thus also applied in the development of recreation, entertainment, and shopping zones in cities, often as part of redevelopment projects. Harbor Place in Baltimore, MD, Waterside in Norfolk, VA, and the Riverwalk in San Antonio, TX are examples.

Special events are a second major category in the entertainment services domain of commercial recreation. Thousands of special events occur annually in many forms and sizes. For example, even though the United States has become urbanized and suburbanized, people still enjoy activities like agricultural fairs, rodeos, and folk festivals. In Michigan, often perceived as an industrialized urban state, there are over 50 agricultural festivals each year celebrating everything from asparagus to blueberries to tulips. Special events create a sense of excitement and opportunity among visitors and local residents alike. Some of the more famous and largest annual special events include New Year's Eve in Times Square, Mardi Gras in New Orleans, the Kentucky Derby in Louisville, and the Indianapolis 500. Many small towns across the country also have 4th of July celebrations, street fairs, and arts-and-crafts festivals.

Special events are promoted in many ways. Some communities package their natural resources in combination with special interests, like the Strand Festival held in Galveston, TX, which combines its beaches with a literary festival. Other communities capitalize on folk themes. Spivey's Corner, NC (population 200) is internationally known for its annual Hollerin' Contest. Thousands of people congregate each June in Spivey's Corner for a week-end of hollering, folk dancing, and socializing.

Spectator events make up a third major category in the entertainment services domain. Despite some fluctuations due to labor disputes or changing tastes, spectator sports have enjoyed an extended period of growth. Professional sports receipts in 1997 were $10 billion (US Bureau of the Census, 1999). Also included in the spectator events category are circuses, traveling shows, and various theatrical or musical productions. These particular events had 1997 receipts of $22 billion. In 1997 people attended jazz concerts (12 million), classical music (16 million) and opera performances (5 million), musicals (25 million), plays (16 million), and ballet performances (6 million). Leisure and recreation professionals are more often prepared to program for participation rather than spectating, but some spectator event businesses employ them to assist with marketing, scheduling, and event management.

Natural Environment-based Recreation Services

Although many people associate outdoor recreation with the public sector, natural environment-based recreation services are a major component of the commercial recreation sector. Commercial campground operators provide over half of all campsites in North America. For example, Kampgrounds of America (KOA) began business in 1964 and operated over 700 franchises over the years (US Department of Commerce, 1985). In 1997 over 47 million camped, 9 million downhill skied, 2.5 million cross-country skied, 12 million went backpacking, and 16 million owned some type of recreational boat (US Bureau of the Census, 1999). All these people spent money in some way, whether on entry fees for private land or facilities, equipment and supplies, equipment maintenance, or guide and outfitting services. The sheer scale of natural environment-based recreation makes commercial recreation services attractive. Growth areas such as rock climbing, hang gliding, and wind surfing include needs for specialized equipment, knowledge, skills, and instruction. Commercial recreation enterprises are often better positioned to provide these services than are the public or not-for-profit sectors.

Retail Outlets

Retail outlets sell products and services directly to customers. The volume of sales related to leisure and recreation is astounding. For example, in 1997 consumers spent $64 billion on sporting goods (US Bureau of the Census, 1999). In 1996 people bought $90 billion worth of recreational video, audio, musical, and computer equipment and spent $50 billion on books, magazines, maps, newspapers, and sheet music.

Products. One important tie between retail sales and recreation is suggested by the proliferation of shopping malls. Retail shopping has become a recreation activity. Malls are designed to make visiting them seem less like a shopping trip and more like an excursion. Larger malls sometimes even hire special event planners or coordinators, including recreation and leisure professionals. Malls often provide performance space and facilities for concerts, art exhibits, craft shows, fashion shows, and dramatic productions. Such diversions not only draw people to the malls in the first place, but also encourage customers to stay longer. Children's entertainment is provided to encourage parents to shop there. Some malls offer free rides for smaller children and amusement arcades with video games attract older kids. Coffee shops and specialty food vendors attempt to re-create a sidewalk café environment within malls where shoppers can relax. Open-air markets, farmers' markets, and even flea markets use some of the same techniques to attract customers. These are all places people go in their free time—sometimes buying and sometimes not—just to watch others, visit with friends, and absorb the atmosphere.

There are over 35,000 malls in the United States and Canada. Some are constructed around a theme while others are simply a collection of shops. Recently shopping areas have been developed in renovated mills and warehouses like The Cannery and Ghiradelli Square in San Francisco. At the center of Old Chicago there is a seven-acre park with nearly three dozen major rides. Quincy Market in Boston attracts more than 10 million visitors annually and combines shopping and entertainment featuring street musicians and artists. The largest malls have actually become tourist destinations. The huge West Edmonton Mall in Alberta, Canada is a city within a city. It includes a diverse range of recreation attractions including a water area large enough to accommodate scuba diving, submarine rides, and wind surfing. It also offers ice rinks, a roller coaster, and several hotels. The Mall of America outside Minneapolis is nearly as large, and offers a similar array of recreation possibilities.

Another tie with sales is the link retailers provide in connecting merchandise and recreation activities. Salespeople have always advised customers on appropriate equipment and its proper uses. Now, however, retailers often sponsor workshops and demonstrations to educate existing and potential customers about specific recreation activities. Some retailers, particularly larger ones, now provide recreation activities as well as merchandise, offering everything from weekend excursions to major expeditions. Recreation Equipment, Inc. (REI) provides seminars and workshops as well as merchandise at its locations around the country.

Recreation sales volume grew from $48 billion in 1990 to an estimated $67 billion in 1998. Recreation and sporting goods consistently make up 2.5 percent of total retail sales (US Bureau of the Census, 1999). Caution is necessary when interpreting these figures, however. For example, although fewer than half of those people who purchase jogging shoes *participate* in jogging, not everyone who bought jogging shoes *intended* to use them for jogging. On the other hand, people who buy bicycles or weightlifting equipment probably *intend* to ride or lift, but only 52% of bicycle owners and 49% of those who bought weightlifting equipment *actually used it* at least once a year (Brooks, 1988). These sales figures do, however, tell us about discretionary spending patterns and suggest how shopping has become a recreational activity. Some specialized retail outlets employ skilled recreationists to sell merchandise since the availability of expert advice is an incentive to buy from such retailers. Other retailers, particularly mass merchandisers, use pricing to attract customers. Organizations as the National Sporting Goods Association and the American Recreation Equipment Association provide important information and support to such retailers.

Services. Service providers are perhaps more commonly associated with the recreation industry than are retail outlets. Examples of commercial recreation service providers are aquatic centers, bowling lanes, racquet sports complexes, aerobic dance studios, video arcades, and billiard parlors. Commercial recreation businesses increased their market shares during the 1970s and 1980s by utilizing a variety of marketing strategies (Warnick & Howard, 1990). Commercial recreation enterprises are vulnerable to changing market conditions, however. Long-term viability depends on distinguishing fads and long-lasting trends, and responding accordingly.

Conventional wisdom held, for example, that the 1980s fitness boom would increase through the 1990s and into the new century. Participation data are tricky, however, when used to predict market trends, and there is now considerable evidence that fitness activities have not necessarily increased. Baby boomers who exercised regularly in their 20s and 30s have begun to turn 50. Their preferences seem to be changing toward buying home exercise equipment, which they may or may not use, and walking instead of working out at fitness centers or jogging. Exercise walking is participated in more often than any other sport activities (US Bureau of the Census, 1999). The numbers of participants in both tennis (19.5 million in 1997) and jogging (22 million in 1997) appear to be increasing somewhat. Again, caution is necessary in comparing these figures because of differences in measurement procedures and because aggregate totals tell us very little about frequency of participation (i.e., whether individuals participate once a year or once a month).

Commercial recreation enterprises can implement several strategies to adjust to changing market conditions, but no substitute exists for good marketing data. The key is to understand the motives that determine individual recreation and leisure behaviors and the forces that modify them. A wide range of information sources are available to help with this, including government agencies, universities, general trade and business groups, and industry-specific organizations like the International Racquet Sport Association and the National Golf Foundation.

Hospitality and Food Services

Private commercial recreation enterprises provide lodging, food, and other services to local community residents as well as travelers. Between 1985 and 1997, the number of pleasure trips taken in the United States increased from 301 million to 443 million, and the number of vacation trips increased from 264 million to 389 million (US Bureau of the Census, 1999).

Resort communities have become a major component of the commercial recreation domain. Frequently planned around activity clusters (e.g., performing arts, gambling, the visual arts, skiing, golf, tennis), resorts try to provide a total recreation experience. Resort communities have a dual nature—home for permanent residents and travel destination for temporary residents and tourists. Two types of recreation and leisure professionals are thus often found in resort communities: those professionals who provide services for the permanent residents of the community, and those professionals who work with temporary residents and tourists. Ideally, all recreation and leisure professionals work together to plan and utilize a community's resources effectively.

Resort communities are not all developed along the same pattern. Some feature different complexes while others are single communities. For example, there are an estimated 1,300 ski communities in the United States and Canada. To cope with the effects of seasonality, many of these areas serve as conference centers or develop golf and tennis facilities to attract year-round business. The Resort and Commercial Recreation Association and Council on Hotel, Restaurant, and Institutional Education give leadership to the growing number of recreation professionals employed in this commercial recreation domain.

Another hospitality/resort business that has enjoyed much success recently is the cruise ship industry. Its popularity can be traced to a variety of factors including nostalgia, strong marketing, and favorable sociodemographic trends (e.g., more single professionals, more double-income married couples, a rising number of healthy and affluent senior citizens). Cruise ships provide millions of passengers with experiences as varied as traveling the Mississippi on paddle wheelers, island hopping in the Caribbean on luxury liners, and scenic and educational tours along the coasts of British Columbia and Alaska. Two trade groups serving the professional in this industry include the Cruise Line International Association and the International Passenger Ship Association.

Issues Surrounding Commercial Recreation

Commercial recreation professionals differ from their public sector counterparts with respect to organizational motives (Yoshioka, 1990), job characteristics (Yen & McKinney, 1992), and work motivators (Lankford, Neal & Buxton, 1992). Studies reveal that many participants perceive differences both between the type of services and facilities offered by public sector and commercial sector enterprises and between the people employed in the two sectors (Havitz, 1989; Bogle, Havitz & Dimanche, 1992). Commercial recreation professionals see the world differently from their public sector counterparts, as do their customers. The private commercial recreation sector is, for example, regarded as more responsive to changing market conditions than is the public sector. This and other differences raise problems for those wishing to unify all sectors of recreation and leisure services.

Commercial recreation enterprises and businesses enjoy significant advantages in developing projects that require large capital investments and expose owners and investors to financial risks. Commercial recreation professionals often embrace new technologies for their recreation and market potentials. In some instances, the technologies become the experience. Walt Disney's EPCOT Center (Experimental Prototype Community of Tomorrow) is a classic example of technology as a recreational attraction. The public sector is simply unable to respond to market potential as rapidly and decisively as did Disney.

Safety and legal issues form another significant difference between commercial and other sectors providing recreation and leisure opportunities. Commercial recreation operators generally push risk boundaries more than their public and not-for-profit sector counterparts. They treat leisure and recreation as ends rather than as means toward desirable policy and social outcomes, though these goals are not necessarily mutually exclusive. With their focus on profit margins, commercial recreation enterprises may regard as acceptable some activities like drinking or gambling that are regarded as unsuitable for public sector agencies. The ability to exploit market opportunities characterizes the history of commercial recreation (Cross, 1990; Butsch, 1990).

The three sectors of the recreation and leisure industry have different missions. Public and not-for-profit recreation agencies emerged to meet specific social needs. Most public and not-for-profit recreation professionals continue to believe that even if market-based approaches to the delivery of recreation and leisure services must be implemented, these services must nonetheless be intended to be socially and environmentally beneficial. Public recreation professionals are accountable to elected officials and ultimately to citizens. Public professionals also operate under the scrutiny of the media, appear at public hearings, respond to citizen advisory boards, and comply with requirements for open meetings. The commercial recreation sector, on the other hand, faces none of this external oversight. These professionals and employees receive much less pressure to consider the social and environmental consequences of their programs, goods, and services. Many commercial recreation operators consider themselves less obligated to educate and inform customers than to "give them exactly what they want." Retailers of jet skis, snow machines, and all terrain vehicles, for example, quite likely have different views on the value of those products than public employees charged with preserving both natural resources and the civil peace. Just because a product *can* be sold or used does not mean it *should* be.

Unlike the public and not-for-profit sectors, commercial recreation providers have less responsibility to serve underrepresented or disadvantaged members of the community. Commercial recreation providers target not just the 5% of a community's population who play racquetball, the 10% who play golf, or the 30% who swim, they target those segments of racquetball players, golfers, and swimmers who are *willing* and *able* to pay for related goods and services. The bottom line is that private commercial recreation enterprises generally must be concerned with profit margins.

Many jobs exist in the private commercial recreation sector. This area is growing rapidly, and knowledgeable and socially responsible professionals are needed for these businesses. The market-driven mission of most commercial recreation providers is different from the mission of the public or not-for-profit sectors that focus on social services. All sectors, however, have a role to play in providing a variety of recreation and leisure opportunities for people in communities. Their relationship must be complementary, not competitive.

Reflection Questions

1. What are the classifications of commercial recreation? List three examples of each.

2. What are the primary missions of commercial recreation, public recreation, and not-for-profit recreation?

3. What are some advantages and disadvantages of commercial recreation growth in a community?

4. What types of recreation services and products do commercial recreation enterprises have advantages in providing?

5. What reasons can you give for *including* retail sales of leisure goods and services as part of the recreation and leisure profession? What reasons can you give for *excluding* them?

6. Illustrate a significant issue facing private commercial recreation providers and present your ideas on how it could be addressed.

3.10   Sustainable Tourism

As an area of study within the field of recreation and as a specific aspect of commercial recreation, tourism is a newcomer. Prior to 1980 you likely would not have found a chapter or even a section that dealt exclusively with "travel and tourism" in a text on recreation. Like therapeutic recreation or youth services, today tourism is recognized as a vital element of the leisure service delivery system and a specialty within the profession.

The previous chapter described the broad field of commercial recreation and some of the ways that tourism is one aspect of private commercial recreation. This chapter focuses more specifically on tourism and travel services and describes how tourism can be sustainable and compatible with social and environmental issues.

Descriptions of Tourism

The field of tourism, with its many facets, is difficult to define. Several university departments across the United States have a title like Department of Recreation, Parks, and Tourism Management. Some professionals argue that tourism should be an area of study in business because it is a collection of industries. Others see it as a part of the hospitality field. Some people view tourism as a profession in its own right. The way that tourism is defined is debatable, but no doubt exists that tourism is a growth industry tied to recreation behaviors and interests.

Travel for trade and religious purposes dates back to ancient times, yet tourism is a modern industry—perhaps the most dominant form of commercial recreation behavior. Its growth as a major economic force and as a leisure interest for millions is due to both technological advances and affluence. Tourism is also an outgrowth of the people's desire to see other cultures, visit other environments, and have new and different experiences away from their everyday routines. These reasons have motivated pleasure travel for generations, but only in the last 100 years has tourism become fashionable enough to warrant a system to accommodate it.

Tourist behavior ranges from trips to the beach to sunbathe and shop to trips to Antarctica to study its fragile ecosystem. Tourism involves traveling to an outdoor destination to ski, swim, or hike, but it can also mean taking a trip to Las Vegas to gamble, to New York to attend a Broadway play, or to London to sightsee and shop at Harrods. Tourism may mean visiting friends or relatives or taking a sightseeing trip to Busch Gardens or to the Grand Canyon. Given its complexity, most professionals tend to define it by its characteristics or elements rather than offering a single description. The elements most frequently mentioned are distance traveled, motives of travel, and the time required for the visit.

The first characteristic of tourism generally involves a distance traveled. Definitions of a tourist based on the distance traveled vary. The United Nations definition requires one to cross an international border, while the US Census Bureau defines a trip as traveling one hundred miles away from home. Both definitions are problematic. For example, skiers traveling from Denver to many of the Colorado ski resorts would go less than a hundred miles, but their behavior and impact on the local economy would be similar to those skiers coming from points several hundred miles away. On the other hand, it is highly unlikely that the residents of Juarez, Mexico, feel as if they are tourists when they cross the border each morning to work in El Paso, Texas.

The second characteristic is the reason for the trip. The US Travel Data Center includes in its definition all motives for travel except those related to commuting to and from work, school-related travel, or travel involved in operating a transportation vehicle such as plane or train. All the motives cited for other forms of recreation hold true with travel and tourism. Tourism is stimulated by a desire to learn, to experience, and to have new adventures. Travel is encouraged by the mass media, popular literature, and a perception of high status. Given the opportunity to travel, people generally do. When they do not, typical reasons include the costs involved, a lack of free time, health limitations, fear and safety factors, or family situations.

The final consideration is the length of time one stays away from home while traveling. Most definitions of tourism include a time frame, such as the UN's definition that requires a stay of at least 24 hours. Such a restriction, however, would eliminate many day trips in excess of a hundred miles for recreational purposes. In these day trips, the traveler exhibits the characteristics of a tourist. Consequently, most students of travel and tourism are less concerned about the duration of the trip than the motives and distance traveled.

Given these parameters, one could define a tourist as an individual who travels to a destination for recreation purposes. This definition allows the business traveler to become a tourist when that portion of the travel is recreational rather than work required. All tourists are travelers, but not all travelers are tourists.

Perhaps the area that has the greatest tie to recreation and leisure is *mass tourism*—that segment of the industry that appeals to the majority of recreational travelers. It requires little of the traveler to adapt to the culture of the host to see attractions or to explore an area. It is convenient tourism. Travel may be with a tour group or individually planned, organized or spontaneous.

It is system-dependent and relies heavily upon travel agents, promotion materials, tour guides, travel organizations such as the American Automobile Association (AAA), and hotel and motel chains.

The Travel Industry

Other than the recreational component associated with tourism, it is difficult to separate the tourist industry from the travel industry. Both depend upon the same infrastructure and types of accommodations and services. Travelers of all types need accommodations and a means of transportation. Hotels would exist with or without tourists. Likewise, airlines would operate even if no passengers were flying to destinations for recreational purposes. These industries, however, would not be as significant if there were no tourists, especially the mass tourists.

In addition to these basic elements of the travel industry, tourism requires the additional component of attractions. Activities, sites, and relationships bring the traveler to a given destination for recreational purposes. The activities generally include shopping, sightseeing, dining, active participation (e.g., skiing, horseback riding, attending the opera) or structured tours. The success of travel and tourism largely depends upon the successful interaction of the traveler, host, private businesses, and governmental policy. Each of these contributors to tourism has its own motives, expectations, and roles.

The first perspective is that of the *traveler*. People expect trips to be pleasurable and to be worth their time and effort. They usually expect amenities at the destination in a form familiar to those of the home community (e.g., similar food and lodging accommodations). They often want the local population to be open to questions and stop what they are doing to meet the tourists' needs of the moment. In short, tourists expect to be accommodated because, after all, they are paying for it.

Those people residing in tourist destinations, also called the *hosts*, often have a different perspective. Depending upon the importance of the tourist industry to them, hosts can have a love/hate relationship with tourism. Sometimes host community residents are not universally happy to see their area become a travel destination (Milman & Pizam, 1988). They understand the positive economic impact it brings to their communities, but they also know that with the tourists come longer lines at local restaurants, crowded highways, increased criminal activity, and inflated prices on local goods and services. They understand the symbiotic relationship that exists between the traveler and his or her needs and the host environment with its services and attractions. The degree that local citizens are involved in tourism planning and development directly relates to the attitude the host has toward its visitors and the visitors' view of the community's hospitality.

From a marketing standpoint, local *private businesses* need to differentiate the host from the tourist. By knowing something of the tourists' origins and behaviors (e.g., their cultural traditions, interests, income, and motives), local merchants better know how to stock for them. These private sector businesses also know if these same products and services will be needed or wanted by local residents and can make adjustments accordingly. Tourism-related industries do differentiate tourists from other travelers. For example, airlines and hotels/motels generally use a different pricing policy for tourists and business travelers because business travel is usually less flexible than recreational travel. Hotel operators have found that it is in their best interest to encourage the tourist to travel mid-week and to stay over a weekend when business travel is less significant. Many motels and hotels reduce their rates considerably to attract weekend guests.

Local governmental officials are interested in tourism for a number of reasons. Travelers and guests will have an impact on government services such as police and fire protection, the transportation system, health and sanitation, water treatment facilities, and operations of local parks and public areas. Officials in local governments must consider the impact of tourist activities before embarking on a course of action to attract visitors. For example, the building of a sewage treatment plant with a capacity many times greater than that required by the local residents may be necessary to meet the demands of its visitors. This undertaking was necessary at Rehobeth Beach, Delaware, where the community's population grows tenfold over the weekend, especially in the summer.

The Impact of Tourism

The economic and social impact of tourism is significant. Government and industry must work closely to assure controlled growth and development and to minimize host community and visitor conflicts. Mass tourism implies that both the necessary money and time are available in large segments of the population to engage in pleasure travel. The more affluent the economy, the more travel and tourism generated. Other factors that influence tourism are job opportunities, speed of travel, infrastructures, marketing, freedom of movement, and climate.

From a global perspective, the tourist industry is worth trillions of dollars with a growth potential of $5.5 trillion by 2005. Should that occur, an additional 30 million new jobs will be created globally. At the national level, the statistics are equally dramatic. In 1997, people in the United States spent over 386 billion dollars in domestic travel and 51 billion dollars in travel abroad. Nearly half of their travel was for personal or pleasure reasons. International travel to the United States reached almost 34 million people in 1997—40% from overseas and 60% from Mexico and Canada. The United

States has experienced a trade surplus in most years. More money was made from international travelers to the United States than expended by US citizens in other countries.

At the local level the economic impact of tourism can be significant. For example, the Charlotte, North Carolina, Chamber of Commerce estimated that a recent National Basketball Association all-star game had a $15 million impact on the Charlotte region. The sales tax generated from visitors to the Coca-Cola 600 stock car race was equal to having 22 new property owners paying property tax.

As a less obvious connection to tourism, consider the laundry operator who has a contract with a local convention hotel, or the food wholesaler who provides hamburgers and salad materials to a theme park, or the furniture company who provides beds, carpets and television sets for a regional motel chain. Probably none of these workers (the local laundry worker, the farmer, or the furniture maker) would consider himself or herself being employed in the tourist industry, yet their jobs directly relate to it, as do the jobs of travel agent, events manager, or state director of travel and tourism.

Speed related to travel mode is a factor for a society that values time, but with speed comes cost. It is three times more expensive, but three times faster, to fly the Concorde than it is to fly first class trans-Atlantic on a 747. Distance, preference, and income also determine the mode of traveling. The RV may provide great flexibility for a family of four taking the grand tour of the western United States. It may be a little demanding, however, for an older adult who would prefer a packaged bus tour.

Infrastructures also influence tourism. When President Eisenhower signed the bill to create the interstate highway system in the 1950s, few anticipated its size or the impact it might have on the travel and tourism industry. Today, much of the over 40,000 miles of interstate highway is heavily traveled, old, and undergoing repair. Further, the demand for air transportation is often greater than the capacities of airports to handle the number of planes. Massive investments are required to maintain what exists and to develop new systems for this century. Beautiful islands in the Caribbean might be attractive to tourists, but without a major airport or a port deep enough for large cruise ships, they will not visit. A healthy infrastructure goes beyond transportation. A tourist destination must be able to accommodate outsiders with adequate water and sewage systems, police, fire, medical, and other social services as well. Often these necessities require the cooperation of state and local officials to assure both visitors and hosts that they are cared for during peak periods of activity. The role the quick food industry has played in travel and tourism as well as its influence on our dining habits also must be acknowledged. Like the franchised motel chains, they give travelers a sense of security and familiarity.

Marketing is a critical dimension of tourism. The key is having something people want to see or experience, and generally being able to attract the capital necessary to build new tourist attractions. Consequently more attention is being focused on existing attractions, natural resources, and the promotion of festivals and events. Tourist areas tend either to promote themselves as destinations because of their natural resources (e.g., mountains, lakes or shores) or their attractions (e.g., theme parks, events, or cultural aspects). Sports tourism, for example, has become a growing area as people travel to many types of major athletic events in cities throughout the country and in the case of the Olympics, throughout the world. The Internet has also affected marketing and promoting the tourism industry. Having easy access to the air and hotel bargains and sales has encouraged more people to travel. In addition, discount travel networks that flag the lowest rates and allow consumers to bid on the price they want to pay has also promoted travel and tourism throughout the United States and the world.

Freedom of movement is taken for granted in the United States. This freedom, however, is not universal. Even the US government restricts the travel of its citizens to certain countries during periods of unrest or when there are political disagreements. For example, in the 1950s Cuba was a major tourist destination for thousands of Americans, but was placed off limits to travelers once our government broke off diplomatic relations. Government approvals can change without warning. International tourism requires numerous agreements covering air and ground transportation, what products can be taken across borders, and what tariffs must be paid.

Finally, a successful tourist experience or tourism destination somewhat depends on its climate and weather. For example, hurricanes on the seacoast can cause billions of dollars of damage and negatively affected these tourist destinations. Even a single event can have an impact. Tourists have the choice to go or not to go to a locale, but the destination itself cannot move due to weather or natural disasters.

Issues Facing the Tourism Industry

Like all industries undergoing growth and change, travel and tourism has its challenges. The federal government addresses promotion and regulation. Regulations to protect the safety of tourists, whether in the United States or traveling abroad, are important. How much tourism promotion is done to attract people is also important. Some politicians believe that tourism promotion should be left to the individual states, local communities, or to the private sector and not involve the government. Others believe the government should be concerned because of the economic impact that tourism has on communities.

A second problem confronting the industry is its variety. The tourism industry comprises many subsystems. For example, at least thirty federal industrial codes have been developed by different agencies related to travel and tourism. At the local level, each state has its own set of laws governing operations. Coordination among levels of government, among the various interdependent industries, and between these industries and governments is critical to the operation and growth of the travel and tourism industry. This coordination does not exist to any great extent.

The effects that tourism has on a destination's social system and culture is a third issue. Many people view tourism as a savior for economically depressed areas, especially if the region has a strong natural resource base as one of its attractions. Potential negative costs must be considered as well as economic gains. Pollution, infrastructure costs, increased social problems, and seasonal unemployment issues must be considered. Tourism promoters must also consider whether an area really has destination potential given the competition and the choices travelers have. Often overlooked by local officials is the concept of clustering as a necessary ingredient to generate enough attractions to entice travelers to change destination preferences. An underdeveloped infrastructure or poor labor market can negatively affect a destination in much the same way that undercapitalization may negatively affect a start-up industry.

Numerous cases exist where tourism has transformed or destroyed local traditions and crafts. Rather than reflecting the values and interests of the community, local traditions can come to reflect the market. The designs of many Amish quilts, for example, no longer have meaning to the Amish because they are the designs most popular with the tourists. Dance rituals of American Indians once performed for their own sake are now sometimes done at specific times for monetary reasons. Commercial rugs are often advertised as Indian designs implying American Indians made them. Trinkets have replaced native crafts and the demand for inexpensive souvenirs causes a decline in craft quality. Before a community embarks on the path of becoming a tourist destination it should carefully weigh the gains and losses.

Tourism and the Environment

A great concern expressed by many individuals is the impact of tourism on the environment. Tourism depends almost wholly on the environment. If the environment degrades, many forms of tourism diminish. Sustainable tourism development can have impetus for structural change within society by moving away from a strictly socioeconomic focus toward preserving resources for the future (Fennell, 1999). Sustainable tourism relates to not consuming natural resources at a higher rate than they can be replaced, maintaining biological diversity, recognizing and valuing the aesthetic appeal, following ethical principles that respect local cultures, and involving and consulting local people (Williams, 1998). Mass tourism is typically not sustainable. In a world that values humans more than other life forms, the principles of ecosystem management and human ecology embodied in sustainable tourism can help us to better understand the place of humans in the natural world (Fennell, 1999).

Ecotourism connects tourism to the environment. Ecotourism, nature tourism, appropriate tourism, ethical tourism, and responsible tourism are some of the tourism descriptors emerging in recent years with overlapping and imprecise meanings that might be grouped under *alternative tourism*. The appeal of ecotourism is the opportunity to see and possibly become connected to endangered cultures, lands, and animals. Properly practiced, ecotourism is multifaceted with its low-impact, small-scale nature that educates the traveler. Ecotourism can also provide funds for conservation, help empower local communities, and foster respect for different cultures and human rights. Further, people who earn their living from ecotourism are more likely to defend natural resources against destructive activities. The most remote corners of our delicate planet are now easily accessible by modern transportation. Making people aware that these areas exist through ecotourism might protect them. Ecotourists often fight to keep the wild places wild because they have seen these areas and have been touched by their beauty.

If travel and tourism professionals care about the future of leisure, they must adopt a greener agenda. Fennell (1999) illustrated that perhaps the most important aspect facing tourism planners and managers is not to insert small numbers of environmentally aware people into pristine environments, but to improve the sustainability of ethical and responsible mass tourism. One role may be to demonstrate the ability of the industry to become more ecologically accountable. Sustainability should be the philosophy and cornerstone of the development of the tourism industry, since the natural environment constitutes most of its primary resource base. New forms of tourism bring with them new environmental challenges and more demanding standards for sustainable development. Tourism in all parts of the world will need to face more stringent conditions on growth and development. The industry must look at and manage change to address the ethics of environmental concerns.

The Future of Tourism

Travel and tourism will likely increase in popularity. Postindustrialism and a growing service economy have their effects, as do political and social changes. For example, with the aging population in the United States, the tourist industry likely will provide more package tours (i.e., having the travel agent attend to all the travel details so all the tourist has to do is participate). Considerable evidence suggests that even the more seasoned travelers are turning over the lodging and transportation details to the travel professional so that they might spend more of their energies and time enjoying the pleasures of the destination. Perhaps this reason is why the cruise ship industry has experienced such success.

Given the dimensions of the tourism industry, the federal government likely will become more involved in travel and tourism. The large amounts of capital required to build the necessary infrastructure and attractions to sustain tourism suggest the need for government involvement. This government involvement should encourage more public debate and a clarification of government's role in travel and tourism, especially at the local level.

Tourism involves a variety of corporations and businesses: airlines, rental car companies, hotel and motel chains, and entertainment groups. Big corporations like the Marriotts and Walt Disney Worlds are involved, but the majority of the tourist operations in the United States are operations employing 25 or fewer persons. The major theme parks may get our attention, but the small operators serve as the backbone of the industry. Within tourism, countless opportunities exist for individuals who want to test their entrepreneurial skills, whether it be providing travelers with information, services en route to their destination or home, programming for tourists at their destination or during their travels, or memories (e.g., videotapes and photographs) of their experience.

Local governments are becoming more involved with tourism activities. Working cooperatively with their chambers of commerce or tourist bureaus, local recreation and leisure providers schedule events marketed as attractions. They sponsor cultural activities, street fairs, and sporting events, as well as make their aquatic areas, tennis courts, and golf courses available to their guests. They may even receive a percentage of the guest taxes charged by local hotels and restaurants to expand or support those programs and facilities that have tourist appeal.

Tourism affects everyone. Many times each year we are either a tourist or a host interacting with those visiting our home communities. Like so many forms of commercial recreation, tourism is often criticized as being a contributor to pollution, immorality, urban blight, and related social problems. On the other hand, it also has the potential for bringing to the public creative, stimulating experiences and aesthetic surroundings. Tourism has the potential to create more understanding between people and to infuse life into economies.

Sustainable tourism can be maximized when government and industry work cooperatively to provide quality recreation opportunities. Every time a community develops an attraction for its visitors, it also provides additional recreation opportunities for its citizens. Every time a community develops its public recreation areas or encourages private entrepreneurs to operate an attraction, it adds to the attractiveness of the area as a tourist destination. The systems are interactive and interdependent.

Travel and tourism are major areas in the recreation and leisure services system. This form of recreation offers a variety of opportunities and has a major economic impact on areas. The future of tourism will lie in how it can be sustained in a way that results in economic development but also maintains human and environmental character.

Reflection Questions

1. What is a tourist?

2. What is ecotourism? Should this leisure option be continued? Why or why not?

3. Identify three of the benefits of tourism for local communities.

4. Describe the relationships between travel and tourism.

5. What aspects of tourism need to be addressed if it is to be sustainable?

3.11   Recreation Leadership

The future of recreation and leisure services, regardless of the sector, depends on leadership. We began this unit with a discussion of careers in recreation and leisure services and how one might think about some of the opportunities. This chapter describes some of the dimensions of leadership related to the profession and the provision of leisure services. Over the past 100 years, recreation and leisure opportunities that add meaning and quality to a person's life have grown tremendously. Further, the complexities of today's world have resulted in the need for a strong professional base for recreation and leisure and a commitment to providing positive environments and experiences for all people. We define leadership broadly to include direct contact with participants, management of an organization, and a commitment to the profession.

The Evolution of Recreation Leadership

Most of us can recall recreation experiences that were positive in one situation and yet negative when in a different context. When trying to understand why we had such a different reaction, we often reach the conclusion that the people in charge dramatically influenced our reactions and impressions. For many participants the key to a quality and enjoyable recreation experience often depends upon the environment and activities established by recreation leaders. In a rapidly changing society like the United States, where recreation is seen as an important social service, demands on leaders exist regardless of the type of provider system. These leaders, however, do not operate in a vacuum. Recreation leaders' styles, approaches, and values are influenced by social factors (Russell, 2001).

As previously described in the historical overview, the early recreation programs of the late 1800s grew from a strong commitment to develop a social service that would raise the quality of life for people, especially the poor and children. The early leaders faced many economic and political problems but exerted strong leadership that established the foundations for today's recreation programs and facilities. In many cases this leadership was autocratic, dogmatic, and reflected the passions of the few key recreation leaders of the day.

Leadership in current recreation sectors has changed from the early days in several ways. First, society has become increasingly more democratic with greater input from participants, especially in local communities. Second, most people recognize that not just anybody can be an effective recreation professional, since particular positions in recreation and leisure services require both general and specialized knowledge, skills, and training. In addition, the growth of the recreation industry has increased the diversity of participants and needs. Further, recreation leadership styles and approaches have been altered by increased facility resources (Russell, 2001). The role of the recreation leader has gone from making all of the decisions to developing systems and processes through which participants become active in the decision-making process (Davis, 1978). Recreation leaders must know how to manage change. Without flexibility to assess trends and issues and knowledge to apply research, our recreation leaders will face daunting challenges. The key rests in the ways recreation professionals are prepared to become leaders with positive attitudes toward change and the skills necessary to promote social change through recreation.

Leadership Qualities

Russell (2001, p. 12) defined leadership as "interpersonal influence exercised by a person or persons, through the process of communication, toward the attainment of an organization's goals." Jordan (1996) proposed leadership is a

> dynamic process of interactions between two or more members of a group which involves recognition and acceptance of leader-follower roles by group members within a certain situation. (p. 8)

Although many definitions exist, they all seem to suggest that leadership is a dynamic, ongoing process that influences the behaviors of individuals in the group.

Most people attribute certain kinds of qualities and characteristics to a leader, such as being trustworthy, honest, dedicated, confident, visionary, motivational, and articulate. Most people believe that a good leader inspires other people in the group to become good followers. Depending upon the style of the leader, a follower may have influence over the course of action for the group after some input from the leader (democratic style), may have opportunities to acquire leadership experience within certain aspects of the activity (participatory style), or may need to follow the specific instructions of the leader (autocratic style). In some situations, a leader may use a variety of leadership styles within the context of any given experience and may even accept a follower role while leading an activity.

Someone who provides leadership has a variety of expectations for performance. Direct leadership aspects include understanding and programming for the benefits and outcomes desired by participants, providing a safe and positive environment, and interacting with participants. Many recreation leaders also exert supervisory leadership when responsible for overseeing staff or running facilities. For recreation professionals at the highest levels of leadership, they also have administrative expectations that require additional and specialized leader skills. As a way to better understand the need for trained professional recreation leaders, we will look into the professional life of a public recreation leader, Chris.

Chris has a bachelor's degree in recreation and has been hired to be a program specialist in the community's park and recreation department. The job description specified skills were needed in several technical and conceptual areas. Many aspects of Chris's job required skills learned as a part of the recreation major undertaken at college. Chris learned how to plan, organize, and implement programs. Other skills included writing goals and objectives that fit the mission of the agency and reflect their philosophy. These goals also help participants achieve the benefits and desired outcomes from the recreation experience. Additional programming skills learned included budgeting, marketing, scheduling, risk management, volunteer and staff training and supervision, activity analysis, specific activity skills, and evaluation. New technologies continue to develop, but the coursework and experience with computers and software applications, the Internet, geographic information systems (GIS), and other new advances in recreation areas and facilities management provided a sound foundation for this first job.

The human relations dimension of Chris's job is pertinent every day. Chris continually interacts with the public, whether with participants in a specific recreation program, community leaders interested in new recreation initiatives, or political leaders concerned over budgetary demands. Chris puts into practice the communication skills learned in college when asked to give a speech to the Kiwanis Club, provide a training workshop for summer camp staff, partner with social services to facilitate a support group for people with AIDS, or write the news release about the midnight basketball league for young women and men in the community. The classes Chris took in college about human development, understanding diversity, community development, and leadership training contributed to a strong professional foundation for relating to the wide array of constituencies encountered daily by the recreation professional.

The conceptual skills required for Chris's job have continued to develop from the basic understandings acquired during college to the more specific applications in the current job. To be a good leader, a recreation professional must understand the big picture and have a vision for the future. The classes in recreation administration helped Chris understand the importance of a mission statement and the way it becomes a map for everything done by the department. Discovering the history of the profession gave Chris a better understanding of the past and helps to set future directions. Chris also understands more completely the political processes at work in the community with the background from political science, sociology, and public policy. Even though Chris is not a recreation administrator, these conceptual skills are still critical to the day-to-day happenings in the office.

Chris's job is quite complex. Could any college graduate do this job? Maybe, but having a sound background in recreation should make Chris a better leader in addressing the challenges of the field of recreation and leisure studies. If recreation is to be a symbol for a civilized society concerned with the highest quality of life possible for all people, well-educated leaders in the recreation profession will be a critical component of the plan. We need recreation professionals who can dream, motivate, problem-solve, teach, organize, adapt, innovate, facilitate, and make good decisions. We need professionals to lead.

Therefore, the task of creating and implementing effective leisure and recreation programs for all facets of America is ongoing. In the formative years of recreation and leisure services, the professional was seen as one who developed and supervised activities such as nature hikes, tennis tournaments, and playground programs, or one who managed a physical resource such as a park. Today, the professional is more than an activity instructor or park ranger. The roles assumed by park and recreation professionals include manager, administrator, community organizer, therapist, educator, and policy formulator. These roles require a different set of skills and understanding than were required by those who served the park and recreation movement in the past.

Reflection Questions

1. Describe what skills it takes to be a good recreation professional.

2. How is recreation leadership different today than a century ago?

3. Provide an example where you believe the leadership of a recreation activity made a difference in the quality of the experience.

UNIT FOUR: TRENDS AND ISSUES IN RECREATION AND LEISURE SERVICES

In a static society with no change, the future is like the present. In a dynamic society, the future is being created each day and requires people to modify their behaviors accordingly. The world we live in continually changes. The present intersects the past and the future, and our actions in the present play a significant role in determining our future. Each individual creates her or his own future each day. Therefore, we must examine both the *probable* future as well as the *preferable* future to see what each individual can do to influence a future that promotes a high quality of life.

Speculating about the future can be great fun—the possibilities are endless. This unit offers some ideas about the future trends and issues affecting recreation and leisure. Many of the problems presented here do not have definitive solutions. We encourage readers to consider the emerging issues related to recreation and leisure in society, as well as issues that might be significant for individuals contemplating a career in this field. As the 21st century unfolds, a number of dimensions influence available recreation and leisure services. These emerging areas include the economy, demographic and social trends, technology and time-use patterns, and evolving management strategies.

4.1   Planning in the 21st Century

Recreation and leisure are dynamic. As you have seen throughout this book, what people want from these enjoyable experiences changes in relation to how society changes. Since recreation addresses personal interests as well as social justice, changes in programs and facilities are needed as new issues and trends emerge. If the field of recreation is to maintain its viability, professionals must consider the emerging issues and develop strategies to address new trends.

A variety of techniques have been developed to forecast the future. One technique, known as trend extrapolation, examines past trends over a period of time to project the future. Another technique, the Delphi technique, relies on the intuition and judgment of experts to identify dynamics of change and assess likely influences on specific areas of life. Regardless of the technique or method used, the key is understanding how present issues will affect people in the future. This requires identifying the forces in the present most likely to shape the future. One example is the relation between population trends and public services. The baby boom between 1947 and 1965 was followed by a declining birth rate. This changed the nature of public services with the anticipation that the primary demand for future services would come from an aging population. Once the baby boom generation began to establish families, however, a baby boom echo occurred with an increase in children born. As a result, not only did the demand for public services increase in addressing the aging baby boomers, but also public services were needed aimed at a younger generation. The results were expanded educational and recreational programs as well as expanded healthcare and senior programs. Changing patterns in wealth, education, and work needed to be assessed. Clearly the issues are complex and controversial. Sound policy decisions can only be made on the basis of sound analysis. Many issues must be addressed if we are to create a future for ourselves, the recreation profession, and the communities where we live.

Forces of Change

Some value changes seem to be occurring as America moves into a new century of great change due to emerging postindustrial values (Plummer, 1989, p. 10). By examining the meanings of these value changes, recreation professionals can begin to see what future trends might occur. Many topics in this chapter stem from action planning by various groups, particularly the "Creating Community in the 21st Century" California Action Plan (California Parks and Recreation Society, 1999).

Industrial Values	Postindustrial Values
Self-denial ethic	Self-fulfillment ethic
Higher standard of living	Better quality of life
Traditional sex roles	Blurring of sex roles
Accepted definition of success	Individualized definition of success
Traditional family life	Alternative families
Faith in institutions	Self-reliance
Live to work	Work to live
Hero worship	Love of ideas
Expansionism	Pluralism
Patriotism	Less nationalistic
Unparalleled growth	Growing sense of limits
Industrial growth	Information/service growth
Receptivity to technology	Technology orientation

Recreation and the Economy

Going into the 21st century, the US economy is dynamic, with changes occurring daily. Jobs abound throughout the United States, even though some of those jobs are not as meaningful as some people would like. Access to higher education has risen, and thus, an overall higher quality of life is available to many people. In addition, a healthy entrepreneurial spirit exists. Everyone "wants to be a millionaire" and many people have gained and lost wealth due to investments in the stock market and particularly in technology. Unfortunately, a number of people in the United States are becoming poorer due to underemployment and other issues that prevent them from working at the capacity that they could. Although the overall economy is good, not everyone enjoys the good fortune.

Adding to the overall economic well-being of the country, in general, is the growing tourism and hospitality industry. Many communities look for ways to enhance their economy through tourism. Recreation as a field directly contributes to this economic growth. Professionals address the incorrect perception that recreation is unimportant or superfluous. The benefits-based approach has helped to show the numerous positive outcomes that can occur when recreation opportunities are abundant. More strategic marketing, however, must continue to establish recreation as a key factor for increasing the quality of life in communities.

Recreation enhances business and community vitality. For example, property values increase noticeably when homes and businesses are located near parks, greenbelts, and wetlands. Recreation and leisure professionals also continue to seek ways to partner with community groups to enhance the image of recreation. In addition, the growing number of entrepreneurs and the privatization of recreation services result in cost-effective recreation opportunities. The challenge will be to ensure that people who are qualified to conduct and manage recreation experiences have the skills and resources to do their jobs.

Recreation providers are becoming more aware of political and legislative trends as they relate to economics. When monies become available for various social mandates, recreation professionals need to try to obtain that funding. For example, money has been made available through juvenile justice programs to offer after-school programs for youth from high-risk environments. Recreation professionals have an important role to play and must be able to show how recreation can have a positive impact on people and why people should invest in recreation. Political issues and atmospheres differ by communities, so recreation professionals must heed changes that occur in terms of priorities and emphasis areas.

Recreation and Demographic, Social, and Cultural Trends

Unit one identified some of the demographic and social changes occurring in our society. The growth and change in the population will require investments in recreation to meet the needs, interests, and preferences of people. The population is growing in many areas of the country, and the nature of that population is changing in terms of ethnic diversity, age, and income inequality. These demographic changes have raised concerns about crime and violence, a focus on sustainability and environmental preservation, and the need to balance personal autonomy with social good.

With a larger population base comes the need to provide more recreation opportunities. Similarly, greater usage requires continued maintenance and evaluation for improvement. Alternative funding in all of the recreation sectors assures that usage and usability are balanced. Changes in the population require that recreation professionals be sensitive to different recreation preferences based on cultural differences.

The aging population, particularly the boomers who began to reach age 50 in the mid-1990s, is also significant and will continue to be important as we move into the 21st century. People living longer and healthier will likely change patterns of participation as recreation and leisure become lifelong pursuits. Older people in particular demand more physical and intellectual activities. Recreation professionals will need to consider safety and access as they program for these individuals. The boomers have grown up expecting more opportunities for themselves, and they will continue to have those expectations from recreation providers into the future.

Although a number of people in the United States are economically well off, many individuals are not. Income inequality is an issue for many people due to lack of training, lack of education, or inability to adapt to the changing job market. Many lower income people are clustered in communities, whether in urban areas or rural enclaves. Bifurcation (the haves and the have-nots) occurs regarding access to recreation. The 21st century requires that recreation providers be aware of the problems with access to recreation, whether in urban neighborhoods or rural areas. User fees are another issue that will require greater consideration. The solutions to income inequality will not be easy to solve, but they must be addressed or US society will experience greater segregation.

Crime and personal safety concern almost everyone, but more police and longer jail terms are not necessarily the answers. Evidence suggests that crime rates drop when open space and recreation opportunities are expanded and improved in cities. Recreation professionals work to address the importance of facilities and programs in lowering the crime rate. For example, the success of midnight basketball programs in some cities has resulted in lowered youth crime rates. Recreation is not the only solution, but it may be an important one. Collaboration with police departments and other community services will be needed. The more groups that address this problem of crime and violence, the more likely we are to find positive solutions.

People also express concern for the environment and sustainability of natural resources. Tension exists, however, between the need for preserving natural areas and meeting the demand for business and residential opportunities. Living in harmony is important to most people, but their behaviors do not always reflect those values. Recreation professionals address these issues by examining the environmental impact that programs have. Further, recreation providers must seek to continually develop new parks and open spaces to meet the increasing demand for natural areas. With rapid population growth and urban sprawl, acquiring land for recreation will become a greater challenge in the future. Issues related to sustaining natural resources while increasing economic development will not be easy to address in the coming years. This problem does not solely belong to recreation providers, but since recreation often occurs in the outdoors, the responsibility cannot be abdicated.

People want autonomy in their recreation, and they expect to be treated as customers. Recreation providers must seek ways to make information about opportunities easily available. The diversity of needs must also be kept in mind. Recreation providers cannot forget the mandate they have to provide for all participants, to promote the social good of communities, and to address environmental impacts.

The commercial sector of recreation is likely to experience continued growth in the future because of the focus on individual needs. This growth is not a problem as long as other recreation providers address the leisure needs and interests of individuals who may not be able to afford or rely on the commercial sector. We hope the leisure service sectors (public, not-for-profit, and private commercial) will use healthy competition and cooperation to meet the demand for the desired variety of experiences for all individuals.

Recreation, Time Use, and Technology

Unobligated time becomes difficult to address as American life speeds up in response to a greater focus on productivity. Technology was going to make life easier for us, but rather has resulted in us expecting more from ourselves. The backlash has been that people also tend to approach their recreation like their work by packing a number of recreation activities into a small amount of time. This behavior has been referred to as *time deepening*—doing more than one thing at a time (Godbey, 1997). A good example is to simultaneously eat dinner, watch television, and help the kids with homework during the commercials. Recreation professionals concerned with this pattern must emphasize the *quality* of the experiences they provide as well as the role of recreation in stress reduction. Programs that address stress management, lifestyle management, and values clarification may be central in the future.

People today tend to spend more free time in physically passive activities, as evidenced by the high rate of obesity in US society. A trend toward passivity may be because people are so busy in work that they just want to relax and do nothing in their leisure. Being a couch potato does not require much learning, discipline, or commitment. Recreation providers, therefore, inform people about the recreation options available to them and the health benefits and higher quality of life associated with active lifestyles. This issue goes beyond providing services to include aspects of education and communication.

Technology greatly impacts the way people use their time to live, work, and play as we enter the 21st century. The influence of rapidly evolving technological changes will continue to have dramatic effects on our lives. For example, the separation between where people work and where they live will likely be blurred in the future. Many professional people will likely do more of their work from their home rather than travel to an office. Recreation providers will need to provide recreational opportunities that are accessible to people working in a variety of locations. Partnerships with industries and among recreation providers may be necessary for the future. Recreation providers will need to be creative in getting people to take time to get out of their homes and virtual communities and into their immediate neighborhoods to recreate.

Recreation and Leisure Services Management

New management techniques within all sectors of recreation and leisure services will be required if recreation professionals are to succeed in the future. We would like to briefly note some of the management issues that will need to be addressed as recreation professionals contemplate the future in the 21st century.

Funding is a critical issue that includes a variety of alternatives depending on the recreation sector involved. In addition to taxes and fees, many recreation agencies rely on charitable donations. For example, companies now support programs that promote their commercial interests. They also have moved away from silent donations toward taking credit for their contributions and even helping to market and promote programs. Giving money and volunteering time in America has been on the decline since the 1980s (Coolidge, 1995). In light of the increased competition for charitable dollars, leaders of recreation agencies need to become astute in fundraising concepts and strategies. Many donors no longer reward only good intentions; they reward good results. These results often rest on sound evaluations of programs that document accountability. Besides donations, recreation providers will need to explore a variety of other funding opportunities such as partnerships and other forms of creative financing.

The effective management of recreation organizations requires the continual reforming of processes and practices to realize the vision shared by the organization. Programs need outcome-based processes that are monitored and evaluated. The effects of this type of management organization are often dramatic. For example, the success of program delivery measured in the past by numbers of participants and a sense of a job well done has to be revised. Staff has to clarify a vision of how quality of life improves because of the recreation services provided, and rethink their relationship to funding sources and other agencies to explore collaborative projects (Penuel, 1997). The focus on outcomes, monitoring, and evaluation as an outgrowth of organizational learning will continue to influence the management, funding, and accountability of most recreation organizations.

All organizations have to be managed for success. Commercial organizations use the financial bottom line, but professionals must also consider what difference they make in people's lives. At the same time, recreation professionals in public and not-for-profit organizations are most concerned with "what difference will we make?" These professionals, however, cannot abdicate their responsibility for good fiscal management. As suggested by Stubbs (1998), the following strategies link organizational practices with effective management:

- Planning based on a clear mission

- Agenda focusing on priorities

- Recruitment that seeks quality leadership

- Fundraising organized for intended purposes

- Goals that fulfill the mission

- Responsiveness in reflecting community expectations

Although strategic management is not new, the emphasis on doing it within recreation organizations in all sectors may become more critical. To remain competitive in the business world, recreation agencies will need to more fully utilize effective strategic management processes.

Volunteering is a recreation activity and can be valuable to the organization for program delivery as well as fundraising. Professionals need to know how to share the vision of the organization with their volunteers in a way that builds a passion and commitment.

The workforce is changing and will continue to change rapidly within the next decade. Recreation providers must be aware of these personnel changes. Within the next few years, 85% of the new employees entering the workforce will be women and minorities (Barner, 1996). The workers who will be most valued in the future may be those individuals who can thrive within a diversified work team and who are managed by an administrator sensitive to perspectives that may vary by gender, race, ethnicity, sexual orientation, disability, religion, and age (Barner, 1996). As boomers age and move into retirement, the mass exodus from the workforce will likely be one of the single most important policy challenges to face the country in the next 30 years (Johnson, 1998). The need for workers may go unmet in some areas while greater benefits may be seen for employing older workers as well as understanding the needs of older clientele (Barner, 1996). Another solution may be to have fewer permanent employees and more part-time workers, short-term project workers, or teams of specialists assembled quickly to address tasks and issues as they arise (Swimming with Tomorrow's Sharks, 1997). The successful workers may the ones who remain flexible and involved with continuing education so they can stay marketable within this new work environment.

Reflection Questions

1. What is the value in thinking about the future?

2. What are the current major influences on recreation and leisure services?

3. What demographic changes will affect the leisure service industry in the near future?

4.2   Time for Work and Leisure

Time is the most equally distributed of all leisure resources—no one gets more than 24 hours in a day. Time is also the scarcest and most valuable of resources. A sense of control over one's time and a sense of having a sufficient amount of time are important elements in individual satisfaction with life (Campbell, Converse & Rodgers, 1976). How much time people have at their disposal is important in any assessment of leisure in contemporary society. To understand time, however, it is necessary to examine how work and leisure are connected in most people's lives.

Historical Perspectives

In surveying the history of leisure, we saw that workers resisted the imposition of longer work hours and of time-disciplined work as early as the medieval and renaissance eras. With the emergence of modern work in the 18th and 19th centuries, workers, employers, politicians, social reformers, economists, and many others struggled to define how long people should reasonably be expected to work. Resolving this question proved to be extraordinarily difficult because it involved seriously conflicting economic, moral, political, religious, and social interests. A brief historical sketch gives a useful perspective on the current debate over how much time people work and how much time they have available for leisure.

Cross (1989) estimated that English and French workers in 1840 labored between 57 and 69 hours weekly. Over the next century work hours declined steadily, to between 31 and 38 hours a week. Reasons for this decline included demands by workers for more leisure, concerns about the effects of overwork on workers and their families, and employers' searches for competitive advantages in the market. These reasons also applied in the United States. Without time free from work, people could not be effective citizens (Roediger & Foner, 1989). Workers' resistance to long hours took on other meanings as it reappeared throughout the United States during the 19th century. By 1900, when the US workweek was approximately 60 hours (Hunnicutt, 1985), work hours reduction was a central issue for the US labor movement and for many social reform organizations. The length of the workweek was reduced to 42.7 hours by 1948 and to 42.5 hours in 1975 (Owen, 1976). Owen identified three reasons the workweek failed to decrease further. Foremost was the release of consumer demand pent up during the Depression and war years. The desire to catch up on consumer goods assumed greater priority among Americans than reduced work hours. The second reason was the baby boom. Childrearing entailed long-term costs that made the potential loss of income through shorter work hours unacceptable to new parents. Third, the boomers stayed in school longer than previous generations and those going to college added about three years of formal education. Additional schooling not only imposed costs on parents, it also delayed their children's entry into the workforce.

Business, labor, and government interpreted fluctuations in work hours as the effect of business cycles. Work hours decreased when business conditions deteriorated and rebounded during periods of recovery. Leisure was increasingly recognized as an important element in maintaining sufficient consumer demand to minimize these fluctuations. Emphasis on consumption permanently altered leisure while also contributing to the constancy of work hours.

The Work Hours Debate

Just how much Americans work was hotly debated during the last years of the 20th century. Conflicting research findings prevent any easy answers to this question. Although some studies (e.g., US Department of Labor, 1999) suggested that work hours have remained stable since the 1970s, this seems increasingly unlikely in the light of other analyses.

Increased Work Hours

Much recent discussion of work hours resulted from the publication of Juliet Schor's *The Overworked American* (1991). Schor, an economist, argued that Americans worked an average 163 more hours annually in 1990 than they did in 1970, the equivalent of four additional 40 hour weeks. Noting that women continued to do the bulk of housework and childrearing while being more frequently employed outside the household, Schor calculated that this resulted in the equivalent of 7.5 additional workweeks annually. Men's work hours also increased, by the equivalent of an additional 2.5 workweeks annually. Schor's book seemed to confirm the growing perception that work hours and time pressures had increased substantially in American society. *The Overworked American* was generally well-received in the popular media, but academic and professional reviews were more reserved. Although some researchers agreed work hours had increased, there was no consensus on the size of the increase or how the additional work hours were distributed in the population.

Decreased Work Hours

Data on time allocations and the amount of time people devote to different activities are generally collected using one of two basic methods. With the time diary method, people record their activities at regular short intervals (e.g., every 15 minutes) over several days or when prompted by the researcher (e.g., using a beeper). With the recall method, people are typically asked by survey researchers how much time they spent on certain activities (e.g., work, free time, watching television) during the preceding day, week, or month.

The studies discussed earlier in this section relied on data collected using the recall method. After reviewing alternative methods for collecting time allocation data, Juster and Stafford (1991) concluded that estimates of work hours based on the recall method were consistently higher than estimates based on time diaries. They also found that the differences between the two methods had grown after 1965, a finding endorsed by Robinson and Godbey (1999). Two explanations for the growing discrepancy were suggested by Robinson and Bostrom (1994), who reported that overestimates were greatest among people who recalled working the most hours, and that women overestimate work hours more than men. Reports of long hours and the number of women in the workforce may have contributed to the growing disparities between estimates of work hours based on the recall and the time diary methods.

When Robinson and Godbey's *Time for Life* first appeared in 1997 (second edition 1999) it generated considerable discussion. The authors directly challenged Schor's findings and the widely held belief that work hours had increased. Using time diary data, Robinson and Godbey claimed instead that work hours had *decreased* for both women (from 36.8 hours weekly in 1965 to 34.3 hours in 1985) and men (from 46.5 hours weekly in 1965 to 42.6 in 1985). The second edition of *Time for Life*, however, reported an *increase* in women's work hours between 1985 and 1995, to 37.3 hours weekly, which was a half-hour more than women had worked in 1965. Men's work hours, on the other hand, *decreased* between 1985 and 1995, to 42.3 hours weekly, or 4.2 fewer than in 1965. For both men and women, time diary estimates of work hours remained lower than estimates based on the recall method.

Reconciling the Differences

These discrepant findings remind us that we cannot be indifferent social science research methods. This research has significant implications for what we learn about our social world. The analysis of work hours illustrates the importance of considering research methods when evaluating research findings.

Note that researchers using the recall method reported their findings as average *annual* hours worked while researchers using the time diary method used average *weekly* hours worked. These two averages are not strictly comparable. Average annual hours worked provides a more accurate understanding of time allocated to work. It minimizes the distorting effects of seasonal or temporary employment, variations in holidays or vacations, and unusual events in the economy like strikes or major disasters. Researchers can capture not only how much time people allocate to work but they also can note changes in the structure of the workforce and the economy.

According to the US Department of Labor (1999) the entire increase between 1969 and 1997 in full-time year-round workers ages 25 to 54 resulted from women entering the workforce. In 1969, 27% of women in this age range were employed full-time, year-round. By 1997 women's workforce participation rate for this age range had climbed to 50%. During the same period the number of men ages 25 to 54 employed full-time year-round declined. Moreover, the percentage of workers with average workweeks longer than 40 hours increased more rapidly among women than men. Not only are more women working throughout the year, but more of them are also putting in longer workweeks.

A second structural change in the workforce is the substitution of overtime for employment (Hetrick, 2000). Rather than hire new workers, employers in the manufacturing sector have found it more profitable to pay overtime to their present workers. This practice was not unusual during periods of recovery after economic downturns, but work hours usually returned to normal levels within several years as new workers were hired into the workforce. After the 1981–82 and particularly the 1990–91 recessions, however, work hours remained higher after recovery was well underway, indicating that new workers had not been hired (Bluestone & Rose, 1998). Despite the unprecedented economic expansion after 1992, manufacturing employment remained well below its level prior to the 1990–91 recession. Overtime, however, reached record levels at 4.9 hours weekly in January 1998 (Hetrick, 2000) and declined to only 4.7 hours weekly by May 2000 (US Bureau of Labor Statistics, 2000). Overtime reduced the number of manufacturing jobs. As more workers take nonmanufacturing jobs, which tend to have shorter workweeks, the average length of the workweek decreases.

Decreased employment security is a further important structural change in the workforce. The average length of employment with the same employer has been decreasing. Employers have become more willing to dismiss workers to increase profitability (i.e., downsizing or, from the employer's point of view, rightsizing) and to ask remaining employees to intensify their work efforts. Employers also increasingly contract for services once considered core business functions (i.e., outsourcing). For more workers, employment now depends on such contracts for a fixed term that may or may not be extended. In this volatile labor market, workers experience frequent cycles of high and low work hours (Bluestone & Rose, 1998). They must often accept longer work hours now to guard against the likelihood of reduced work hours in the future. These cycles do not always register when average weekly hours worked are examined, but they become apparent when taking a longer view.

Finally, a fourth structural change in the workforce is the rising percentage of married couples with both partners employed outside the home. In 1969 about 43% of married women ages 25 to 54 years were either working or looking for work. By 1998 this number increased to 74%. Married couples added about 14 more hours to their workweeks from 1969 to 1997, while the percentage of couples with both partners working full time increased from 24% to 43% (US Department of Labor, 1999).

Burdens and Benefits of Increased Work Hours

Americans as a whole have increased the number of hours they work annually. Work hour trends are not uniform throughout society, however. Women's annual work hours have risen while men's have fallen. Bluestone and Rose (1998) estimated that between 1967 and 1989 men's work hours fell an average 2.6 hours annually and women's rose an average 18.8 hours annually. A closer look reveals a disproportionate average loss of 7.7 hours annually by African-American men compared to 2.1 hours annually for

Table 4.2:	Annual Growth in Combined Hours Worked by Change in Real Earnings of Husband-Wife Couples Ages 25–54 from 1973–1976			
Couple Type	Growth in Combined Hours Worked per Year*	Annual Percentage Growth in Combined Hours Worked	Annual Percentage Change in Combined Real Earnings	Percentage Change in Combined Real Hourly Earnings
All couples	34.2	16.3	18.5	1.8
African-American couples	22.8	11.8	15.8	3.6
White couples	35.1	17.1	19.8	2.2
High school dropout (husband)	24.5	11.6	−8.2	−17.7
High school graduate (husband)	33.0	16.1	3.7	−10.7
College graduate (husband)	36.4	16.6	32.5	13.6

*data from 1967–1988

Adapted from Bluestone and Rose (1998)

White men. In 1989 African-American men worked the equivalent of 3.75 fewer 40-hour weeks than they did in 1967 (p. 27). White men worked approximately 2,300 hours in 1989, African-American men 1,950 hours. The difference is roughly equivalent to two months. During the same period White women added the equivalent of 10.3 additional 40-hour weeks, compared to 5.4 additional 40-hour weeks for African-American women.

People with higher levels of education on average work longer hours than people with less education. Men who did not graduate from high school worked six fewer hours weekly in 1969 than college-educated men. By 1998 the difference grew to 13 hours weekly; this trend also held for women (US Department of Labor, 1999). Given their responsibilities, professionals and managers are usually expected to work longer hours, even though longer hours do not necessarily mean increased earnings. Other occupations, such as transportation or sales (i.e., commissioned sales) require longer hours to increase earnings (Rones, Ilg & Gardner, 1997). The rate of employment in these occupations increased for women by 12.7% between 1985 and 1993—more than double the 5.1% rate increase for men.

Combining these factors allows us to assess the results of increased work hours. As Table 4.2 shows, race and education make a difference when examining the combined work hours of heterosexual married couples. White couples increased work hours substantially more than African-American couples. Couples with a husband who did not graduate from high school experienced a much smaller increase in work hours than couples with a husband who had more education. Real earnings increased for all couples except when the husband did not graduate from high school. Real earnings are calculated using a constant value for the dollar, removing the effects of inflation to allow more accurate comparison of income levels in different years. Not surprisingly, couples in which the husband was a college graduate showed a much higher rate of earnings growth.

The last column in Table 4.2 shows the percentage change in combined real hourly earnings. We can think of this as the change in a couple's hourly wage, or how much the couple was paid per hour worked. This is determined by dividing the couple's combined annual work hours into their combined annual earnings. If wages and salaries increase faster than hours worked, the change in combined hourly earnings will be higher. On the other hand, if hours of work grow faster than wages and salaries, the change in combined hourly earnings will be lower.

Although most couples increased their annual combined earnings between 1967 and 1988, they did so only by *increasing their combined hours of work*, not because wages and salaries increased (Bluestone & Rose, 1998). Among all couples combined real hourly earnings grew only 1.8%, calculated by Bluestone and Rose as equivalent to an increase of about two cents per hour annually. The value of an hour's work decreased by over ten percent for all other couples. These couples had to increase their combined hours of work just to maintain their existing standard of living. This trend has continued throughout the 1990s (Mishel, Bernstein & Schmitt, 2001).

At the end of the 20th century work hours do not follow a uniform pattern in society, nor do they continue to decrease as many people anticipated earlier in the century. Even in the midst of economic boom times and as work hours increase among the well-educated, secure employment still remains elusive for many workers. In some occupations people are rewarded for their long work hours, while most others must increase their work hours simply to hold on to their present lifestyles. As people work longer hours, whether they earn more or not, they surrender more of their scarcest resource—time.

Reflection Questions

1. Explain why you believe people have more/less leisure time today than in the past.

2. Do you believe that gender still influences time for leisure? Provide three examples to illustrate your point of view.

3. Is quality of life enhanced or worsened by increased work expectations?

4. One aspect of the shorter work hours debate was the question of how wealth generated by rising productivity should be used. Should it be converted into shorter work hours so people have more free time? Or should it be converted in higher earnings so people are able to consume more goods and services?

5. How much time would you trade for earnings and how much earnings for time?

6. Why does it matter to recreation and leisure professionals how many hours people work and what they do? How can providers of leisure services use information about work patterns to better meet leisure needs?

7. Does more time equal more and/or better leisure?

4.3   The Meanings of Work

From the time we are very young, we are encouraged to think about work.
As children some of us had tasks to do for an allowance. We had guidance
counselors trying to help us decide future work roles. We worked to get our
first car, to go to college, or to buy clothes, CDs, or other desired items.
We all know the most popular question asked by family and friends is "So
what job do you hope to get when you graduate?" Ironically, many of us
have a hard time defining what work means to us. We know work is among
the constants in human life, but it has had different meanings in the Western
tradition. Work is a curse and a burden, a salvation and release, selfish and
selfless. Many of these meanings remain current in contemporary debates
about work.

Historical Themes

The story told in Genesis (3:14–24) reminds us of the meaning of work
historically. Having failed to respect divine commandment by daring to eat
from the tree of knowledge, Adam and Eve were cast from the Garden of
Eden. God had placed Adam in the garden "to dress it and keep it" (Genesis
2:15). Now his punishment was to see it turn to thistle and thorn bushes,
condemned to work: "In the sweat of thy brow shalt thou eat bread, till thou
return unto the ground" (Genesis 3:19).

Throughout most of Western history, work indicated inferior status—
the only avenue open to those men and women without rank. Thomas
(1964) commented, "A contempt for manual labour permeates aesthetic,
educational, scientific and religious assumptions until very early modern
times" (p. 57). In the ancient world the Egyptians, Athenians, and Romans
all regarded work as demeaning in various ways and this attitude persisted
among the medieval nobility and clergy. In the renaissance a greater acceptance of work as a means for social advancement based on wealth occurred, while in the reformation Luther and Calvin taught that diligent
work was a sign of faith. To work throughout their mortal lives became a
means for human beings to redeem themselves.

Contemporary Meanings

Morse and Weiss (1955) studied the meanings of work among a sample of
United States males employed in managerial and working class jobs using
data collected in 1953. They concluded: (1) that work was more than a means

to an end, and (2) for most people work served nonmonetary purposes that varied depending on the type of work done. When asked whether they would continue to work even if they no longer needed to earn an income, 80% of the respondents answered yes, with 63% of these respondents giving positive reasons for their choice (e.g., keeping busy is good, enjoy work, self-respect) and 37% giving negative reasons (e.g., would feel lost or "go crazy" without work, boredom, feel useless). When asked what they might miss the most if they were not working, only 12% of the respondents indicated they would miss the kind of work they did and only 2% indicated they would miss the money they earned in their current jobs. Respondents most frequently said they would miss social contacts and friends at work (31%) and a feeling of doing something (25%). Respondents also said they would miss a sense of self-respect, a regular routine, and being part of something.

These findings suggest that the meanings of paid employment lie outside the work itself. Most of what the respondents would miss if they were not working could easily be found in other forms of activity. For these respondents, however, jobs were the primary context where they received these nonmonetary gains. Morse and Weiss (1955) did not ask about leisure, so we do not know whether their respondents did not think of it as a context to pursue these purposes, or whether they did not find leisure an attractive arena in which to do so. It is important to remember that when these data were collected the labor market was relatively stable. People worked in the same business for many years and sometimes for life, and businesses remained located in one place. The mobility of individual workers and the relocation of businesses characteristic of the contemporary labor market had not appeared.

In market economies, a primary justification for work is that the income it provides not only allows people to satisfy basic needs but also increases their access to other goods and services that enhance their quality of life, such as leisure. This postmaterialist culture shift idea was based on the work of Inglehart (1977, 1990). A later analysis by Lane (1978) called this justification of work further into question. Ironically, his evidence suggested that as income levels increase, people feel decreasing levels of satisfaction. Once a certain level of economic prosperity is achieved, noneconomic factors contribute more to life satisfaction than does income. Lane argued that at the individual level, actual income is not as related to a sense of well-being as are noneconomic sources of life satisfaction. Noneconomic sources might be the number of friends a person has and the absence of time pressures. A balanced sense of time, satisfying nonwork activities, and family life contribute to an individual sense of well-being. Work has meaning because it provides a sense of control that allows people to pursue other life satisfactions, such as leisure-related activity (Andrews & Withey, 1974).

Hunnicutt (1996) studied workers' responses to the six-hour workday implemented at the Kellogg's cereal plants during the Depression as part of a strategy to reduce unemployment and enhance workers' lives. The six-hour day continued, albeit for fewer and fewer workers, into the 1980s. Kellogg workers were divided in their opinions about the six-hour day. Some workers, many of them women, welcomed it as an opportunity to develop nonwork interests to enrich their lives and communities. They participated in community affairs, increased their family involvement, and pursued creative activities. Other workers, many of them men, felt uncomfortable with the extra free time. Accustomed to working full time and without nonwork interests, they lost their sense of usefulness and self-respect. They engaged in diversionary activities that passed time but did not enrich their lives. Eventually they began to press for a return to the eight-hour day, accusing the remaining supporters of the six-hour day of being slackers who did not want to work. The many contradictory meanings of work are evident from Hunnicutt's analysis.

A study of agriculture, manufacturing, retail, service, and government workers in Ontario, Canada by Mannell and Reid (Reid, 1995) provided a comparison of the satisfactions found in work and leisure. They identified eight possible personal satisfactions and asked respondents to rank them in order of importance for both work and leisure. Table 4.3 shows the results. Note how work satisfactions are similar to those reported forty years earlier by Morse and Weiss (1955). The greatest satisfaction was "keeping busy," followed by "socializing." Morse and Weiss also found these the two most frequently mentioned meanings of work. The rankings of "being competent" and "service to others" were the third and fourth satisfactions derived from work. Interestingly, the satisfactions found in leisure in general were ranked in reverse of those found in work, with the exception of "keeping busy." Mannell and Reid's respondents regarded leisure as an arena where

Table 4.3:	Satisfactions from Work and Leisure	
Personal Satisfactions	**Work Rank**	**Leisure Rank**
Keeping busy	1	3
Socializing	2	6
Being competent	3	5
Service to others	4	7
Developing friendships	5	2
Maintaining physical fitness	6	4
Exercising power	7	8
Escaping pressure and stress	8	1

Adapted from Reid, 1995, p. 67

they could escape their problems elsewhere and cultivate friendships away from work, but they apparently remained uneasy with the notion of leisure as idleness.

In his reflections on the personal and social meanings of work, philosopher Gini (2000) observed that the close link between modern individual identity and a person's occupation has hidden costs. Some people are what they do in their work. For other people work means "you do what you gotta do" (p. 219) to make a living, even if this means a job without much social status or letting go of other hopes and ambitions. The stable post-World War II labor market studied by Morse and Weiss (1955) suggested that work rested on doing one's share and meeting one's responsibilities. A trade or craft like plumbing was a respectable occupation. Now, however, with all the emphasis on high-tech jobs in the "new economy," estimates suggest that in 2005 only 22% of all jobs will require a college degree 78% will not (US Bureau of Labor Statistics, 1992). This fact does not deny the unquestionable desirability of advanced training in the contemporary economy. It does suggest, however, that unglamorous work will remain more fundamental in our daily lives than e-trading or software coding. Perhaps we need to consider whether the meanings and status of work should reflect connections to other aspects of life, such as leisure.

In the volatile labor market that accompanied the economic restructuring that began in the 1980s, the meanings of work became increasingly uncertain, as the old rules changed. Layoffs and downsizing were once reserved for blue-collar workers in manufacturing industries. Now they are occurrences at all levels in organizations and throughout the economy. As Sennett (1998) illustrated in his description of IBM managers laid off from jobs once thought secure, the absence of meaning in work is disorienting and paralyzing.

Work remains a source of personal dignity and growth (Wolfe, 1997), but only for those who can work (e.g., some people with disabilities are unable to work), and for people whose work is respected in society and in the workplace. Reid (1995) commented that

> while for a few work is increasing in intensity and time commitment, for many it no longer maintains its capacity to provide traditional satisfactions, either because of reduced employment opportunities or because many of the tasks have been truncated, making them meaningless and unfulfilling. (p. 11)

In such circumstances, the need for leisure and quality recreation professionals, programs, and facilities becomes even more compelling. If the meaningfulness of work has become uncertain, leisure must become all the more meaningful.

Reflection Questions

1. Explain the impact of people working for personal rather than economic needs.

2. How can personal needs be met through leisure?

3. Escape was cited as the major satisfaction in leisure. How is this idea inconsistent with the comments about personal needs being met at work?

4. Imagine that you are a recreation programmer working in a public or not-for-profit agency. What sort of programs might you design and offer to demonstrate that leisure can be central to an individual's life, regardless of the kind of work he/she does?

5. How will you balance work and leisure once you enter the working world?

6. If work and leisure both contribute to identity, why do you think we place more value on the work part of our lives?

4.4   An Aging Society

Opportunities and services for persons over the age of 65 years will gain significance in the 21st century. No matter where you work in leisure services, you will work with older adults. Nine states are home to 52% of all persons over the age of 65 in this country: California, Florida, New York, Texas, Pennsylvania, Ohio, Illinois, Michigan, and New Jersey (Hooyman & Kiyak, 1999).

Historically, the United States population has been triangular with the greatest number of persons being very young and the fewest number being very old. We expect the pyramid to dissipate into a rectangular graphic of age cohorts as childbirth continues to decline and more people move into older age categories. Never before has any society faced a situation where the oldest age groups equal the numbers of persons in the youngest ages groups. Leisure services professionals will find services and expectations altered by this new configuration.

Demographics Today and Projections

A multitude of information and future predictions are available describing the current group of older adults. The American Association of Retired Persons (AARP, 1999a) suggests that people over the age of 65 years are the fastest growing segment of the US population, and persons over the age of 85 years represent the greatest growth of all groups. Since 1900, the number of people over the age of 65 has increased from 3.1 million to over 34 million. People who are 65 in 2000 can expect to live 17 more years, and will be joined by the surge of baby boomers entering older adulthood. According to the Administration on Aging, by 2030 almost 22% of the US population will be over 65 years. Further, the percentages of persons over 65 who are minorities are growing at a rate faster than Whites.

Older adults make up a heterogeneous collection of individuals with differing interests, values, experiences, health, income, and education. Many myths exist about older adults in our society. First, not all older adults are feeble and live in nursing homes. In reality, approximately 95% of older adults live in the community and the majority own their own homes. Only about 5% live in nursing facilities and the largest proportion of nursing home residents are over the age of 80. Minority older adults are even less likely to live in a nursing home. Many older adults live with a family member. About 75% of men over age 65 are married and an additional 5% live with another family member. The marriage rate for women is lower than for men, but the majority (52%) are married. With age and mortality of partners, the marriage rate decreases steadily for both sexes as they age.

Similarly, not all older adults are poor, lonely, or have debilitating impairments. Although about half of persons over age 65 years do have some type of chronic impairment such as arthritis, hypertension, or hearing loss, over 80% function independently in activities of daily living such as self care, mobility, and leisure. The 1994 National Health Interview Survey found that over 70% of older adults living in the community described their health as good to excellent. Older minority adults reported a less favorable perception of their health with about 50% expressing good to excellent health (National Center for Health Statistics, 1997). Not all older adults are happy, though. The highest suicide rates in this country are for older White males. This is possibly due to the significant role (e.g., work opportunities and parenting roles) loss during old age and retirement. The loss of identification as a worker, physical functioning, or a spouse is associated with higher risk of suicide.

In 1970, only about 28% of persons over 65 years had completed high school. In 1998, that number had grown to 67% although graduation rates are still low for ethnic minority seniors. Historic discrimination in education is responsible for this discrepancy. Of today's older adults, both White and African-American women are more likely to have finished high school than are men. Of all older adults who finished high school, men were more likely than women to finish college. Educational attainment is aligned with economic status, resulting in continued disadvantage for older minority persons and women who may not have had opportunities for higher education. As baby boomers reach old age, they will have higher education levels and more discretionary money than previous cohorts.

Other variations also exist. Many older adults are economically independent. From 1989 to 1998 the median net worth decreased for people under the age of 55 but increased for people over the age of 55 (Gist, 2000). This average, however, is not true for all older adults. A greater percentage of minority older adults live in poverty than do Whites. Approximately 26% of African Americans, 21% of Hispanics, and 35% of American Indians over the age of 65 live near poverty, while only 9% of Whites over 65 are near poverty levels (AARP, 1999a). In addition, women outnumber men at age 65 by a 14 to 1 ratio, and this ratio increases as people age. Women are more likely to live alone and to live near poverty than are men. Combining sex and ethnicity, 49% of older African-American women live alone. Unlike other groups, Hispanic men outnumber Hispanic women, primarily because more Hispanic men than women immigrate to this country.

Social Security is the major source of income for many older adults. Although some of the monies in Social Security were deposited during the working life of today's older adults, the viability of this program is influenced by the current working population. The dependency ratio is the proportion of working adults (aged 18–64 years) compared to the number of persons over the age of 65. This ratio is not exact since many older adults continue to work and many persons under 65 are unemployed, but the ratio provides a good estimate of the available support to older adults. In 1910 the ratio was approximately ten working people for every older adult. Today that ratio has decreased to five working adults for every older adult and expected to continue to decline well into the 21st century as birth rates remain low and numbers of older adults increase (Hooyman & Kiyak, 1999). The future role of Social Security is highly speculative. The age when people can begin to receive Social Security has risen and other changes are also likely to occur. Social Security has been considered a right and will likely continue to be so.

These demographics have implications for leisure. For example, minority older adults face additional factors that influence leisure participation. More minorities than White seniors live with family members and maintain social roles within that unit; they tend to use recreation facilities at a lower rate. The changing numbers of older people, their health, the education and minority status, and government programs including Social Security's future will effect the potential and opportunities for leisure for older people in the coming years. These demographics raise issues of what successful aging means and how leisure might be embodied.

Theories of Aging

Many conflicting and complementary theories exist to explain successful aging. A few of the ideas pertinent to thinking about the impact of the aging on society and leisure services will be discussed here.

Activity theory (Havinghurst, 1963) assumes that older adults adjust to aging in direct proportion to their activity levels. More adjusted and successful older adults have larger numbers of productive roles and activities. These people belong to groups, volunteer, exercise, and remain active. Although on the surface this theory appears congruent with the leisure services, activity theory omits the value of individual choice, values, personality, and resources. For example, some people do not have transportation, so they cannot stay active in community activities. Other people may feel they have earned the right to be lazy in their old age.

Continuity theory (Neugarten, Havinghurst & Tobin, 1968) explains successful aging as a person's ability to continue the patterns developed during middle adulthood. People are happiest when they continue their lifelong social behaviors. Successful aging relates to the development of a satisfying lifestyle during middle age. This tie between middle and late life stages suggests the feasibility of a life span approach to understanding successful aging.

Neither the activity nor continuity theories place emphasis on an individual's interaction with a changing society. Continuing or increasing activities of middle adulthood may not hold the same value or reward in a changing world. Contemporary theories attempt to view successful aging from both micro (individual) and macro (societal) frameworks. A Golden Girls television episode provides an example:

> Dorothy, concerned about leaving her mother at home alone, conspires with a nursing home administrator to convince mom (Sophia) that Sophia is volunteering as Activity Director for the center. In this role, Sophia takes charge of the situation. She is very active, eagerly awaits work each day, and is satisfied with the arrangement. When trouble occurs in one of her programs, and the secret is revealed that she is really attending the home as a participant and not as Activity Director, enthusiasm changes, and she quits attending the center.

Person-environment theory helps us understand this situation. Theories based on the interaction of the person with the environment propose that to successfully age a person must balance what is important to her or him individually with what society expects. In this situation, both the person and the environment influence change in each other. The environment can be the community, society, neighborhood, or family. Successful aging occurs when a match is found between personal competence and the environment where one lives (Hooyman & Kiyak, 1999). Older adults need to feel they have a stimulating environment that does not put limits on their personal control. This desire is a challenge when considering how older adults might experience leisure.

Successful aging comes from a variety of influences. No theory gives us a prescription for successful aging. Rather, leisure service providers should approach the task of supporting older adults from a blended perspective.

The Potential of Leisure

Recreation and leisure professionals must consider a number of issues to meet the leisure needs and interests of older adults in the coming years. Leisure service professionals will encounter issues never before faced by the profession. As more people reach older ages, the probability of disability increases. Thus, services and supports for people with disabilities will continue to be important. Similarly, as larger numbers of minority persons enter old age, the issues of cultural sensitivity increase. Predictions estimate that women will continue to outnumber men in the older adult population so issues of sexual equity will remain important.

As a greater percentage of our population reaches old age, issues of family caregiving also will increase. Older en are more likely than older women to be married or living with a family member. Thus, adult women are increasingly faced with the role of caregiver for a spouse or a parent. Often these women, referred to as the *sandwich generation*, provide care for an older parent while raising their own children and maintaining employment. As society ages, the probability of an older person being the caregiver for another older person increases. A caregiver might well benefit from a leisure respite. Providing a program for the caregiver, however, is not enough. Caregiving is often a 24-hour-a-day job, and the leisure participation of the caregiver is one of the first things given up to fulfill the role. The caregiver is unable or unwilling to leave their family member for a trip to the recreation center. Often the guilt associated with taking time for oneself is greater than the benefit. In these situations, the recreation program might also offer a leisure program for the care recipient. Even then, the caregiver may not experience freedom from worry. If the programs are in the same building, the caregiver may feel required to check on their family member. If programs are in separate facilities, timing is crucial to allow for transport between facilities. Issues are much the same as for parents and child-rearing. This example of caregiving, nevertheless, represents some of the major issues that individuals as well as leisure service providers will need to address in the future.

Politics also influences leisure. Older adults constitute a growing and significant political and social force. The American Association of Retired Persons (AARP) is the largest membership organization in this country with over 30 million members. Local and state AARP chapters organize voter education programs, volunteer transportation options, and political debates. Older adults have lived in their current communities for years, are connected to that community, and vote more frequently than other age groups. In the 1996 national elections, people over 65 years of age represented 20% of all voters (Federal Elections Commission of USA, 1997). It is expected that political candidates will seek the older adult vote more in the future than ever before. Thus, the influence of their values and desires will be influential. For recreation professionals, the influence of older adults, their needs for recreation programs and facilities, and their voting power cannot be ignored.

Work and leisure issues are magnified in retirement. Since people are living longer and the Social Security system supplements their income, retirement has become a common choice of later years. You have probably heard your parents' or grandparents' dreams of retiring and living the good life. As more people live longer and as more people are needed in the labor force, this pattern could change. People now consider working part-time rather than taking full retirement because of economic constraints or because they are looking for meaningful activities (AARP, 1999b). Work patterns may change to where people stop work for a number of years and then rejoin the workforce later. Since its inception in 1935, the Social Security Administration has set 65 as the magic age for retirement and receipt of Social Security benefits. That age is being systematically raised and will affect the time when people can afford to retire fully.

We mentioned earlier that the possibility of disability increases with age. On a related note, people with lifelong disabilities are now living to old age. This trend means that service systems for older adults and services for persons with disabilities will need to work together. Until recently, few persons with a developmental disability were expected to live to old age. Further, many had never worked so retirement had no meaning. With the aging of society, this situation will no longer be true. Systems are needed to support the retirement options of persons with developmental disabilities, including access to community senior programs (Mahon, Mactavish, Mahon & Searle, 1995). This issue is made more complex by current financial regulations that prohibit persons receiving Social Security disability income from accumulating retirement investments. These individuals face a Catch-22. If they accumulate savings, they loose government benefits and must spend their savings to exist. Without investments or pension plans, these persons are destined to work until they die, because they do not have the financial means to retire. This financial conundrum is also true of older adults moving into long-term care facilities such as nursing homes. Another related issue for people who live in supported housing situations is who is responsible for providing leisure options for residents—the residential provider or the community service network. Rather than argue about responsibility, a cooperative approach is needed.

The age makeup of American society is changing. As the number of older adults continues to grow, recreation and leisure service providers will be faced with changing policies and programs to meet these needs. The demographics of the older adult population will become more diverse, as will examples of successful aging. Many more jobs may develop based on the changing needs of this population of participants. Leisure service professionals, as well as personnel in all areas of human services, will need to continue to learn about and respond to our aging population.

Reflection Questions

1. What are some common, but not necessarily true, myths about older adults?

2. How will an increased percentage of older adults influence leisure services? What will the impact of baby boomers retiring early be on leisure service provision in this country?

3. Explain two theories of aging and how those theories relate to leisure services.

4. What will be the greatest challenges to recreation professionals when trying to meet the needs of our aging society?

4.5   A Segregated Society

As Americans move into the 21st century, high hopes for a better society have not materialized the way some people had envisioned. Many people thought that tensions and divisiveness around individual characteristics like race, gender, age, income, sexual identity, and religion would be an unpleasant memory of the past. We can look around us, however, and still see many examples of segregation and prejudice. For example, African-American students sit together on one side of the cafeteria, and European-American students on the other. Women still dominate professions such as teaching and nursing. Communities are designed exclusively for older retired people, or for people who could afford a $400,000 home.

While many people point out that legislation prohibits discrimination based on such characteristics as race, gender, and religion, the reality of equity does not necessarily exist for all people. Facilitating recreation and leisure experiences challenges a society that has remnants of segregation. Another related issue concerns segregated opportunities and when they should be allowed within recreation and leisure services. This chapter examines selected examples of how leisure professionals might begin to think about the impact of an implicitly segregated society.

Social Segregation

Some people think segregation is a notion of the past. They may have grown up in a community where great diversity could be seen in the neighborhood, within groups of friends, and in the places where they played, went to school or church, or shopped. Others, however, grew up in communities where everyone looked and acted alike with few differences based on skin color, religious affiliations, and economic advantage. If anyone was different (e.g., gay or lesbian, had a disability, unmarried), they were often segregated or isolated, and sometimes treated differently from the rest of the community. Many people feel uncomfortable saying that segregation exists in their community. Most of the time, we just say that some people like being with their own kind and no one is being separated from the rest of the community. A challenge is to get people to critically evaluate how society continues to be segregated.

We use income as an example of how class segregation can be found in US society. Most people agree that society is divided along economic lines. Morganthau (1997) suggested that 21st century America will be a crowded, mean-spirited, and balkanized society with a huge chasm between the rich and the poor. Sklar (1995) suggested that all of us are a part of an economic pyramid that has vast inequalities in the distribution of wealth. In this pyramid, 1% of the population controls 48% of the wealth, another 19% controls 46% of the wealth, and 80% of the population divides up the remaining 6% of the wealth in the United States.

Many of us are not aware of the great economic inequality and the resulting segregation based upon income level that exists and continues to be perpetuated in society. To stay powerful, the 1% who control almost half of the wealth need for the majority to work hard, stay healthy, have basic literacy skills, break up their work with some fun in their lives, and find a little security. The middle group (19%) comprises buffer professions and occupations that encourage demands for political and economic participation by the poor. These professionals in jobs like social welfare work, teaching, counseling, healthcare, and recreation receive a better education, better pay, and a little more security and respect in exchange for providing services for the people on the bottom of the pyramid (80%). As members of this buffer zone, professionals do enough to keep the workers on the bottom, as well as themselves, alive and well. If someone does not succeed economically, it is considered his or her own fault (Sklar, 1995). Older adults, people of color, immigrants, single-parent families headed by women, and people with disabilities overrepresent the people who comprise the have-nots.

Integrated Leisure

As recreation professionals, we need to examine our role in economic segregation. As providers of structured recreation activities, we do not want to set up a "we-they" situation that further segregates us from the people who most need our services. Some recreation and leisure professionals live in the communities where they work but many do not. Recreation professionals need to understand the positive and negative aspects of how leisure services are programmed and managed. For example, most professionals know that they need to do a better job examining benefits not from what they assume participants need and want, but from what the participants say they need and want. Recreation professionals might assume larger advocacy and facilitator roles through recreation services that help empower participants regardless of their class status. Offering facilities and programs in poor inner-city areas that raise the quality of life for that segment of the population is as much a priority as maintaining the golf courses and marinas for the upper-class.

Most people can think of numerous ways that recreation brings people together. For example, public recreation providers often sponsor community-based festivals that celebrate many forms of cultural diversity. Adults play on sport teams in leagues from throughout the community. Parents in an at-risk neighborhood devise ways to offer an after-school program in a nearby church through the facilitation efforts of several recreation staff. Grandparent Buddy programs bring together older adults with children in an intergenerational program. A social support group for people living with AIDS and their caregivers meets at the community center near their hospice. Efforts such as these are ways that recreation can bring people together even in situations that could be potentially divisive. Rather than accentuate the differences, recreation can bring people together in common experiences and teach respect and appreciation for the wide array of differences.

While segregation is usually considered an undesirable state, one might wonder if there is ever a time when it might be beneficial. As we noted when we talked about people with disabilities in unit three, sometimes environments are so unwelcoming and uneducated that it is far more comfortable for people with disabilities to stay in segregated situations. This obviously is not a beneficial outcome, but it is often the justification for keeping groups segregated.

To illustrate the problems and benefits of segregated groups we will briefly examine women-only outdoor recreational experiences. Past research has suggested that some women want a safe, supportive environment that frees them to learn new skills, establish bonds with other women, and recreate in an atmosphere free of gender expectations. These women may feel constrained in a coed situation and unable to experience the freedom and choice found in leisure. While most people do not want segregated recreation experiences, many people make a case for special programs that allow individuals an opportunity to maximize their leisure. On the other hand, if coed environments felt safer, more supportive, and if they were free of gender expectation and roles, many women might not feel the need for all female groups.

Leisure programs that focus on a targeted homogeneous group might be appropriate in some cases. Perhaps justifications are found when the program is a choice, and not the only option. For example, to allow a person with a physical disability to only participate with other people with physical disabilities limits that person to a preconceived idea of need and ability. Rather than segregate based on disability, inclusive programming would encourage greater awareness about disabilities and promote individual growth based on ability. That way, the individual makes the decision about which environment is most conducive to his or her needs at that time. The individual may choose a segregated program designed specifically for people with disabilities until they acquire the skills necessary to participate comfortably in a nonsegregated activity.

Society has many challenges to address concerning integrated leisure. It is difficult to understand how to solve segregation problems, especially when we hear about situations such as the 1999 Supreme Court ruling that allow the Boy Scouts to deny gay leaders a place in their organization. Hate crimes and sexual assault often make participation in leisure with like groups much easier, more comfortable, and safer. Recreation professionals, however, must be aware of these larger social issues and attempt to make sure that leisure services do not contribute further to the problems that exist in society.

Recreation and leisure can make a difference in the quality of life of our community members in ways that can bring people together rather than isolate and separate. Ending segregation and making programs inclusive depends on consistent and concerted efforts. Through recreation programs, inclusive management, and staff training, recreation professionals can advocate for greater respect and understanding for individuals in their communities while developing opportunities and skills to empower all individuals including those people most at risk for being invisible or marginalized within our social institutions and structures.

Reflection Questions

1. When, if ever, should public recreation agencies provide segregated activities? When is it not acceptable for agencies to provide segregated activities?

2. Why might there be a need for recreation-based programs that target certain populations, such as gay, lesbian, or bisexual youth?

3. In what ways do you see recreation in your community continuing to segregate programs and people? In what ways does it integrate people?

4.6   Education for Leisure

For generations, the public school system has prepared students for a life where work is primary and leisure is secondary. As a high school student, you likely met with a guidance counselor who helped you match your interests and skills with job possibilities. You took certain courses to prepare you for college or technical school. Everyone was interested in what kind of work you would pursue as your career. In school you also had numerous opportunities to explore leisure interests through such extracurricular activities as sports, band, chorus, drama, debate club, and service clubs. It is doubtful, however, that anyone really talked with you about how to find balance in your life, how to find outlets for stress, or even how to maintain an emotionally and physically healthy lifestyle. Some of these outcomes were certainly encouraged and implied in what you did after school and in your free time, but they were likely not discussed.

We assume that people need to learn how to work, but that somehow we know how to experience leisure without any planning or forethought. This emphasis on the "work self" is a clear indication of the values we hold in US society. Work has been the central interest of industrial Western society. Elementary, secondary, technical, and higher education have all emphasized the skills and attitudes necessary to support a work-oriented value system and way of life. We define ourselves by our jobs more than by our leisure interests, no matter how central those interests might be in our lives.

On the other hand, schools have provided some education in areas that support leisure life choices in unarticulated but major ways. Leisure education occurs in many forms related to skill development, such as music, arts, reading, physical activity, and extracurricular activities. Education for leisure, however, is more than teaching specific activity skills or the providing of facilities for extracurricular activities. Education implies developing attitudes about life that free individuals to discover who they are and what is meaningful to them. Leisure education also suggests developing the attitudes and skills necessary for future explorations and involvement in new leisure pursuits.

Typically the higher level of education a person has achieved, the greater their leisure repertoire. This trend can be partially explained by exposure to leisure venues and by social learning through observation of other's leisure behaviors. Mundy (1998) proposed, however, that with the recent emphasis on academic basics and the elimination of art, music, and physical education programs at schools throughout the country, the true onus to educate the citizenry for leisure will fall primarily on recreation and leisure professionals. She argued that as a profession we have assumed that possessing knowledge and skills about recreation activities opportunities for participation will lead to enriching, enhancing leisure lifestyles. She also stated,

> the primary emphasis of the field of recreation, park, and
> leisure has been on the provision of recreation activities,
> areas, and facilities. If there has been any educational empha-
> sis, it has been on developing knowledge and skills needed
> for participation in specific recreation activities. (p. 1)

She admonished that it can no longer be assumed that people have the ability to find satisfying recreation and leisure on their own.

Educating for Leisure

Education for leisure is a necessity. If recreation and leisure professionals really believe in the right of all people to freely choose and participate in leisure, they must be willing to provide the education that will allow informed choices. People should be prepared for living a meaningful existence. Education for leisure should include instruction about leisure awareness, attitudes, and knowledge; an understanding of personal values and how values influence leisure choices; resource identification and utilization; and leisure planning and decision-making skills.

Most people can define leisure, but many do not explore the real value of leisure in their life. Leisure is a concept easily taken for granted. The idea of leisure rarely elicits deep reflection or contemplation for the average citizen, although many people articulate that they do not have enough time for leisure. Without an understanding of the value and role of leisure in one's life, however, we have difficulties in identifying leisure resources. Many people feel their lives lack leisure, but they cannot explicitly identify why constraints exist. Increasing people's understanding of leisure in their lives and improving their attitudes toward it is a foundation for taking control of leisure choices. It leads to the possibilities for leisure planning and decision making. Leisure planning skills can reduce stress by allowing an individual to build sufficient leisure activity into the daily routine.

People complain far less about being bored at work than at home. What to do with unstructured time is an uncomfortable decision for many people. In such situations we often find it easiest to just turn on the television and be entertained. Having choices in our leisure, or being free to participate sounds like a simple concept, but if an individual is unaware of the multitude of leisure options available, choice is difficult to apply.

Venues for Education for Leisure

Leisure education has primarily been a technique used by therapeutic recreation specialists and counselors. As we discussed in unit three, these professionals often work with specialized groups of people who need help with their leisure lives. People in the general society as well as people in marginalized groups also need to have educational opportunities that will help them better understand the importance of leisure in their lives.

The typical advertisement by way of posting a flyer or putting an ad in the newspaper regarding a class on leisure education might not be the best way to educate people. Rather, recreation and leisure professionals might operate as leisure advocates by doing outreach such as guest presentations at school, clubs, and organizations. These presentations should not only explain what programs a recreation agency offers, but also help people see why leisure is important and how they can make choices within their lives to include leisure. Participating in preretirement planning seminars is another opportunity to provide education for leisure. People anticipating their retirement often attend instructional seminars to determine their values, needs, and preferences related to retirement. Most of these seminars focus on finances, but the money people have will only be useful if it leads to a more satisfying life. People want to enjoy retirement and make choices about leisure behavior no longer regulated by work life.

Other groups besides retirees need education for leisure. For example, young adults who graduate from high school or college and move to a new city to take their first job need the skills to facilitate leisure involvement in their new situation. If someone does not have options to choose, she or he may do what is easy like watch television or do nothing at all. Similarly, if a person does not know where to find a leisure activity, participation is inhibited. Leisure service professionals have an obligation to educate a broad base of society about the multitude of leisure options and resources that are often available in communities. An example of one way that some professionals are reaching out to community members is by accessing community cable channels in their city. This venue is another way to provide education for leisure to someone unaware of the opportunities that exist in a community.

Learning and leisure are lifelong processes. As we become aware of alternatives and develop attitudes that encourage exploration and decision making, freedom of choice in leisure is broadened. If recreation and leisure are to be meaningful to individuals, they must possess the skills and attitudes that affirm their choices. Leisure education is a central challenge to facilitators of recreation and leisure services in all sectors.

Reflection Questions

1. Who should be responsible for leisure education?

2. Justify the inclusion of leisure education as a part of an elementary or secondary school curriculum.

3. How might the provision of leisure education perpetuate the status quo rather than freeing people to choose?

4. Why do people need to be educated about leisure?

4.7   Wellness and Healthcare

Health and wellness are central to leisure. Positive leisure lifestyles result in improved physical and mental health. This chapter explores the relationships that exist between leisure and wellness and why people are more concerned about health than ever before.

Identifying the Issues

In the 1990s consumer prices grew by 59%, while the consumer price index for healthcare grew by 117% (Moon, 1996). At its current rate, healthcare spending will soon consume 20% of the gross national product, compared to 12% in 1990 (Chenoweth, 1998). The advent of managed care has helped to slow the growth of healthcare costs, but other factors (e.g., the increasing older adult population, expensive medical equipment) impact that growth. Further, the patterns of health and illness in this country have changed. Historically, people died of infectious diseases such as smallpox, diphtheria, and yellow fever. Today, people are living longer and affected more by chronic degenerative illnesses such as heart disease and cancer (Whitman, Merluzzi & White, 1999). Stress is also linked to physiological and mental health and is the most common problem found in health screenings. Stress may reduce productivity, cause accidents, and result in fatigue, headaches, and anxiety. Reducing the cost of healthcare is expected to continue to be a pertinent issue for politicians and economists.

Health and wellness implies more than just the absence of illness. To be healthy is to have

> a state in which the individual has (a) a capacity for joy and happiness; (b) a sense of self-worth, confidence, and efficacy; (c) a sense of personal identity and meaning; (d) a sense of belonging to a meaningful and supportive group; and (e) the motivation to be involved in the maintenance of social order. (Shain, 1996, p. 328)

This broad view of health and wellness has led to

> a shift from a medical model that favors treatment of disease, illness, and medical maladies to wellness, focusing on health, quality of life, and health promotion . . . from a competitive model to a collaborative model. (Shain, 1996, p. 2)

Today, healthcare emphasizes health maintenance and the prevention of disease. It is accepted that prevention is less costly than cure. With the shift of emphasis from treating disease to health maintenance, greater attention will be given to those behaviors that maintain or improve health. Healthcare providers will become responsible for the health of their communities and be forced to collaborate with other service providers to meet the needs.

Prevention efforts, intricately associated with the leisure service profession, emphasize the importance of healthy lifestyles. For example, physical active involvement focuses on prevention of disease more than on treatment. Some insurance providers have even begun to finance prevention and education programs because these programs can reduce healthcare costs. It is estimated that 50% to 70% of all disease is caused, or at least stimulated by, poor health behaviors such as smoking, poor diet, sedentary lifestyle, and alcohol and drug abuse (Whitmer, 1993). Behaviors that are controllable by the individual through efforts such as stress reduction programs can reduce physician visits by up to 50% (Saving Money by Reducing Stress, 1994; Scott & Jaffe, 1994).

Benefits of Healthy Living through Leisure

Even with the plethora of information about healthy living, the health of the average American has not improved during the past decade (Chenoweth, 1998). If the new paradigm of healthcare is preventive, holistic, and focused on healthy lifestyles, then leisure services can have potentially beneficial impacts on people's health. A few of the benefits of leisure participation include physical fitness, social connections, and stress relief through humor.

Physical Fitness

Physical fitness is a major contributor to wellness. Studies demonstrate that physical activity

(1) decreases health risks for cardiovascular disease including high blood pressure, obesity, and high cholesterol (Anspaugh, Hunter & Dignan, 1996);

(2) increases energy, body strength, and self-esteem (Paffenbarger, Hyde & Dow, 1991);

(3) decreases tension and symptoms of depression (Lampinen, Heikkinen & Ruoppila, 2000); and

(4) effectively manages non-insulin-dependent diabetes.

The aging of our society will continue to impact healthcare costs. The majority of aging persons have at least one chronic illness, and many have multiple ailments. Many of the factors associated with chronic diseases are related to lifestyle choices such as smoking, excessive alcohol or caffeine use, long-term dieting, and sedentary lifestyles. Exercise combined with medical treatment has been found to be more effective than medical treatment alone in decreasing a number of the effects of aging (Hooyman & Kiyak, 1999).

Various prescriptions have been offered to increase the fitness of American citizens. Running, walking, and aerobics have become popular fitness activities. Many experts consider a total of 30 minutes of moderate exercise most days of the week as a minimum. Other experts propose several five-minute workouts per day. Whatever the approach, prescribing fitness regimens is not enough. People have to be willing to adhere to a fitness routine. Most people will stick to doing physical activity if they enjoy it. Leisure service professionals have a role to play in helping people find enjoyment in having healthy lifestyles.

Social Connections

A recent study reported that organizational membership is down in the US society (Putnam, 2000). People are not joining civic groups, churches, or other organizations as frequently as in previous years. This could have potential impact on healthcare in the future. Social belonging has been found to relate to overall well-being, compliance with medical regimen, and onset of illness (Frank et al., 1997; Seigley, 1998). Jaffe (in Padus, 1992) stated, "It's as though a breakdown in the social support structure precipitates a breakdown in the body's immune system" (p. 18). For example, a study of Japanese Americans found that with other risk factors controlled, those older people who maintained traditional Japanese values emphasizing the importance of community had lower heart disease than those seniors who adopted a less community-focused value system. In a similar study Berkman and Syme (1979) found that older adult participants with strong social ties lived longer than people without social connections, regardless of other risk factors. Leisure service providers can offer opportunities for social interaction in the activities they facilitate.

Stress Relief through Humor

Norman Cousins (1979) in *Anatomy of an Illness* was one of the first medical professionals to promote the value of laughter to overall health. Laughter activates muscles and increases heart rate and oxygen exchange similar to the desirable effects achieved through exercise. Laughing heartily releases endorphins that in turn elevate people's moods. Further, a good strong laugh reduces muscle tension and thus, stress. Laughing can be a mini workout for the internal organs. All of us can probably remember a time when we laughed so long and so hard that our muscles ached.

Laughing is inherently associated with play. Cousins (1979) contended that adults forget how to play, and this lack of spontaneous enjoyment is related to physiological ills. Certainly the joy and camaraderie of play and other forms of recreation participation enhance laughter and reinforce a sense of humor.

Recreation Programs to Improve Health

Improving the wellness of citizens will become the responsibility of multiple service providers. Recreation and leisure professionals will need to be leaders in this effort. Throughout the book we have discussed venues for recreation and their contribution to the overall leisure profession. These agencies, businesses, and organizations can all contribute to wellness and the prevention of increasing healthcare costs.

Public recreation agencies offer fitness and sport programs for all ages. Further, participation in programs such as art or drama can contribute to improved self-esteem and a sense of belonging. Often the leisure professional is limited in knowledge of the broad influences on health. To overcome this deficit, recreation agencies can collaborate with healthcare professionals. Health fairs cooperatively offered by local healthcare providers and recreation agencies strengthen the tie between quality leisure and overall well-being.

Recreation and leisure services cannot provide all the remedies for health. You need only visit a bookstore to see the myriad self-help remedies available. Leisure service providers, however, can supplement this interest by sponsoring speakers and demonstrations related to self-help topics, or by providing facilities where participants can design their own wellness opportunities.

Leisure providers are not the only ones reaching out to the fitness needs of America. In recent years, over 300,000 hospitals have opened fitness centers (MacStravic & Montrose, 1998). Most hospitals started these centers to serve as a revenue source as well as to lower healthcare costs. One example is the Tom Landry Center, an affiliate of the Baylor Hospital System in Dallas. The Landry Center offers state-of-the-art wellness services, including fitness facilities, nutritional counseling, and psychoeducational groups. Similarly, hospitals are frequent sponsors of wheelchair sports teams and clinics.

The employer's share of America's total healthcare bill increased form 18% in 1965 to more than 30% in 1997 (Chenoweth, 1998). To combat this increase, employers frequently offer recreation and fitness programs. These employee recreation programs provide benefits of reduced time needed for sick leave and better health of participating employees. Healthier employees are more productive, but motivating employees to participate is often a problem. Many companies find that few employees choose to participate, and those who do are typically already fit. To reach greater numbers of employees, business programs now offer a wider variety of programs and services for employees, including fitness, smoking cessation, preretirement planning, and financial counseling. All of these programs are offered to increase the quality of life of employees and to enhance their well-being.

Choice is central to leisure. As recreation and leisure professionals determine ways to handle future needs related to wellness and health, they must focus on giving people information and choices. This freedom to choose should provide a powerful avenue for people with differing interests and abilities to find a route toward improving their overall life while simultaneously fighting off the onset of chronic conditions that may require healthcare interventions. Strong leisure education will maximize participants' freedom of choice, raise awareness about the benefits of recreation especially related to health and wellness, and instill a greater appreciation and value for leisure as a central part of life.

Reflection Questions

1. What are four health benefits of leisure?

2. How can leisure influence the onset of chronic illness and disease?

3. How does stress impact health? How can leisure be a tool to manage stress?

4. How might you as a recreation professional promote healthy lifestyles in your community?

4.8   Technology and Leisure

Advances in technology have given people new ways to communicate, innovative places to play, better equipment to facilitate their adventures, and new activities to pursue. Some of the advances have helped recreation professionals streamline or remove tedious work tasks like league scheduling, improve communication efforts with participants, and manage services more efficiently and effectively. Many of these positive advances, however, have come with often overlooked costs. In this chapter we explore some of the positive and negative influences of technology on recreation and leisure.

Technology and Positive Influences on Leisure Pursuits

Every one of us can look around and see the influence of technology on our leisure lives. Walk into almost any household in the United States and you will likely find one or more televisions with cable (and maybe Internet service), a VCR or DVD player, radio and laser disc player, and enough remote controls to confuse any technophobe. Many households have a computer, timesaving appliances like microwaves, and maybe a cell phone. We buy recreational vehicles like personal watercraft, motor homes, and the latest bicycles, tennis rackets, and in-line skates. We can make vacation reservations, access maps, and find tourist information over the Internet. More people are doing activities like backpacking, climbing, and paddling because technology has improved the equipment needed to make the activities more comfort and safer to attract a wider range of individuals. The next time you put on your Gortex jacket, a Coolmax shirt, or your Teva sandals, remember how much even the clothes we wear are influenced by technology. Four impacts will be discussed briefly: access to information about activities, the creation of new recreational pursuits, new possibilities for people with disabilities, and tourism with a global focus.

Access to Information

Many examples exist of technological advances that help people to access information and pursue new recreation interests. The Internet has become the biggest information center available in our society. Within seconds people can access information about new hobbies, places to do these activities, and connections with other people interested in the same activities. People can access websites to buy the needed equipment or supplies, make reservations, acquire permits, or just chat with other interested people. Advances in fiber optics, laser technology, and other forms of transmission continue to make this access faster, easier, and cheaper.

New Recreation Pursuits

Technology has also led to new recreational activities and significant changes
in older forms of recreation. A quick look through a recreational store,
catalog, or online shopping site provides evidence of these advances. For
example, we have dozens of new pursuits directly related to the prevalence
of computers such as computer games, virtual reality gaming centers, online
chat groups, MP3 music, DVD players for computers, online auctions, and
just surfing the net. People do not even need a computer for this access since
cable can bring these experiences to the home through a television. New
recreational equipment is available such as jet skis, all-terrain vehicles,
snowmobiles, and hang gliders. Some of our old recreational activities have
been enhanced by the development of new materials (e.g., titanium) for
softball bats, backpack equipment, and bicycles. We use technology to make
our equipment stronger and lighter, our clothing warmer or cooler, and our
activities more exciting and innovative. We use sonar to locate fish and
modify target equipment to produce opportunities like paint ball. We row
and bike in our living rooms and rock climb indoors on artificial walls.

Opportunities for People with Disabilities

Technology has also allowed whole new worlds to open for people. For
example, some people with physical disabilities can ski, run, climb, garden,
paint, and lead an active life because of technological advances that facilitate their movement, their senses, and their personal interactions. People
with communication impairments have computers that can speak for them.

Tourism with a Global Focus

Lastly, technology has influenced the way people travel and visit other people
and places. More people than ever before fly to varied destinations around
the world. Tourism has emerged as one of the leading economies in many
countries because of the ease of travel due to better technology. People around
the world want to experience different cultures, visit historic areas, and see
the natural beauty of the world. For example, people are now able to visit
the penguin colonies of Antarctica, trek in the remote areas of Nepal, float
the Amazon River to see some of the remaining rain forests, bike tour
through ancient Greek ruins, or visit the Great Wall of China. For much of
the tourism industry, technology has helped make these experiences more
accessible with comfort-enhancing amenities. Families unable to afford the
cost of travel can still learn about distant lands through television, videos,
and websites. Some people suggest that the technological influence on the
future of tourism is barely tapped as entrepreneurs explore the possibility
of space travel, orbiting resorts, and moon-based recreational adventures.

The Negative Side of Technology

Technology has left its mark on recreation activities, but not everyone views all the advances positively. For example, although some people value forms of recreation such as jet skis and snowmobiles, other people view them as negative. These vehicles seem incompatible to some people's leisure ideals because of the noise, pollution, resource depletion, and habitat destruction they cause. Some people believe the technology behind these machines should not have been developed and marketed to the general public.

Although recreational issues may not seem critical to the "life and death" of an individual, they are often critical to the quality of people's lives. We will address four negative issues that have resulted from technological advances in recreation: passivity, violence, consumerism, and social isolation. These complex issues raise questions about personal values. They also provide a context for examining basic concerns about technology development.

Passivity

Technological developments are often touted as laborsaving devices that free people from the drudgeries of manual work. "Free time" should provide opportunities to enjoy leisure and pursue an active, healthy life. Technology, however, has often taken away many physical demands of life and offered passive opportunities instead. For example, many experts are increasingly alarmed at the lack of physical activity of Americans (US Department of Health and Human Services, 1996) and often link this passivity to television viewing and growing interest in computer-based entertainment. In 1996 over 18% of all nine-year-olds watched six or more hours of television a day. When analyzed by gender and race, 20% of all boys and 39% of all Black non-Hispanic children were in this category (US Department of Health and Human Services, 1998). According to Nielsen Company (1998), the average American watches 3 hours and 46 minutes of television each day, but the television is actually on in the average home for 7 hours and 12 minutes (TV Free America, 1999).

Although television watching has declined slightly over the last ten years, the difference is being picked up by increased use of computer-based entertainment (Kaufman, 2000). Rather than use free time to pursue active leisure pursuits, more people (especially children) resort to passive hours before a screen. As one 16-year-old teen responded when asked if he had ever been told he spent too much time on the computer:

> All the time. From 5 p.m. until 11 p.m., I'm on. The most time I've ever spent online was 218 hours one month.
> (Teens on the Web, 2000)

While the positive aspects of television and computers have been highlighted, the negative impacts on physical activity cannot be denied. Physical and mental health concerns as a result of less physical recreation is a direct challenge brought about by human responses to marketing that promotes watching television or a computer screen instead of being an active participant.

Violence

Violence also arises from increased technology in recreation. Violence has been a part of leisure for centuries (e.g., gladiators in ancient Rome). Concern exists today that some recreational activities promote violence and technology exacerbates this violence. For example, violence has been associated with sports like football and soccer, and with the advent of televised games, millions of people view these events. Not only is the violence seen on the field, but also some people suggest it carries over into the living room. The media have suggested that domestic violence increases on Super Bowl Sunday, although little data has supported that claim (Adams, 2000).

New activities such as paint ball—where camouflaged participants actively pursue and shoot other players with gel bullets from realistic looking guns—raise questions of violence. Parents worry that violent computer games with realistic blood and gore send a message of permissible violence, especially when reinforced by similar images on television and lyrics in popular songs. Pornography accessed through the Internet is one more way that some people suggest violence is perpetuated. It is too simplistic to blame violent behavior on technology alone, but these behaviors raise the ethical issue of whether a person should be free to access and pursue violence through technologically enhanced leisure opportunities.

Consumerism

Increased consumerism has a strong tie to technology. As more activities and equipment are developed, many people feel they must have the latest, biggest, or fastest model available. We view these technological advancements as symbols of our expertise, wealth, or status. Further, every day new advances come on the market. The need for more can range from the latest Airs by Nike, the most powerful laptop, the largest entertainment center with DVD and surround sound, or the largest motorboat on the lake.

The message is you must buy your way in, and even if you may not be good at an activity, you can at least look the part. The slogan that appeared on a T-shirt several years ago, "He who dies with the most toys, wins" has become an anthem for our consuming culture. As the richest society in the world, people in the United States are also the greatest consumers of resources for recreation. The techniques used to market this notion of consumerism, as well as the advancements used to produce the items, are examples of the double-edged sword of technology.

Social Isolation

Social isolation is often linked to technological advances, particularly to the use of free time. We can e-mail, fax, talk on cell phones, videoconference, and search the world's libraries and databases from the comforts of home. People who work outside the home often return at night without setting foot outside the door until they leave again the next day. We can buy groceries and shop online. We visit friends over the phone, use our computer to send pictures or videos, and interact anonymously in chat rooms. In his article "Bowling Alone," Putnam (1995a) suggested that our society is becoming more socially isolated, even in our recreation. The example of individuals going bowling by themselves rather than bowling on teams as the trend used to be, is indicative of decreased social interaction and increased self-absorption.

With technological advances, many people can choose to have minimal contact with other people. With reasons that vary from weak interpersonal skills to being too tired from work demands, people have become more isolated socially, although more technically linked. While social isolation can be seen as individual choice, particularly in leisure, professionals worry about the long-term effects. This isolation can result in a decrease in community involvement and negative impacts to individuals who lack social support groups and companions.

Technological Influences on the Recreation Professional

Just as technology influences individuals' recreation and leisure, technology also affects the recreation professional. Technology has a direct bearing on the programs offered by any sector of leisure services providers, whether a parks and recreation department, a YWCA, or a whitewater rafting company. For example, people with disabilities who find that technology can minimize their disabilities demand opportunities to take part in all aspects of recreation programs. Professionals must keep abreast of the influences that technology has on the potential participants.

Many technological changes occur in the management and administration of recreation services. For example, a typical office has a computer on the desk with a network system that allows professionals to use the latest software for budgeting, database development, desktop publishing, registration, and athletic league schedules. Most recreation departments have websites for information and marketing, and many communications are handled by e-mail. The phone has voice mail and there is a fax machine for information unable to be sent as an e-mail attachment. The professional has a pager and a cell phone for 24-hour contact. GPS (geographical positioning system) units are common in the field, with the professionals taking advantage of the extensive mapping systems available to help them understand their communities and resources. Professionals can conduct training or take continuing education courses online or through interactive video hookups.

Ever-changing recreation activities have placed new demands on many agencies for programs and facilities. Recreation professionals must respond to consumer demands for new facilities like skateboard parks, indoor climbing walls, and laser tag spaces. Participants want state-of-the-art fitness centers with spinning bikes, saunas, and weight-training machines. Participants also want trained personnel to teach them how to use this equipment. Professionals must respond to consumer expectations for such amenities as multiple ways of registering for programs, downloadable maps of local parks, and immediate posting of results on the World Wide Web after tournaments or other events.

For many recreation and leisure professionals, the challenge in the future will be how to balance the demands and expectations that arise from technological advances without losing the personal touch that has been the foundation of our everyday lives and of the recreation profession. The profession has grown out of concerns for the social welfare of all members of a community and a commitment to the advancement of a higher quality of life based on choice, freedom, and intrinsic satisfaction. Recreation and leisure professionals must be vigilant that they do not lose this.

Reflection Questions

1. How do you see technology continuing to influence leisure behavior?

2. Is social isolation bad or just a different way of living not in line with the current dominant culture?

3. How is technology being used to increase the effectiveness and efficiency of leisure services? What are some of the challenges to recreation and leisure services presented by technology?

4. Explain five technological innovations in the past five years and how they have increased leisure opportunities.

5. Technological advances merely promote consumerism within recreation. Do you agree with this statement? Why or why not?

4.9   Environmental and Human Interfaces

The relationship between the environment and humans has been an ongoing source of scrutiny for the recreation and leisure profession. Aldo Leopold (1949) summarized the situation over fifty years ago in the classic book, *A Sand County Almanac*, by stating:

> We abuse the land because we regard it as a commodity
> belonging to us. When we see land as a community to which
> we belong, we may begin to use it with love and respect.
> (pp. xviii–xix)

The political, social, and economic significance of outdoor activities and the environment have been analyzed, debated, and recorded in the professional literature. People need only watch television or pick up a magazine to see the current obsession with the status of outdoor activities. Sport utility vehicles (SUVs) are the hottest cars in the showroom and are marketed by appealing to people's sense of adventure and the potential to go into the rugged environment while riding in luxury. Clothes originally designed for outdoor experiences are now found on racks in the most exclusive stores to be worn on the streets of any major city. People do not just buy a bike to ride, but spend time and money on buying specialized equipment, including a LiteSpeed Titanium for serious road racing, a Specialized Stumpjumper for mountain biking on trails, and a Trek for riding around town. Although outdoor recreation is enjoying this popularity phase, consequences can be found when looking at the environmental and social impacts. In this chapter, several of these issues will be discussed to illustrate the relationships that develop from this human and environment interaction.

Outdoor Recreation

Wilderness and its symbolism have become an obsession for the American public. This sense of connection with grand, wild landscapes has been a fascination for American society since the mid-1800s and has served as the primary motivation for a preservation focus not found in any other country in the world. Outdoor spaces are seen as natural laboratories to study and preserve undisturbed ecology. These outdoor areas are also places for people to visit and play where they can become renewed spiritually, challenged physically, and engaged socially. Wilderness and other natural environments provide a foundation for recreation and play opportunities.

Outdoor recreation has been a component of our society for centuries. The need for the preservation and conservation of outdoor spaces was the impetus for the national park movement and a commitment to provide outdoor areas and facilities as a component of government services. The concept of eminent domain was designed as a way that government could override the land rights of individuals if the need for recreation land was deemed a social good for the welfare of the people. Since recreation enjoys this designation as something important for the social good and welfare, many examples exist where eminent domain and condemnation processes were used. This power allowed the establishment of the Smoky Mountains National Park. Landowners were forced to sell their land to the government because the establishment of the park was seen to be more important than the needs of the individual. Such sacrifices are indicative of the hidden costs often unappreciated by park users who take that environment for granted.

The establishment of outdoor recreation environments and the pursuit of outdoor experiences were particularly important in the 20th century. A comprehensive national review by the federal government in the late 1950s and early 1960s focused specifically on opportunities and facilities for outdoor recreation. During the 1980s a similar national study was undertaken as a part of the President's Commission on Americans Outdoors. These studies indicated that the general public was enthusiastic about outdoor recreation and concerned about the environments needed for varied outdoor interests.

As an outcome of the growing awareness about outdoor recreation, a debate intensified between advocates for commercial and industrial development of natural resources and proponents who wanted to preserve the land. Continued interest in outdoor recreation and the environment by people in the United States has resulted in the emergence of recreation resource management as one of the recognized specialties within the recreation profession.

Environmental and Outdoor Education

Considerable interest has developed during the past 25 years in protecting the outdoors and the environment from pollution, unneeded industrial development, rampant residential sprawl, and wanton destruction of the natural resources. This movement has taken many forms. Special interest groups such as the Sierra Club, Defenders of Wildlife, the Audubon Society, and the Wilderness Society have mounted large public information efforts. These campaigns have been directed toward congressional legislation (e.g., Clean Air and Clean Water Acts), activities of regulatory governmental units (e.g., the Environmental Protection Agency and their enforcement of public laws), and various schools (e.g., outdoor education and resident outdoor school programs). Although all of these efforts have had an impact on the recreation movement, resident outdoor school and environmental education efforts have had the closest relationship to recreation and leisure systems.

The basic assumption of the outdoor education movement is that outdoor education best occurs in the outdoors and that nature provides the best learning environment for the study of nature. The philosophy is based on four premises:

(1) development of a land ethic that treats the land and its resources with respect and results in ethical ecological action toward stewardship of the land;

(2) development of the cognitive aspects of knowledge about the interrelationships of all facets of the ecosystem, including a basic understanding of ecological, sociological, and cultural principles that prepares the person to weigh the impact of action on the environment, the culture, and humanity;

(3) knowledge of how to live comfortably in the outdoors and how to recreate with a minimum impact on the environment; and

(4) the belief that outdoor education must be taught at all levels and pursued throughout life (Council on Outdoor Education, 1989).

The terminology used to describe various outdoor education efforts is often confusing because people tend to use the terms interchangeably. Table 4.9 (page 344) provides a summary of some of the common terms used to describe a variety of aspects of environmental and outdoor education.

Although public schools have been a focal point for much of the early education in the outdoors, several agencies offer educational experiences for adults. The most widely recognized programs are Outward Bound and the National Outdoor Leadership School (NOLS). Outward Bound is an adventure-based program that provides challenging opportunities in wilderness settings that foster self-discovery and leadership training. NOLS offers courses that develop fundamental knowledge, skills, and experiences necessary for minimum impact use and enjoyment of wilderness environments by emphasizing safety, judgment, leadership, teamwork, outdoor skills, and environmental studies. These courses are specifically tailored to people who want to work professionally as wilderness educators. Some universities and colleges have embraced these outdoor leadership and training programs by offering college credits to participants. These trainings, as well as a variety of other experientially based programs, continue the efforts to offer outdoor learning experiences throughout the adult years. Another option available to students interested in developing outdoor leadership skills is the Wilderness Education Association, which offers programs in a number of universities in the United States.

Table 4.9:   Definitions Regarding the Outdoors

Adventure Education: Activities purposely including elements perceived by the participants as having risks. The activities are not inherently dangerous as taught under qualified instruction, but they appear to be to the participant, so they generate a sense of adventure. Adventure activities include such aspects as rope courses, whitewater rafting, mountaineering, and rock climbing.

Conservation Education: Study of the wise use of natural resources that tends to focus on animals, soil, water, and air as single topics in relation to their use for timber, agriculture, hunting, fishing, and human consumption. It is not usually concerned with preservation, recreation, or human relations and as such is narrower than outdoor education. This term has declined in use since the 1960s.

Environmental Education: Education about the total environment, including population growth, pollution, resource use and misuse, urban and rural planning, and modern technology's demands on natural resources.

Environmental Interpretation: Technique used to help visitors understand the meanings of natural resource or cultural phenomena on display while simultaneously arousing curiosity for more information. Usually associated with visitor centers administered by parks, forest service, or other outdoor centers.

Experiential Education: Learning by doing or by experiencing. Many experiential education activities are synonymous with adventure activities and outdoor pursuits; however, experiential education can also mean any form of pragmatic educational experience. In many ways, outdoor education may be viewed as experiential, especially when learning takes place through outdoor experiences.

Outdoor Education: Study of natural resources that usually does not include the wide sense of the world environment. Many people, however, think of outdoor education in its broadest sense and prefer the term outdoor/environmental education.

Outdoor Pursuits: Nonmechanized outdoor recreation activities done in areas remote from the amenities of telephone, emergency help, and urban comforts. To many people, the terms outdoor recreation and outdoor pursuits are similar.

Outdoor Recreation: Broad spectrum of outdoor activities participated in during leisure time purely for pleasure or some other intrinsic value, including swimming, boating, winter sports, cycling, and camping.

Resident Outdoor School: Process of taking children to a residential camp during school time for a period of usually three to five days to extend the curriculum through learning in the outdoors. Originally called camping education, it was later referred to as school camping. These phrases were discontinued when parents and taxpayers believed they meant the same thing as summer camp, which seemed to be more recreational than educational.

Adapted from the Council on Outdoor Education (1989)

Issues Concerning the Interface between People and Outdoor Recreation

Interest in outdoor recreation and the environment has paralleled the growth and development of the interstate highway system, the travel and tourism industry, and the sports equipment industry. As one expanded, so did the others. As more people turn to the outdoors to pursue some of their recreation interests, they exert stress on these outdoor areas. People seem to be "loving the wilderness to death." Simultaneously, the environment receives extreme pressures from industries, developers, and citizens who demand the amenities provided by the exploitation of natural resources. This clashing of perceptions about the environment results in heated debates about how best to manage the natural environment. Four current issues of concern to participants and recreation professionals interested in the outdoors are discussed: use versus preservation of natural resources, nature and spirituality, liability and adventure/extreme recreation, and gender and cultural influences on outdoor recreation.

Use versus Preservation of Natural Areas

The accessibility, availability, and use of the natural resources versus the preservation of these areas is a controversial issue. The problem focuses on the amount of use an area can withstand before severe or irreparable damage is done (i.e., carrying capacity), whether an area is left entirely in its natural state or developed for recreational or business enterprises (e.g., timber harvest, mining, oil exploration), and visitor management.

Carrying capacity implies that a resource has a natural level of productivity that must be controlled for the resource to be sustained. Recreational carrying capacity refers to the relationship between the recreational experience sought and the recreation resource. This relationship can be translated into the maximum number of people and type of use an area can sustain over a specific time without impairing the environment or the visitor experience (Fogg, 1975). For example, when someone goes hiking in the mountains, they have a different experience if they do not see another person all day than when the trail looks like a superhighway. How much a visitor can tolerate before their experience is diminished because of the number of people is one way carrying capacity might be explained. This broader perspective of recreational carrying capacity acknowledges the role of social capacity as well as ecological capacity. The determination of recreational carrying capacity becomes a sociopolitical process as well as a biophysical one (Burch, 1984). Therefore, carrying capacities are the product of value judgments as well as science where the values of managers and users are used to reach a collective judgment (Hendee, Stankey & Lucas, 1990).

Convenience and accessibility determine to a great extent the amount of use an area will receive. People come to see areas such as the Great Smoky Mountains, Yosemite, Yellowstone, and the Grand Canyon every year by the millions. Visitor management is important. The negative impact of these large numbers of people is seen in pollution from vehicles, large amounts of garbage and sewage, crime and vandalism, deterioration of facilities and areas, and increased presence of emergency medical care and rescue. Park managers confront increasingly complex management decisions at a time when fiscal and human resources are often lacking. Policies such as daily visitor quotas, access by permit, a reevaluation of facilities needed to be located within the park, and traffic plans are among the possible solutions to the problems of high use or overuse.

Politicians and recreation and park professionals also note that many national parks are inaccessible to the majority of the population. The majority of national parks are in the western half of the United States where the population density is low. The parks are basically out of reach of the urban masses, particularly less affluent people. The National Park Service reports regularly that about a quarter of people's visits are to national recreation areas located primarily in suburban and urban areas; however, these national recreation areas only comprise four percent of the total acreage of the national park system. Sixty percent of the acreage of national outdoor areas is in western US national parks that are quite a distance from most major cities. Therefore, while a small number of federal areas may be subject to heavy use, others are virtually unreachable for the general public.

Another aspect of how natural resources should be used centers on preservation and conservation. Preservation of natural environments includes maintenance of long-term ecological processes and management to protect the resource from human influence (Hendee, Stankey & Lucas, 1990). Conservation is usually associated with renewable natural resources and using resources in the most beneficial manner over time while avoiding waste. Conservation involves a cycle of intelligent use and timely replenishment of resources as they become damaged or partially depleted. Timber harvesting done appropriately is an example of conservation but not preservation.

Some individuals would like to see all natural areas, particularly wilderness areas, preserved for all time (LaPage & Ranney, 1988). Wildernesses are areas whose primeval character and influence have been primarily affected by the forces of nature, where the imprint of humans is unnoticed, and where the opportunities for solitude are significant. Although certain types of minimum-impact outdoor recreation may occur in these settings, management would be for the natural environment. This value structure is inherent in a biocentric philosophy of the outdoors. This philosophical stance acknowledges humans as only one piece of an interconnected web of natural relationships where situations exist that do not necessarily place the needs and desires of humans first. For example, in a biocentric approach, wilderness areas would be used for backpacking trips under primitive conditions but the management focus would remain with maintaining the integrity of the environment when using the resource for recreational purposes. The result may be that some of the desires of the backpackers are unmet if they are ultimately incompatible with the optimum maintenance of the natural resource. For example, in Denali National Park, people might be prohibited from backpacking in a particular sector of the park when the bears "frenzy feed" in the fall. The bears' need for food outweighs the backpackers' rights to share that area of park with them, since people might make a nice addition to the bears' menu if the opportunity presented itself.

Other people like to see natural areas conserved with recreation being one of many uses of these renewable resources. A broader selection of outdoor activities would be accommodated than in a biocentric perspective because more supportive facilities and amenities are permitted to provide a balance between human activity and the environment. This anthropocentric perspective stresses the development of the environment to best accommodate people's wishes even if it may take away some of the integrity of the natural environment. An application of this view can be seen in most national parks, where a central core area of the park is developed to meet visitor needs. These accommodations may include lodging, stores for buying supplies and souvenirs, equipment rental, educational areas, and structured recreational activities. Some economic gain may accrue to local communities through wilderness recreation, but the key is to balance tourism with conservation. The partnership requires an understanding of the needs of the visitors, outfitters, and resource managers (Wallace, Tierney & Haas, 1990).

Lastly, some people would advocate for human uses of the natural resources as the leading priority. Although no universal agreement exists for this approach, we refer to it as the maximizing perspective. The development of extensive facilities and the maximized use of the resource to meet the demands of people would be the first priority. Resorts and commercial outdoor recreation facilities that offer a variety of amenities to try to meet everyone's needs are examples of this type of perspective. The proposed development of the Arctic Wildlife Refuge for oil production is also an example of the desire to put human needs as the priority when a conflict arises between use and preservation.

Safety relates to resource development and use regardless of the perspective taken. Crime has increased greatly in society, and parks and recreation programs are not exempt from this trend. Women in particular may be perceived as more at risk for personal physical violence in their outdoor pursuits (Bialeschki, 1999). Some of the problems of fear and violence are larger social issues that have no easy solution when identified in relation to outdoor activities and settings. In resource development for the future, however, planners will be able to consider issues of safety through the design of areas and the consideration of security systems for areas and facilities. Parks are safer when they are filled with programs and people, and this philosophy also has implications for the kind of use that might occur. In addition, if people can be convinced that they have some ownership of outdoor areas and facilities, empowered citizen groups may organize themselves to address problems of vandalism or crime in local parks. Safety issues and issues of fear, unless addressed directly by leisure service providers, may be one of the major constraints to people's leisure in the coming years (Bialeschki, 1999; Shaw & Whyte, 1996; Whyte & Shaw, 1994).

The preservation and development of resources in the future will be challenged by the conflicting demands between people and the environment. Different recreational behaviors require particular types of settings. A balance between biocentric, anthropomorphic, and maximizing perspectives will be needed. Recreation spaces are public commons, limited in number and type of experiences they can accommodate. Parks and recreation professionals must make full use of nontraditional recreation areas such as shopping centers, libraries, public gardens, private lands wildlife refuges, and open spaces such as cemeteries. These areas also afford possibilities for leisure satisfactions and must be considered as complements to those fragile areas and outdoor facilities managed by park and recreation agencies. A systematic approach to planning, development, and maintenance of all potential recreation and environmental resources is needed.

Nature and Spirituality

Two broad views about the environment can be found in American culture. These views reflect the heritage and spiritual connection of the people who contributed to the development of society. Native American and transcendentalist tradition celebrated in ways that sought harmony with all life and natural elements. Western tradition promoted a belief in the superiority of humans to all other life and a belief that the universe exists to serve human needs (Driver, Dustin, Baltic, Elsner & Peterson, 1996).

The Native American philosophy links the spiritual experience directly to the environment. Most indigenous Native Americans view themselves not as the masters, but as a part of a balanced universe. In this belief system, they often perceived an imbalance caused by humans, so they developed ceremonies that would retain and reestablish the harmony with nature. These rituals and ceremonies maintain a belief in the unseen powers and the unity with fundamental life forces inherent in all things (Ibrahim & Cordes, 1993).

The Western view often portrayed nature as dangerous or something to be use and dominated. Other life forms were important only in terms of their usefulness to humanity, especially when development and profit motives were foremost. Spirituality became tied to beliefs that civilization, not nature, conveyed the sacred lifestyle. Nature as a spiritual connection became further removed from daily existence.

A renewed interest in the spiritual side of life, including moral values, compassion, and respect for other humans and life forms, is emerging in American culture and finding its way into the management of natural areas in which we play. In reaction to urbanism, impersonal transactions, and industrialism, a growing number of people are exploring their inner feelings to develop a sense of belonging. They are discovering values that rise from direct contact with the beauty, complexities, and mysteries of nature. Recognition seems to exist that modern technical knowledge has neglected the natural at the expense of human needs. This new "ecospirituality" stresses a reverence for all living (e.g., animals, trees) and nonliving (e.g., water, rocks) things. For some people, outdoor recreation has become a forum for spiritual attainment with activities like wilderness camping as central to the experience.

Others see the outdoor spirituality movement as antidevelopment and idealistic. To them, camping is spending the weekend in a park, using the mobile camper as home base, using a portable satellite television, staying connected with a cell phone with Internet capabilities, and cooking on a propane stove. The weekend in the outdoors is merely a continuation of their urban values that uses nature as a backdrop, not as an integral part of the experience. Accommodating both perspectives is a growing challenge to the outdoor recreation professional.

Liability and Adventure/Extreme Recreation

Liability, especially from adventure and extreme sports, confronts every recreation professional. Previously, laws of sovereign immunity protected public agencies from potential lawsuits. Today, however, government is not immune and is expected to provide safe recreational experiences and environments. Liability occurs when a recreation professional becomes legally responsible for an individual's welfare as opposed to being morally responsible. Most cases in outdoor recreation involve negligence, which means that a person in charge failed to perform responsibilities at the expected level of a prudent person under the same circumstances (Ibrahim & Cordes, 1993).

Liability is often discussed related to opportunities and environments for adventure activities and extreme sports such as rock climbing, hang gliding, and whitewater paddling. Outdoor participants argue their right to risk during their pursuit of recreational experiences, but resource managers strive for a clearer interpretation of their obligations and reasonable options for adventure. The values of adventure programming are important, but the challenge may be how to offer these activities in a way that allows excitement and risk without jeopardizing the provider or the environment. As more people push their personal boundaries (and pay large sums of money to reach their goals) care must be taken to prevent incidences such as the May

1996 Mount Everest disaster, when eight people died because the goal of reaching the summit was more important than their safety. Sound leadership and decision making need to be mitigated with the pressures on commercial recreation providers because of a belief that the adventure customer is immune from disaster and owed a successful adventure.

Gender and Cultural Influences on Outdoor Recreation

Another topic of current interest is the influence of gender and cultural differences on outdoor recreation. Contrary to popular notions, women's involvement in outdoor recreation is not a phenomenon of the past twenty years. Since the first outdoor recreation activities were undertaken, women have been involved. Their accomplishments were often obscured, however, by the exploits of their male counterparts, by their relegation to the role of helpmate, and by their achievements being questioned or minimized (Bialeschki, 1992). For example, soon after the Sierra Club was founded in 1892, women made up nearly half the club memberships, went on group expeditions, and comprised a third of the mountain climbers (Kaufman, 1986). History, however, has not acknowledged the accomplishments of these outdoorswomen.

Statistics suggest that at the turn of the century almost as many women are involved in most outdoor activities as are men (Kelly & Warnick, 1999). Many women use the outdoor environment as a source of empowerment and resistance, particularly when they participate in all-female groups. Women and girls often choose same-sex outdoor groups for a number of reasons, including the opportunities to:

- Learn and practice skills;

- Share common interests;

- Gain self-understanding;

- Live in stereotype-free environments;

- Gain a sense of renewal or spiritual connection;

- Work on fear and safety issues; and

- Interact in a supportive group environment. (Bialeschki, 1999; Yerkes & Miranda, 1982)

The benefits of these experiences often result because of increased self-esteem that leads to feelings of empowerment (Bialeschki, 1999; Mitten, 1992). Programs offered by outdoor groups such as Outward Bound, National Outdoor Leadership School, Girls in the Woods, and Adventure Associates often have specific courses designed for older women, girls from at-risk communities, women who have been battered or abused, and women who have been victims of sexual assault. These programs build upon the values associated with experiences in the natural environment.

The influence of cultural heritage is only beginning to be addressed by researchers interested in outdoor recreation (Allison, 1988; Chavez, 1992; Floyd, 2000; Hutchinson, 1987, 1988; West, 1989). A great debate exists on why cultural and ethnic differences are experienced in outdoor recreation. According to some studies, the rates for participation differ significantly. For example, African Americans are less likely to go hiking and camping than European Americans, but they have a higher rate of participation in many urban outdoor activities such as sports and picnicking (Dwyer & Gobster, 1992). Speculations focus on the differences in socioeconomic backgrounds and to other factors related to inherent cultural, ethnic explanations. Many people of color have not had the same traditions in outdoor activities as have middle class White people. With more people of color comprising the voting block in the United States, the funding of federal and state public lands may be reduced because many people of color have not experienced outdoor recreation opportunities. People who do not appreciate the outdoors and wilderness areas are less likely to support preservation and conservation policies. Only recently have researchers begun to examine the role that recreation and leisure may play in the acculturation process as participants become integrated into the dominant culture and the ways that recreation may also encourage the maintenance of traditional culture. All of these research efforts are designed to increase awareness and understanding about diversity issues in recreation and to provide information that will be useful in policy development and management techniques.

This chapter provided an overview of the issues facing recreation and leisure professionals when examining the relationships between people, outdoor recreation activities, and the environment. Challenges relate to the philosophies held, the desires for risk and adventure within ever-changing safety needs, and the influence of gender, race, and culture on personal experiences. In a society that seems to value consumptive behaviors even in our outdoor experiences, the balance between human need and environmental need is often precarious.

Reflection Questions

1. Should humans have priority for environmental resources? Why or why not?

2. What is the difference between preservation and conservation?

3. How do issues of safety influence the experience of leisure and the outdoors?

4. What do you believe are the three greatest challenges facing recreation professionals interested in the environment? Why?

5. Do you believe outdoor pursuits should be limited if they negatively impact the environment? How would you define a negative impact?

4.10   Leisure around the World

Recreation and leisure are global issues. The discussion of leisure around the world must start with a willingness to step outside of our own cultural viewpoint of leisure. Most of us have grown up in the United States where our political focus on individuals and their rights and the industrialization of the United States shapes our concept of leisure. Most of this book examines leisure in Western cultures. In other societies around the world, however, leisure often has a different connotation. This section will require that you put views about the US culture alongside other ideas and look broadly at the underlying issues about leisure from different viewpoints.

Western Views

Most Western cultures have significant technological development, stable economies, and a history of world leadership. Countries such as the United States, Canada, Australia, Britain, France, and other countries of western Europe tend to value leisure because it enhances the quality of life for individuals and provides economic benefits for the country. These countries share a basic cultural heritage that has been strongly influenced by Christianity, a Protestant work ethic that has gradually balanced with the importance of leisure, and an emphasis on national pride that comes about through excellence in sports and cultural arts.

Media greatly influence many of these Western societies. The media can shape messages about leisure by the television programs aired, opportunities available through the Internet, types of music played, books read, and art performed. For example, some suggest that outdoor recreation has grown in popularity because it is portrays the ideal image of young, energetic, beautiful, popular people who have the ability to spend large sums of money to buy the desired equipment or experiences. On the other hand, leisure also informs the media. The demands by the public for certain media opportunities for their leisure has fueled such interests as satellite television (with hundreds of channels that guarantee something for everyone) or greater coverage of women's sports in newspapers and magazines.

Most Western societies have developed a consumerism approach to leisure. Leisure is often viewed as a commodity to be bought and sold. This market sector has generated hundreds of millions of dollars for national economies, often through commercial recreation opportunities that include entertainment, sporting equipment, spectator events (e.g., concerts, sport events, theatre), travel, and tourism. In many Western countries, the amount, size, and type of possessions and the type and destination of leisure experiences have become status symbols. While pockets of nonconsumers can be found, the overriding philosophy seems to center on possessing whatever and as much as you want without a thought to the repercussions of excessiveness and resource allocations in other parts of the world. This consumerism around leisure has led some people to believe that leisure is a class-defined experience primarily for the wealthy.

The modernization dream has always been to use technology to free humans from the drudgery and demands of work. A life of leisure seemed to be eminent for these technologically advanced societies. An examination of the lives of people in these societies, however, seems to indicate more work and stress with less time and less emphasis placed on relaxing, fitness, social responsibility, stewardship of the natural environment, and commitment to community. Instead of working fewer hours, we actually are working more with less time for leisure (Schor, 1991). Although recreation and leisure seem to be ideal ways to achieve a higher quality of life, the reality may be more "talking the talk" than "walking the walk."

Countries with Emerging Economies

Many countries in the world are termed developing because the full productivity of their resource potential has not been realized. The concept of development implies a general level of technology, economic sophistication, and standard of living (Russell, 1996). Some of these countries face overwhelming issues related to poverty, education, health, and environmental degradation that has resulted in a low standard of living and quality of life. The act of modernization has placed pressure on traditional social structures by replacing long standing cultural values with lifestyle standards that emulate the unfamiliar values of Western societies.

Leisure within these developing countries has a divergent image. From one perspective, leisure is an integral component of all village life. The celebration of rituals and traditions through stories, dance, music, art, and games is often the cornerstone for the life of the community. From another perspective, leisure intimately ties to the environment, where certain landscapes and places are sacred and cared for as an honored responsibility. The appreciation of the environment reflects a connection to all things of nature. Another perspective is that recreation and leisure could become exploitative tools for increasing economic gains such as can occur in mass tourism. This problem occurs when leisure becomes a product being sold rather than an experience that is everyone's right.

Although the exploitation of leisure may immediately alleviate some of the harshness of people's lives, the long-term consequences may not be fully appreciated or understood. For example, the Sherpas of Nepal realize economic gain on every mountain expedition, but the cost of that leisure opportunity for wealthy Western tourists may have resulted in the loss of cultural traditions, new materialism that results from Western contact, and immense environmental stress and degradation of fragile ecosystems. A positive outcome has developed over the last decade with the advent of *ecotourism*. This form of tourism emphasizes adapting to the culture and the environment of the area visited with the least amount of impact. This approach provides economic exchange while emphasizing the importance and appreciation of the natural environment and local customs without Westernizing the experience. The issue of the rainforest is an example. Cutting the trees may help local families to subsist if the cleared ground can be planted for crops for several years before the soil is depleted. However, selling the rainforest in its natural state to ecotourists results in economic gains that are long-lasting without destroying the important natural resource. These families can become a part of the ecotourism business, valuable outside money can be generated for the area, and a resource saved from destruction.

The term *leisure* may not be a familiar concept in many of these countries, nor does the experience necessarily manifest in ways similar to Western views. For example, in some South American or Latin American countries, no equivalent for the term leisure can be found. The closest word is similar to the American words for free time or play. In Korean, the word leisure is equated with expensive pastimes of the rich and implies a negative connotation of laziness. The emphasis of leisure in developing countries is often not on the individual, but rather on the family or community. Leisure in this viewpoint is less about the rights of the individual to pursue self-benefiting experiences but more about the shared benefits to a larger social structure (i.e., extended family, neighbors, community).

Many developing countries do not have the variety of leisure services systems that North America or western Europe do. Nongovernmental organizations, similar to our not-for-profit groups, may be more likely to become responsible in some places. Some of the countries have forms of government such as dictatorships based on nondemocratic principles that view recreation and leisure within a narrow framework. Governments control the natural resources that could become national parks or sites for industrial economic development. There may be scant money to provide facilities to support the arts, sports, children's play spaces, programs for older persons, and parks when people do not always have enough food. The government, however, may support forms of tourism that attract Western dollars.

The leisure exploitation of developing countries concerns many people. From environmental damage to coral reefs to the huge impact of sex tourism from the exploitation of girls and women by Western tourists, the outcome is similar. The focus on economic gain, no matter the cost to humanity or environment, can have serious repercussions with no clear course for correction. The desire to be like Western countries may ultimately eliminate or completely alter these developing countries.

The Right to Leisure

The right to leisure is a global concern. The World Leisure and Recreation Association (WLRA) is a worldwide, nongovernmental, professional organization dedicated to discovering and fostering those conditions best permitting leisure to serve as a force for human growth, development, and well-being (http://www.worldleisure.org). WLRA is involved with research and advocacy that promotes the goals of the association. The interests include tourism, park and recreation services, arts and culture, sport and exercise, theme parks, entertainment centers, and children's play. WLRA offers services to members and nonmembers through conferences, workshops, and media forums to discuss trends and issues. They form partnerships with the United Nations, other world government bodies, and international organizations, including recreation and leisure associations. They offer innovative programs such as a graduate education program at the WLRA International Centre for Excellence in the Netherlands and WLRA professional services (WPS) to public and private sector agencies and enterprises throughout the world.

Through the efforts of WLRA, and in cooperation with the United Nations, a Charter for Leisure Rights was drafted and first approved in 1970 (see Table 4.10). This proclamation reinforces the importance and value of recreation and leisure in the lives of the world's citizens. The statement addresses a belief that the individual has the right to experience freely chosen activities that lead to self-fulfillment, improved quality of life, and the attainment of community values.

The role of recreation and leisure around the world is often culture-dependent and mitigated by many factors. As noted throughout this book, leisure experiences are a part of every society on earth with rich histories that go back thousands of years. The role of leisure may be primarily linked to the individual in one culture or a collective group in another. Further, leisure may have strong economic influence whether provided by the government, a not-for-profit, or a commercial enterprise.

Table 4.10:   Charter for Leisure

Introduction

Consistent with the Universal Declaration of Human Rights (Article 27), all cultures and societies recognize to some extent the right to rest and leisure. Here, because personal freedom and choice are central elements of leisure, individuals can freely choose their activities and experiences, many of them leading to substantial benefits for person and community.

Articles

1. All people have a basic human right to leisure activities that are in harmony with the norms and social values of their compatriots. All governments are obliged to recognize and protect this right of its citizens.
2. Provisions for leisure for the quality of life are as important as those for health and education. Governments must provide their citizens a variety of accessible leisure and recreational opportunities of the highest quality.
3. The individual is his/her best leisure and recreational resource. Thus, governments should ensure the means for acquiring those skills and understandings necessary to optimize leisure experiences.
4. Individuals can use leisure opportunities for self-fulfillment, developing personal relationships, improving social integration, developing communities and cultural identity as well as promoting international understanding and cooperation and enhancing quality of life.
5. Governments must ensure the future availability of fulfilling leisure experiences by maintaining the quality of their country's physical, social, and cultural environment.
6. Governments should ensure the training of professionals to help individuals acquire personal skills, discover and develop their talents, and to broaden their range of recreational opportunities.
7. Citizens must have access to all forms of leisure information about the nature of leisure and its opportunities, using it to enhance their knowledge and inform decisions on local and national policy.
8. Educational institutions must make every effort to teach the nature and importance of leisure and how to integrate this knowledge into personal lifestyle.

Approved by the World Leisure and Recreation Association Board of Directors, July 2000 (http://www.worldleisure.org)

Reflection Questions

1. Describe three reasons why developing countries should not necessarily follow a Western view of leisure.

2. Do you think the Leisure Bill of Rights is a reasonable expectation for the world's societies? Why or why not?

3. Why is it important for us to consider leisure in other countries?

4.11   Leisure and Social Capital

Earlier in this unit, we noted that work hours have risen for many Americans, and that many people must work longer to maintain their existing standards of living. The amount of free time available, however, does not determine the quality of leisure. What people *do* during the time available is more important than *how much* time they have. This chapter examines the different ways individuals use their free time.

Free Time Allocations

Time diary studies examine the patterns of daily life. They track how people undertake daily obligations and opportunities. Several important national and international research projects have provided time diary data relevant to the analysis of leisure. The most current detailed time diary study is Robinson and Godbey's *Time for Life* (1999). Changes have occurred in the weekly patterns of women's and men's time allocations among three broad categories: productive activity, personal care, and free time. Robinson and Godbey (1999) defined productive activity as paid employment, commuting, and family responsibilities; and personal care as sleeping, eating, and grooming. Remaining unallocated time is available for leisure. The most controversial finding they reported was an increase in weekly free time for both women and men between 1965 and 1995. Looking further inside the data, however, we find that women's weekly work hours increased between 1975 and 1985 and that work hours increased for both women and men between 1985 and 1995.

Robinson and Godbey (1999) used four categories to analyze allocations of free time. Recreational activities was a broad category to which they assigned many different activities ranging from working out to hobbies to adult education. Socializing, taking part in clubs or associations, and attending church were categorized as social and organizational activity. Reading and listening to the stereo formed the third category. Watching television formed the fourth.

The data collected by Robinson and Godbey (1999) suggested that free time allocations increased between 1965 and 1995. During the average week in 1995 women devoted almost three more hours (a 28% increase) to recreational activities than they did in 1965, and men had over five additional hours (a 57% increase). Women and men also watched more hours of television in 1995.

The magnitude of television watching merits special attention. In 1965 television viewing already consumed over a quarter of women's free time and one-third of men's. By 1975 it was the most frequent free time activity for both women and men, and has remained so ever since. Perhaps most alarming is the proportion of the increase in free time that has been allocated to watching television. From 1965 to 1995, women's viewing time increased by almost six hours weekly which is equivalent to 121% of the additional hours of free time women gained during that period. The entire increase in women's free time was more than consumed by television viewing in 1995. Men watch television just over two hours more weekly than women, allocating 68% of their gain in free time since 1965 to television. Women and men now view television for just about the same percentage of their weekly free time.

Time is a finite resource. If people wish to allocate additional time to one activity, they must reduce the time allocated to other activities. Increases in time devoted to television viewing and recreational activities have meant decreases in time available for other forms of leisure. Reading and listening to the stereo were the least frequent free time activities in each of the four years for which Robinson and Godbey collected data and they decreased 0.8 hours for women and two hours for men between 1965 and 1995. Time allocated to social and organizational activities shifted significantly. In 1965 women devoted more weekly free time hours to this activity category than to any other, while men devoted more time to viewing television and the same amount of time to recreational activities. The time allocated to social and organizational activities decreased every year since 1965 for both men and women except 1995, when it increased a slight 0.4 hours weekly for men. In 1965 women devoted 33% of their weekly free time to social and organizational activity compared to only 21% in 1995. The pattern for men was similar with 27% in 1965 and 20% in 1995.

Several recent developments may have significant implications for free time allocations. These changes include the increasingly structured nature of children and adolescents' time in and out of school, and the growing tendency of older adults to remain in the workforce rather than take early retirement. These changes affect the periods in life when free time is assumed to be most plentiful and flexible. Another development is the explosion of home computer use. Reliable research on the effects of the widespread availability and use of computers is scarce. The dire predictions made about the ultimate consequences of computer usage during free time are not likely to occur. Computer usage has not simply replaced other more socially interactive forms of leisure. Instead, people who frequently use computers appear to reallocate some of their time otherwise devoted to media like television or television-based games. Nevertheless, evidence exists that intensive use

of computers during free time is associated with higher rates of social isolation and depression. Little can be said with certainty about this growing use
of time associated with computers other than that it is a subject deserving the
continuing attention of both recreation professionals and leisure researchers.

Leisure and Social Capital

The allocation of free time is important if leisure professionals are to understand how people find meaning and make sense of their lives. People ought to
have freedom to do as they wish in leisure within the limits of responsible
citizenship. People have expressed concern over the loss of community, the
dissolution of social ties, preoccupations with self, and lifestyles characterized as narcissistic (Bellah, Madsen, Sullivan, Swidler & Tipton, 1985;
Lasch, 1979; Marcuse, 1991; Riesman, 1961). The content of leisure is not
exempt from the issues raised in these exchanges (e.g., Goodale, 1985;
Hemingway, 1991). Whether people allocate more time to television viewing,
to bowling alone, or to participating in clubs or other social forms of leisure,
makes a difference. This difference can be seen when analyzing the relationship between social capital and leisure. Consider the following two examples
of social capital in action, using leisure settings.

1. A long weekend is coming up. You want to do something exciting
   and challenging that you have not done before. When you mention
   this idea to an acquaintance in one of your classes, she invites you
   on a whitewater rafting trip and assures you it will be safe for nov-
   ices. This person offers to provide the necessary gear. The other
   people going on the trip are lots of fun and won't mind if you come
   along. Having worked with your acquaintance on several class
   projects, you know she is reliable. You decide to accept the offer,
   have a great time despite swimming accidentally in one of the
   rapids, and make some new friends.

2. Packing up after their weekly bowling league, Ellen happens to
   mention to Charlie that her child is having trouble with calculus
   in school. She wonders if tutoring is available, but isn't sure how
   to find out. It happens that Charlie has a neighbor, Diane, who is a
   teacher in the school attended by Ellen's child so he promises to ask
   her about this when he gets the chance. The next evening Charlie
   talks with Diane over the backyard fence and she tells Charlie that
   Ellen should give her a call at school the next day.

Social capital is a resource, just like financial capital (e.g., money) and
human capital (e.g., knowledge). Unlike financial and human capital, however, social capital is not "owned" by anyone. It is created and exists only
through participation in social structures and relations among individuals

occupying specific social roles. A social role is constructed around expected behaviors appropriate to someone who occupies that role. The examples above include several social relations defined by social roles—acquaintance-ship and group project partner in the first, and team member, parent, and neighbor in the second. When we interact with people occupying social roles like these, we anticipate that they not only understand the associated expectations but also accept them and have a sufficient sense of obligation to fulfill them.

Social capital enables people to accomplish their goals more effectively. Instead of developing their own independent resources, people in environments rich with social capital have access to resources held by their counterparts in social relations. In the first example, you had a specific goal for the weekend (an exciting and different experience). Rather than searching for different possibilities, trying to assess them, and then making your choice, through your acquaintance from class you had access to a whitewater rafting trip along with the required knowledge and equipment. Your prior interaction as group project members created a sufficient level of trust to allow your acquaintance to invite you to come along, and for you to accept. This existing trust was transferred from one social relation (group project members) to another (acquaintances). The success of the trip increased the level of trust, allowing you to become friends.

In the second example, Ellen's goal was to find calculus tutoring for her child. She had no expectation that Charlie himself could meet this need, but just mentioned it casually to him. To Charlie, the role of team member included helping other team members when possible. Thus, Ellen gained access to assistance from Charlie's neighbor Diane, who did know how to get calculus tutoring. Charlie knew nothing about calculus, but he did know Diane. Diane did not know Ellen, but offered to help her because she trusted Charlie as a neighbor. Once Ellen understood the procedures for requesting tutoring assistance for her child, she was then able to share this information with other parents she met. Even though these other parents were not part of the original social interaction among Ellen, Charlie, and Diane, they nonetheless benefited because Ellen had relevant information and felt a sense of obligation to share it. Social capital tends to reproduce and expand the more it is used.

These two examples illustrated two basic types of social capital: bonding and bridging (Gittell & Vidal, 1998; Putnam, 2000). *Bonding* social capital builds up the social relations between people who were already connected in some fashion. The new friendship with a whitewater rafting classmate is an example of bonding social capital. *Bridging* social capital brings together people who previously had no social relation. Charlie served as the bridge between Ellen and Diane because his acquaintanceship with each of them independently enabled them to establish a relation more effectively than would otherwise have been possible.

Putnam's research (1993) uncovered an association between specific forms of leisure activity and higher levels of social capital. The mutual knowledge and trust required for the formation of social capital has a greater opportunity to develop when people participate in social forms of leisure like active memberships in leisure-oriented clubs and associations, or participate in creating recreation opportunities (Storrmann, 1996). In Putnam's essay "Bowling Alone" (1995a) and book of the same title (2000), however, Putnam argued that Americans are withdrawing more from the forms of leisure that facilitate social capital formation. The primary culprit in his view (1995b) was the steady domination of free time by television viewing and the gradual replacement of generations whose leisure activities had been formed when television was less influential. A widespread concern exists that Americans are presently less engaged in their communities and in social capital producing activities than at any time since the 1950s.

In the light of Putnam's work, the time diary findings reported by Robinson and Godbey (1999) take on added significance. People have allocated less time to the categories of free time activity identified as conducive to social capital formation. As people increase their work hours, much of their social interaction may occur in settings favoring competition (e.g., the workplace) rather than settings that develop the mutual trust and knowledge necessary for cooperation (e.g., in the home or community). Both forms of social capital can develop together, but bonding social capital appears to be nurtured in settings more characteristic of leisure, while bridging social capital develops more readily in work-related settings. There is a dark side to both forms of social capital. Bridging social capital may emphasize instrumental relationships among self-interested individuals intent on gaining the best advantage for themselves. Bonding social capital may reduce the diversity and richness of social relations. Research on social networks consistently reveals that the stronger the tie connecting two individuals, the more similar they are (Granovetter, 1973; Mardsen, 1990). These aspects of social capital should not go unnoticed when discussing its formation during leisure.

Leisure is an important arena for generating social capital (Hemingway, 1999). The recreation profession can create opportunities for socially interactive leisure that include a diverse range of people. These opportunities extend beyond simply providing programs and facilities to administering them in an open, democratic fashion. Recreation professionals might facilitate social capital formation more through the manner of administering programs and facilities than through the programs and facilities themselves. Recreation and leisure professionals have a fundamental ethical and professional obligation to nurture social capital development, especially when the focus is on inclusive recreation programs, settings, and facilities.

Reflection Questions

1. What is social capital? How do you think recreation and leisure services in communities help to create it?

2. How might the concept of social capital be used in addition to the traditional concept of economic capital?

3. Distinguish between *bonding* and *bridging* social capital. What examples of each can you observe during your own leisure activities? As a recreation programmer, how could you facilitate the development of each?

4. How might social capital be increased through leisure involvement?

4.12   Inclusion

The United States is undergoing a transition in its political and social attitudes, just as it is undergoing economic and technological change. An emerging idea that occurred during the 1990s (and the theme of this textbook) is social inclusion. Although inclusion has often been used within the field of recreation in relation to people with disabilities, a much broader meaning can be found as we summarize how recreation and leisure can create opportunities for all. Inclusive recreation means that all individuals, regardless of their position in society, will have opportunities to find identity and connections through socially responsible recreation and leisure opportunities. Inclusive recreation, however, will not occur unless we put recreation within the context of a society that currently examines attitudes toward human rights, work, and leisure.

Throughout this book we have identified changes occurring as America moves into the 21st century. How these societal changes will affect the way people experience leisure in the future is not always easy to predict. A focus on meanings and a better quality of life, along with alternative views of family, pluralism, and self-help will mean that more people will likely seek recreation opportunities. Inclusion involves having choices for people to consider for their leisure.

The Nature of Inclusion

Inclusion assumes a concept of social justice. Sometimes the notion of inclusion is linked to just recreation, which relates to the idea that leisure and recreation contribute to social justice (Henderson, 1997). To do harm to any group through unethical leisure behavior or inequitable leisure provision is to diminish us all (Henderson, 1997; Shogan, 1991). A discussion of recreation and leisure services requires a continuing focus on social and environmental ethics. The examination of leisure and ethics began long ago, but today the discussions have moved beyond the realm of philosophers. The nature of ethics as the science of right action precludes tidy and simple answers. To illustrate an aspect of equity, we will use a metaphor described by Molotch (1988):

> In many public buildings, the amount of floor area dedicated
> for the men's room and the women's room is the same. The
> prevailing public bathroom doctrine in the United States is
> one of segregation among the genders, but with equality as

the guiding ideology....Such an arrangement follows the
dictum that equality can be achieved only by policies that
are "gender-blind" (or "color-blind" or "ethnic-blind") in
the allocation of a public resource....Women and men have
the same proportion of a building to use as rest rooms.

The trouble with this sort of equality is that, being blind,
it fails to recognize differences between men as a group and
women as a group. . .(such differences include hygiene needs,
different physiological functions, and the use of toilets versus
urinals). . .By creating men's and women's rooms of the same
size, society guarantees that individual women will be worse
off than individual men. By distributing a resource equally,
an unequal result is structurally guaranteed. (p. 128–129)

Molotch goes on to describe the specific situation of intermission time
at a theatre where long lines for women and no lines for men are not unusual.
The liberal policy or solution is to make women's rooms larger than men's.
An alternative solution (one he calls conservative) would be for women to
be like men and to change the way they do things, rather than for society to
change the structuring of rest room space. In other words, a conservative
approach would say there is no need to overturn the principle of equality of
square footage among the genders. Instead, women need to use their allot-
ted square footage more efficiently. This conservative argument, however,
discounts the role that men have in the problem. For example, most men want
women to be demure and beautiful so women need more time and privacy
in the bathroom. What if the problem is not because women primp and
gossip in the rest room, but the fact that men expect them to be beautiful?
Another possible solution might be called a radical approach where women
are allowed to decide for themselves what they will need for rest room space
and how they will use it. This approach will also enable them to resist
dominant (patriarchal) views about how women use rest rooms.

Molotch (1988) concluded that figuring out equality and equity is not
a matter of arithmetic division, but social accounting and justice. We need
to realize how equal treatment of groups may create unequal opportunities
for individuals. The story provides a foundation for examining the outcomes
of inclusion in all sectors of leisure services. We will explore three aspects
pertaining to inclusion: equality and equity, diversity, and leisure opportunities. Ultimately, an ethical examination of these areas may lead to further
questions concerning recreation and leisure as tools for social change and
the empowerment of participants.

Inclusion and Equality versus Equity

Inclusion is not likely to occur until we have noted the important, but often subtle, differences between equality and equity. *Equality* is a matter of fact (e.g., women have as many rest rooms as men, or women have the same sports programs as men) and is basically objective. *Equity* is a matter of ethical judgment (e.g., women need more rest rooms than men because of the way they use rest rooms, women need more sports skills development opportunities than men because women have not had the same learning opportunities when younger) and takes subjective assessments into account. Therefore, equity is equated with fairness. Although equality and equity are both important considerations for recreation professionals, equality connotes sameness while equity connotes fairness.

The goals of equity are reflected in social movements that allow individuals (e.g., low income, disabled, female) to go from roles to rights, from best interests to choice, from paternalism to self-determination, and from invisibility to visibility (Rioux, 1993). Leisure service providers have a moral imperative for inclusion and for ensuring everyone is a full participant in recreation programs. Equity results in power, ability, and willingness to help others make changes in their lives. It applies to all groups including individuals who were previously underserved or disadvantaged related to leisure and recreation.

A discussion of inclusion and equity often results in questions about whether freedom is more important than equality. Justice and equity are equivalent if we redress distributional inequalities. Rawls (1971) argued, however, that a society is just even in the absence of equal distribution of social and economic benefits as long as inequalities are arranged so that they can reasonably be expected to be to everyone's advantage and not limit anyone's freedom. For example, it won't hurt men if women have more rest rooms, and giving girls additional sports skills may result in more playing partners for men in the future. Fairness rather than sameness is required to achieve justice. Rawls also suggested that distributional equity should occur only when it does not interfere with freedom.

Any recreation professional committed to service must also be committed to the fundamental values of justice, fairness, and empowering others. Recreation provision is deliberately designed to develop worthwhile states of mind and character in participants. This act assumes that if inclusion is to occur in recreation and leisure experiences, then we must intentionally set it as a goal and not leave matters to chance. Inclusion is embodied in demonstrating an interest in the protection, growth, health, and well-being of all people whether they are coworkers or participants.

Inclusion and Diversity

Inclusion cannot occur without acknowledging the power of privilege and the diversity among people. Differences between men and women are one aspect, as are differences among women and among men. For example, even if women and men were to obtain equal rights, the diversity that exists due to race, class, physical ability, sexual orientation, age, and other issues of privilege needs to be addressed.

Recreation professionals in the future will need to focus on gender, race, class, and ability inclusivity rather than neutrality. Ignoring differences and suggesting they are not important, as Molotch (1988) described in the bathroom story, does little good. Arguing that no differences exist, however, draws attention away from actual differences in power and resources among groups (Rhode, 1990). For example, ignoring ethnic differences does not challenge the existing social structures and assumes that particular groups of people have no special needs. Affirming the similarity between women and men, Black and White, gay and straight, or other heterogeneous groups may inadvertently validate norms of the dominant social groups. These norms often have not addressed diverse interests, experiences, and perspectives for groups participating in recreation activities.

Knowledge of differences must be addressed when analyzing inclusion. Inclusion is more than recognizing differences or even celebrating them. Differences must be taken into account if the provision of leisure services to underserved or marginalized groups are to be understood.

To change anything about leisure behavior, however, we must know what differences we seek to change. For example, more opportunities for evening sports participation for women (i.e., making the opportunities equal to men's) would not be warranted if women do not feel safe going out in a particular neighborhood to play sports at night. Different schedules or different accommodations may be needed for certain groups such as for Moslem women who are not allowed by doctrines of their religion to be seen in swimming attire when men are present. The Americans with Disabilities Act now states that people with disabilities have the right to participate in recreation programs, and the ethical approach is to train staff and other participants in how to create a welcoming environment for all individuals who have the right to participate. Claiming and acknowledging differences are not enough without exposing and disrupting previous understandings of the divisiveness of differences. The challenge to leisure professionals lies in making sure that the differences are considered and that leisure services providers are inclusive of gender, race, class, and other potentially dividing characteristics.

Inclusion and Leisure Opportunities

Recreation professionals at all levels will be challenged with how to provide recreation opportunities for community groups that will enable them to become empowered, not only in leisure, but also in other areas. Inclusive recreation programming means that all participants will be encouraged to participate and to learn enjoyable activities because they possess the confidence and skill levels necessary to be successful. Inclusive recreation can help groups see others as equals, respect people as role models, and offer appropriate support. Inclusive recreation should ensure that both behaviors and attitudes change.

No magic formulas exist to help leisure service professionals facilitate for inclusion, but some approaches are better than others (Henderson, 1997). Traditionally, we have followed the liberal philosophy of treating people equally. This approach, however, is almost always defined according to the dominant culture's terms, with minority groups striving to get more of what the dominant group has always had. Making everything the same assumes a cultural barrier removable through rational intervention. The approach offered in the name of equality and fairness has been effective in offering more opportunities for particular groups and for calling attention to the inequalities that have existed. As implied throughout this chapter, the liberal equality model has advantages but generally it is not enough. Recreation professionals cannot assume that all activities are important to all individuals just because they are important to some. Equality will not work if it means some people have to adjust and others do not. Activity does not have to be the same for all, but everyone should have a choice.

Another approach to programming for inclusion is based on an equitable education model (Bailey, 1993). Achieving equity means equally recognizing and rewarding the achievements of all individuals.

> A wider range of choices will be genuinely available to
> girls only when an equally wide and nontraditional range
> of choices is available to boys as well. (Bailey, 1993, p. 322)

This model also seeks to counter stereotypes and behaviors that diminish the value of recreation. Equitable recreation means that stereotypes must be addressed. Frequently when a person from a marginalized group does not perform in some way, attributions are made to that person's group affiliation. For example, if a woman cannot shoot a bow and arrow well, the assumption is that females can't shoot well. If a man cannot shoot a bow and arrow well, he's just not a good shot. Recreation professionals will be challenged with addressing stereotypes they hold that are also held by others in society.

If professionals can agree that inclusive recreation is defined as recreation and leisure opportunities that provide a wide range of choices for all individuals, then a number of strategies will be necessary to implement inclusive programs. For example, clearly worded, widely distributed, and strictly enforced policies requiring equitable treatment of all participants and staff must be established. Staff must acquire techniques to address imbalances, and criteria must be developed for what defines an equitable situation. Further, promotional and training materials must be reviewed to assure no gender, racial, or other biases exist in said materials.

In inclusive recreation, all participants must have an opportunity to learn a variety of skills with the focus on the process and not necessarily the outcome. Inclusion for all participants may occur by professionals encouraging individuals to feel emotionally and physically safe trying various activities and being supportive of differences in participants' needs. The personal power available to all participants is based on participation and involvement, not history or gender expectations. Along with this notion of power would be the desire to allow all participants to learn so that they might assume leadership positions within recreation agencies, organizations, and businesses.

If what leisure professionals do in practice is to have meaning from an ethical and a practical point of view, we must contribute to positive social change. The work of recreation professionals ought to result in inclusion and just alternatives to enhance current practice. When all individuals in our society have comparable life, leisure, and employment choices, no need will exist for discussions about inclusion and justice. If recreation and leisure are to contribute to a better world and a higher quality of life, all of us must be concerned about inclusion. The challenge is ours whether we are participants, community citizens, or recreation professionals.

Reflection Questions

1. What is inclusion?

2. Who is responsible for inclusion?

3. How can a recreation service be equal but not equitable?

4. What skills are needed to promote inclusion?

5. How can leisure services professionals develop inclusive leisure programs?

6. How does inclusion relate to our earlier discussion of marginalized groups, disability, and just recreation?

4.13   Partnerships

Although recreation and leisure services are provided in different ways, the future of recreation services and their effectiveness depends on working collaboratively in partnerships. This chapter provides information about partnership issues and why they are important and identifies the ways that partnerships occur within and among public, not-for-profit, and the private commercial sectors.

The Nature of Partnerships

Partnerships in various forms have always existed, but recently they have become more significant. Dollars for public services have been more difficult to acquire while at the same time citizen demand for services has increased. People (and organizations) must find ways to do more with less—partnering is one way to accomplish this. Partnerships can be advantageous for citizens in a community as well as the agencies and businesses that provide leisure services. Partnerships of all types will be paramount in the 21st century.

The challenge of any partnership, whether it is in recreation services or in a marriage, is to make sure that each partner benefits from the relationship. It is also imperative that each partner understands the obligations and responsibilities that are necessary for the partnership to work. Some partnerships work better than others because the benefits and the costs are clearly identified in the beginning. Partners can then work diligently to make sure that the outcomes promised and the responsibilities delineated are consistent over time.

Partnerships may occur within sectors or across sectors with two partners or numerous partners. For example, a local parks and recreation department might work with state government to develop a bicycle path, or a local department might work with a local manufacturing company to get swim passes for employees. Some partnerships include primary partners and numerous other contributors or sponsors. One only needs to look at something like a T-shirt given at a road race to see examples of partnerships in action. For example, while Raleigh (NC) Parks and Recreation might sponsor a race, they may partner with the local Boys and Girls Club, a fitness center, a local corporation, Coca-Cola, local restaurants, and various other groups. Each event or program is likely to offer many potential avenues for involvement, but successful professionals will determine what partners are needed and how they can best work together.

Advantages of Partnerships

Many advantages to partnerships exist. Professionals need to assess these advantages and the purpose of partnerships for any proposed undertaking. One advantage is that the increased interaction among partners can lead to more informed decision making and more effective programs. By their nature, partnerships involve people. A by-product of these partnerships is also a better-informed public, with more people potentially available to show support for parks, recreation, and leisure programs and businesses.

Another advantage is that in today's complex society, it is more difficult to compartmentalize recreation services. Therefore, it is necessary particularly in the public sector to determine how and where to invest funds in personnel and space to provide the broadest and most inclusive leisure services possible. In addition, without cooperation and partnerships, competition and duplication of services (and thus a waste of time and money) could occur. Communities that have adequate and effective partnerships are likely to be places where staff in the various sectors of recreation coordinate, communicate, and work together.

Partnerships can add energy and enthusiasm to a recreation service, program, event, or facility. They can offer an opportunity to focus on the patterns of recreation services needed and provide creative ways to address social and leisure issues. They also provide a way for professionals, business leaders, and citizens to learn from one another. In essence, partnerships can allow people and organizations to contribute their strengths to a situation. Depending on the type of partnerships, a number of other outcomes can occur such as greater profits or sales, tax deductions, improved quality of services, and the development of a sense of ownership among the partners.

Disadvantages of Partnerships

No disadvantage is insurmountable, but the potential disadvantages must be assessed. One of the biggest disadvantages occurs if the roles of the partners are not clearly defined. Some partnerships may be defined as one partner, like the public park and recreation department, being responsible for the actual programming of an event with the partners providing advice and money. If one of the partners believes they should be running an event and this relationship has not been clearly defined ahead of time, problems can occur. Policy and program control must be clearly identified for each partner. It takes time and energy to determine how a partnership will work, including who will be served, how quality standards will be met, and definitions of the relationships.

A problem that can undermine partnerships is the perceived competition that can occur in a community between potential partners. For example, if a community recreation program and a YMCA exist in a community, they may be perceived in some cases as competitors for the same customers. To some extent, these agencies may have some similar target audiences, but that fact does not preclude examining how they might work together to provide better opportunities for individuals. The success of both organizations may depend on recognition of the interdependence between sectors that can result in a reevaluation of how groups can mutually support one another.

Any partnership might result in the need to negotiate differences among the partners related to policies, scheduling, financial constraints, legal restriction on public use of private facilities (and vice versa), mutual protection of spheres of influence, available information, and the specialized nature of particular groups. None of these problems are intractable but they must be taken into account when embarking on opportunities to work together.

Partnerships in Outdoor Recreation

Partnerships among recreation providers and community groups are not new. The value of these partnerships, however have become evident in recent years. For example, the report of the President's Commission on Americans Outdoors in the late 1980s called for a greater involvement of the private and voluntary sectors in the expansion of outdoor recreation opportunities. Given that over two billion acres of land and water (about 60% of the total acreage in the United States) was in private ownership, that only 6% of national shoreline was under public auspices, and with less governmental funds available for capital development, it was essential that the private commercial sector be involved in outdoor recreation planning and management. These efforts at partnerships, however, also raised issues about public and private relationships. For example, who is to maintain private areas when they are opened to the public—government or the private landowner? Why should the private sector become involved and what costs will the public assume in the form of incentives (e.g., tax credits) to encourage their involvement?

In this scenario, the views of the private sector are mixed. Some corporations and individuals feel it is their civic responsibility to make their outdoor resources available to the public when the activities pursued are not injurious to the resource. Partnerships result in good public relations and a potential source of income, assuming they are able to assess a fee or operate a concession. Other people have argued that these relationships negated their privacy, interfered with the resource's current and primary use, and often resulted in vandalism. The reality of these assumptions varies from place to place, and more research is needed. It is obvious, however, that without the not-for-profit and commercial sectors' involvement in outdoor recreation, further expansion of opportunities and services are limited. The options remain simple: continue to rely upon government to provide and maintain the resource, have the private sector make available its resources for public use, or allow private development on governmental property for both private and public use.

Other Examples of Partnerships

Many other ways of developing partnerships exist. Partnerships usually take on forms to meet different community needs. These range from the need to attract or invite investment capital to gaining efficiency through coordination. The joint ventures can range from shared responsibility on the part of partners to minimal involvement by one or more of the partners. The opportunities and options are virtually limitless given the many providers of recreation services and the needs that exist in communities. Here are some other examples to consider:

- One common way to set up a partnership is for the public agency to provide facilities and a not-for-profit or commercial organization to offer services. An example would be a commercial group providing refreshment services at a public athletic field, or a canoe club providing instruction at a lake in a local park. Another example is a community organization such as a Lions Club that adopts a park or a greenway and is responsible for litter pickup.

- Public, not-for-profit, and private commercial organizations might undertake a joint venture to provide facilities. In this case the public agency might provide the basic facility and the private group could make improvements. An example might be a golf course operated on public lands.

- Partnerships also occur in the form of lease agreements. These agreements have specific legal functions. An example is the case of a marina that might be leased for operation on a public lake owned by a state.

- Coordinating councils within communities are another example of partnerships. A coordinating council frequently consists of individuals from organizations representing different sectors. An example that occurs in several places around the United States is a community coordinating council that looks at the needs of a particular group such as people with disabilities or youth services.

- The use of sponsorships is a common example of partnerships. Sponsorships at different levels provide the chance for several commercial businesses or other groups to work together. An example suggested earlier was the road race coordinated by a specific group but offering numerous opportunities for others to be involved either with monetary gifts or volunteer resources.

• Partnerships might also exist with people offering technical assistance to one another. If an organization such as a youth-serving agency has particular expertise in youth programming, they might assist another organization to set up a program or address some of the issues that need assistance.

• Funds can be raised for special events through partnerships, including a direct solicitation for money as well as the use of in-kind donations or material goods that can be given away (e.g., free refreshments) or door prizes.

• A number of other examples exist, such as loaned executive programs, loaned equipment, volunteer labor, shared facilities, joint purchases, joint public relations or advertising, and endorsements.

Facilitating Partnerships

To develop any type of recreation partnership will require that several steps be taken. First, each recreation organization must examine its mission and goals to determine if recreation might be further enhanced in a community through the use of partnerships. Collaborative goals can be reached through a pooling of resources. A needs assessment might be done in conjunction with this step. The second step is to identify what resources might be available in a community from other agencies, businesses, or citizen groups. The third step is to begin a dialogue to see how partnerships might be mutually beneficial. The variety of ways that partnerships might be coordinated might also be considered.

In today's society one sector alone does not meet the interests and needs of all citizens, particularly when the goal is inclusive recreation. Initial partnerships can open the door for many other endeavors in the future. Therefore, partnerships may be one important way to extend the services and provide more and better opportunities. Partnerships often have financial advantages, but they also provide a way to enhance services and develop a broader base of support for community recreation opportunities.

Reflection Questions

1. What are the advantages of partnerships? What are the disadvantages?

2. How is it justified that commercial services partner with public services?

3. Describe a recreation partnership in your community or university, including both positive and negative aspects.

professionals and leaders may become more like facilitators and educators for recreation opportunities and experiences. For example, perhaps a group of parents from a low-income area talk with the recreation professionals in their community about the possibilities of having a soccer league for their children, who are currently not participating in after-school sports programs. These parents have found space to offer a program in a vacant lot and have volunteers to staff a program. However, they need help in structuring programs, training volunteers, and getting equipment. They turn to the public recreation professionals for help. People, especially in local communities, need to feel empowered to meet their needs while the professional facilitates this personal and community growth. Recreation programs can evolve from an expressed grassroots need that maintains authority and control with the participants rather than always a top-down program. Such examples of facilitative styles of programming and leadership may become more common in the future.

The role of women, people of color, and other marginalized people is an issue that will likely influence the leadership of recreation and leisure systems in the future. Currently more females than males are majoring in recreation and leisure studies in universities and colleges, but the number of people of color entering the profession is still very low. Women and people of color are becoming more visible in leadership in leisure services; this is also occurring gradually in other professions. Issues will need to be addressed concerning how work environments can be more hospitable to these professionals from historically marginalized groups. For example, work environments will need to become more flexible for many women who still have primary childcare responsibilities in this society. In addition, issues in other professions that confront women and other marginalized people, such as sexual harassment, wage discrimination, and the glass ceiling, still exist. A diverse workforce employed in recreation and leisure will likely result in more diverse participants.

Citizen involvement, particularly in the planning and policy aspects of recreation and leisure services, will continue to be essential. All monumental social changes (e.g., civil rights, environmental, nuclear disarmament) have occurred because of citizen grassroots movements. Citizen involvement offers the most potential for change in the future. In the public and not-for-profit sectors, and to some extent the private commercial area, various political forces affect recreation and leisure services. The lay leadership is often in a better position to address political forces than are most professionals. Likewise, citizen involvement in program planning, facility acquisition and development, and evaluation assures a recreation future of their own choice and content. Recreation professionals have recognized that the involvement of the community in the planning process is almost as important as the

4.14   The Future and the Profession

The one certainty about the future is that things will change. The profession and the leaders who work in recreation and leisure services will experience challenges unimagined today. The need for flexibility, creativity, vision, and cutting-edge leadership will be imperative if recreation and leisure are to remain essential in our society. No blueprint exists to create the perfect role for the profession. Several aspects, however, will continue to be important as the profession grows and develops: leadership responsibilities, financial support, and professional identity.

Leadership Responsibilities

Leadership is paramount when considering the future of leisure services. There are two kinds of leadership: (1) professional leadership that gives direction to techniques and program strategies; and (2) citizen involvement that gives the program validity and the movement political credibility. As discussed in unit three, recreation and leisure services as a profession offers employment opportunities for individuals with a variety of backgrounds, skills, and professional orientations. Sociologists, economists, landscape architects, gardeners, maintenance workers, computer specialists, dance specialists, and technicians are all a part of the leisure delivery system. The recreation professional who is uniquely prepared to give leadership to the overall operations of a recreation, park, leisure, or tourism agency or business will be needed as the guiding force that integrates all of the many employees into a cohesive service.

The role of the recreation professional is distinct from the technician or activity leader. Being a professional requires broad understandings of interpersonal relationships and dynamics, interagency relationships and partnerships, the need for long-term and short-term planning, and the significance of leisure and recreation in contemporary life. The technician or activity leader is more concerned with the implementation of day-to-day activities and decisions that provide the professional with the data necessary for planning and action. In the future, recreation and leisure organizations will likely increase their use of part-time workers and volunteers who will need supervision and leadership from professionals.

Another possibility is for the leadership of recreation programs to become more shared. Some professionals believe that the future holds more collaborative programs and partnerships that grow from interests expressed by individuals as well as other community agencies. In addition, recreation activity itself. Recreation professionals must continue to nurture and develop opportunities for citizen participation in all sectors for the future.

Financial Support

The future economy is always an issue of concern for participants and professionals alike. Recreation and leisure services professionals, especially in the public and not-for-profit arena, have recognized the need to strengthen and broaden the base of financial support. This change will occur through a combined effort of greater citizen support, the exploration of new funding sources, and improved long-range planning. For example, public recreation and leisure systems cannot afford to rely solely upon property tax revenues for operating budgets. The first revenue source often used by public recreation professionals is increased fees and charges. These new charges, however, should not make programs and facilities inaccessible to people who have typically been underserved and marginalized.

Recreation organizations might also apply some of the proven market strategies developed in the commercial sector to the provision of program services. Among the techniques that may be used to expand park and recreation budgets and services are grants, trusts, endowments, bequests, gift catalogs (which itemize the needs of an organization and solicit donations), Friends of the Parks or "adopt-a-park" programs, cosponsorships and corporate assistance, and volunteer services. Privatization, the assignment or contracting of certain functions to private and commercial organizations, may be another alternative way to expand services without increasing taxation.

A broader base of public support and citizen involvement through a more diversified program approach should result in a greater potential for financial support. Getting citizen response to potential solutions for critical problems may be the major challenge before professionals in recreation and leisure services. People who want high quality programs and organizations must make sure that quality is not sacrificed for quantity and funding possibilities. Hopefully, more enlightened and devoted participants will result in a commitment that includes being willing to pay for quality environments and programs.

Political attitudes affect financing recreation services, particularly in the public sector. If citizens view recreation and parks as a necessity, they tend to support bond issues and the expenditure of tax dollars for recreation operations. They do not expect recreation professionals necessarily to be entrepreneurial. Rather, they want their local parks and recreation department to work for the betterment of the community. When recreation and parks have been viewed as a luxury, public recreation has not always fared well. With the economic turnaround in the late 1990s and political activism of citizens on behalf of the environment, legislation such as the Conservation and Reinvestment Act (CARA), introduced to Congress in 2000, received political support but no funding at the time Congress adjourned. The message seems to be that recreation professionals must be politically smart and foster a strong loyalty from their grassroots citizenry if the value of recreation is to stay in the forefront as an essential component of our quality of life.

Professional Identity

As the future unfolds, recreation and leisure professionals will be valued by members of communities based on the services and facilities offered and the human and environmental values upheld. Pressures will exist to evolve into identities that differ from the current sense of who we are as a profession. Just as personal identities are shaped by environment and experiences, the same type of forces will be encountered within our developing professional identity. Some of those forces will lead to positive change but some may not.

Professional identity within the recreation and leisure field will result from clearly defined roles that are different from the roles assumed by other groups, professionals, and organizations. Our emerging body of knowledge obtained through research, as well as our programs of voluntary certification and accreditation, are assisting the profession in establishing its uniqueness. The activities of the National Recreation and Park Association and other professional associations can aid that endeavor. The burden of professionalism, however, lies with individuals who identify themselves as professionals.

A fragmentation of the recreation movement into subspecialities or special interest groups who do not identify with the broad area of leisure services will slow and confuse the identification of recreation and leisure services as a unique profession. The field of recreation and leisure services has a long and rich history that supports interests in the preservation and use of the environment as well as concerns for social welfare programs, marginalized groups, and opportunities for individual and community development. Our future professional identity will be influenced by the past and will evolve with the economic and political climates of the future. How recreation and leisure services evolve as a profession depends on the directions taken by future recreation professionals along with citizens in communities.

Reflection Questions

1. What will be the impact of a diverse society on the future of the profession?

2. How will increased consumption and an increasing gap between rich and poor influence leisure service provision?

3. How do you think professional leadership and citizen involvement will need to come together to offer the best recreation services in the future?

4. What effect will the changes in population, social, and economic patterns have on recreation and leisure services?

5. What is the appropriate level of response for all sectors, including public, not-for-profit, and private commercial, in providing recreation services?

6. What is the appropriate role for citizen participation in the decision-making process concerning the development, operation, and expansion of recreation and leisure opportunities?

Epilogue

Over 30 years ago the Heritage Conservation and Recreation Service (1979) addressed "Future Directions." They identified what they considered to be the more difficult problems, questions, and issues confronting public park and recreation systems during the coming decades. The concerns expressed are still valid today:

1. What effect do the changes in population, social, and economic patterns have on recreation and leisure services?

2. What is the appropriate level of response for all sectors, including public, not-for-profit, and private commercial, in providing recreation services?

3. What is the appropriate role for citizen participation in the decision-making process concerning the development, operation, and expansion of recreation and leisure opportunities?

Answers to these broad questions can be found through more comprehensive thinking about the role of recreation and leisure in people's lives and in communities. Every public service, profession, and social movement needs support to prosper in the future. The recreation and leisure system has made rapid gains in the past, but these gains are small in comparison to the plethora of opportunities that lie ahead. As discussed throughout the text, the future of the leisure service delivery system is dependent upon the relationship and partnership of all its segments: public, not-for-profit, and commercial agencies and businesses. All are needed, and all have important roles to play.

For recreation and leisure to meet the needs of the world's citizens in the future, research is needed. The progress of recreation and park systems in the future will depend upon the quantity and quality of research undertaken. A well-defined approach is needed to carry out a continuing program of research. This research system must involve and utilize resources of the academic community, private research firms, and research units of federal agencies. It also requires the support of foundations and private interest groups who are willing to underwrite the needed studies and investigations. Research is essential to the development of sound public policies and effective administrative practices.

Leisure will be important in the world of postindustrialism. People are experiencing a change in the structure of their lives related to uses of time, the value systems that structure existence, and the technology that provides for survival as well as an enhanced quality of life. In the past these forces have offered more disposable free time, more disposable amounts of human energy, more disposable income, and an approach to life that stresses doing something satisfying and productive. The potential for leisure results from further advances in technology and the emergence of a holistic view of life, which has people in tune with nature's rhythms rather than those of the clock or the bureaucracy. Recreation and leisure expression can give people opportunities to empower themselves to be in control of their lives and to create social capital in their communities. The opportunities for leisure and recreation experiences must be freely chosen for the satisfaction derived from involvement. The potential for leisure is enormous and worthy of a system to protect and nurture it. The challenge exists for all people to experience leisure joyfully and responsibly, and for recreation and leisure professionals in all sectors to provide inclusive and socially just opportunities.

About the Authors

This book was undertaken as a joint project when all the authors were affiliated with the University of North Carolina at Chapel Hill. The chapters were planned together with individuals taking the lead on this new edition of the book with its number of changes from the past. The book reflects the authors' commitments to inclusion and social justice within the broad field of recreation services and leisure studies. The authors have both a diversity of interests within the field as well as a unified commitment to the value of leisure and recreation services in the lives of all people.

- **Karla A. Henderson** is a Professor and the Chair in the Department of Recreation and Leisure Studies at the University of North Carolina at Chapel Hill where she has been for 15 years. She grew up on an Iowa farm and received her Ph.D. from the University of Minnesota. Karla is a member of the Academy of Leisure Sciences, the American Academy of Park and Recreation Administrators, and the American Leisure Academy. She has served as president of the Society of Park and Recreation Educators and the Research Consortium of the American Alliance of Health, Physical Education, Recreation, and Dance. Her academic specialties include gender and leisure, research and evaluation methods, and camping. Her personal leisure commitments are to playing a musical instrument, running, and writing just for fun.

- **M. Deborah Bialeschki** is a Professor in the Department of Recreation and Leisure Studies at the University of North Carolina at Chapel Hill where she came shortly after receiving her Ph.D. at the University of Wisconsin—Madison. She is a member of the UNC Academy of Distinguished Teaching Scholars and has also served as president of the Society of Park and Recreation Educators. Her research interests include alternative families and leisure, fear in leisure, and research and evaluation methods. She enjoys playing with her dog, traveling, running, being in the mountains, and playing her trumpet.

- **John L. Hemingway** is an Associate Professor in the Department of Recreation and Leisure Studies at the University of North Carolina at Chapel Hill. He received his Ph.D. in Political Science at the University of Iowa, where he also studied recreation. John has been on the faculties of Old Dominion and Washington

State Universities. His academic interests lie in the political dimensions of leisure, recreation management, and the historical analysis of leisure. John's leisure passions are the Philadelphia Flyers and paddling his canoe.

• **Jan S. Hodges** is currently an Assistant Professor at University of North Texas where she also completed her Ph.D. She was a faculty member for three years with a specialty in therapeutic recreation at the University of North Carolina at Chapel Hill. Jan spent eight years with Dallas Parks and Recreation. Her current research interests include inclusion and community-based therapeutic recreation services. For fun, Jan likes to putter with her plants and enjoys a good stout beer.

• **Beth D. Kivel** is an Assistant Professor in the Department of Recreation and Leisure Studies at the University of North Carolina at Chapel Hill. She received her doctorate at the University of Georgia and taught for a short time at the University of Northern Iowa. Prior to coming into academia, Beth was a community activist in San Francisco, California and brings her commitment to public service in the work that she does. Her research and academic interests include identity development, leisure ideology, youth and not for profit agency management. She enjoys going to movies and playing tennis.

• **H. Douglas Sessoms** is an Emeritus Professor in the Department of Recreation and Leisure Studies at the University of North Carolina at Chapel Hill where he taught for over 40 years before his retirement in 1996. Doug received his Ph.D. at the University of Illinois. He has been active in numerous professional organizations, including being president of the Society of Park and Recreation Educators, Academy of Leisure Studies, and the American Academy of Park and Recreation Administrators. In his retirement, Doug enjoys traveling, collecting Native American pottery, and watching soap operas.

References

Academy of Leisure Sciences. (1993). Leisure: The new center of the economy? Available online: http://www.eas.ualberta.ca/elj/als/als1.html

Act of August 25, 1916. Stat 39. 535.

Adams, C. (2000, April). Does violence against women rise 40% during the Super Bowl? The Straight Dope. Available online: http://www.straightdope.com/columns/000414.html

Adams, M., Bell, L. A., and Griffin, P. (Eds.). (1997). *Teaching for diversity and social justice.* New York, NY: Routledge.

Alberti, L. B. (1969). *The family in renaissance Florence* (R. N. Watkins, Trans.). Columbia, SC: University of South Carolina Press. (Original work published 1443)

Allison, M. (1987). Kaleidoscope and prism: The study of social change in play, sport, and leisure. *Sociology of Sport Journal, 4,* 144-155.

Allison, M. (1988). Breaking boundaries and barriers: Future directions in cross-cultural research. *Leisure Sciences, 10,* 247-259.

American Association of Retired Persons. (1999a). *A profile of older Americans.* Washington, DC: Author.

American Association of Retired Persons. (1999b). *Baby boomers envision their retirement: An AARP segmentation analysis.* Washington, DC: Author.

American Camping Association. (2001). Available online: http://www.acacamps.org

Andrews, F. M. and Withey, S. B. (1974). Developing measures of perceived life quality: Results from several national surveys. *Social Indicators Research, 1,* 1-26.

Anspaugh, D. J., Hunter, S., and Dignan, M. (1996). Risk factors for cardiovascular disease among exercising versus nonexercising women. *American Journal of Health Promotion, 10,* 171-174.

Austin, D. (1998). The health protection/health promotion model. *Therapeutic Recreation Journal, 32,* 109-117.

Austin, M. M. and Vidal-Naquet, P. (1977). *Economic and social history of ancient Greece: An introduction* (M. M. Austin, Trans.). Berkeley, CA: University of California Press.

Babbie, E. (1986). *Observing ourselves: Essays in social research.* Belmont, CA: Wadsworth.

Bailey, S. M. (1993). The current status of gender equity research in American schools. *Educational Psychologist, 28*(4), 321-339.

Barbee, J. and Calloway, J. (1979). The courts and correctional recreation. *Journal of Physical Education and Recreation, 50*(2), 40.

Barner, R. (1996). The new millennium workplace: Seven changes that will challenge managers and workers. *The Futurist, 30*(2), 14-18.

Bedini, L. (1990). The status of leisure education: Implications for instruction and practice. *Therapeutic Recreation Journal, 24*(1), 40-49.

Begun, B. (2000, January 1). USA: The way we'll live then. *Newsweek*, 34-35.

Bellah, R. N., Madsen, R., Sullivan, W., Swidler, A., and Tipton, S. (1985). *Habits of the heart: Individualism and commitment in American life*. Berkeley, CA: University of California Press.

Bennett, J. T. (1980). The Youth Council approach: An alternative to the street. *Parks & Recreation, 15*(6), 34-36.

Berkman, L.F. and Syme, S. L. (1979). Social networks, host resistance, and mortality: A nine-year follow-up study of Alameda County residents. *American Journal of Epidemiology, 109*, 186-204.

Berlin, I. (1969). *Four essays on liberty*. London, UK: Oxford University Press.

Betzig, L. L. and Turke, P. W. (1985). Measuring time allocation: Observation and intention. *Current Anthropology, 26*, 647-650.

Bialeschki, M. D. (1992). We said "Why not?": A historical perspective on women's outdoor pursuits. *Journal of Physical Education, Recreation, and Dance, 63*(2), 52-55.

Bialeschki, M. D. (1999). *Negotiations of fear: Women's resistance to social control of outdoor recreation space*. Paper presented at the 1999 National Recreation and Park Association Leisure Research Symposium, Nashville, TN.

Bluestone, B. and Rose, S. (1998). *The unmeasured work force: The growth in work hours* (Public Policy Brief 39). Annandale-on-Hudson, NY: The Jerome Levey Economics Institute of Bard College.

Bogle, T., Havitz, M. E., and Dimanche, F. (1992). Sector biases in adults' recreation fitness facility selection. *Journal of Park and Recreation Administration, 10*(3), 49-74.

Bolino, A. C. (1998). *From depression to war: American society in transition—1939*. Westport, CT: Praeger.

Braden, D. R. (1988). *Leisure and entertainment in America*. Dearborn, MI: Henry Ford Museum and Greenfield Village.

Bregha, F. (1991). Leisure and freedom re-examined. In T. Goodale and P. Witt (Eds.), *Recreation and leisure: Issues in an era of change* (3rd ed., pp. 47-54). State College, PA: Venture Publishing, Inc.

Brooks, C. (1988). Armchair quarterbacks. *American Demographics, 10*(3), 28-31.

Brucker, G. A. (Ed.). (1971). *The society of renaissance Florence: A documentary study*. New York, NY: Harper & Row.

Bullaro, J. and Edginton, C. (1986). *Commercial leisure services: Managing for profit*. New York, NY: MacMillan.

Burch, W. (1984). Much ado about nothing: Some reflections on the wider and wilder implications of social carrying capacity. *Leisure Sciences, 6*, 487-496.

Burke, P. (1987). *The Renaissance*. Atlantic Highlands, NJ: Humanities Press International.

Butsch, R. (Ed.). (1990). *For fun and profit: The transformation of leisure into consumption*. Philadelphia, PA: Temple University Press.

California Park and Recreation Society. (1999). *Creating community in the 21st century*. Sacramento, CA: Author.

Campbell, A., Converse, P. E., and Rodgers, W. L. (1976). *The quality of American life: Perceptions, evaluations, and satisfactions*. New York, NY: Sage Publications, Inc.

Carcopino, J. (1940). *Daily life in ancient Rome: The people and the city at the height of the Empire* (E. O. Lorie, Trans.). New Haven, CT: Yale University Press.

Carter, L. B. (1986). *The quiet Athenian.* Oxford: Clarendon Press.

Ceram, C. (1971). Gods, graves and scholars. In R. Kraus, *Recreation and leisure in modern society.* Englewood Cliffs, NJ: Prentice Hall.

Chamoux, F. (1965). *The civilization of Greece* (W. S. Macguinness, Trans.). New York, NY: Simon and Schuster.

Chavez, D. (1992, May). *The wildland/urban interface: Hispanics in the national forest.* Paper presented at the Fourth National Symposium on Society and Resource Management, University of Wisconsin-Madison, Madison, WI.

Chenoweth, D. H. (1998). *Worksite health promotion.* Champaign, IL: Human Kinetics.

Chick, G. (1998). Leisure and culture: Issues for an anthropology of leisure. *Leisure Sciences, 20,* 111-133.

Chubb, M. and Chubb, H. (1981). *One third of our time.* New York, NY: John Wiley & Sons.

Cipolla, C. (1994). *Before the industrial revolution: European society and economy, 1000-1700* (3rd ed.). (C. Woodall, Trans.) New York, NY: W. W. Norton.

Clawson, M. and Knetsch, J. L. (1966). *Economics of outdoor recreation.* Baltimore, MD: The Johns Hopkins University Press.

Connolly, P. and Finegan, J. (1996, October). *Therapeutic recreation: From basics to the future.* Paper presented at the National Therapeutic Recreation Society Institute, Kansas City, MO.

Coolidge, S. D. (1995, October 16). Corporations can take tips from non-profits. *Christian Science Monitor, 87*(224), 8.

Council on Outdoor Education. (1989). Outdoor education—Definitions and philosophy. *Journal of Physical Education, Recreation, and Health, 60*(2), 31-34.

Cousins, N. (1979). *Anatomy of an illness.* New York, NY: Norton.

Crandall, R. (1980). Motivations for leisure. *Journal of Leisure Research, 12*(1) 45-54.

Cross, G. (1989). *A quest for time: The reduction of work in Britain and France, 1840-1940.* Berkeley, CA: University of California Press.

Cross, G. (1990). *A social history of leisure since 1600.* State College, PA: Venture Publishing, Inc.

Crossley, J. (1990). Multi-ties programming in commercial recreation. *Parks and Recreation, 25*(3), 68-73.

Csikzentmihalyi, M. (1975). *Beyond boredom and anxiety: The experience of play.* San Francisco, CA: Jossey-Bass.

Csikzentmihalyi, M. (1990). *Flow: The psychology of optimal experience.* New York, NY: Harper & Row.

Davis, J. M. (1978). Leadership in leisure service. In H. Ibrahim and F. Martin (Eds.) *Leisure: An introduction.* Los Alomitos, CA: Hwong Publishing.

de Toqueville, A. (1945). *Democracy in America.* New York, NY: Vintage Books. (Original work published 1835)

de Vries, J. (1994). The industrial revolution and the industrious revolution. *Journal of Economic History, 54,* 249-270.

Deaux, K. (1992). Personalizing identity and socializing self. In G. Breakwell (Ed.), *Social psychology of identity and the self-concept* (pp. 9-33). New York, NY: Surrey University Press.

Decker, J. and Crompton, J. (1990). Business location decisions: The relative importance of quality of life and recreation, park and cultural opportunities. *Journal of Park and Recreation Administration, 8*(2), 26-43.

Devine, M. A. and Kotowski, L. (1999). Inclusive leisure services: Results of a national survey of park and recreation departments. *Journal of Park and Recreation Administration, 17*, 56-72.

Dewey, J. (1916). *Democracy and education.* New York, NY: Macmillan.

Dickason, J. (1985). 1906: A pivotal year for the playground movement. *Parks & Recreation, 20*(8), 40-45.

Driver, B. L., Brown, P. J., and Peterson, G. L. (Eds.). (1991). *Benefits of leisure.* State College, PA: Venture Publishing, Inc.

Driver, B. L. and Bruns, D. H. (1999). Concepts and uses of the benefits approach to leisure. In E. L. Jackson and T. L. Burton (Eds.), *Leisure studies: Prospects for the Twenty-first Century* (pp. 349-369). State College, PA: Venture Publishing, Inc.

Driver, B. L., Dustin, D., Baltic, T. Elsner, G., and Peterson, G. (Eds.). (1996). *Nature and the Human Spirit.* State College, PA: Venture Publishing, Inc.

Dulles, F. (1965). *A history of recreation in America.* New York, NY: Appleton-Century-Crofts.

Dumazedier, J. (1967). *Toward a leisure society.* New York, NY: The Free Press.

Dustin, D. and McKenney, A. (1999). A night at the opera. Fine arts as rehabilitation? *Parks & Recreation, 34*(3), 85-99.

Dwyer, J. F. and Gobster, P. H. (1992). Recreation opportunities and cultural diversity. *Parks & Recreation, 27*(9), 22-31, 128.

Ellis, G. and Witt, P. (1985). Conceptualizing leisure: Making the abstract concrete. In T. Goodale and P. Witt (Eds.), *Recreation and leisure: Issues in an era of change* (pp. 105-117). State College, PA: Venture Publishing, Inc.

Ellis, J. J. (1973). *Why people play.* Englewood Cliffs, NJ: Prentice Hall.

Erikson, E. (1968). *Identity: Youth and crisis.* New York, NY: W.W. Norton & Co

Fain, G. S. (1991). Moral leisure. In G. S. Fain (Ed.). *Leisure and ethics: Reflections on the philosophy of leisure* (pp.7-30). Reston, VA: American Association for Leisure and Recreation.

Federal Elections Commission of the USA. (1998). Voter registration and turnout in federal elections by age: 1972-1996. Available online: http://www.fec.gov/pages File: agedemong.htm

Fennell, D. A. (1999). *Ecotourism.* London, UK: Routledge.

Ferguson, W. K. (1940). *The Renaissance.* New York, NY: Holt, Rinehart & Winston.

Ferguson, W. K. (1968). The interpretation of the Renaissance. In P. O. Kristeller and P. P. Wiener (Eds.), *Renaissance essays* (pp. 61-73). New York, NY: Harper Torchbooks.

Finney, C. (1984). Corporate benefits of employee recreation programs. *Parks & Recreation, 19*(8), 44-46, 71.

Floyd, M. (2000, September). *Interregional migration patterns of Hispanics: Research, management, and policy implications*. Paper presented at the 2000 Outdoor Recreation Trends Conference, Lansing, MI.

Fogg, G. (1975). *Park planning guidelines*. Alexandria, VA: National Recreation and Park Association.

Foner, E. (1994). The meaning of freedom in the age of emancipation. *Journal of American History, 81*, 435-460.

Frank, J. C., Hirsch, S. H., Chernoff, J., Wallace, S. P., Abrahamse, A., Maly, R., and Reuben, D. B. (1997). Determinants of patient adherence to consultative comprehensive geriatric assessment recommendations. *Journal of Gerontology, 52*, 44-51.

Franklin, B. (2000). *Wit and wisdom from Poor Richard's Almanack*. Mineola, NY: Dover Publications.

Fraser, A. (1966). *A history of toys*. New York, NY: Delacorte Press.

Freud, S. (1964). *The standard edition of the complete psychological works of Sigmund Freud*. London, UK: Hogarth Press.

Fryer, D. and Payne, R. (1984). Proactive behavior in unemployment: Findings and implications. *Leisure Studies, 3*, 273-295.

Garin, E. (1965). *Italian humanism: Philosophy and civic life in the Renaissance* (P. Munz, Trans.). New York, NY: Harper & Row.

Gini, A. (2000). *My job, my self: Work and the creation of the modern individual*. New York, NY: Routledge.

Gist, J. R. (2000). *Wealth distribution in 1998: Findings from the survey of consumer finances*. Washington, DC: AARP Public Policy Institute.

Gist, N. and Fava, S. (1964) *Urban society*. New York, NY: Crowell.

Gittell, R. and Vidal, A. (1998). *Community organizing: Building social capital as a development strategy*. Thousand Oaks, CA: Sage Publications.

Godbey, G. (1988). The sociology of leisure: Past, present and future research. In L. Barnett (Ed.), *Research about leisure: Past, present and future* (pp.35-46). Champaign, IL: Sagamore Publishing.

Godbey, G. (1997). *Leisure and leisure services in the 21st century*. State College, PA: Venture Publishing, Inc.

Goetz, H. W. (1993). *Life in the Middle Ages from the seventh to the thirteenth century* (A. Wimmer, Trans.; S. Rowan, Ed.). Notre Dame, IN: University of Notre Dame Press.

Goodale, T. L. (1985). If leisure is to matter. In T. L. Goodale and P.A. Witt (Eds.), *Recreation and leisure: Issues in an era of change* (Rev. ed., pp. 44-55). State College, PA: Venture Publishing, Inc.

Goodale, T. L. and Godbey, G. C. (1988). *The evolution of leisure*. State College, PA: Venture Publishing, Inc.

Granovetter, M. (1973). The strength of weak ties. *American Journal of Sociology, 78*, 1360-1380.

Green, T. H. (1964). Liberal legislation and freedom of contract. In J. R. Rodman (Ed.), *The political theory of T. H. Green: Selected Writings* (pp. 43-74). New York, NY: Appleton-Century-Crofts. (Original work published 1881)

Gross, D. R. (1984). Time allocation: A tool for the study of cultural behavior. *Annual Review of Anthropology, 13*, 519-558.

Gunn, C. (1988). *Tourism planning* (2nd ed.). New York, NY: Taylor & Francis.

Gutman, H. G. (1977). *Work, culture, and society in industrializing America.* New York, NY: Vintage Books.

Haggard, L. M. and Williams, D. R. (1991). Self-identity benefits of leisure activities. In B. L. Driver, P. J. Brown, and G. L. Peterson (Eds.), *Benefits of leisure* (pp. 103-119). State College, PA: Venture Publishing, Inc.

Haggard, L. M. and Williams, D. R. (1992). Leisure symbols of the self. *Journal of Leisure Research 24*(1), 1-18.

Hansen, M. H. (1991). *The Athenian democracy in the age of Demosthenes* (J. A. Crook, Trans.). Oxford, UK: Blackwell.

Harper, W. (1986). Freedom in the experience of leisure. *Leisure Sciences, 8*, 115-130.

Havinghurst, R. J. (1963). Successful aging. In R. Williams, C. Tibbits, and W. Donahue (Eds.), *Process of aging.* New York, NY: Atherton.

Havitz, M. (1989). The empirical development of a taxonomy for classifying recreation participants based on their attitudes toward the public and commercial sectors. *Leisure Sciences, 11*, 229-243.

Hayes, G. (1969). Recreation services for the mentally retarded in the state of Kansas. *Therapeutic Recreation Journal, 3*(3), 13-19.

Heath, S. B. and McLaughlin, M. W. (1993). *Identity and inner city youth: Beyond ethnicity and gender.* New York, NY: Teachers College Press.

Hemingway, J. L. (1988). Leisure and civility: Reflections on a Greek ideal. *Leisure Sciences, 10*, 179-191.

Hemingway, J. L. (1991). Leisure and democracy: Incompatible ideals? In G. D. Fain (Ed.), *Leisure and ethics: Reflections on the philosophy of leisure* (pp. 59-81). Reston, VA: American Association for Leisure and Recreation.

Hemingway, J. L. (1996). Emancipating leisure: The recovery of freedom in leisure. *Journal of Leisure Research, 28*, 27-43.

Hemingway, J. L. (1999). Leisure, social capital, and democratic citizenship. *Journal of Leisure Research, 31*, 150-165.

Hemingway, J. L. and Parr, M. (2000). Leisure research and leisure practice: Three perspectives on constructing the research-practice relation. *Leisure Sciences, 22*,(3), 139-162.

Hendee, J., Stankey, G., and Lucas, R. (1990). *Wilderness management.* Golden, CO: North American Press.

Henderson, K. A. (1992). Invisible pioneers? The impact of women on the recreation movement. *Leisure Sciences, 14*, 139-153.

Henderson, K. A. (1993a). "The changer and the changed:" Leisure research in the 1990s. *Journal of Applied Recreation Research, 18*(1), 3-18.

Henderson, K. A. (1993b). A feminist analysis of selected professional recreation literature about girls/women from 1907-1990. *Journal of Leisure Research, 25*(2), 165-181.

Henderson, K. A. (1993c). Rediscovering spirituality. *Camping Magazine, 65*(4), 23-27.

Henderson, K. A. (1997). Just recreation: Ethics, gender, and equity. *Journal of Park and Recreation Administration, 15*(2), 16-31.

Henderson, K. A., Bialeschki, M. D., Shaw, S. M., and Freysinger, V. J. (1996). *Both gains and gaps: Feminist perspectives on women's leisure.* State College, PA: Venture Publishing, Inc.

Hendry, L. (1993). *Growing up and going out: Adolescents and leisure.* Aberdeen, Scotland: Aberdeen University Press.

Heritage Conservation and Recreation Service. (1979). *The third nationwide outdoor recreation plan (The assessment).* Washington, DC: Government Printing Office.

Hetrick, R. L. (2000). Analyzing the recent upward surge in overtime hours. *Monthly Labor Review, 123*(2), 30-33.

Hooyman, N. and Kiyak, H. A. (1999). *Social gerontology: A multidisciplinary perspective.* (5th ed.). Boston, MA: Allyn & Bacon.

Hoschild, A. and Machung, A. (1990). *The second shift.* New York, NY: Viking Press.

Howe-Murphy, R. and Charboneau, B. G. (1987). *Therapeutic recreation intervention: An ecological perspective.* Englewood Cliffs, NJ: Prentice Hall.

Hunnicutt, B. K. (1985). Economic constraints on leisure. In M. G. Wade (Ed.), *Constraints on leisure* (pp. 243-286). Springfield, IL: Charles C. Thomas.

Hunnicutt, B. K. (1988). *Work without end: Abandoning shorter hours for the right to work.* Philadelphia, PA: Temple University Press.

Hunnicutt, B. K. (1996). *Kellogg's six-hour day.* Philadelphia, PA: Temple University Press.

Hutchinson, R. (1987). Ethnicity and urban recreation: Whites, Blacks, and Hispanics in Chicago's public parks. *Journal of Leisure Research, 19,* 205-222.

Hutchinson, R. (1988). A critique of race, ethnicity, and social class in recent leisure-recreation research. *Journal of Leisure Research, 20,* 10-30.

Ibrahim, H. and Cordes, K. (1993). *Outdoor recreation.* Madison, WI: Brown & Benchmark Publishers.

Inglehart, R. (1977). *The silent revolution: Changing values and political styles among western publics.* Princeton, NJ: Princeton University Press.

Inglehart, R. (1990). *Culture shift in advanced industrial society.* Princeton, NJ: Princeton University Press.

Iso-Ahola, S. (1980). *The social psychology of leisure and recreation.* Dubuque, IA: Wm. C. Brown.

It makes a difference…The starfish parable. (1992, August). *Footnotes: North Carolina Chapter of the Sierra Club,* p. 2.

Jackson, E. L. and Scott, D. (1999). Constraints to leisure. In E. L. Jackson and T. L. Burton (Eds.), *Leisure studies: Prospects for the twenty-first century* (pp. 299-321). State College, PA: Venture Publishing, Inc.

Jardine, L. (1996). *Worldly goods: A new history of the renaissance.* New York, NY: W.W. Norton.

Jenkins, A. (1977). *The forties.* New York, NY: Universe.

Jensen, C. R. (1977). *Leisure and recreation: Introduction and overview.* Philadelphia, PA: Lea and Febiger.

Johnson, D. (1998). The consequences of living longer: A cure for aging could create difficult choices for society. *The Futurist, 32*(5), 8-9.

Jordan, D. J. (1996). *Leadership in leisure services: Making a difference.* State College, PA: Venture Publishing, Inc.

Juster, F. T. and Stafford, F. P. (1991). The allocation of time: Empirical findings, behavioral models, and problems of measurement. *Journal of Economic Literature, 29*, 471-522.

Kaplan, M. (1991). *Essays on leisure: Human and policy issues*. Rutherford, NJ: Farleigh Dickinson University Press.

Kasson, J. (1978). *Amusing the million: Coney Island at the turn of the century*. New York, NY: Hill & Wang.

Kaufman, P. (1986). Early women claim park lands for adventure and aspiration. *Courier, 31*(10), 16-18.

Kaufman, W. (2000, June 26). The way we play. *The changing face of America*. National Public Radio Morning Edition. Available online: http:www.npr.org/programs/morning

Kaza, S. (1996). Comparative perspectives on world religions: Views of nature and implications for land management. In B. L. Driver, D. Dustin, T. Baltic, G. Elsner, and G. Peterson (Eds.), *Nature and the human spirit* (pp. 41-60). State College, PA: Venture Publishing, Inc.

Kelly, J. R. (1978). Situational and social factors in leisure decisions. *Pacific Sociological Review, 21*, 313-330.

Kelly, J. R. (1983). *Leisure identities and interactions*. London, UK: George Allen & Unwin.

Kelly, J. R. (1987). *Freedom to be: A new sociology of leisure*. New York, NY: Macmillan.

Kelly, J. R. (1996). *Leisure* (3rd ed.). Boston, MA: Allyn & Bacon.

Kelly, J. R. and Warnick, R. B. (1999). *Recreation trends and markets*. Champaign, IL: Sagamore Publishing, Inc.

Kidder, R. (1995). *How good people make tough decisions*. New York, NY: William Morrow & Co.

Kivel, P. and Kivel, B. (2000). Beyond cultural competence: Building allies and sharing power in recreational programs. In M. T. Allison and I. E. Schneider (Eds.), *Diversity and the recreation profession* (pp. 263-277). State College, PA: Venture Publishing, Inc.

Kleiber, D. A. (1979). Fate control and leisure attitudes. *Leisure Sciences, 2*, 239-248.

Kleiber, D. A. (1999). *Leisure experience and human development*. New York, NY: Basic Books.

Kleiber, D. A. (2000). The neglect of relaxation. *Journal of Leisure Research, 32*, 82-86.

Knapp, R. and Hartsoe, C. (1979). *Play for America*. Arlington, VA: National Recreation and Park Association.

Krinsky, A. (1992). Therapeutic recreation and the homeless: A clinical case history. *Therapeutic Recreation Journal, 26*(3), 53-57.

Kuhn, T. (1970). *The structure of scientific revolution*. Chicago, IL: University of Chicago Press.

Kunstler, R. (1993). Serving the homeless through recreation programs. *Parks & Recreation, 28*(9), 16-22.

Lampinen, P., Heikkinen, R. L., and Ruoppila, I. (2000). Changes in intensity of physical exercise as predictors of depressive symptoms among older adults: An eight-year follow-up. *Preventive Medicine, 30*, 371-380.

Lane, R. E. (1978). Markets and the satisfaction of human wants. *Journal of Economic Issues, 12*, 799-827.

Lankford, S., Neal, L., and Buxton, B. (1992). An examination and comparison of work motivators in public, private/commercial, nonprofit, and armed forces leisure service organizations. *Journal of Park and Recreation Administration, 10*(4), 57-70.

LaPage, W. and Ranney, S. (1988). America's wilderness: The heart and soul of culture. *Parks & Recreation, 23*(7), 24-31, 66.

Larson, R. (1994). Youth organizations, hobbies, and sports as development contexts. In R. K. Silbereisen and E. Todt (Eds.), *Adolescence in context: The interplay of family, school, peers, and work in adjustment* (pp. 46-64). New York, NY: Springer-Verlag.

Lasch, C. (1979). *The culture of narcissism.* New York, NY: Warner Books.

Le Goff, J. (1980). *Time, work, and culture in the middle ages* (A. Goldhammer, Trans.). Chicago, IL: University of Chicago Press.

Le Goff, J. (1989). *Medieval civilization, 400-1500.* New York, NY: Basil Blackwell.

Leopold, A. (1949). *A Sand County almanac.* New York, NY: Oxford University Press.

Linder, S. B. (1970). *The harried leisure class.* New York, NY: Columbia University Press.

Lundberg, G. A., Komarovsky, M., and McInerny, M. A. (1934). *Leisure: A suburban study.* New York, NY: Columbia University Press.

Lynd, R. S. and Lynd, H. M. (1929). *Middletown, a study in contemporary American culture.* New York, NY: Harcourt, Brace and Company.

MacCallum, G. C., Jr. (1967). Negative and positive freedom. *The Philosophical Review, 76*, 312-334.

MacStravic, S. and Montrose, G. (1998). *Managing healthcare demands.* Gaithersburg, MD: Aspen.

Mahon, F., Mactavish, J., Mahon, M., and Searle, M. (1995). *Older adults with mental disabilities: Exploring the meanings of independence.* Winnipeg, MB: University of Manitoba.

Males, M. (1996). *The scapegoat generation: America's war on adolescents.* Monroe, ME: Common Courage Press.

Mannell, R. and Kleiber, D. A. (1997). *A social psychology of leisure.* State College, PA: Venture Publishing, Inc.

Mannell, R., Zuzanek, J., and Larson, R. (1988). Leisure state and "flow" experiences: Testing perceived freedom and intrinsic hypotheses. *Journal of Leisure Research, 20*, 289-304.

Manville, P. B. (1990). *The origins of citizenship in ancient Athens.* Princeton, NJ: Princeton University Press.

Marasco, D. (n.d.). Jackie goes to Wrigley. Available online: http://pubweb.acns.nwu.edu/~dmarasco/jrwrig.html

Marcuse, H. (1991). *One-dimensional man: Studies in the ideology of advanced industrial society.* Boston, MA: Beacon Press.

Mardsen, P. (1990). Network diversity, substructures, and opportunities for contact. In C. Calhoun, M. Meyer, and W. Scott (Eds.), *Structures of power and constraint: Papers in honor of Peter M. Blau* (pp. 397-410). New York, NY: Cambridge University Press.

Martin, T. R. (1996). *Ancient Greece: From prehistoric to hellenistic times*. New Haven, CT: Yale University Press.

McDaniel, W. B. (1924). *Roman private life and its survivals*. Boston, MA: Marshall Jones.

Meacham, J. (2000, September 15). The new face of race. *Newsweek*, 38-41.

Mead, G. H. (1963). Mind, self and society. In C. W. Morris (Ed.), *Perspectives in the social order* (pp. 139-141). New York, NY: McGraw-Hill.

Meyer, H. and Brightbill, C. (1964). *Community recreation*, (3rd ed.). Englewood Cliffs, NJ: Prentice Hall.

Meyer, L. E. (1977). A view of therapeutic recreation: Its foundations, objectives and challenges. In G. C. Zaso (Ed.), *Dialogues in development: Concepts and action* (pp. 1-27). Durham, NH: University of New Hampshire.

Meyer, P. (1990). State parks in a new era. *Parks & Recreation, 25*(4) 28-32.

Milman, A. and Pizam, A. (1988). Social impacts of tourism on central Florida. *Annals of Tourism Research, 15*, 191-204.

Mishel, L., Bernstein, J., and Schmitt, J. (2001). *The state of working America 2000-2001*. Ithaca, NY: ILR Press/Cornell University Press.

Mitten, D. (1992). Empowering girls and women in the outdoors. *Journal of Physical Education, Recreation, and Dance, 63*(2), 56-60.

Molotch, H. (1988). The rest room and equal opportunity. *Sociological Forum, 3*(1), 128-132.

Moon, M. (1996). *Medicare now and in the future* (2nd ed.). Washington, DC: Urban Institute Press.

Moore, K. A. and Glei, D. A. (1994). Taking the plunge: An examination of positive youth development. *Journal of Adolescent Research, 10*(11), 15-40.

Morganthau, T. (1997, January 27). The face of the future: Demographics. *Newsweek*, 58.

Morse, N. C. and Weiss, R. S. (1955). The function and meaning of work and the job. *American Sociological Review, 20*, 191-198.

Mundy, J. (1998). *Leisure education: Theory and practice* (2nd ed.). Champaign, IL: Sagamore Publishing, Inc.

Munn, N. D. (1992). The cultural anthropology of time. *Annual Review of Anthropology, 21*, 92-123.

Munson, W. W. (1991). Juvenile delinquency as a social problem and social disability: The therapeutic recreator's role as ecological change agent. *Therapeutic Recreation Journal, 25*(2), 19-30.

Nash, J. B. (1960). *Philosophy of recreation and leisure*. Dubuque, IA: Wm. C. Brown.

National Center for Health Statistics. (1997). Advance data (No. 28). Washington, DC: Author.

National Center for Public Analysis (1999). The Recreation Standard. Available online: http://www.ncpa.org/pd/economy/pd062899f.html

National Park Service. (2001). Available online: http://www.nps.gov/legacy File: mission.htm

National Recreation and Park Association. (1968). *Supply/demand study: Professional and pre-professional recreation and park occupations*. Washington, DC: Author.

National Recreation and Park Association. (1994). *Comprehensive leisure and aging study: Final report*. Ashburn, VA: Author.

National Recreation and Park Association. (1999, October). Board of Trustees meeting.

National Recreation and Park Association. (2000). Discover the benefits of parks and recreation [Brochure]. Ashburn, VA: Author.

National Recreation and Park Association. (2001). Available online: http://www.activeparks.org

Neugarten, B., Havinghurst, R. J., and Tobin, S. S. (1968). Personality and patterns of aging. In B. L. Neugarten (Ed.), *Middle age and aging*. Chicago, IL: University of Chicago Press.

Neulinger, J. (1981). *To leisure: An introduction*. Boston, MA: Allyn & Bacon.

O'Laughlin, M. (1978). *The garlands of repose: The literary celebration of civic and retired leisure: The traditions of Homer and Vergil, Horace and Montaigne*. Chicago, IL: University of Chicago Press.

Owen, J. D. (1976). Workweeks and leisure: An analysis of trends, 1948-75. *Monthly Labor Review, 99*(4), 3-8.

Padus, E. (1992). *The complete guide to your emotions and your health*. Emmaus, PA: Rodale Press.

Paffenbarger, R. S., Hyde, R. T., and Dow, A. (1991). Health benefits of physical activity. In B. L. Driver, P. J. Brown, and G. L. Peterson (Eds.), *Benefits of leisure* (pp. 49-57). State College, PA: Venture Publishing, Inc.

Palmer, R. R. and Colton, J. (1965). *A history of the modern world* (3rd ed.). New York, NY: Alfred A Knopf.

Parker, S. (1971). *The future of work and leisure*. New York, NY: Praeger.

Patterson, C. (1994). The case against Neaira and the public ideology of the Athenian family. In A. L. Boegehold and A. C. Scafuro (Eds.), *Athenian identity and civic ideology* (pp. 199-216). Baltimore, MD: Johns Hopkins University Press.

Patterson, O. (1991). *Freedom: Freedom in the making of Western culture*. New York, NY: Basic Books.

Pausanias. (1918). *Description of Greece* (Vols 1-4). (W. H. S. Jones and H. A. Ormerod, Trans.). Cambridge, MA: Harvard University Press.

Pennsylvania Cable Telecommunications Association. (n. d.). The history of cable TV. Available online: http://www.pcta.com/history.html

Penuel, W. R. (1997). *Organizational learning in the nonprofit sectors: Lessons from working with the Girl Scouts*. Paper presented at the Annual Meetings of the American Educational Research Association, Chicago, IL.

Peterson, C. A. and Stumbo, N. (2000). *Therapeutic recreation program design: Principles and procedures* (3rd ed.). Boston, MA: Allyn & Bacon.

Piaget, J. (1962). *Play, dreams and imitation in childhood*. New York, NY: W. W. Norton and Company.

Pieper, J. (1963). *Leisure: The basis of culture* (A. Dru, Trans.). New York, NY: New American Library.

Plummer, J. T. (1989). Changing values. *The Futurist, 23*(1), 8-13.

Public Health Reports. (1993). *Measuring the health behavior of adolescents: The youth risk behavior surveillance system and recent public health reports on high-risk adolescents.* Public Health Reports, 108 (Supp. 1). Rockville, MD: Public Health Services.

Pullan, B. (1973). *A history of early Renaissance Italy: From the mid-thirteenth to the mid-fifteenth century.* London, UK: Allen Lane/Penguin Books.

Putnam, R. (1993). *Making democracy work: Civic traditions in modern Italy.* Princeton, NJ: Princeton University Press.

Putnam, R. (1995a). Bowling alone: America's declining social capital. *Journal of Democracy, 6*, 65-78.

Putnam, R. (1995b). *Tuning in, tuning out: The strange disappearance of social capital in America*, pp. 664-683.

Putnam, R. (2000). *Bowling alone: The collapse and revival of American community.* New York, NY: Simon and Schuster.

Quinnet, P. (1994). *Pavlov's trout.* Sandpoint, ID: Keokee Co.

Rainwater, C. (1922). The play movement in the United States. Chicago, IL: The University of Chicago Press.

Rawls, J. (1971). *A theory of justice.* Cambridge, MA: Belknap Press of Harvard University Press.

Reid, D. (1995). *Work and leisure in the 21st century: From production to citizenship.* Toronto, ON: Wall and Emerson.

Rhode, D. L. (Ed.). (1990). *Theoretical perspectives on sexual difference.* New Haven, CT: Yale University Press.

Reisman, D. (1961). *The lonely crowd: A study of the changing American character.* Yale University Press: New Haven, CT.

Rifkin, J. (1995). *The end of work: The decline of the global labor force and the dawn of the post-market era.* New York, NY: G. P. Putnam.

Rioux, M. H. (1993). Rights, justice, power: An agenda for change. In M. Nagler and E. J. Kemp (Eds.) *Perspectives on disability* (2nd ed.). Palo Alto, CA: Health Markets Research, pp. 515-523.

Robinson, J. P. and Bostrom, A. (1994). The overestimated workweek? What time diary measures suggest. *Monthly Labor Review, 177*(8), 11-23.

Robinson, J. P. and Godbey, G. (1999). *Time for life: The surprising ways Americans use their time* (2nd ed.). University Park, PA: Pennsylvania State University Press.

Roediger, D. and Foner, P. (1989). *Our own time: A history of American labor and the working day.* Westport, CT: Greenwood Press.

Rojek, C. (1989). Leisure time and leisure space. In C. Rojek (Ed.), *Leisure for leisure: Critical essays* (pp. 191-204). London, UK: Macmillan Press.

Rones, P. L., Ilg, R. E., and Gardner, J. M. (1997). Trends in hours of work since the mid-1970s. *Monthly Labor Review, 120*(4), 3-14.

Russell, R. V. (1996). *Pastimes: The context of contemporary leisure.* Dubuque, IA: Brown & Benchmark Publishers.

Russell, R. V. (2001). *Leadership in recreation* (2nd ed.). Boston, MA: McGraw-Hill.

Salamon, L. M. (1999). *America's nonprofit sector: A primer*. New York, NY: Foundation Center.

Santrock, J. W. (1990). *Adolescence*. Dubuque, IA: Wm. C. Brown Publishers.

Saving money by reducing stress. (1994). *Harvard Business Review, 72*(6), 12.

Schor, J. (1991). *The overworked American: The unexpected decline of leisure.* New York, NY: Basic Books.

Scott, C. and Jaffe, D. (1994). Stress and stress management in the workplace. In M. O'Donnell and J. Harris (Eds.), *Health Promotion in the workplace* (pp. 390-427). Albany, NY: Delmar.

Scraton, S. (1994). The changing world of women and leisure: Feminism, 'postfeminism' and leisure. *Leisure Studies, 13*(4), 249-261.

Seigley, L. (1998). The effects of personal and environmental factors on health behaviors of older adults. *Nursing connections, 11*(4), 47-58.

Sennett, R. (1998). *The corrosion of character: The personal consequences of work in the new capitalism.* New York, NY: W. W. Norton.

Sessoms, H. D. (1990). On becoming a profession: requirements and strategies. *Journal of Park and Recreation Administration, 8*(4), 33-42.

Sessoms, H. D. (1993). *Eight decades of leadership development: A history of programs of professional preparation in parks and recreation 1909-1989.* Arlington, VA: National Recreation and Park Association.

Sessoms, H. D. and Orthner, D. (1992). Our growing invisible populations. *Parks & Recreation, 27*(8), 62-65.

Seven, S. (1979). Environmental interpretation for the visually impaired. *Therapeutic Recreation Journal, 13*(1), 12-17.

Shain, M. (1996). Work, employment, and mental health. In R. Renwick, I. Brown, and M. Nagler (Eds.), *Quality of life in health promotion and rehabilitation: Conceptual approaches, issues, and applications* (pp. 327-341). Thousand Oaks, CA: Sage Publications, Inc.

Shaw, S. M. and Whyte, L. B. (1996). An analysis of the hierarchical model of leisure constraints: Using fear of violence as a case study. In D. Dawson (Ed.), *Proceedings from the 8th Canadian Congress on Leisure Research* (pp. 245-249). Ottawa, ON: University of Ottawa.

Sherlock, J. (1999). The fifties: A brief history. Available online: http://www.joesherlock.com/fifties.html File: 50s history

Shogan, D. (1991). Understanding leisure experiences: The contribution of feminist communitarian ethics. In G. Fain (Ed.), *Leisure and ethics: Reflections on the philosophy of leisure* (pp. 141-151). Reston, VA: AAHPERD.

Silbereisen, R. K. and Todt, E. (1994). *Adolescence in context: The interplay of family, school, peers, and work in adjustment.* New York, NY: Springer-Verlag.

Singh, B. R. (1989). Neutrality and commitment in teaching moral and social issues in a multicultural society. *Educational Review, 41*(3), 227-242.

Sklar, H. (1995). *Chaos or community? Seeking solutions, not scapegoating for bad economics.* Boston, MA: South End Press.

Smith, H. (1991). *The world's religions.* New York, NY: HarperCollins Publishers.

Smith, R. W., Austin, D. R., and Kennedy, D. R. (2001). *Inclusive and special recreation: Opportunities for persons with disabilities.* Boston, MA: McGraw-Hill.

Snodgrass, A. (1980). *Archaic Greece: The age of experiment.* Berkeley, CA: University of California Press.

Snow, R. (1984). *Coney Island: A postcard journey to the city of fire.* New York, NY: Brightwaters Press.

Spigner, C. and Havitz, M. E. (1993). Social marketing or social justice: A dialogue on access to recreation for the unemployed. *Parks & Recreation, 28*(11), 51-57.

Statistical Abstract of the United States. (1993). *Television and radio use, 1950, 1970, and 1990.* Washington, DC: US Government Printing Office.

Statistical Abstract of the United States. (1999). *Parks, recreation, travel and natural resources.* Washington, DC: US Government Printing Office.

Stebbins, R. A. (1982). Serious leisure: A conceptual statement. *Pacific Sociological Review, 25,* 251-272.

Stebbins, R. A. (1999). Serious leisure. In E. L. Jackson and T. L. Burton (Eds.), *Leisure studies: Prospects for the twenty-first century* (pp. 69-79). State College, PA: Venture Publishing, Inc.

Storrmann, W. (1996). Recreation's role in community development. *Journal of Applied Recreation Research, 21,* 143-164.

Strayer, J. R. (1955). *Western Europe in the Middle Ages: A short history.* New York, NY: Appleton-Century-Crofts.

Stubbs, R. A. (1998). A recipe for non-profit success: Managing the linkages and key elements of successful organizations. *Fund Raising Management, 28*(11), 17-21.

Sugrue, T. J. (1996). *The origins of urban crisis: Race and inequality in postwar Detroit.* Princeton, NJ: Princeton University Press.

Swimming with tomorrow's sharks: Managers must "keep moving or die." (1997). *The Futurist, 31*(3), 13-14.

Tedrick, T. and Henderson, K. A. (1989). *Volunteers in leisure: A management perspective.* Reston, VA: AAHPERD.

"Teens on the Web." (2000). Available online: http//www0.mercurycenter.com/svtech/news/special/webteen

Thomas, K. (1964). Work and leisure in preindustrial societies. *Past and Present, 29,* 50-62.

Thompson, E. P. (1967). Time, work-discipline, and industrial capitalism. *Past and Present, 38,* 56-97.

Toalson, R. (1980). Special districts. *Parks & Recreation, 15*(7), 29-30.

Toner, J. P. (1995). *Leisure and ancient Rome.* Cambridge, MA: Polity Press with Basil Blackwell.

TV Free America. (1998). Cited in TV Statistics. Available online: http://www.oc-profam-net.org/media/tv_statistics.htm

US Bureau of Labor Statistics. (1992, July). *Monthly Labor Review, 115*(7), 15.

US Bureau of Labor Statistics. (1999, December 22). The editor's desk. *Monthly Labor Review* Available online: http://stats.bls.gov/opub/ted/1999/Dec/wk3/art03.html

US Bureau of Labor Statistics. (2000, August 4). The employment situation: July 2000. Available online: http://stats.bls.gov/newsrels.html

US Bureau of the Census (1999). Statistical abstract of the United States. Available online: http://www.census.gov/prod/www/statistical-abstract-us.html

US Department of Commerce (1985). *Franchise opportunities handbook*. Washington, DC: Author.

US Department of Education, National Center for Education Statistics. (1993). *Youth indicators 1993: Trends in the well-being of American youth*. Washington, DC: US Government Printing Office.

US Department of Health and Human Services. (1996). *Physical activity and health: A report of the surgeon general*. Atlanta, GA: Centers for Disease Control and Prevention, National Center for Chronic Disease Prevention and Health Promotion.

US Department of Health and Human Services. (1998). *Trends in the well-being and health of America's children and youth*. Office of the Assistant Secretary for Planning and Evaluation. Washington, DC: US Government Printing Office.

US Department of Labor. (1980). *Exchanging earnings for leisure: Findings of an exploratory national survey on work time preferences*. Washington, DC: US Government Printing Office.

US Department of Labor. (1999). Report on the American workforce. Available online: http://www.fedstats.gov

Ventura, S. J. (1995). *Births to unmarried mothers: United States, 1980-1992* (NCHS Series 21, No. 53). Washington, DC: US Department of Health and Human Services.

Wallace, G., Tierney, P., and Hass, G. (1990). The right link between the wilderness and tourism. *Parks & Recreation, 25*(9), 63-66, 111-112.

Walvin, J. (1978). *Leisure and society 1830-1950*. London, UK: Longman.

Warnick, R. and Howard, D. (1990). *Market share analysis of selected leisure services: an update—1979 to 1987*. Presented at the Outdoor Recreation Trends Symposium III, Indianapolis, IN.

Warren, K. (1996). Educating for environmental justice. *Journal of Experiential Education, 19*(3), 135-140.

Wearing, B. (1998). *Leisure and feminist theory*. London, UK: Sage.

Weber, M. (1930). *The Protestant ethic and the spirit of capitalism* (T. Parsons, Trans.). London, UK: Unwin Hyman.

West, P. C. (1989). Urban region parks and Black minorities: Subculture, marginality, and interracial relations in park use in the Detroit metropolitan area. *Leisure Sciences, 11*(1), 11-28.

Whitman, T. L., Merluzzi, T. V., and White, R. D. (1999). *Life-span perspectives on health and illness*. Mahwah, NJ: Lawrence Erlbaum.

Whitmer, R. W. (1993). Why we should foster health promotion. *Business and Health, 11*(13), 68, 74.

Whyte, L. B. and Shaw, S. M. (1994). Women's leisure: An exploratory study of fear and violence as a leisure constraint. *Journal of Applied Recreation Research, 19*(1), 5-21.

Wilhite, B., Keller, J., and Caldwell, N. (1999). Optimizing lifelong health and well-being: A health enhancing model for therapeutic recreation. *Therapeutic Recreation Journal, 33*, 98-108.

Williams, S. (1998). *Tourism geography.* London, UK: Routledge.

Wilson, A. and Wilson, P. (1994). *Theme parks, leisure centers, zoos, and aquaria.* New York, NY: John Wiley & Sons, Inc.

Wolfe, A. (1997, September/October). The moral meanings of work. *The American Prospect.* Available online: http://www.prospect.org/archives/34/34wolffs.html

Wood, D., Halfon, N., Scarlata, D., Newacheck, P., and Nessim, S. (1993). Impact of family relations on children's growth, development, school function, and behavior. *Journal of the American Medical Association, 270*, 1334-1338.

World Leisure and Recreation Association. (2000, July). Charter for leisure. Available online: http://www.worldleisure.org File: Charter of Leisure

Yen, T. and McKinney, W. (1992). The relationship between compensation satisfaction and job characteristics: A comparative study of public and private leisure service professionals. *Journal of Park and Recreation Administration, 10*(4), 15-36.

Yerkes, R. and Miranda, W. (1982). Outdoor adventure courses for women: Implications for new programming. *Journal of Physical Education, Recreation, and Dance, 53*(4), 82-85.

Yoshioka, C. (1990). Organizational motives of public, nonprofit, and commercial leisure service agencies. *Journal of Applied Recreation Research, 15*, 59-70.

Zill, N., Morrison, D., and Coiro, M. (1993). Long-term effects of parental divorce on parent-child relationships: Adjustment and achievement in early adulthood. *Journal of Family Psychology, 7*(1), 91-103.

Zuefle, D. M. (1999, September). The spirituality of recreation. *Parks & Recreation*, 28-33, 48, 197.

Author Index

Subject Index

*The A•B•Cs of Behavior Change: Skills for
Working With Behavior Problems in
Nursing Homes*
by Margaret D. Cohn, Michael A. Smyer,
and Ann L. Horgas

*Activity Experiences and Programming
Within Long-Term Care*
by Ted Tedrick and Elaine R. Green

The Activity Gourmet
by Peggy Powers

*Advanced Concepts for Geriatric Nursing
Assistants*
by Carolyn A. McDonald

Adventure Programming
edited by John C. Miles and Simon Priest

*Aerobics of the Mind: Keeping the Mind Active
in Aging—A New Perspective on Programming for Older Adults*
by Marge Engelman

*Assessment: The Cornerstone of Activity
Programs*
by Ruth Perschbacher

*Behavior Modification in Therapeutic Recre-
ation: An Introductory Manual*
by John Dattilo and William D. Murphy

Benefits of Leisure
edited by B. L. Driver, Perry J. Brown,
and George L. Peterson

Benefits of Recreation Research Update
by Judy M. Sefton and W. Kerry Mummery

*Beyond Bingo: Innovative Programs for the
New Senior*
by Sal Arrigo, Jr., Ann Lewis, and Hank
Mattimore

*Beyond Bingo 2: More Innovative Programs
for the New Senior*
by Sal Arrigo, Jr.

*Both Gains and Gaps: Feminist Perspectives
on Women's Leisure*
by Karla Henderson, M. Deborah
Bialeschki, Susan M. Shaw, and Valeria
J. Freysinger

*Dimensions of Choice: A Qualitative Approach
to Recreation, Parks, and Leisure Research*
by Karla A. Henderson

*Diversity and the Recreation Profession:
Organizational Perspectives*
edited by Maria T. Allison and Ingrid E.
Schneider

*Effective Management in Therapeutic Recre-
ation Service*
by Gerald S. O'Morrow and Marcia Jean
Carter

*Evaluating Leisure Services: Making Enlight-
ened Decisions*
by Karla A. Henderson with M. Deborah
Bialeschki

*Everything From A to Y: The Zest Is up to
You! Older Adult Activities for Every
Day of the Year*
by Nancy R. Cheshire and Martha L.
Kenney

*The Evolution of Leisure: Historical and Philo-
sophical Perspectives (Second Printing)*
by Thomas Goodale and Geoffrey Godbey

*Experience Marketing: Strategies for the New
Millennium*
by Ellen L. O'Sullivan and Kathy J.
Spangler

*Facilitation Techniques in Therapeutic
Recreation*
by John Dattilo

*File o' Fun: A Recreation Planner for Games
& Activities—Third Edition*
by Jane Harris Ericson and Diane Ruth
Albright

*The Game and Play Leader's Handbook:
Facilitating Fun and Positive Interaction*
by Bill Michaelis and John M.
O'Connell

*The Game Finder—A Leader's Guide to
Great Activities*
by Annette C. Moore

*Getting People Involved in Life and Activi-
ties: Effective Motivating Techniques*
by Jeanne Adams

*Glossary of Recreation Therapy and Occupa-
tional Therapy*
by David R. Austin

Great Special Events and Activities
by Annie Morton, Angie Prosser, and
Sue Spangler

Group Games & Activity Leadership
by Kenneth J. Bulik

*Hands on! Children's Activities for Fairs,
Festivals, and Special Events*
by Karen L. Ramey

*Inclusive Leisure Services: Responding to the
Rights of People With Disabilities*
by John Dattilo

*Internships in Recreation and Leisure Services:
A Practical Guide for Students—Second
Edition*
by Edward E. Seagle, Jr., Ralph W.
Smith, and Lola M. Dalton